The Nightfisherman:
Selected Letters

The Nightfisherman

Selected Letters of W.S. Graham

EDITED BY
MICHAEL & MARGARET SNOW

CARCANET

First published in Great Britain in 1999 by
Carcanet Press
Floor 4 Alliance House
30 Cross Street
Manchester M2 7AQ

A CIP catalogue record for this book
is available from the British Library.

ISBN 9781857544459

The publisher acknowledges financial assistance
from the Arts Council of England

Supported using public funding by
ARTS COUNCIL
ENGLAND

Set in 11/12pt Bembo by XL Publishing Services, Tiverton
Printed and bound in England by SRP Ltd, Exeter

Contents

List of Illustrations

(following p. 180)

Photographs 1, 5, 6, 8, 9, 11, 14, 16, by Michael Snow; 4, 18, by Margaret Snow; 7, P.W. Jarrett; 12, Nicholas Elder; 17, Nancy Wynne-Jones; 19, Eric Wynter

Introduction

In 1938, after completing his engineering apprenticeship, Sydney Graham went for one year to Newbattle Abbey, studying Literature and Philosophy. He had already been writing poetry for some time but it was during this year that he decided he wanted to be a poet. Full-time. That was the important qualification which made his situation unusual and ensured a difficult life for him. The delight and revelation he had received from reading and making poetry so thoroughly engaged him that it was to inform his whole understanding and way of life, becoming an intrinsic part of his perception and means of expression:

> My poems tell me and let me peer through to something real and more elemental which has to do with all I breathe and make and am made.[1]

Graham's love of Scotland remained all his life and Scottish references abound in his poems and letters, particularly to his childhood in Greenock itself and the whole region of mountains and islands to the north and west of Glasgow. But in 1943 he was able to live in a caravan in Cornwall, free of charge, and begin his career as a full-time poet. From a later statement it was clear that he had an objective:

> The thing is to find or create (in this case the same thing) a language, a timbre of thought or voice which I will live in. It will never be adequate except for its moment but it will be the nearest to my soul speaking and as I change so it shall. A way of speaking, if it is any good, as it persists creates its understanders. Its early idiosyncracies become solid currency. It is alive, changing and organic. And at last works.[2]

The progress he made in developing his own original voice was confirmed some fifteen years later when T.S. Eliot, writing of *The Nightfishing*, said 'some of these poems – by their sustained power, their emotional depth and maturity and their superb technical skill

– may well be among the more important poetical achievements of our time'. Graham's later collections, *Malcolm Mooney's Land* (1970), and *Implements In Their Places* (1977) explored new territories and drew even stronger praise. Damian Grant described him as 'one of the rarest talents in English poetry... a profound, humane and generous poet'.[3]

Graham's letters record the financial difficulties he experienced and the embarrassments created by his determination to devote himself completely to poetry. Without the support of his wife, his friends and admirers he would never have been able to accomplish what he did. Even in later life his work never produced what anyone now thinks of as a living wage. He was stoical about this fact and, apart from alcohol, not particularly self-indulgent. His letters are frequently positive, even optimistic, often concerned about the stress being experienced by others. There were fees for publication and in later life he was given a small pension and occasional grants of money. If we are ever tempted to criticise his strategy for survival perhaps we ought first to ask why we are prepared to pay poets if they will first become teachers, critics and, above all, entertainers, but we have not yet developed adequate methods for properly identifying and supporting the seriously committed individualists like Graham who only require subsistence in order to concentrate on their work. To call such a person 'unemployed' would seem at least inaccurate.

Sydney Graham's poetry represents an unusually powerful and autonomous body of achievement and his letters contain much of interest about his ideas and working methods. Initially searching for his comments about poetry, we found ourselves inevitably illustrating a great deal of his life as well, the two being so intertwined that attempts to separate them became artificial. While poetry is not autobiography (even when closely based upon personal experience), and there is an important distinction between the life of the writer and that of his work, there are interesting perceptions, underlying preoccupations and assumptions that are developed both in the poems and in the letters. Some of these were stated in Graham's extraordinary article called 'Notes On A Poetry Of Release' first published in 1946 and reprinted here as still very relevant to all his later work (see Appendix). He had a strong curiosity about life which found both encouragement and discipline at Newbattle Abbey WEA College in 1938–9. It remained constant. Sometime in the 1960s he wrote to Roger Hilton:

> I want to know a wee bit about where I am now before I go away. And I don't mean Madron. It is one of the few things possible. I would have hated to be put into the world either as a pig or a milkjug and gone out again never knowing anything about where I had been.[4]

For someone permanently influenced by the writing of James Joyce, with its emphasis on life/art as a stream of consciousness, the imaginative ideas of Heraclitus, which formed part of the Newbattle Philosophy course, must have appeared delightfully apposite. There are numerous correspondences between them and some of the themes in Graham's later work, the most obvious being those in which the world is seen as a phenomenon of perpetual change, a state of flux. 'One cannot step twice into the same river, nor can one grasp any mortal substance in a stable condition, but it scatters and again gathers; it forms and dissolves, and approaches and departs.[5] In *The Nightfishing* we have 'I cupped/My hand to the glass chimney./Yet it was a stranger's breath/From out of my mouth that/Shed the light.' Some Heraclitean ideas were extensively developed in the twentieth century by Heidegger, whom Graham also read. It is obvious that Graham quite naturally explored these ideas for their wider poetic resonances rather than as a study of philosophy, but the rigorous attention to language demanded by the course must also have served him well. He knew that the language one used governed what it was possible to say with it, and later would no doubt have appreciated Werner Heisenberg's comment that 'what we observe is not nature itself but nature exposed to our method of questioning'.[6]

The concept of perpetual change applied to language itself was, for Graham, no academic theory but a perceived everyday reality. Words are ambiguous. 'Each word is touched by and filled with the activity of every speaker. Each word changes every time it is brought to life.'[7] In an environment of such fluidity language is freed to create and be a new reality, the finished poem. In poetry words embody and present meaning, they are not restricted merely to narrating some 'extractable' message. Today it is important to understand that Graham was not an abstract theoretician with a complex hidden agenda. His realisation of the fundamental 'extraordinariness' of existence and of language was a deeply personal, practical, everyday fact. His creative response was his poetry. Because he spoke about perceptions and experiences available to all of us (if we will pay attention) he both touches and challenges our imaginations:

> I mean no harm, I say. But of course I mean every sort of harm by speaking with a degree of articulateness above the average about the things which should disturb us all I hope.[8]

Graham's courageous subversion of both cliché and complacency strips existence down to its essentials. The chilling scenario of cosmic isolation, the essential discrete loneliness of every individual, is presented with great integrity but always accompanied by the possibility of love and communication between people:

> Art expression is a voice between two things. Abstract formality and the very human gesture. And one doesn't work without the other.[9]

In the letters, as in the poems, the 'alone reader' is addressed with unusual directness, summoned to attend, his presence as another consciousness insisted upon as an essential element. He is enlisted as a natural companion for anything from the observation of a foxglove to reflections on the isolation of man. The letters, like the poems, assume an imagined response from their readers: 'I say / This silence here for in it I might hear you'.[10]

For Graham, poetry was not an optional luxury. He knew that the full appreciation of any art does indeed require from the participant what he described as 'his best effort of beholding' because it may challenge and subvert lazy or conventional established habits of perception and consequently meet with resistance.[11] In some of the later work his language was so starkly elemental that each word seemed to have had a struggle to be born at all and then to have found its place, its exact place, in the carefully modulated silence that both inter-penetrated and supported the whole structure of the poem. He spoke his poems with strong, measured clarity and his audiences, large or small, had their attention captured and transformed. His dramatic skills were impressive. There was no sense that this was some sort of esoteric or élitist enterprise requiring specialist knowledge before it could be undertaken. The wit and humanity of the man and the work was both implicit and obvious as he spoke.

A good introduction to the letters of a poet is familiarity with his poetry and perhaps the letters are most usefully seen as the poet's parallel activity, something concurrent with the poetry which also gives an indication of Graham's background, his enthusiasms, critical ideas, aims and personality. The letters add to our knowledge both of the genesis of the poetry and the evolution of the poet. They extend our awareness of Graham and they show us something of his routines, emotions and temperament. The letters' unusual clarity, honesty and humour reveal a remarkable man. Some of them are so imaginative that they almost become the continuation of poetry by other means. They were obviously addressed to individuals instead of a larger audience but he could not suddenly anaesthetise his sensitivity to words simply because he was writing a letter, or become dulled to the strangeness and the ambivalence of the words before him, their waywardness, the unexpected awkwardness they could produce or the equally unexpected gifts, from near poetry to awful puns. One of the first questions Graham asked of his own or other people's poetry was 'Does it disturb the language?' and the letters often retain that very Joycean intoxication with words so characteristic of his early poetry, long after the later poems have developed less strenuous and more transparent voices.

The poems themselves have no room for, or need of, explanatory apparatus by virtue of the very compression and economy of speech and imagery that makes them autonomous. They become resonant poetic objects by the finality with which they have made words fuse 'meaning', form and image into one. The letters show what a very lengthy process this could sometimes be and they show aspects of that process more clearly than the finished poems can do.[12]

The letters also seem to have had a very practical usefulness for him: 'I only write (even to you) to help myself as well'.[13] There is in them a sort of 'five-finger exercises' quality, a playing with the materials of the craft of words, the sort of relaxed but aware, intelligent play that creative artists neglect at their peril. He seems to allow the words to participate in his intention, to partly form it or enable him to investigate what it might become on the particular day. This improvisation can be of interest in itself, quite apart from what the letter might actually be about. The passages of luxuriant polyvalent language, puns and all, give small insights into his sources, the current objects of his attention and interest. They provide him with an arena for language to toss its head and gallop all the way through high seriousness to the absurd and back. The fact that the letters often contain verse is yet another indication that the writing of them was sometimes a kind of 'aware practice', parallel to the pursuit of poetry, even a way of starting work again. As he says himself:

> What a mysterious unsubstantial business it is, writing poetry. After one finishes a poem which seems to work one says Ha Ha now I'll write another because I know how to do it but it is not so. There is the silence before one just as difficult to disturb significantly as before. What one has learned is inadequate against the new silence presented.'[14]

Many of the poems (and letters) were written during the undisturbed night hours, listening to that silence.

The range of Graham's poetic achievement is extraordinary. He has been described as 'a poet of spectacular sophistication and originality and the supreme comic poet of our time'.[15] From *The Nightfishing* onwards Graham created a stark and dramatic interior poetic landscape, home equally to the intrepid sailor or explorer, or to the prisoner of communication in his cell. Metaphors for search and for suffering. Yet in the same period of work we may find poems of love and tranquillity, elegiac and serene, counterbalance to chaos.

Graham was not a 'joiner' of groups, social, literary or political. He shared something of William Blake's dismay at the repression or coercion of the individual by authority and convention and, having been disturbed by the moral destruction of war, was deeply suspicious of propaganda in art or politics. As a companion he might at different times be an irritant, a convivial wit, a clown, a stringent critic, or a master of revelatory language. His letters show him being all of these things but above all they show us a man totally dedicated to the pursuit of poetry and capable of uninhibited warmth to his friends, forever alive to the paradox:

> To be always alone is necessary.
> One would not ever be otherwise.
> Yet our nature is such that we
> Want to share our souls with others.[16]

MICHAEL SNOW
Devon, 1999

1 To Edwin Morgan, 22 September 1943.
2 To Ruth Hilton, 22 March 1967.
3 Damian Grant, 'Walls of Glass: the poetry of W.S. Graham' in *British Poetry since 1970*, eds Peter Jones and Michael Schmidt (Manchester, 1980).
4 To Roger Hilton (undated), letter no.140.
5 C.H. Kahn, *The Art and Thought of Heraclitus* (Cambridge, 1979). This transcription is from Plutarch.
6 Werner Heisenberg, *Physics and Philosophy* (New York, 1962).
7 W.S. Graham, 'Notes On A Poetry Of Release' (See Appendix).
8 To Roger Hilton, 24 September 1969.
9 To Ruth Hilton, 24 January 1966.
10 W.S. Graham, 'The Constructed Space'.
11 To C.H. Sisson, 31 December 1967.
12 Music, for example, was an important part of Graham's life and Ruth Hilton (the professional musician Ruth David) described him as 'a very "musical" man – one to whom music spoke directly as a familiar language exploring every nuance of feeling and thought'. She also sent him Johann Joachim Quantz's *On Playing the Flute* (1752). (See Ruth Hilton, 'The Influence of Music' in *The Constructed Space*.)
13 To Elizabeth Smart, 8 September 1978.
14 To Robin Skelton, 8 December 1972.
15 'W.S. Graham: Professor of Silence', Dennis O'Driscoll, in *The Constructed Space*.
16 To Roger Hilton, 7 November [1966].

Note on the Text

We eventually found more letters than could be included in this book and we wished to use as many of them as possible in their entirety. Not all were of equal interest and they were certainly not evenly spread through Graham's life. They did not constitute a complete record of Graham's circle of friends; some were not represented here, others saw him so often that writing to them was usually unnecessary. We hope our selection is reasonably representative of the material collected.

The volume is divided into chapters to coincide, very broadly, with the completion of a major poem or collection. The biographical information and comment preceding each section is based on conversations with Nessie Graham and other friends, works listed in Further Reading, other published and unpublished letters, many other books and articles not listed here and our conversations with Sydney Graham over a period of more than thirty years.

We have tried to minimise repetition and where extracts have been used this is indicated. For ease of reference longer addresses have been abbreviated after first use. Punctuation and spelling have also been regularised for clarity but where variant spellings might be seen as creative they have been left alone. Editors' notes are enclosed in square brackets [ ]. Omissions are indicated by the sign [...]. A few small omissions have been made to avoid pain to persons still living or unnecessary intrusion into personal privacy.

The majority of the original letters were typewritten, others were sometimes in a striking calligraphy. Several were decorated. We have not attempted to reproduce the varied layouts and occasional drawings or paintings *in situ* but some examples of Graham's drawings and handwriting have been reduced in scale and distributed through the text. They originally fitted the large foolscap (or, later, the standard A4) pages of most of the letters. Graham sometimes wrote on much larger sheets of paper and made much larger paintings on old sheets of cardboard. One of the photographs taken inside the Coastguard Houses shows a painting done on a broken mirror.

Acknowledgements

In 1993 we began to search for Sydney Graham's letters. Their importance to a better appreciation of Graham's ideas and achievements was obvious. We are deeply grateful to all the correspondents included in this book and/or their personal representatives who shared their letters with us. Their help was crucial and their memories were irreplaceable. Special thanks are also due to correspondents whose letters were not included in the final selection but who also helped with our research. We record with great regret the fact that a number of the contributors did not live to see their letters printed in this volume. Nessie Graham's death in May 1999 at the age of eighty-nine closed a friendship with us which had lasted for over forty-four years. Her knowledge of Sydney's poetry and ideas was unparalleled and she gave us unwavering support throughout our project.

We should like to thank the Trustees of the following institutions whose Librarians kindly provided access to copyright material housed in their collections: the National Library of Canada, Ottawa; the National Library of Scotland, Edinburgh; the Library of University College, London; the University of Manchester John Rylands Library; the Library of The Royal College of Art, London; the Tate Gallery Archive, London; the University of Texas, Harry Ransom Humanities Research Center.

For additional help in locating material and for information we wish to thank Ricky Atkins, Elspeth Barker, Ilse Barker, W. Barns-Graham, Vicki Beatson, Trevor Bell, Stella Benjamin, John Bodley, Alan Bold, Georgina Buxton, Robert Calder, Biddy Crozier, David and Judy Gascoyne, Geoffrey Godbert, Martin Green, Rose Hilton, Robert Hunt, James Keery, Marius Kociejowski, Helen James, George and Helen Lanyon, Tony Lopez, Bet Low, Malcolm Mackintosh, Richard and Myra Nimmo, Wendy Prahms, Roger Slack, Frances Spalding, Chris Stephens, Matthew Thomas, David and Tina Wilkinson, the publishers Faber and Faber and The Greville Press.

For local information about the Graham family history and Sydney Graham's youth we are much indebted to the researches of David Allan, and Len McDermid, and for information to Jack Dooley, Alastair Graham, Ronald McNeil, Margaret Millar and Christine Shaw.

For helpful comments on our text we wish to thank Anthony Astbury, Alex Currie, Ronnie Duncan, Matthew and Creina Francis, Harold Pinter, Christopher Reid and Michael Schmidt. We are indebted to the staff of Carcanet Press for their help, to our patient copy-editor, Robyn Marsack, and to Dot and Colin Milton for technical assistance with word-processing. For permission to use an extract from the correspondence of Hugh MacDiarmid we thank Deirdre Grieve, also Rose Hilton for permission to reproduce the drawing 'They travel without hope' by Roger Hilton (p. 220).

Publication of *The Nightfisherman* may well result in the discovery of additional letters and we should much appreciate information about any which come to light and could thus be preserved, as originals or copies, in the National Library of Scotland.

When all the magic silver stars of love
Have fled before the weary winter years
And slow old tunes of sleep come flowing in
To fill our eyes and dry our last love-tears,

When we are with the night-sea round our feet
And feel the music of green-weeded shores,
And even when the salt death-breeze of night
Is on our faces with impatient breath,
Then we will turn and look along the way
That we have come, along the shining stream,
Right to its misty birth.

WSG April 1939

One

'I AM A POET' – THE FIRST SEVEN YEARS

1938–1945

GREENOCK AT NIGHT I FIND YOU

1

As for you loud Greenock long ropeworking
Hide and seeking rivetting town of my child
Hood, I know we think of us often mostly
At night. Have you ever desired me back
Into the set-in bed at the top of the land
In One Hope Street? I am myself lying
Half-asleep hearing the rivetting yards
And smelling the bone-works with no home
Work done for Cartsburn School in the morning.

At night. And here I am descending and
The welding lights in the shipyards flower blue
Under my hopeless eyelids as I lie
Sleeping conditioned to hide from happy.

2

So what did I do? I walked from Hope Street
Down Lyndoch Street between the night's words
To Cartsburn Street and got to the Cartsburn Vaults
With half an hour to go. See, I am back.

3

See, I am back. My father turned and I saw
He had the stick he cut in Sheelhill Glen.
Brigit was there and Hugh and double-breasted
Sam and Malcolm Mooney and Alastair Graham.
They all were there in the Cartsburn Vaults shining
To meet me but I was only remembered.

'To Set The Scene'

William Sydney Graham was born on 19 November 1918 in Greenock, a Clydeside industrial town set in beautiful surroundings. Its prosperity was based on the docks, shipyards, and sugar refineries (all of which have declined in recent years) and is still evident in the large number of well-built and set out houses surviving amongst areas of reconstruction necessitated by considerable war damage.

No. 1, Hope Street, where Graham was born 'in a set-in bed', still stands, a four-storey sandstone house where the street door opens onto a central broad stone staircase dividing each floor into two rented flats. All of these originally had stained glass panels and brass fittings to their individual front doors and were typically divided into a bathroom, living-room and kitchen, both the latter being high-ceilinged spacious rooms which also contained sleeping accommodation. The Grahams lived on the top floor with a spectacular view over 'the massive cranes in Scott's ship-yard and the blue lights made by the welding machines' to the Clyde, Loch Long, Gare Loch, and the mountains around Arrochar.[1] Half way down Hope Street Graham could see over to a railway marshalling yard and station and, from the high kitchen window and from the docks where he sometimes carried his father's lunch, he watched vessels from all parts of the world steaming up and down the (then) busy Firth of Clyde. His father, Alexander, was an engineer who had travelled on the convoys to Murmansk during the First World War and his uncle, Tom Lockie, was a marine engineer. The images of travel and construction were a pervasive part of his environment and for most of his life he lived near the sea.

Graham said that his mother Margaret (McDermid), came from an Irish family in Galway.[2] She had managed shops for the Buttercup

Dairy and later ran her own small general shop in Ann Street. Alexander Graham played the violin and piano, was particularly active in local musical entertainments, taught himself painting and etching and taught his son watercolour painting. There seems to have been a convivial social life; half a dozen couples in their immediate circle took it in turns to give hospitality and Jean Laird, a family friend, recollected helping Margaret Graham to push back the furniture and roll up the living room carpet for the dancing.[3] Throughout most of the Depression Alexander remained in work and neither Sydney nor his younger brother, Alastair, born in 1926, thought their childhood at all deprived. Indeed the steadiness of the family finances was reflected in their 'upward' move in 1932 to the locally better regarded and more spaciously laid out area of Brisbane Street, where they lived in a five-roomed top floor flat in a house of broadly similar design to that in Hope Street.

Sydney Graham had little interest in his local elementary school (Cartsburn) and was impatient to be wandering out of doors. From the corner of Hope Street it was a short walk up past the sugar refinery to the Whinhill, beyond which lay the open country, the Renfrewshire hills, Loch Thom and the western views over to the islands of Arran and Bute. He often went off alone, walking in the hills, taking a bag of provisions and a small telescope for looking at the stars. At Greenock High School he seems to have received some encouragement from an English teacher, Jack Gillespie, but had no wish at that time to pursue formal education or go to university. He was a member of the Trinity Church choir where the choirmaster and organist, Willis Calder, thought so highly of his voice that he encouraged him to have it professionally trained, even offering to pay for the initial lessons. Graham studied for three months but had no wish for a professional singing career either, though music was always an important part of his life. He did take part in the Operatic Society, joined the Tennis Club, and was by no means unsociable though some thought him slightly fey or eccentric. Relationships within the family seem to have been affectionate, though his strong will and independence caused some anxiety as he began to lead an increasingly separate life.

At fourteen he left school to take up an engineering apprenticeship, introduced by his mother's brother, John, a manager, to P. and W. McClellan (Structural Engineers) at a time when such opportunities were difficult to find. Graham seems to have enjoyed the early training in draughtsmanship (which included, amongst other things, writing the Lord's Prayer on a postage stamp) but his interest in engineering as a career was not very strong. During the later stages of his training he was often following up other interests more energetically and attending evening classes in art and literature at Glasgow University, in preference to mathematics and engineering subjects prescribed. He read voraciously and submitted poems to the *Greenock Telegraph*, at least one of which was published (under a pseudonym). In 1937 a friend, Norman Thomson, introduced him to Edwin Morgan (aged seventeen), leading to a strong friendship and a correspondence between the two young poets which continued at intervals over many years.

At the end of his apprenticeship Graham managed to obtain a bursary enabling him to spend the 1938–9 academic year at Newbattle Abbey, the residential College for mature students, near Edinburgh. A few fellow students thought him a 'poseur' because of his eccentric humour and increasing dedication to poetry, but it seems to have been a very rewarding year for him. All students took a course in Economics and two afternoons a week were spent in outdoor activities such as forestry or gardening. Graham's other courses were English Literature (including Anglo-Saxon poetry, Coleridge, Wordsworth, and modern writers such as Yeats, Synge, Joyce, Pound, and Eliot), and Scottish Literature (including Early Scottish Poetry). The courses were taught with thoroughness and he much enjoyed them, as he did the amateur theatricals and the music. At Newbattle he met Nessie Dunsmuir from Blantyre. She was a frequent companion and later provided much moral and practical encouragement in his life. She described his being, at this period, about 5ft 8ins in height and of slim build with fair skin, dark brown wavy hair with chestnut glints (which may have accounted for his once being described as red-haired, which he was not) and particularly piercing blue eyes. He was clean-shaven, walked with a springy step, 'and knew more about most people in five minutes than they knew about themselves'.

'I am a poet'. The first seven years.

TO ND

No two can meet the way that we have met
Completely like the marriage of fused stars
That streak their meteor'd lights each into each
And shuddering to the life of leaping light
Start down the sky charged to a double blaze.

No two can come the ways that we have come,
Like silver moonlight creeping over stones
On stream-banks, lighting every crystal vein
To Beauty's sadness. No, they have no dreams
To break the steady darkness of their night.

A draft of the poem 'To ND' fell out of his pocket at Newbattle Abbey and was picked up by the Assistant Warden, John Mack, who, on the strength of it, recruited him to the class in Philosophy during the second term. Here he became particularly interested in the Pre-Socratic philosophers. His interest in Heidegger developed later.

Some Newbattle students were strongly 'left-wing' but Graham appears to have remained 'as against the Left as the Right'.[4] His existing enjoyment of Scottish culture appears to have been enlarged and encouraged without, in his case, becoming especially politicised. His Scottish accent was never 'Englished', Scottish words and forms of speech occurred entirely naturally in his poetry throughout his life, but the pursuit of a specifically nationalist literature by some Scottish writers was to him an interference with the freedom necessary for poetry.[5] His family upbringing and the evidence of working-class poverty in the area had impressed on him the need for greater social justice but he appears to have had little confidence in political parties and theorists as agents of change. He was radical in a different way, one more directly connected to his medium of poetry.

As war drew closer, Graham's objection to conscription or coercion of any kind was typical of many writers and artists at the time, who similarly found that their genuinely held beliefs usually received no recognition from the Tribunals which questioned conscientious objectors unless they appeared to be based on conventional religious grounds. Independent philosophical convictions were not encouraged. Graham briefly took refuge in Ireland but eventually submitted to a medical examination. This disclosed that he suffered from an unsuspected ulcer and he found work in the Torpedo Factory at Fort Matilda near Greenock. One of his companions there recalled Graham's workmates being in some awe of him, as he so obviously had his mind on other things but there were lively evenings in the local pub, fuelled by whisky and 'Graham's Port', when he sang 'Who is Sylvia?' and 'Il Mio Tesoro' by popular request, 'as though to an audience of thousands'.[6] Another friend found that Graham's influence gave him an interest in literature which lasted for the rest of his life.[7]

It was probably during this period that his hill-walking enthusiasm got him into difficulties.

> I walked through Glencoe thinking I would get a lift not knowing the pass was blocked at the other end and went unconscious on Rannoch Moor – was found in early morning by a shepherd who took me back to his croft and gave me brandy. Snow everywhere – had no coat or food – had been in open air for three days sleeping out with 8d. in pocket (aged 21). Before I became unconscious sitting huddled in a sheepfold I imagined I heard girls laughing, that foxes came right up to me in the dark, that avalanches were starting. I wasn't frightened at all but enjoyed a lovely drugged kind of richness sitting in the numbing darkness – bloody pitch black.[8]

Most of Graham's factory work was at night. He kept a notebook in his drawer there and, when he had finished his quota of machining parts, was able to continue work on his first book of poems, *The Seven Journeys*. Although this was his first completed collection of poems it was not published until 1944. His second collection, *Cage Without Grievance* (a phrase used in the last poem of *The Seven Journeys*) was published in 1942 by David Archer's Parton Press. David Archer was a most generous and sympathetic patron of the arts. At the suggestion of the Scottish painter Robert MacBryde he had come from London to Glasgow to avoid the bombing. He was no businessman (his friends noticed that, as a bookseller, he refused to stock books he disliked and frequently gave away those books he particularly liked) but as a publisher he had a great eye for talent and had already published the first books of George Barker, David

Gascoyne and Dylan Thomas. Graham always freely acknowledged the influence Thomas had on his own early poetry and Thomas strongly supported Graham's work, on one occasion reading a Graham poem at the end of a performance of his own work. Both men first met in Glasgow and shared an over-arching enthusiasm for James Joyce.[9]

During the war Glasgow benefited from an influx of continental refugees. The artist J.D. Fergusson, born in 1874, had lived in France from 1905 to 1914 and again from 1929 to 1939, been a member of the Salon des Independants and known many of the modern French painters. His wife, Margaret Morris, was interested in non-classical forms of modern dance with an emphasis on music, rhythm and naturalistic movement. Fergusson was instrumental in starting The New Art Club in Glasgow at the end of 1940. The Polish painters Josef Herman and Jankel Adler came to the city, Herman having an influence on the evolution of a 'social realist' art and Adler an influence on artists such as Colquhoun, MacBryde and Minton. Graham helped Adler to translate his article on Paul Klee, whom Adler had known well, for the magazine *Horizon* in 1942.

By providing his Scott Street Art Centre in 1941 as a meeting place and resource centre at nominal fees, David Archer stimulated artistic life in Glasgow even though the Centre itself lasted only eighteen months. Many artists belonged to both clubs. Archer also provided a flat in Sandyford Place. Benjamin Creme and Robert Frame were able to stay there rent free and, when Graham left his job, Benjamin Creme invited him to stay at Sandyford Place too. Josef Herman, Jankel Adler, Helen Biggar, Julian Orde, Douglas Campbell, Jacky Hyams, Isabel Gourlay and many others became associated with The Centre and Christine Shaw (*née* Cramond) recalled politely asking Sydney Graham there if he was an artist. 'I'm a poet. I'm a bloody good one. I'll be the best', was his confident reply.[10]

Archer's connections were useful; he helped several local artists to visit London and some London artists came north. Later Graham became a familiar figure in Soho, staying with 'the Roberts', Colquhoun and MacBryde, in Bedford Gardens, where Adler also had a studio, or with Julian Orde in Highgate. For whatever reason he continued to drink far more than was good for him. Throughout his life he was usually a courteous man but when drinking he often appeared to adopt an unnecessarily challenging manner which could become tedious to those unfamiliar with him. Similarly, although he was grateful for the hospitality he often received, he sometimes interpreted it as patronising and responded with unnecessary shows of independence. It is also true that his eccentricities, though sometimes owing simply to nervousness, were often quite consciously adopted as a way of poking fun at friends he thought over-solemn. Graham was not physically aggressive (despite Maclaren-Ross's description of him as 'prickly')[11] and was often so lively and original as a companion that he began to earn respect for his work. One of his friends was the painter John Minton who often visited him later at the caravans in Cornwall. The warmth of Graham's affection for Minton is apparent in his invitation to him to visit the Graham family in Scotland in December 1945. Apparently the visit was a great success.

By 1942 Graham was working as what might be called a 'poet in residence' at Kilquhanity, a progressive school in Galloway, where he proved to be an effective teacher. He also formed a close relationship with a colleague, Mary Harris, who had taken First Class Honours in English at Oxford and pursued a serious interest in writing. In 1943 they left the school and went to live in Germoe, Cornwall, where Mary had two caravans which Sydney named 'The Wheelhouse'. Mary stayed there for a short time but they had already amicably agreed to separate and that their daughter Rosalind should be born and brought up by Mary in Scotland, as Sydney did not want to assume responsibility for a family.

The caravan was to remain Sydney's home until December 1947. In 1944 Nessie Dunsmuir joined him there and they struggled to live off the land, casual labour, growing violets and the infrequent publication fees from magazines. Both of them were writing and by 1945 the volume *2ND Poems* (**To N**essie **D**unsmuir)[12] was ready for publication.

1 The quotation is from a letter to the Editors, one of several interesting contributions written by David Allan. Much of our information about Graham's early life and family comes from visiting sites with Margaret Millar and David Allan, from David Allan's and Len McDermid's searches in local records, and from Sydney's brother Alastair.

2 Letter to Elizabeth Smart (undated, probably 1951). Margaret Graham herself was born in Greenock but her mother Julia McDermid was born in Ireland.

3 Jean Laird (information supplied by her grandson Ronald McNeil).
4 Letter to Alex Comfort, 12 December 1945.
5 To William Montgomerie, 20 August 1944, and to Moncrieff Williamson, undated, probably January 1949.
6 Jack Dooley (in conversation).
7 J. Johnston (conversation with Robert Calder).
8 Note to David Wright, *Edinburgh Review* 75 (Feb. 1987).
9 Thomas appeared to value Graham's opinion on his work. David Wright described Thomas in a Soho pub showing Graham an early draft of 'Fern Hill', written on the back of an envelope, and asking for comments. Mary Harris was present when Graham was asked to give an opinion on the first version of 'Poem in October'.
10 Letter to the Editors, 2 December 1994.
11 Julian Maclaren Ross, *Memoirs of the Forties* (London, 1965).
12 See letter to Peter Moldon, 4 May 1979, for significance of the '2ND' in the title.

1. *To Edwin Morgan*

[1938] 13, Brisbane St., Greenock

Dear Morgan,

It is indeed myself, Graham. I was reading over some of your poems the other night, aloud. The room was singing and dreaming with the sound of them. Three of the dream poems fused into me and made me cry – They must be good – 'or what does this signify to you.'

Mozart's 'Jupiter' plays upon.....I feel I am disintegra.....

[fragment of a torn page dated by E.M.]

2. *To John Lehmann*

7 October 1941 Greenock

John Lehmann,

I met David Gascoyne in Glasgow. He read some of my poems and liked 'The Narrator' particularly. He said he would write to you.

If you can't publish any of my poems will you please advise me where I might send them for I have had nothing published yet.

yours sincerely, W Sydney Graham

3. *To William Montgomerie*

10 June 1942 23, Windsor Terrace, Glasgow N.W.

William Montgomerie,

It is good to get your letter. I would be pleased to be published in a Scottish number of LIFE AND LETTERS and I hope you can find something suitable here.

I have had absolutely nothing published yet although the Parton Press (first publishers of Gascoyne, Barker, Thomas) are putting out a small book of my poems and I am now making arrangements with MacLehose the printers here in Glasgow. None of the poems I send you here will be included.

Yours sincerely, WSGraham

4. *To William Montgomerie*

5 July 1942 Glasgow

William Montgomerie,

I don't know why the making of a Scottish number of LIFE AND LETTERS has been put off because of poor material. I would have thought a worthwhile selection could have been made from poets like Muir, Grieve, Ruthven Todd, Scott, McCaig and myself. I don't think there is much good poetry being made in Scotland just now but there could have been a Scottish number surely equal to the Welsh one.

Dylan Thomas has been staying here with us for a week. He left for London yesterday. He agreed with me about the Scottish selection.

My book called CAGE WITHOUT GRIEVANCE is at MacLehose now. I wait for the proofs. Dylan likes it very much and will help me about reviewers etc.

I am interested in the Contemporary Group idea and hope to hear more about what it's doing.

The Centre just doesn't exist anymore and there is definitely no chance of it reopening again soon. It was my first experience of a crowd of people artistic intellectual. It sickened me a bit though I made a few good friends from the wreck and the talking parties.

When you come to Glasgow again I would like to see you. You can write beforehand and say when you will be.

sincerely, W S Graham

5. *To Edwin Morgan*

22 September 1943 Wheelhouse, Pengersick Lane, Germoe, Marazion, Cornwall

Dear Morgan,

I am pleased to hear from you and sorry you are disappointed for I mind what you think of my poetry. Mostly I don't care what people say about my poetry. You are one of the few poets I have talked to whose poetry was poetry. Now, at this time (is it 3 or 4 years later) what have we changed to? For me, Edwin, your letter goes on so much a stream of vague and complicated ingredients that poetry must have that maybe it is different things we want to make out of words and find in the poetry of others. I must try to answer parts and point out some values. Now, at this time, I know what is my poetry in all I do, I have the feel of it more, I know what I want to make more nakedly and in its element than ever in my life. And yet at this time I feel it a great task to write against your say. I promise it will not be so long again.

You say about my success or failure. I don't know – successes, failures, they occur often and continually to the heartbeat, as mixed and fused one in the other as a sorrow or a joy or a below or an above. My successes or failures are my own. Indoors they run riot and ruin or create and no one knows them even their names or for what they are and on them I sink and swim.

'unreal, without meaning, severed from true and naked emotion and shy of true thought'. People write and write so sweating that it should say something worthy and valuable to humanity that some comparative wisdom is tortured into the world, recognisable and able to be valued on its plane of the world's philosophy, so that the poet is assured and a bit certain that it is good (for does it not measure favourable with the things we know) and the public are a bit certain they are not being hoaxed (for here is something we understand) and another bad poem is made, a nice rivetted up wagon whose wheels all go silently round over the tested and known-to-be-good rails with its cargo of 100 tons Thought which is known to be a good weight.

The poet does not write what he knows but what he doesn't know. At this time I am more alive and creative in my thinking and intellect than ever I have been. I have read more, there are more things I am more sure of, I am more single and more constantly in my days a poet. Here, I find I am being driven into a protesting that my poetry has thought which wraps me up in a ridiculous bundle of I am's which cannot touch the other side of the territory where you simply find my poetry shy of true thought. Well, lastly in this, I, in the way I live and in what I make, outside on the bright paper, inside in my head above my heart, today am more widely an intellectual. (Christ the words Edwin so difficult and are so unspeaking when you want them to help). With you I am as sick of the poet's poetry today for many of the same reasons. Most poems today, their justification is not in their poetry but in some worthless overtone incidental to true poetry. The poets set up fishops to sell fish to the people who want fish and they all call the fish poetry and the fishmongers they call poets. And poetry is not fish but another stuff entirely. People want always just to do with the stuff they can weigh, the mapped part where things always fall down and never fall up into Heaven. Never have I written my poems slower with greater care with a prayer that I might burn bright enough to see out through the window which my poem is. Maybe it is that now what I am trying to make, you don't want. My poems tell me and let me peer through to something real and more elemental which has to do with all I breathe and make and am made.

You say you don't see how I can but admit your criticism but I don't. What you say is yours, and what I say about my poetry does not agree with it.

What you say about poetry I agree with. But the strange thing is that I would point out to people how in this line there is real poetry and quote 'Who longingly for violetcells prospect the meads.' or maybe 'Birches erect The ephemeral mechanism of welcoming.' and think of it with 'Cataracts are ephemeral to this fall' or quote all of (because of 'EPHEMERAL') O Gentle Queen, I, no more real than evil and Here next the chair I was when winter went, the three poems in my book which I would firstly let stand. So when I agree about poetry with you I then turn to my poems and say, yes that's right. I am always so first to say love the words the single words that have a heart and a world in them which beats and changes to a new rhythm in every new position of context. And I think now words are saying more for me. Please Morgan and even after all you've said be patient with the poems they are great poems only to me but they should not be so bad for you. What is it I wonder? I find now I'm wondering about going on like this protesting against this and that you say and I hate it. There's something wrong. This is not the way to do it. Good diction, emotion, height of intellect, shape form sincerity falseness tricked out not tricked out, they all make and are made from the minute life of the reader coming to the poem, being born into the first word of the first line, and being passed out of the world again at the last line's last word. We'll finish with it, eh Edwin?

CAGE WITHOUT GRIEVANCE is a first book of poems. It's all right, better than most first books, because I am potentially a greater poet than most today which does not make me very great but I am. The three poems I mention earlier will stand with me I think. The chief value is the realisation that my voice is heard and the involuntary responsibility which comes down on me and makes me more hard working at my poems. And there is the worth of the book as a shout which makes people turn their heads so that if I can shout some good it will be heard. From me, I don't think much of it. It's a start. The poems are hardly poems but have more to do with what poetry is than most poets in England today. The poems now are much better. There are two in a new magazine coming out shortly. POETRY SCOTLAND I'll send you a copy. I don't know if you see many poetry magazines. There are some new ones. I'll send a list of them to your mother so that she can send the ones you haven't seen. When you write again I will reply quickly. Have you any new poems I can see? I don't know why you joined the forces. When do you come back? Have I an unavoidable bias? (I'm looking through your letter before I finish.) Christ it's a great letter Morgan you can fairly write like a wee minister of a good gospel. I don't know what you want to be there for. I have my self said and then all you say I still say it's when it comes to my poetry, there's the bother. 'There are innumerable things to speak of and questions to ask.' I hope you write soon. It was Norman [Thomson] told me you wrote to him. Right, here's the end and I can't write more. I seem to not be stimulated up to replying good to your letter. I don't know why. It seems not to matter. Yet it does matter to me very much that you are disappointed. Its raining now on the roof. I'm living in a caravan a friend's lent me in Cornwall, lonely and by the sea. I fish and gather mushrooms and write and cook.

Yours sincerely, W S Graham

6. *To Ben Nicholson*

16 October 1943 Germoe

Ben Nicholson
Dear Sir,

I'm living here near Praa Sands in a caravan a friend's lent me. I've been here three months and I would like to talk to someone. I'm quite alone here. Could I please visit you. I'm interested in poetry. Parton Press published my first book about a year ago. If it's all right will you let me know when to come. I can ride over on my bike.

Yours sincerely, W S Graham

7. *To William Montgomerie*

19 January 1944   c/o [Helen] Biggar, 8 Grovepark St.,Glasgow.

Dear William Montgomerie,

Thanks for your letter and yes I would like fine to come up to Dundee and have a talk with you and with the group about poetry and making poetry. I've never been in Dundee. I would like to see the countryside. Just now I am in no official job, so the date can be as soon as you want. I might have some job out of Glasgow by March. How many people might be there? Does the group meet in Dundee or Broughty Ferry? If you can give me a bed and my fare that will be all right.

The Braque quotation is interesting and has to do with what I believe about each (say) poem being an addition to the world, not a distortion or mathematic of known digits of what we have already. After each poem there should be such an apparent addition to the world that it will be as obvious as a new over-4000ft mountain added to the Grampians. It is plainer to see when we remember the block of words which is Blake or even lately, Yeats. It's almost as physical as a geographical change. I've read Stein's PICASSO. I liked it very much. The Apocalyptics, have they [a] 'line' about surrealism? Their work doesn't show any definite approach to it. Here's a quotation concerning the position of surrealism to making poetry, from Edith Sitwell's introduction to Helen Rootham's translation of Rimbaud's LES ILLUMINATIONS.

'Rimbaud, masculine and powerful, provoked the unconscious by perfectly voluntary methods, and at the same time remained master of the treasure-trove of his draggings; Surrealism and its imitators, all of them feminine, are passive, and endure the inner word.'

The poet must make use of the 'inner word' but with it construct carefully and certainly.

I didn't get a copy of the Scottish LIFE AND LETTERS. They must have sent it to Cornwall. I'm interested in Scottish Nursery Rimes. I'm sorry I didn't see your article. Do you know

Water water wallflower..growing up so high
We are all children. We all must die.
Except Nessie Dunsmuir, the fairest of them all.
She can dance and she can sing
And she can turn her face to the wall.

and a rime-game called 'Sclim the lether'?
Thanks for the poem and I hope to hear from you soon
Yours sincerely, W S Graham

8. *To William Montgomerie*

10 February 1944 Glasgow

Dear William Montgomerie,

I have not written sooner because I have been trying for a job as deckhand on a boat which sails from Greenock round the islands. It is still not completely arranged yet and I don't think I'll be away before the 19th. So I would like to come. If I have any word from the Steamship people I'll wire you directly, but I don't think this is likely.

I am completely broke just now and the people I might borrow from are also broke. Would it be possible to send me my fare. Let me know soon about this so that I can have time to find some way. Shall I come straight to your address in Broughty Ferry?

It's good about the chance of the broadcast. I hope it comes off. No, I've not published any book since C W G [*Cage Without Grievance*]. PL [*Poetry London*] (Nicholson and Watson) is putting out a book in the spring called 2ND POEMS. It is made up of 23 poems from 1942 to last October. I think they're an improvement on C W G. I'll type out a few tomorrow of the best and most suitable for broadcasting. If the poems have appeared somewhere or have been accepted for publication in a magazine or journal, do I have to obtain permission for them to be broadcast?

Yours sincerely W S Graham

9. *To William Montgomerie*

24 February 1944 Glasgow

Dear Bill Montgomerie,

Here are the poems I read, A LETTER MORE LIKELY TO MYSELF, MANY WITHOUT ELEGY, and ALLOW SILK BIRDS THAT SEE. And one other, THE HALFTELLING SIGHT. Apart from how good they are the poems which would read easiest are, MANY WITHOUT ELEGY, HIS COMPANIONS BURIED HIM (Poetry Scotland), THE

NARRATOR and THE SERVING INHABITERS (Life and Letters). In the book, the poems which I think are best and easiest for reading aloud, are HERE NEXT THE CHAIR..., I, NO MORE REAL THAN EVIL... and maybe O GENTLE QUEEN OF THE AFTERNOON. I know you will use them in the best way but it might help you to know how I feel about which are the easiest to read. If you want copies of any other poems let me know.

I enjoyed very much my visit to Broughty Ferry and goodness your wife is a lovely woman. And it must be good to have children like Ian and Diane. I will send you some C without Gs and you can give them to people interested. I'll find out the terms and fees of Kilquhanity House School. And more nursery rimes for Norah. Will you remember to send me a copy of the elegy for Soutar when it's finished. I would like to come and see you all at Broughty Ferry in the summertime.

Yours sincerely W S Graham

10. *To John Minton*

4 July 1944 c/o [Julian] Orde, 49, Cholmeley Crescent London

Dear Johnny,

Yesterday a day of rain and now today, a higher sky and the birds singing here among the limes of the crescent, and I wonder what to do today for Norman[1] seems to be making things just *too* difficult, so anyhow Johnny, here I'm writing to you with your lovely letter before me, and I'll be sending it off to go to wherever you are and to meet you coming in from whatever you're doing.

Today I feel lonelier than usual. I think maybe tonight I'll go into the Marquis etc. for a few lemonades. And to suffer the talk and the music, spilled drinks and mopped-up counters and the looks and continual flow of the people through the eye. With the pub and all its grinning hundreds, still the countryside never becomes shut out. It is so true that outside the land is crossed with curving canals and clumped with towns ending in 'wich' or 'burgh' or 'bury'. Christ it will be fine to get to the green, rising and falling, wooded, meadowing, rivering countryside. A gain. Today the shires hold up their trees and cant their rivers to the faroff sea. Always its a looking for

1 Probably refers to Norman Bowler.

something.

'Then lean out, Love, and yearn from the window
That ever you saw from, that far hero,
Some one wandered into imagination
And weed of the way, and word won.'[1]

I'm lost in foxes of falling down. Dear Johnny I can write nothing today I see now I've begun. Christ you are a very good person, and not many I see around. It's so fine that you're not comfortable. For Jesus sake work hard. But phone me as you said you would, remember. It is to write quicker and say why love encumbers as the kiss sets free, and why eye sparks and shines and builds my heart, or why the sky is held aloft over the shires of England by my making, keeping, constructing, own blue eye. We should speak good before I go and something valuable come of talking and shying our thoughts at our glasses, and spinning a hopeless word on those despairatly soaked counters of the povertystricken talkers of London.

'Near farms and property of bright night-time
By mileaway dogbark how there is means to say'[2]

Love *Sydney*

11. *To William Montgomerie*

20 August 1944 Germoe

Dear Bill,

Drinking tea this morning under my neighbour elderberry tree, I begin this letter to write to you specially about SCOTTISH POETRY AND THE TECHNIQUE OF VERSE.

It's difficult for there's nothing in it I disagree with. All you say is important and should be published somewhere, better in Scotland. So I'm left only to talk about the things you haven't dealt with under your heading TECHNIQUE OF VERSE and which your leaving out so completely might give a wrong impression. You keep so completely to the TECHNIQUE OF PHYSICAL (sound) VERSE that the impression might be that the poet builds (I'm now talking about his conscious

1 From 'The Lost Other' in *The White Threshold* (1949).
2 From 'Explanation Of A Map' in *2ND Poems* (1945).

wordcraft) purely out of sound and that there is not a consciously working TECHNIQUE OF MENTAL VERSE. And here I don't mean inspiration or idea. I mean that just in the same cold conscious way as I can construct a line or phrase like

Even this woman to her lover woven

which is active so much through its rime and alliteration, I can construct – More one has good of me and bad breaks way. in which the 'and bad breaks way' is helped by 'makes way. Or 'needle eye', the fact of a needle having an eye makes it organic in the language. Or 'my eyes achieve further through elegy' in which the word 'achieve' does its dictionary meaning and also suggests the word 'move'. Also the conscious use of 'clichéforms' as in -

Without a song backward since spring bleeds the peat (without a glance backward) and – Makes sure example of ... and – To put it springtime the green shepherd, (To put it mildly) and – By far the ghost and surest of all the sea (by far the best) and – Poverty takes over. and – wakens wide. and – At her beck and miracle (at her beck and call) I think this conscious use of clichéforms and associations which I do as technically as I construct in sound, and most poets, should have been mentioned. And if approaching verse from the poet's side why not mention beginnings of poems, lines of poetry which are justified by their different qualities, say we take three lines, all successful but active through different roads to the reader.

a Wiry and white-fiery and whirlwind-swivelled snow
b Nor fret for few who die before I do
c Spins to the widow-making unchilding unfathering deeps

a A sensual experience

b An utterance, disturbing in its suggestions and kept memorable and easy to say by its construction.

c A sensual experience and has all the world significance of b. It has all that physical sight and movement of a, but is so much more significant to me as soon as the widow child father is put in. And it speaks of so many things at once, the ship, widows, the seas, the child, the drowned, the father,

I construct my lines so that each line is justified and (in relation) floated by definitely some activity.

And memorableness. It's something I construct towards, part of my direction. And saying and suggestion [of] many things and overtones from one phrase or line. Maybe successful in – 'My lifetime treads a rolling ball.' And now I know I've gone away from maybe the things under TECHNIQUE OF VERSE. (I'll read over what I've written and see what's to say now.) Yes Bill, it seems to me that almost a wee bit the article might give folk the idea that a line of poetry couldn't exist without riming and alliteration and devices. And there are lines like – 'The senses roll themselves in fear' and 'the voice of him that walketh in the garden in the evening time' and – 'And makes one little room an everywhere.' Anyhow I think the article is very good and I wish we could do something to waken things up and get the National bias down and more poetry in Scotland to be made of words instead of heather and homerule and freedom. The simple thing's that poetry is made of none of them. POETRY'S MADE OF WORDS And yet people keep forgetting it. I liked what you said about the poetry 'O mistress mine, till you I me commend' and how the modern Scottish poets are not conscious of the laws of language as this.

What's to be done?

Please let me hear from you soon and will you be trying to have this published? your article. How is Norah's collection going on? Is she doing any work on her cloots? And the children?

yours sincerely, Sydney

12. *To John Minton*

[September 1944]

Dear Johnny,

Cornwall September mist wind wet bracken noon, a rabbit in the pot and sauce (family size) in cupboard, each day poetrymaking and each night royal thirst and song and tralleeing among the pints. Are you still in the painting working mood? Or is it all gone under the miserable tides beersounds frustrations of London. A hawk over the field, hoverer over me. O what is to become of us poor all of us? You can burn letter to PJ now.[1] All the same if you do see her or hear she's about, tell her to write to me. If you see a magazine called NEW POETRY around could you send me a copy. I'm working very hard each day and poetry growing up into such a garden in me. I'll be maddening.

1 PJ probably refers to Peggy Jean Epstein, as she was known to be one of his friends.

'He takes to himself fleetly the morning
And follows a smoky flock to bring
Him to the apple that rivers his life
And her voice under a tempest leaf.'

At the packet still I'm asked where is my pal the tall one and I say He's a Londoner and an artist and they nod and smile and say g'an drink up man, have one along w'me. And up I drink my eyes full of songs and my lips full of gardens and my feet full of wrong roads. Nessie drinks too and gently smiles. She leaves for Glasgow on todayweek. At night the beer flows down. The words flow in my head. The owls hoot and I get back down the road to sleep and nestle inside my heroshell and ask me how my poem's going. Cheerio for a while, And Love

13. *To John Minton*

[September 1944]

18th September Dear Johnny with good weather here and clouds and swans on the horizons and I'm swimming a lot and at night out ferreting. You find the run. The 'run' may have a dozen entrances and exits. You stop some up and net others up and then take the ferret from the bag. Like a big yellow weasel with ruby eyes and will bite if you don't watch. You coup the weasel. 'Couping' the weasel is tying together the two little rings (steel) which go through the jaws, so that it can't kill the rabbits. Then you bell it. You hang round its neck a wee bell like from a child's rattle. This is so that you can hear it padding about the passages of the run. Well, in it goes and if you're lucky rabbits bolt out like wildfire into the nets. We got none. A bad lot of runs we tried. Not so much pub at night. More writing, longwalks and reading. So I go on. Eating is not too bad. Plenty potatoes and brambles and bread, quite filling though not too tasty. The four shillings are very nice and I'll get something good. You know not to worry in the least about my eating. I always am a very luckyman and always the angels of providence watch over my bed and my house in my head. HORIZON SENT BACK My Definitions and now they've my new poem called THE SEARCH BY A TOWN which they've considered for about six days now but I'm not worrying and I suppose it will be back in a post or two. Christ

I am sorry to hear of you not well but glad you're well on the way to a speedy discovery. And what a carryon with no money and your house full of bills. Work hard how is it going, the work. Thanks for *Listener*. Of course you bet sure thing absolyootly I'll let you know if I get ill or anything from being really hungery. Love to Robert and Robert and how is their exhibition going on?[1] Are you in it too? Are you going to have or what an exhibition soon. Have you made good paintings from the Cornwall sketches? O it's a good day. Sunout and seagentle and hoppers in the grass and cater pillars making Colquhouns and birds here now rooking the blackthorn elderberry hawthorn of their berries. What Brambles O Boy. Is there an Everready blade within reach. Even one. I just can't buy even one anywhere around and uncomfortable with my chin like bracken. Cheerio and Love. Sydney

14. *To John Minton*

20 September 1944 Germoe

Dear Johnny,

Please post this on immediately. As it is it's late and will have to be posted right when it gets to London. I would have posted it to Julian[2] but she's maybe leaving for some A S Neil-type school with wee Emily anytime. Here it's autumn and clear and in me a strange tick-tock of moods. One minute lonely as an abandoned, next minute with joy at my own one self in the centre of my unpeopled moods bracken hill waves pages birdsong blackthorn and the high up and down sky of September. This letter is for you to post this BIPO[3] Johnny and be sure for it means some money maybe in a fortnight and good food. Word from Nessie. She says Frank's[4] a big hit with folks and even her mother thinks she should marry him. No work now for over a week. I'll be beginning soon again and see

1 Robert Colquhoun (1914–62) and Robert MacBryde (1913–66), Glasgow-trained painters, who shared a show with John Minton at the Alex Reid and Lefevre Gallery in 1944.

2 Graham's friend Julian Orde was an actress and poet; Emily was her daughter.

3 BIPO may be a reference to British Institute of Public Opinion; the Grahams did undertake some part-time opinion survey work.

4 Frantisek Koranda from Czechoslovakia was a member of RAF aircrew. He was later reported missing in action in 1944.

what will be made to come out. I've been looking a lot at [Graham] Sutherland's pictures and on the wall and they begin to make good business along with my eye. He's very lyrical and maybe even now and then a bit too sweet. Do you think so? I would like to draw or paint, this weather, but I know it's only an idler's carryon for me shirking my words and problems.

'Of him that walketh in the garden in the eveningtime'

Or do we know a prince bleeding more gently
Away to best the morning at its gates?

He takes to himself fleetly the morning
And follows a smoky flock to bring
Him to the apple that rivers his life
And her voice under a tempest leaf.

Please work hard and make a good helmet round your head. For it is all a battle and the only way is to make an armour from the god and – in us each all. Love. Sydney.

15. *To William Montgomerie*

3 October 1944 Germoe

Dear Bill,

Word came from Maclellan saying that you would like to write a foreword to The Seven Journeys. Yes. I feel very good about it. It would be a help. Can I have the final say as to whether it is suitable? Please don't mind me being careful about this but about the foreword – Usually forewords are too extravagant and the result is worse than none. – (MacD's 'Fury of the Living' foreword – but that was cockeyed as well as being too extravagant). Without wishing to write it or say what you should say (for of course I want it to be your unbiased explanations and pointing-outs of the poems, and a help to the reader) would it be possible to have some discussion by letter while you are writing this? I'm excited about you doing it and sure it will be interesting. Macl. seems quite keen on the idea. Can you let me know soon about this. You're no wizard at answering letters.

How's Norah and children and cloots, nursery rimes, short stories, contemporary group and collected stories? I'm being very quiet this weather, reading Blake and Bible mostly with little bits of Joyce. I've finished a poem called The Search By A Town. I hope you'll like it. Please write soon.

regards to all, Sydney

16. *To John Minton*

13 October 1944

Cornwall winday and night 13 10 44 and the house rocks like a boat bobbing on the graves of night dear Johnny how are you now and what goes on slowly or I should say without speed for inside in head and heart and the invisible country behind the eyes it is all fast and slow with never a break. Dear Johnny how are you? Or to put it back-words, You are how Johnny dear? I wrote a letter but it's lost and with the wind but maybe someone's posted it and it's got you. I am careless but the wind is a bit furious and you know it is not hard to lose a letter some times. It said thanks for wired money and then got a bit shy about the middle and said so sorry to have to ask you Johnny and then finished with a grand flourish about getting away from here for a while and glad when fare comes. If I can remember it said those things. And I am sorry about your brother[1] and you must feel so helpless about it. Today ten shillings came thanks. With Nessie here it's less lonely but time for me to be away for a while. Poor Nessie is so sad and worrying about Frank. I'm sad about it too and wish he and I had been more together. I hope he turns up.

Here great gales have gone on with high white waves on the sea and the wind like a flying wall. You could be knocked down if you didn't hold on to safety somewhere. All the leaves are off and lots of growing things broken and hanging. I am even happier now at the thought that I can go away soon and since Nessie came I've been working every day and a new poem swimming up the channel. I am by the light of the sweet oil lamp and the dark winds go on outside. I wonder what happened to PJ sometimes and hope she's a bit happier. I wonder what happened. Thanks for blades I'll have a fine young shaved face when I come up.

1 John Minton's younger brother, Richard, was killed near Antwerp on 18 September 1944.

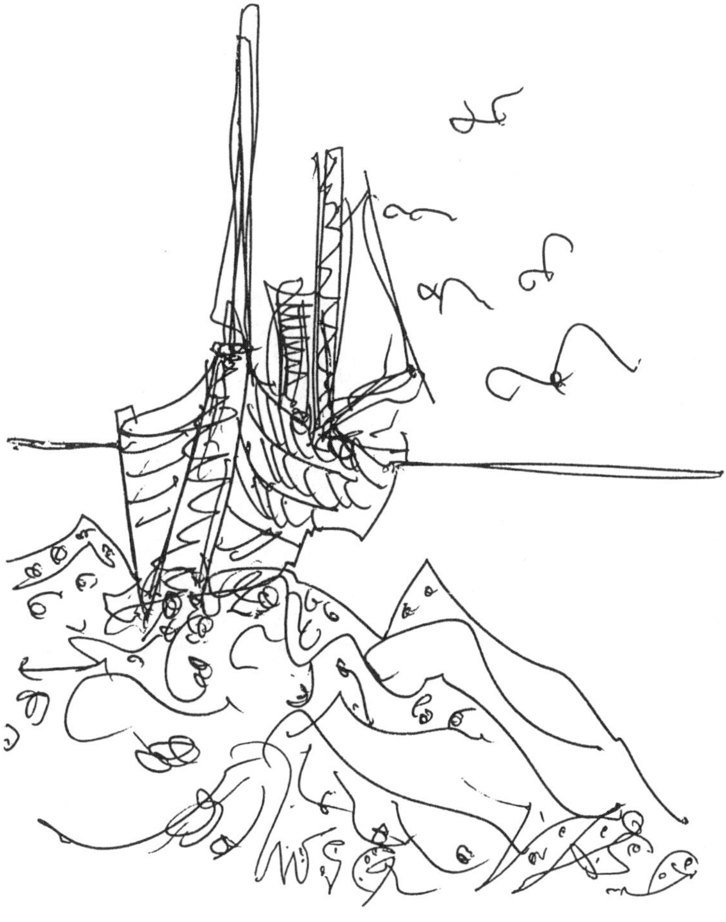

Mary [Harris] the mother of my daughter dear wants me if I go to London to go there for about two days and to see Rosalind Anne my daughter dear. Also I'll be able to go to Julian's if I want. Also I might be able to go to see the actress one. So there's no fear of me staying too long and keeping you off your work. You know I wouldn't would I you know me better than that. Well work hard and good and I do look gently forward to seeing you. Love. Sydney

17. *To John Minton*

[undated]

Dear Johnny,

Some I've wound mercy on. Is lost. I have followed The Fall and like you that ark and ghost of the mist I've stung like a nettle and kissed like a rose. By light I've been made welcome and by dark made fright. So I say there is nothing to do but to make myself proof against. And by being continually the active poet with a garden of lyrical energy behind both my eyes and my helmet moving anywhere. Although, Johnny, I'm off my contraries, I have in me a longing for what I'm empty of and to be what I suppose I'll never become and to meet people who are like Angels and it all drives me into my own countries and to make the journeys and angels and there to act the morals I'm not allowed in 'reality'. I construct my saviour. Work at my poetry is the thing to compensate me for my loss of living, say, in Leeds, a cyclemaker or a shopassistant. I'm so lucky for already I'm of a magnitude enough to myself to be able to suck from and find life from that spring, being a poet and making. Awful if I had been sensitive above the station of the usual shopassistant and yet not any artist in me. There must be people. It's right, I know some. This is all to say don't feel sad alone. And to say therefore how pleased I am that you're working good.

I'm sorry I have to type this letter. Somehow I'm not in a handwriting mood and when I begin a letter I've nothing to say. Your letter and magazines arrived last night and thanks very much Johnny. Try to phone PG now and then. Have you tried the morning, say about 10.30. All the time (don't be feart. I won't run up to London in a sudden) I always would like again to meet you at 6 in the French and begin with two of yon smellers from the dripdrop barrel of ice and then out on the streets and from one to another and the good stuff on the counter and beery floorboards and damp jokes spilled and jostled over giggling chairbacks. And to carry in a helmet of head, rivers, landscape wearing a far seasound over its hills, and saying in my head – 'SAY OIL AND HONEY THEY SWEETLY ANOINT AND RAIN' Man in ten worlds lifts up a griefstruck face. Johnny or many in ten worlds lift up the mastertask, and over the streets (and far seasound) of the city broken to voice and replies from bar and horseshop Paul pints and bluelit underground piss-place, and over the green seas of the bracken and land here, and far blue water, and over my hair and heart quietly like a river go the names and wishes curbs and goods and thousand successes of the moment. The blackthorns are moving in the gentle wind and soon they'll have sloes.

Or do we know a prince bleeding more gently
Away to best the morning at its gates.

Today is the heat back and the sun everywhere. The table's under the elderberries. Beauty's sniffing some heavy robust omelette. I've begun a new Definition and I'll send you a copy when it's finished. I've been ill a bit, but now a bit better; Nessie leaves probably Thursday. I like the pictures, the first one best. Don't drink too much and watch the terrible bombs.

End Here. Sydney

18. *To Norah Montgomerie*

2 December 1944 Germoe

Dear Norah

already midwinter all over me here and shouting through my letterbox. The gales from the sea rock me about and my poor arkvan and flood comes in through the wrenched seams. I'll have to be fixing scuppers round the walls to drain away the waters. Three days now of a constant gale coming up over the shore and lifting sand and salt. The rooks are blown about and the gulls sail well inland. I've a new highnecked navyblack jersey so the cold can't get me. Only there's wind and wet, winter and angry weather. The air has a smell of iodine and drowned fields. Water water wish you well.

It's good to hear from you and you making a design for MANY WITHOUT ELEGY. I do feel very proud and I look forward very much to see it. As well as the excitement over it as a new thing completely separate from my poem I will also be interested in it as a remark of some objectivity on the poem. You know how one's work can be too close and one stands on the paw of the Sphynx and finds it impossible to see the shape of it in any way significant. So he has to climb down off the paw and walk fifteen years away till he sees it across an expanse of wilderness. What do the DAS think of your work? I wish I could see the portrait of Bill sometime.

Yes it's bad about the RIMES not being taken yet or Bill's HAMLET. I don't know. I give up about publishers and what moves them. At the moment I feel very hopeless about them. A publisher said could he have some poems for a certain anthology and then quickly with a not-too-serious emphasis and an ashamed wee giggle adds 'but remember the Great British Public'. It almost becomes a temptation. One has the choice of writing those poems with correct ingredients calculated to squash delightfully on the palate of the reader. Or to make a poem which will release the reader to a responsibility of his own. Christ what a mess it is that the publisher's position should be so much a gateman when he hasn't the eyes to see what his visitors are. You'll keep sending them out I hope. Yes I saw MY CHILDHOOD and it's a grand film. The big mother's dancing was lovely wasn't it. I wish THE SEVEN JOURNEYS was out. The introduction will help. It's just right for the job. I'm so glad you and Bill like the Journeys so much. After your letter I read them again and indeed it's a whole fine country to walk on and breathe on and sail on and with hills and seas and glaciers you can dazzle your eyes with. They're young poems and win by an ascending enthusiasm. It's nice you like them so well. It's like 'thanks' coming for some good I've done. Yes please send your stories. Have I to say anything about them. Or just read them. If you like ask me specific questions to answer about them and I'll try to help. Though I'm not sure about prose.

Certain I'll keep my cottagehunting eye open and I'm glad you're trying to get Bill away from the teaching habit. Unless you're first and never-wanting-to-do-anything-else a teacher, you're better out of it all and all the energy into the right thing.

Emily's lovely with a gentle helmet of brow and brown quick eyes, a straight wee back when she runs after her cooking mother, but can be a powerfully bawlin bairn when she starts. She'll be lovely and a right queen when she's up and about in the love courts of her teens. Julian isn't so well and a bit unhappy there in London.

I'll be going to London I think for Christ Mass and Hogmanay out of this wet and wind for a while to see two Scots painters there called MacBryde and Colquhoun maybe you know them and very good and serious artists. I'll enjoy talking to people again and hearing about their ups and downs and some drink and singing like a bird on a tree. I'll let you and Bill know the new address which will be for about a month, when I leave here. I'll be writing Bill in a day or two. Well Wishes to Dian and Iain and Bill. Water water wish you well. That's like an old rime isn't it. Maybe I'll be able to make a child's verse out of it.

Sydney

19. *To John Minton*

16 December 1944 Germoe

Dear Johnny,

Your letter came to us here this morning Saturday and now I'm going to write you and wire you to send the £2 if you can manage at all. We're very broke but Nessie will be able to travel by train and I'll h[itch]hike. It's lovely to know we can come for we were beginning to give up about coming at all. It's been freezing and wet here and Cornwall's worst rain for years. I'm glad you're going to see Scotland Johnny. Try to visit Glasgow too. There's a bigshot poetry reading being held there in the Stevenson Hall on 29th. Dec. McDiarmid Douglas Young Montgomerie Hendry Lindsay and Bruce will be there. The whole Scots Singers and lyricists. It might be interesting if you had a drink in you. It's a pity Colquhoun might not get off with you. Maybe he'll be able to follow soon. Nessie and I look forward to seeing you on 30th.

Dear Johnny I've nearly finished a very fine poem, I think inspired partly by seeing all the Journeys printed so well and in one book. It is very of the sea and nightwatching sea. 'Cabins the boy in joy in a seadogged lifesave'. Christ Johnny I'm so glad to be seeing you and at the Hogmanay too, please be to Christ you're a bit happier and enjoying yourself better than last time, you insider you. Today to the violets and 15penny hour. Thanks for 5/- and the address book.

Love. Sydney

20. *To William Montgomerie*

3 January 1945 Germoe

Dear Bill

a Happy new year and to Norah and the children. It's a long time since you wrote and I wonder how you are being up there by the firth and if there's any news of the Hamlet book being published and how are the short stories going and Norah's anthology. I've been in London which was specially dreich and over it a freezing damp. I'm at writing again and glad to be back here with the biggest enemies winter and rough weather. We've had the snow too. And frost on top. It lay over all the countryside paleblue in the mornings and pink at nights (it is the west here). We fed the birds with generous crumbs and some mildewed oats, though I was angry at the starlings being pirates to the robins and bluetits who came also. Curiously the starlings were the easiest scared away.

But today I could say it's the first Spring day and I was outside making a fire and cooking a rabbit and easily you could feel the sweet warm sun. The birds are wilder again with the ground soft. I've been writing a lot.

I've begun a poem about Greenock which is to be 'simple' and it begins

Local I'll bright my tale on how
She rose up white on a Greenock day
Like the one first-of-all morning
On earth, and heard children singing.

She in a listening shape stood still
In a high tenement at Spring's sill
Over the street and chalked lawland
Peevered and queened and fancymanned

On a pavement of shouting galleries.
She saw them children of all cries
With everyone's name against them bled
In already the helpless world's bed.

It might not stand like that when I've finished. Also I've finished a poem of 24 lines which begins

The arrival wakes, sunstruck from a million men

which is very much about the sea and 'I am Continual Arrival'. I've the proofs of 2ND POEMS to correct so that should mean it will be out with[in] another year. I soon will have 3RD POEMS[1] ready. Christ I wish they'd hurry up. Please let me know if you've written any poems lately. Could I see Norah's stories she said she would send. I had word from Julian today that she has a job as leading lady at the Harrogate Rep. Address – Opera House, Harrogate. She's pleased but sad about leaving wee Emily. A line from Norah saying congratulations would help to buck her up. Regards to all. Sydney

21. *To Ben Nicholson*

23 January 1945 Germoe

Dear Ben Nicholson,

We arrived here on Saturday and been against the weather since we came down, stopping up leaks and making preparations for keeping warm at nights. But today the sun's out and it looks better for us.

We had a nice time in London and saw our friends and people. Tambi[muttu] is very strange about the book and I'm afraid it's coming out to look very badly.[2] All now I hope is that he might overlook the contract promising him first choice of the next three.

Here are the books and I'm sorry to have kept them so long. I always meant to bring them with me when we came to see you next. The Ramsden book was very good.[3]

Would you send the Gascoyne book here and enclose your phone number. Maybe when the weather's warmer we could come over to see you? Or anytime you might cycle over here. I hope the wee girl is better. Regards. W S Graham

1 *3rd Poems, 4th Poems* etc. were *pro tem* titles for current projects.

2 Editor of *Poetry London* magazine, later of *Poetry London–New York*. Published Graham, Kathleen Raine, David Wright, Dylan Thomas, David Gascoyne and many others. See *Tambimuttu – Bridge Between Two Worlds*, ed. J. Williams (London, 1989).

3 In May 1944 Ben Nicholson wrote to Herbert Read that he had seen Graham several times, was interested in some of his ideas, and that 'his method of working at his writing seems like my method of working at my painting' (Chris Stephens, Introduction to *The Constructed Space* exhibition catalogue, Ilkley, 1994).

22. *To John Minton*

5 February [1945]

5th February dear Johnny for us today here by the sea you can feel the Spring coming on. There's a mild wind and the sun comes warm through the mist. Just outside the caravan, on the nearest blackthorn, the bluetits seasaw and peck at the best brown bread. I've a sprig of honeysuckle in water in a milkbottle on the deskbed here and you can already see the leaves coming out. I feel very happy this weather and a bit contented. I've been writing good and a big lot of work done. My Greenock poem's nearly finished and I've an idea for the start of another. It's so lovely now that the cold spell has gone and we've been down and along the shore and find a good lemon that was swept up by the tide and a boathook and a brush and a rope fender but too heavy with sand and soaking to move.

What a fine morning to get the five pounds. Christ you're very good Johnny. We paid two lots of back rations and some bacon and stuff. Before that we'd been at the vegetables for days. Though all the same it was good fun going up to Curno's field for a cabbage or two and then the field beside us for potatoes broccoli and sprouts. And a rabbit now and then and the beachcombed lemon in the tea. It would be fine if we could live just off the world about us but no it's not Hawaii. We've not been at the pub once and although I could be nudged by thirst easily onto the stuff again I'm not worrying or athirst. The work is the thing. And the Spring and green winds. The hedges and the dykes and the high line of trees trimmed by the offsea Cornish wind. Red Campions still blooming in the shiteplace on the hill. No eggs yet from those Martin hens. I was a little disappointed in Dylan's new poem in HORIZON. Today this morning Nessie's just had word her father's dying, so tears. And I reflect about families and fathers and 'the line'. It brings me to Scotland and I realise I would like to live there in the country-westside and write and be in the place I'm flower of. But there's no family left there for me and when I think of it there's no group of people I would very much like to have around me. But I would like to be among the bens and by burnsides in Glen Orchy. Even I would like just to be on the top of a high mountain again, say Ben Narnaine or Ben Ime or Ben An. Bog myrtle loch long arrochar the rest and be thankful argyle dunbartonshire the bridge strathblane strathyre.

Poor Mervyn. Poor Irish Sean. Poor Sean Black. I hope you're working well. Love to Robert and Robert. I'll write them soon. Love. Sydney

23. *To Norah Montgomerie*

17 March 1945 Germoe

Dear Norah,

Your letter and bestwishes and news and stories came about a month ago and I was sorry to hear about the tonsillitis and glad about at last the rimes being done by Hogarth. I'll have my eye open for them. I don't know about Maclellan and the 20 Collection. I don't think you would get much out of it in money but it might be valuable in other ways. I've quite given up expecting reasonableness from publishers editors and the people at the gates. I got about £3 from Mcl just before the book was published and since then never had a note to say how the book was going. But in my case (obscure modern poetry) it is just that way and I'm not disappointed. I don't know about the efficiency of his distribution methods or advertising but he may be alright. Yes he's a 'good' business man and rarely takes his 'haun oot's pooch'.

Yes I heard about the reading and Bill's demolishing the staging. I wish I had been there with a wee drop of the stuff in me. I'm sorry he's not feeling so well. Is he writing any poetry? Or is it more stories?

About the story, Norah. I like it fine. I think you should find it fairly easy to publish. For me it is not enough an addition to the world for me to get excited about it. I mean that it's not traditional enough. I like very few stories or novels by people writing today. Because Joyce Wolfe [Woolf?] and Hardy have been it's difficult not to look for the new shoots at the top of the tree which have grown from what's grown before. I like the story and it's pleasant and the observation is rare. I enjoyed reading it. Of prose I have not broad appreciation. Very few writers excite me. I just push quickly through the novel to argue with the ideas and see who marries who. In the best prose I think it should work as in poetry (that may be my limitation) that the activity should happen because the words are in a certain order, rather than because the reality recollected by the writer is interesting. O dear it does seem involved when I try to make clear. But I did like the story, Norah and where are you sending it to? Here's a wee poem I made yesterday. [Here follows 'To A Tear']

This poem is an aside poem from a long poem I'm working on just now which begins 'Final my goal, Saint Other in the fields'. Sometimes when you've been working on one thing for a long time it is a relief to come up for breath and make some very different kind of thing. I'm not sure about the title. Maybe when you write again you'll give me your opinion and Bill's.

I don't like the other FRAGMENT at all, Norah. Quite apart from trying to measure it in any way as literature, I don't like it. About whether it's good as writing and publishable, I'm not sure. Maybe my dislike is the result of shock in the images. As surrealism I would criticise the lack of direction in the images and the complete abandonment to them. I think maybe that if I didn't know myself that the defence of Stalingrad was a good and inspired thing for you, I wouldn't know from FRAGMENT. Maybe this isn't important. I wish you could have told me what you think of it yourself Norah. Anyhow about prose I am less sure than I am about poetry. Did you expect me to say anything about them or not? It is just what I think, don't be put out.

Julian's had bad luck again and back in London but maybe you know and she's written you. The spring's coming quickly here and the new rabbits are in the sun already. The birds sing away champion. The flowers are springing fast. And gently the shoures sote. I've been reading Croce Rilke Joyce and The Holy Bible. Also many books about Tibet. Tibet is a strange place and I read a lot about it. There's no more word of my 2ND poems and I never ask. Have you written much. Any poetry? What happened about the design you made for Many Without Elegy? Thanks for the prune jam recipe. Best wishes to Iain and Dian. Please watch that my address next time is correct. Your writing of it fused the Cornish Post Office. Congratulations and best wishes about the rimes. And to Bill. Sydney

24. *To Sven Berlin*

24 April 1945 Germoe

Dear Sven Berlin,

Nessie and I here would very much like to have you over to see us sometime soon. Would you like to come? Can you manage? It's fine here with the sea and the Cornish and the drink but we never have a chance to talk to anyone about books or art. It's very good for working at writing and I'm happy about my work recently. We read Ben Nicholson's article on Wallis and your own.[1] I saw some of Wallis's work. It's like the work of the angel in the man and both not knowing each other very well. I hope you try to come. Can you bring Gascoyne's Poems. But please let me know first and it can be any day but a Thursday.

Yours sincerely, W.S. Graham

25. *To John Minton*

24 April 1945

THE EAR SPEAKS MORE THAN THE TONGUE LISTEN –

Cornwall 24 4 45 after a wee shower gently upon my young friends new planted by the vanside. Though a high wind blows and a bit bread put on the caravan roof for any hungry flyer is blown on to the grass. I'm making a new shithouse today and digging away like a steam shovel but my head buzzing with the ideas of the wide word world like any young girl enamoured with a big bunch of nueroses. Also since you and Roberts hope to be down I must see about getting up some nice new jokes with special victory squeakers and flags on the poop. I've been discussing some with Nessie but they turned out a bit too easilymoving with not the explosive farce of the Burbury Coast. However the wind suffers of flowing and the head of thinking. Love is a fault and the aeronauts of the mind alight on a river like the songed Yarrow or an evening kyle with a single heron. I've just finished the loveliest poem to me I've made. It begins like this

Listen. Put on morning.
Waken into falling light.
A man's imagining
Suddenly may inherit
The handclapping centuries

1 Articles published in *Horizon* magazine in 1943. The fisherman and primitive painter Alfred Wallis had been discovered by Ben Nicholson and Christopher Wood when they visited St Ives in 1928.

Of his one minute on earth
And hear the virgin juries
Talk with his own breath
To the corner boys of his street.
And hear the Black Maria
Searching the town at night.
And hear the playropes ca
The sister Mary in.
And hear Willie and Davie
Among bracken of Narnain
Sing in a mist heavy
With myrtle and listeners.
And hear the higher town
Weep a petition of fears
At the poorhouse close upon
The public heartbeat.
And hear the children tig
And run with my own feet
Into the netting drag
Of a suiciding principle.
Listen. Put on lightbreak.
Waken into miracle.
The audience lies awake
Under the tenements
Under the sugar quays
Under the printed moments.
The centuries turn their locks
And open under the hill
Their inherited books and doors
All gathered to distill
Like happy berry pickers
One voice to talk to us.
Yes listen. It carries away
The second and the years
Till the heart's in a jacket of snow
And the head's in a helmet white.
The song sleeps to be wakened
By the morning ear bright.
Listen. Put on morning.
Waken into falling light. WSG 20 4 45

Well there you are I seem to have typed it all. Do you like it? It's about Greenock a bit. Well my dear Johnny I'm so pleased at you coming down and to see the minton fiddlelong face again. You shouldn't write a wee note like that on the book all about being roaring drunk. It's too much. It makes me want to be able to quietly put the money in the box, dial B[edford] Gardens, and say quietly Yes Minton, Swiss six o'clock. I'm bloody very restless this weather and Ness and I are a bit quiet with each other. Work's the only thing that bucks me up. Christ I would be glad to see someone new. Mary wants me to see the baby a year old but I feel queerly impatient with Mary and Julian and can write like the bees knees to them but no see. I would go to Glasgow for a few weeks only money and no good in Glasgow broke and anyhow when I think it out there's no one I particularly want to go to see and no one to give me a bed. God I wish you were here to talk and have a drink and discuss the questions of the day. It gets that I'm almost ready to start h[itch]hiking just away from Cornwall, the direction being just 'away' not 'to' but I know I'd get to a miserable state and self sorrow. Those are the times the army seems more likely and even war films have an effect on me to get in it. This morning I sang FAITH IN SPRING – Schubert and the solo baritone bit from the Choral I mean Beethoven's Choral. A good aire. [...] The wind blows and the caravan wheels refuse to go round and the brain springs out N, S, E and West but Jock Graham stays here as put as anything was ever put. The wind bebuggered blows and whistles in the ventilator and the OUR TIME review stares me in the moonface (though that's nothing) and the coffee's drunk and I wait on Nessie coming from the post maybe with bipo money and then to get a drink in the brain and the mind starting off like whinfires on the whinhill Greenock when I was a wee boy in hey ho the wind and the fucking rain. Alas Johnny my dear good boy, what's the good of moving about they say. But their wrong their rung and dingdonged for nothing and fall on tone-daft ears. Who wants to hear the word of the wise. The old buggers. Wise bebuggered. You are a good boy. Curiously I notice I write as though I was already drunk and with the spontaneity of the cataracting semen the Lord. When he was talking to Isaiah. What is there to say back to that eh? Eh eh eh eh, ? One's got to face it. Till the heart's in a jacket of snow and the head's in a helmet white and the song sleeps to be wakened by the morning ear bright. Tears. Tears. Like one who has been asleep a long time.

Like one who has been awake too long. Now rest. Fall down on a great past. And rest. I must be shaken up before I stop. Something must happen to me. Poetry bebuggered. That's only an expression and the grass being busy trying to keep somewhat upright doesn't hear a word. Ness is back with 10 so I hope I can talk her up into The Packet. I've written myself a bit further down into the pit. There's not even a pimple or blackhead on my chin I can amuse myself with in front of the mirroir. Dormey vous. Frere Jean. Nachtigal. Let me hear from you Johnny please write and let me hear. Love. Sydney

26. *To John Minton*

[30 April 1945?]

Dear Johnny

a quiet Monday evening with May beginning tomorrow and I sit down to answer your good letter and thank you for the books. Your letter came this morning with me in it like a figure in a landscape Blake or Palmer or Thomas Hardy 'a slow shape careering across the vast night decorated Cornish landscape' and all full of night and sadness. The more I write here (even with my mind on Scotland) the place around becomes intimate landscape and even parts of the roads or 'shortcuts' over fields have you coming into them and I hope the fields and dykes and windmills see more of Minton's long face. Thanks for all those Listeners and things Johnny. Here I can usually get Listeners and LIFE AND LETTERS. Also, when I've a poem in a magazine the editor usually sends me one free. But the bundle coming made a great time of reading the war reports (The Listener), they're very well written and reviews too. Well when I heard about the Freedom Press people I was so angry.[1] Almost I would join something to help shake up this awful frightening system that makes this able to happen. I suppose they would be friends of [Herbert] Read's, [Alex] Comfort's etc. Christ, nine years. I couldn't find an account of it in any newspaper, maybe it was in a Sunday paper. It makes me quite frightened, this world of loonies and the such power

1 The prosecution in March 1945 of four members of the Freedom Press for publishing an anarchic pamphlet, was denounced by (amongst others) T.S. Eliot, E.M. Forster, Herbert Read, and Stephen Spender, as an outrageous interference with freedom of speech.

that flies off them into the hearts of the crowds. There is so much happening just now. Each day it is a new strange growth we find on the body of the people, each day we find people driven to a new unnaturalness we didn't guess before. And Yeats -

'The ceremony of innocence is drowned;
The best lack all conviction, while the worst
Are full of passionate intensity.'

Those fucking poisonous newspapers newspapering up the ears and mouths of the poor in spirit. But to look up once out of the glass in the van the rain's on and the wind up and the clouds black over the coast. On my table a big jar of plum jam and your letter leaning half-folded on a fishy knife and my cup of cocoa. I got NEW WRITING 23 today and find the poetry side a bit too 'profound – responsibilityconscious – and philosophical'. Maybe when I get into Edith's [Sitwell] poem I'll like it better. The Vaughan MAN IN A CAVE is nice but maybe too much like WB but that is all a big question, does it necessarily take away from it if it is very like WB? When are the reproductions of Minton coming out in NW? I've written nothing since LISTEN. PUT ON MORNING. It curiously repeats through my head like some one else's good poem, especially from 'Yes listen. It carries away'. For me myself it's more memorable than any poem I've written. Also maybe a bit like WB too. And a bit like Graham Minton Robert Robert Ness Father Mother Willie Davie Billbrewer Pjean Dylant and Loneheron. Love S.

27. *To John Minton*

[April or May 1945?]

Tonight I walked out of my home
And walked slowly down to the sea.

Dear Dear John

tonight's a humdinger quietly with only an occasional ould owl hooting from among the Pengersick trees. I've been at the writing for days and giving birth to poems wildly in all directions, like a man I saw once in the pictures trying to manoeuvre a vacuum-cleaner that was somehow spraying feathers about the room in which a fat man groaned in the corner with a soft pie thing smeared over his face. Meet the simile. We was mighty glad to get that note and rode into town and got ourselves some grum and likker. This is only a wee note. It's late and I don't really know what to say. A letter came in unexpectedly from California saying my poems were the goods and they were going to print them all maybe (about 6) and that I had sure found a sympathetic reception over there. Also he had said he's sending a Henry Miller book for me. Encouragement. He thinks my poems the very cake. Nessie has been quoting you all day today with 'this is the end' 'wee beed' 'pure hell' and says I'm Hell.

On the other side of this you'll find a rectangle. Could you make me a wee coloured or plain drawing this size. It's to put in the hut. I have a frame which would just hold it with glass and all. This is a book that came to me from a boy who works in a bookshop. It is the thing for you more than me. You could draw in it. Take it anyhow as a gift from me and don't look a gift horse in the mouth. It is all right John there's no need of thanks. It is nothing. Nessie's finished some poems which I quite like. We had a night out drinking with this man Sven Berlin who paints and writes and is having his book on Alfred Wallis published by Tambi[muttu]. He's pleasant and intelligent but knows fuckall about writing or painting. He has a moustache. He's just a big laddie of 32. He's nice but no great excitement to talk to. He has a wife I haven't met yet. He talks about putting up a good show etc. Christ I would like you down here Johnny. I have a new poem beginning -

The ear the answer
Hears the wrecked cry
Of the one-time
Holiday boy who
Feathered his oars
On a calm firth
Held still by hills.

I must write nice letters to this American editor and get him to arrange for me to go to California to help, him eh? I haven't been on a boat, even a riversteamer, for years. I would like to go to Dublin. I would like to go to Cork. I would like to go to Beulah. I would like to go to Lima. To Tibet to beyond where must end the words we say. Love. Sydney

28. *To John Minton*

[undated]

Dear Robert Johnny and Robert

typewriting here this misty Sunday evening before the dark comes on I'll make up this wee note to go in the envelope where you'll find letters to please post. I've started recently a long poem (about 400) with lines and lines to be called NARNAIN. I've this evening just finished the first section which is about the sea a lot. I think it will be principally a 'slow' poem and not crammed as much as some I've done. To be so long and yet stand as a whole, parts will have to be more prosaic in form. And yet I don't want to get up a kind of diluted poetry to last out the length. Every new poem has a crop of new difficulties I never thought of.

By accident I found wee bit about me in the TRIBUNE in an article about poetry called 'Summing Up'. It took the usual line so I better stop copying Dylan Thomas. NEW POETRY, the magazine with the cover by Freud has a wheen of very bad poetry. I was disappointed. And my LOST OTHER is to appear in the next number. I wish I knew someone on a Newspaper. I would like to have a poem in, say, THE DAILY EXPRESS or some paper that's looked at by millions. Or on a billboard between marmalade and somebody's corncure. Poems and pictures should get the chance of being seen by the crowds that are not interested in poetry or art. Say, pictures in postoffices banks pubs undergrounds etc. I hope one day to be able to try the bill-board idea and see the result if any. Well, as the old blues lyric says 'Who's sordid now?' (Joke 345, section V)

If it's news you want. Nessie's been weeding. We've been offered two young cats. Lemon the tea is verbottom. We'll soon be against Russe. Alastair, my young soldier brother is stationed near London. Ness and I have cleaned out the henhouse and scrubbed floor and walls preparatory to painting a light colour so there'll be plenty room. Let me know as far ahead as you can when you will be down because if I know I might try to get some money somehow and (if convenient) h[itch]hike up a week before and come down with you. That's what I would like because I'm a bit sick of the continual pastoral, but it may not work out. The potatoes are sprouting and I'm praying they'll dodge the blight. Still no sign of that book of mine 2ND POEMS.

Tambi's had the MS a year and a half now.

To be a labourer carrying the bricks of his time, and on the scaffolding of an unknown construction. The Jock of Grahams.

Is there anything more Minton Colquhoun McBride? Maybe the sun or the sudden migration of those fancy but sincerely birds of a funeral to be. What a dismal omen. Or the man who comes in the French with a headful of continents and a pocket of loaf sugars for horses, sour metaphors or the incandescent, beautiful words behind the eye. Dreaming of Liberty and all it rubs up we must stand with the right foot out and have another draught Bass in the Irish. And drink it the Gaelic way with a packet of liquid ells dissolved in the glass. Wow. Rumshiduamshidum shedum shedum O Rimshedumshedi. That's the lass of the sweet brown now but well I'm not in voice. It's the local cords. O What an audience. What are you looking so glaikit [daft] about? Eheeeeeheh?

Now it's no time for the funnies and the gentle lamp goldenly is by my side. The sea roars with the long shore aslant as the waves come in. The stones roll back with each wave. 'Who in a squad of the dead pecked by the tides...' ('Those famed old trundlers of the dead') I stand typing in the light with my face towards the light of the paper. Say we end gently and say quietly. Good this night. 'Good stars above you, night pedestrian'. Love and good watching over each one. Sydney.

29. *To John Minton*

[undated (7 May 1945?)]

Dear Johnny,

SHORT HAPPY NOTE

I'm an ashamed boy to be sending so many selfsorry notes to you. It was when I had a drop taken. Today I am very much enjoying the summer for certainly (a lovely word 'certainly') this is the first day of summer. Mit blumen beladen. Everywhere within flagpole distance is a union jack but we stay here quietly in our surrounded field filled with butterflies ladybirds flying birds campions speedwell. And all this morning I've been singing, Early one morning, Sound an alarum, He that dwelleth in Heaven shall laugh them to scorn, and How sweet I roamed from field to field and tasted all the summer's pride. There must be a great commotion there in London. We have lovely coffee this morn. The lettuce are 2 inch high and turnips sprouting. I've been at Milton. Are you at the art? This is the poetic weather full of zephyrs perfumes blossom.

The only good thing about this victory is that the soldiers who were fighting will be saved. Outside that the future is black and the effort to swivel the masses to a new direction has begun. It is an ominous peace and but conceals the germs of something worse than before.

But on such a highskyed blue and green day what is there to greet about? It is hard enough to blow the time by the dandelion clocks and scare off the lesser emerald backed chariotbeetle. 3d. worth of ham bones scraped makes a tidy wee breakfast and then boiled with split peas and you have soup.

My long poem is coming on well and it becomes like the work of a composer making up a new movement to follow after the rapid shortlined beginning. And a kind of counterpointing idea going all through. I saw a bad poem on a picture of Picasso's in the LISTENER. And silliness by [Michael] Ayrton. Let me know how you're doing and what goes on. Your old pal. Jock Graham. Love.

30. *To David Wright*

26 May 1945 Cornwall

Dear David,

It is nice to hear from you and that three poems are made that you are happy about, and about you having a hand in the anthology YOUNG MEN AND VISIONS. I'm glad to hear of Hardy being represented. I think he's too-much left out. His poems are so much better than most of the poems of his time. It would be a pity if Joyce is represented by poems from POEMS PENNYEACH or CHAMBER MUSIC and not parts from Ulysses or Finnegans Wake.

THE SEVEN JOURNEYS is having a bad time. O the reviewers fairly go their mile. 'It's a forgery of the poetic currency and of Dylan Thomas.' But I suppose it's to be expected. But I expected maybe one or two favorable reviews. It is nice to hear from you and that you like them a wee.

Yes I'll send something to Lane of THE WINDMILL. At the moment most unpublished poems are out, but I expect some will be back. Thanks for letting me know. Tambi's latest answer about 2ND POEMS is that they are changing the cover. Who is publishing your book, Tambi or Gardiner? I wish it would hurry and I look forward to it. I'll type you a copy of a recent poem I like called LISTEN. PUT ON MORNING. I've been writing some poems in three-feet lines, that metre which Yeats worked in so beautifully. Also a poem which begins (2ft lines)

THE HILL OF INTRUSION

The ear the answer
Hears the wrecked cry
Of the one-time
Holiday boy who
Feathered his oars
On a calm firth
Held still by hills.
Now grey rock clenches
Round..........

It goes on for 46 lines. It's a quieter and less sensational poem than usual. More philosophical. It is already quite engraved and set. I mean I'm not doubting about it. Sometimes I find a poem when finished never sets, never breaks apart from me and becomes a separate organic. Then it's scrapped. I'm moving towards what I call 'a poetry of release'. In LISTEN. PUT ON MORNING. I feel I'm coming near it. A construction of release to accomplish a courageous, other air to breath. If you could let me see some recent work I'd be pleased. Julian's poem THE UPWARD RAIN is good I think. I hope Dylan helps her towards publication. I've been getting some letters of appreciation from America and it's encouraging. Though I feel a bit restless this weather and jump at the chance to write up an expedition to The Pole, Central Tibet or something. There's a slight chance I might be in London in June or July for a week. I'll make it a point to see you. Please write soon David. Cheerio. Sydney

POETRY LONDON X is very bad I think. I can't see any good of publishing most of those poems.

[A copy of 'Listen. Put On Morning' dated 19 4 45 was included, together with the following notes]

I don't think the poem needs notes but you might like to know – the 'Black Maria' is the name the street boys give to the black police van.

'Corner boys' are men from 17 to 100 who usually stood at the corner of our streets and were really called that. My mother would so – 'you'll end up by being a corner boy.'

'playropes' – skipping ropes.

'sister Mary' – the children's skipping rope song began with 'I call in my sister Mary'.

'tig' a game in which you 'tig' someone by touching him on the arm then you run off till he tigs you.

'sugar docks' – the docks where the raw sugar is unloaded for refining in the Greenock sugar refineries.

31. *To Sven Berlin*

[undated] Sunday

Dear Sven Berlin,

I'm sorry so long it's been since I have written. Here I am on a hot day after lifting 564444 potatoes. I've been very busy at the potatoes and then tired at night and trying a drop of poetry. I've finished 16 lines of a poem called THE VOYAGES OF ALFRED WALLIS which I hope you will like. I'm very pleased with it. Our people have arrived and it's (I mean the situation) turned out bloody awful. He seems to have changed so much and somehow it's no good to talk about anything. I don't know what's to be done. Nessie and I go about as though we were the visitors and the visitors make wisecracks. But it's my trouble. What's happened and how is Helga and Paul and wee shy Janet? Have you begun your new job yet. That long black hull of my wallisboat is over the mantelpiece. I may have another visitor in a week. A man called David Archer who first published Dylan Thomas, Barker, Gascoyne and me. He's very interesting and if possible I would like you to meet him. I feel a bit agitated over this business of my visitors and really not in a letter-writing mood but I should have written before this to tell you how much we enjoyed our stay at St Ives. It isn't a good time to ask you back but I hope somehow we can talk more and more about the 'true art' idea in St Ives. I'll send you a copy of the Wallis poem when I finish it. I've lost the address of your friend I was going to send a copy of my book to. Word from America recently about my poetry is encouraging. I have Helga's MODERN READING safe and will return it this week when I read an article on Henry Miller again. Nessie and I had our first bathe today. I found the water too cold.

I'm getting brown as berries. Can you write a wee note and let me know how you are and have you prepared pictures for the pub yet?
Regards, Sydney

32. *To David Wright*

14 June 1945 Germoe

Dear David,

I've been lifting potatoes for weeks and I've been tired hence so long since writing last.

Thanks for letting me see LANDSCAPE OF A MIDLAND SPRING. It's one of your good poems I've seen. Generally it's a good poem and I think a poetic activity occurs between word and word yet I find it difficult. I like the first and second verses except for 'displumager' and the word 'invention' coming where it does. 'hangs Spring' I definitely like. I can enjoy the chime of 'alcoves' near 'escalades' yet I think the presence of those words in the poem along with 'displumage', 'frieze', 'accidia', somehow give it a feeling of too much artifice which overwhelms the speaking poem. Now I think that those kind of words which are a bit exotic in both a language sense and an associative sense are very difficult to position in a poem compared with more 'physical' early English words like wood wind holt dyke busy drunk and so on. 'farewelling' works beautifully here but I don't think such a word can stand being used again so soon by another poet after Barker has written 'Watching I see the farewelling seasons fall' but its your decision. I like the true pastoral quality in the poem 'A season hanging in the woody oaks' ... and then I could go on quoting down the page there are so many lovely parts. I like the description of an acting spring. I've been reading it aloud to Nessie and we both get excited about it. x...Sacred Elegy One.

I like THE MIRROR and I admire its nice steadiness as a construction. The capital L in 'Looking glass' stops me a bit. Even 'looking glass' acting metaphorically and symbolically needn't have a capital so I'm stopped and asked to think what tremendous significance here in this poem a looking glass may have. And I'm stopped for that time and dragged aside from the fast experience which a poem is into a side issue and a question which is an intrusion and which I can't answer. 'Earless motion' is lovely, very truly a mirror, and also 'rinsed lines'. I like the grammar shape of the opening line which is a shape Yeats used a lot and even here it takes an added romance from the memory of certain Yeats poems.

It's nice to hear it's appearing in YOUNG MEN HAVE VISIONS and I'm pleased Spender's taken a poem of mine though I'm a wee bit tired of O GENTLE QUEEN, however... What other writers are represented? I've lent my PLX away to someone at the moment but I remember the translations of his poems and at the time I thought how they looked like they would be good to me in their own language. I'll let you have a copy later of THE HILL OF INTRUSION. So far no one's published it. THE LOST OTHER is about due out in NEW POETRY 2. I corrected more proofs for 2ND POEMS but not hopeful of an early appearance. I doubt I won't be up for a while yet. What will your book of poems be called? How many poems of how many (average) lines?

Write soon and let me know what goes on. Regards. Sydney.

33. *To David Wright*

21 July 1945 Germoe

Dear David,

It's nice to have a letter and poem from you. I'm sorry to hear you're having trouble with the anthology. I'm writing every day and the good weather's begun and we have a goat. No more news of 2ND POEMS. It will soon be two years since I first sent in the ms. What angers me most of all is that it seems to be a oneway communication service with Nicholson and Watson. I never get a reply from any letter I send them and when any letter comes from them they don't even acknowledge receiving mine. I hear from someone that it should be out soon but I don't see any recent PL [*Poetry London*] notices about it. How about your own?

I don't like THE SHELL as well as your other recent poems. Parts and phrases I like very much, like – 'salt plantations fling', 'The dark hone of the sea, and noise of hosts' and 'hanging coasts'. Also I like the quiet, wellgoverned metre. It is a finished poem with no mistakes or embarrassments. In this poem as in other poems of yours I find a kind of artificial classicism which I think comes from your choice of those coldly exotic words like – Lattice alcoves aquatile wreathed Aeolian mezzanine. I know that it is a matter of liking the tone those words produce rather than objecting to a technical poorness. I have no argument about it. For me those words make the poem bloodless and artificial. The sea is not salt enough. The shore does not smell of drying seaweed and salt enough. It is all too mezzanine, aquatile and aeolian for me. 'Spawny' is good but it hasn't a chance among bloodless words. 'sunken hulks' is weak and getting tired. I like very much the first line of the second verse. It is so easy and what lovely rhythms are in it. I find the last seven lines thin for you to be writing. It has the excellent quality of being restrained but is also gutted of any poetic excitement for me. Please send me more recent poems when you finish them. Do you see Julian? Has she seen THE SHELL?

I've been reading Blake a lot. Jerusalem Milton etc. And Donne's Sermons. Your poem in PQ [*Poetry Quarterly*] was lovely. One of your best I've seen. The part about the spiralling feather reminded me of Watkins a bit.[1] It is a good poem. Nice to be all in the one number, you me and J. Write soon. Sydney.

34. *To David Wright*

3 August 1945 — Wheelhouse, Pengersick Lane, Germoe, Marazion, Cornwall, The Beach, Sunbathing.

Dear David,

Thanks for your poem and letter. I'm so sorry, David, but it's all crowded here with all kinds of people (friends of the owner of the caravans) during most of September. Also I'm going to Kent in a fortnight for about a month. I'll be going through London and might be staying a night. I would like to see you and hear how everything is. Johnny Minton is here just now and sends his regards. I don't know Audrey Beecham's work but I've heard the name.[2] Where is she living? Yes, it would be nice if she should turn up. Who do you see in London this weather, Julian?[Orde] The Grey

1 Vernon Watkins (1906–67), Welsh lyric poet and translator probably best known for 'The Ballad of The Mari Lwyd' (1941) and his correspondence with Dylan Thomas.

2 Audrey Beecham (1915–89), poet who was a prominent activist and generous supporter of revolutionary causes in politics and the arts. Her collection *The Coast of Barbary* was published in 1957.

Walls people?[1]

WALKING TO DEDHAM I like much better than your last poem. It begins so beautifully and is so much full of a kind love, then the first phrase which weakens is – 'the wisdom of the year'. 'Year' in itself is not a very physical or visual word but 'flowers of the year' or 'colours of the year' though not very exciting could hold a position in a poem which would fusify them. But 'wisdom' is so difficult a word. Almost like 'death or hate'. The best phrases, or lines, about say, death or hate usually haven't the words in them. For me, David, 'the wisdom of the year' is a letdown after the first five lines. Other parts of the poem where this same abstract, false-profound, quality occurs – 'the world be coming real' – 'central folds of peace'. 'Dazzles the skeleton with thick petals' is lovely. I like the ending – the last line has a lively inevitable feeling. I'm not saying those phrases could not occur successfully in a poem. Every phrase or word has positions where they can work. A word is exciting because of its surroundings. I like it. It will be nice to see it published, I'm glad you're working good, David.

Yes I notice we have changed the government. It doesn't mean much though it's called Labour. Labour is now quite respectable.

Hope to hear from you soon. Sydney

35. *To Sven Berlin*

[undated] Caravans Friday 13th.

My Dear Sven,

Here's the poem. I will be pleased if you like it. But tell me and if you can point out how any lines or phrases strike you it helps me. Thanks so much you helping me up to that excitement about Wallis and to making this. I myself am specially pleased about it. It begins well and has a nice shape and ends with that nice question – What deep seasaint whispered this keel out of its element? It's been finished a week now but I've been letting it recede a bit so that I could have a right look and listen at it before letting it go out. I wish there was some way people about St. Ives who had heard of Wallis could see it.

1 The Grey Walls Press published *Poetry Quarterly*, edited by Charles Wrey Gardiner, from 1940 to 1953.

Since it I've finished three short poems called

CONSTRUCTION OF 92 WORDS
CONSTRUCTION OF 83 WORDS
&
CONSTRUCTION OF 130 WORDS.

Funny names? You'll see them sometime. You might like parts of them. I'm still a little unsure of them myself. I'm still plugging at that bloody article O I'm sick o' it. I would like to see you all again, Helga Paul Janet Sven Berlins. Nessie's hoeing the violets which look like becoming maybe a lifesaver as the winter starts. Here shall he see no enemy but winter and rough weather. By the way, I've sent THE VOYAGES OF ALFRED WALLIS to HORIZON but they've not taken anything of mine for a while and I don't think it will go in.[1] I've not forgotten, tell Helga, her book with Sven Berlin's poem in it. Love. Sydney.

I don't think I'll be over for a while yet. It gets difficulter and difficulter. Write Soon.

36. *To David Wright*

6 October 1945 Germoe

Dear David,

Here I am in Autumn with berries ruby on the tree and leaves settling back to winter. The weather is very clear and rooks in the high trees and still brambles with milk for a breakfast. I ask how you are and what you are doing and writing. Last time I had to leave quickly and ill in the guts for home here and a bit rest and serene. Where love in gardens finds a rest serene. It is then my very best thought for you and what you are at there in London this autumn. Any more news of your book from Tambi? The people go about the streets and the papers are so much madder every day and what is all to happen I would not want to by chance find out. What are you writing David? Any new poems coming out anywhere? Do you see Julian at all. If ever you see Heath Stubbs would you mention I left quickly because I was ill and had no time to phone him as I

1 The poem 'The Voyages of Alfred Wallis' was commissioned for Sven Berlin's book, *Alfred Wallis – Primitive*, published in 1949, but it appeared in *Life and Letters* (vol. 48, no. 3) in March 1946.

maybe promised.[1] Try to see more of Ormond Thomas [Welsh poet] for he is very good and a good heart. This is just those few words to have you writing me now and then again and to know please how you are getting on with the winter blowing his first gusts in a few weeks and the frosts feeling their way nearer the big five and the poor coalless. Nessie, my girl, has two poems in September's LIFE & LETTERS. Do you like them?

Love. Sydney

37. *To John Minton*

28 November 1945 Germoe

My Dear Johnny,

Thanks very much the rent money came and was shunted on to the other healthcure line and is probably there now. It is very good. At last the cold is here and snows lurking in the rooky heavens and the milk coming home frozen in pail and the stove on almost all day and oil has become the golden fleece of the cold weather. That is how it is the weather making the value of things, the turnips out and still a few mushrooms and I met a fisherman this morning who sold me a conger now in the pot with milk flour mustard salt pepper herbs and a bit butter.

I wrote Robert Frame[2] a while ago and told him I sent no to Maclellan and that I said to Macl that maybe one day he would like Robert and I to do a Drawings and Poems book of the Scottish landscape. But no reply. I meant that as suggesting something else rather than do the Journeys over again. But I don't know if it will come to anything. No reply yet anyhow and maybe he's huffed over not given his beloved [Donald] Bain a chance to do a Gorgon's head on the world. What are you doing Johnny and how is your work going? Did you enjoy the countryparty?

Nessie sews tonight and has been at her poetry and the yellow cat died envenomed from a poisoned rat from a farm near. The black

1 John Heath-Stubbs (b.1918), poet, critic and translator.

2 Robert Frame and Benjamin Creme illustrated Graham's *Cage Without Grievance* (1942). The dust-jacket and frontispiece of *The Seven Journeys* (1944) were designed by Robert Frame. Both artists were founder-members of the Scott Street Centre.

one is very lonely but growing very big. The cat is on the mat. Give me the pen of my aunt. Chanson the poison who purrs the good pussy. O the French they are so sensualle. The violets brought in 3/- this week and we are so hoed and picked by it all. I am hoed by the world and might ask what shall I do with this little hoe. Yet humour is the truth of sitting down rather to weep than affect a strenuous conversation. O I don't know what is to become of me the young man cried. That's reading Dostoyevsky does that. What lousy embarrassing translation they make of it and yet what is told, the narrative, is so good. Lately I've read The Idiot. Very good. Also by other people, Moll Flanders, The War With The Insects, The Power House. That is all.

The Watkins book is very good and I'm glad to have it. The poems are maybe too like Yeats. But it is all much better than the poems with news and journalism in them. Please Rite Johnny and say what you do. This is a quick letter I'm going back to a poem I'm writing. Please tell your mother our love and Nessie asking for her. You are very good. Love. Sydney.

How are the Roberts. O I better write them and see.

38. *To Alex Comfort*

12 December 1945 Germoe

Dear Alex Comfort,

This needn't be replied to. Last night I read an article of yours in NOW 4 and I feel so strongly sympathetic to it that I must write and say at least thanks. I am as against the Left as the Right and see myself related to that political scene you describe very much as you write about it. I find it difficult to talk to people about me not being on the side of this present freedom which is being fought for and yet of course not with Fascism. The words now, 'Democracy' and 'Fascism' seem to have become completely soluble in each other and unite into one mistaken Progress. Your article again starts in me that almost destroying indignation against not just the tyrants who lash the people but against the (in each heart) inherent lack of life which makes the act of lashing possible and which also I have no choice but to put up with and see its implications in every gesture of us all. I have that feeling in me which I suppose we all have to deal with. The dual of, a steady hate for people for not being better, a love for people when there is a sudden unexpected goodness and courage.

I read THE POWER HOUSE and I liked it very much.

Yours sincerely, W S Graham

39. *To John Minton*

13 December 1945 Germoe

Almost Business Note Please Reply By Return

Dear Johnny,

Recently word from home that Alastair is to India for two years and old Dad sad and a bit worried. And he wants me up for Christmas and New Year. Also a nice letter from Alastair (he's really very good I would like to see him and because he's had dysentery already I feel a little worried.) about being fed up (but not a whine) with the army and about extemporising on the piano with jazz. He also mentions my father's a bit worried about me. Nessie and I have both a homesickness for Scotland. Not only because of the New Year coming but a bit accumulative I think.

So. We have decided to hitchhike up to Scotland. Nessie will go to Blantyre of course and I to Greenock. I will see her now and then in Glasgow I suppose. We've been saying we'll go to Scotland for so long and putting it off but we may as well set out and go. Now Johnny would it be alright if you kept the £4 till the 17th. of this month. We plan to start out on a Wednesday morning early on the twentieth. I don't know how long we'll take but I won't push Nessie too much for she's not feeling so good now with the wind and the cold here and if we have to stop at nights she will be going to a salvation army hostel or some kind of bed and me too. But we might be lucky and do it quickly. Will that be all right? The money to arrive here on the 18th. at the very latest. Let me know. Now that we have made up our mind about it we are both very excited and Nessie sewing and patching for me to make a good impression on my father and new mother and be looking like not a complete failure anyhow.[1]

1 Graham's mother, Margaret, had died unexpectedly in 1940 after an operation. His father later married Agnes Hughes, referred to in the letter as 'new mother'.

Now curiously we both thought at the same time and when I said it to Nessie she said yes I was just going to say that and wouldn't it be nice. I said how about Johnny. It would be nice to have him there seeing the Firth of Clyde and the big hills on the other side of Greenock. The thing is this, would you like to come up. And arrive at my home in Greenock on say 22nd, 23rd or 24th of this month. And stay a week or so. Nessie and I would probably be staying till about a fortnight or three weeks after the new year. Now Johnny can you let me know soon. But remember this and don't be put out. I haven't seen my father for a long time. I have to write yet that I am coming up. And I will mention that there is a chance of a friend of mine an artist, very nice and easy, wanting to come up. So you see Johnny there is a slight chance he'll say he'd rather I didn't bring anyone. I don't know. He might be frightened of a person he didn't know from England, or there might be no room. But I would love to have you there. Please write even a wee note by return about those two things, the money, and you wanting to come or not. That is all. That is all.

You can tell the Roberts we are going and you never know they might like to go up this year too and we could see them in Scotland.

I've been writing a lot. And reading that Watkins book. Also a biography of Herman Melville, a strange great man. I would like to see you this new year Johnny. Love. Sydney

40. *To John Minton*

[December 1945] Thursday Cornwall

Dear Johnny,

Thanks for 10/- and your letter and I'm happy to be able to write now Dad's letter's come. He says 'we will be very pleased to have you and your friend come up to Scotland'. And that's good. Dad is not eloquent. Can you bring with you an old copy of THE STUDIO. I think you'll like him.

When you get to Glasgow you take the train from the Central Station to Greenock West (about 40 minutes). Then in Greenock you get a bus to Bow Farm and ask for Graham Street. That's that but please write to me at Greenock (5 Graham St.) and say when your train is due at Glasgow and I'll meet you. I will enjoy janting about Greenock and Glasgow. Write to Ian and tell him you're going up and see where he'll be. Post the money on the Friday to make sure seeing the Christmas is running in so quickly.

Johnny we're both so much looking forward to this. I've never felt so good about going anywhere (yet one's cynical inhabitants lounge about the heart always ready to start something) and seeing you in Scotland. I think you will like to see the Firth and the Cowcaddens Pubs and the Clydebank shipyards. Yes it will be good if Ian can be there. I'll hear from you on Monday here and then write please when your train is arriving in Glasgow. It's strange about that journey from Glasgow to Greenock. I travelled six days a week for five years. But for the right accidents and the courage to be knocked aside by them I might still be doing it. Nessie sings softly all day and we both even already prepare to go off. I have a lovely beginning for a new poem, as good as I've ever written. Some firm wrote me asking if I would consider doing a collected works of WSGraham. Of course No but good now and then to hear from them.

Love, Sydney

SONNET[1]

As brilliance fell I girded me with voice.
Though always all words waste from inward out
I who am fastened to this furious choice
Turned out to be myself a contrary shout.

As the night signed I made making my house.
Yet always all words waste and alter into
A formal ruin lesser than God's voice
So clenched in prison in my mortal tree.

As the blood sang I perished into words.
And always all words illdevise the tongue
That at poor best must sing the beast it guards.
As His blood sang the poem-imprisoned king

Sang me more than myself and made the whole
Descended house of night my house excel.

1 This was later revised and entitled 'As Brilliance Fell'.

Two

TOWARDS THE WHITE THRESHOLD

1946–1949

SHIAN BAY

Gulls set the long shore printed
With arrow steps over this morning's
Sands clean of a man's footprint
And set up question and reply
Over the serpentine jetty
And over the early coaches
Of foam noisily in rows
Driven in from the farout banks.

Last gale washed five into the bay's stretched arms,
Four drowned men and a boy drowned into shelter.
The stones roll out to shelter in the sea.

GIGHA

That firewood pale with salt and burning green
Outfloats its men who waved with a sound of drowning
Their saltcut hands over mazes of this rough bay.

Quietly this morning beside the subsided herds
Of water I walk. The children wade the shallows.
The sun with long legs wades into the sea.

In 1945 Graham began writing his article 'Notes on a Poetry of Release' (reprinted below, pp. 379–83). It took several months and became a most comprehensive and useful statement of his philosophy, criteria and craft. Writing in a language not far removed from that of his poetry (and likewise rewarding careful study), he located himself as simultaneously subject to the changing 'environment flowing in on me from all sides' and to 'language which is obstacle and vehicle at the same time'. Poetry was clearly not to be either a random or a casual expression but a carefully made form of words capable of evoking an individual response from each imaginative reader, while also serving as the exploratory vessel for the poet – 'a man who searches continually'. The searching was to be rigorously attentive to the 'almost physical language', the unquantifiable accidents and associations, and to endeavour to avoid any sentimentality, didacticism, or preconceived 'messages'.

These considerations made an interesting and obviously demanding critical base. They emerge at various times in Graham's letters over a very long period in references to his own or to other people's poetry and clearly continued to be the rationale within which he saw himself working.

Occasional quotations in Graham's letters remind us of the pleasure he took in the sound of Scottish poetry of all periods. His work frequently contains references to the Greenock landscape, real and imagined, and to the language spoken by his parents. Like Joyce in Dublin, he experienced a tension between the deep creative influences of his national culture and the necessity to transmute them into an open contemporary literature uninhibited by the demands of puritanism, nostalgia, provincial or nationalist politics. While Graham felt free to absorb the influence of Scots, Irish, English, American, or indeed any other literature, it is interesting to note that, in the year in which his 'Notes on a Poetry of Release' was published, the Scottish literary scene was dominated by controversy over the perceived English influence on Scottish poetry, an influence to be rejected initially by encouraging poets to write in actual or reconstituted Scottish dialects with the objective of an eventual return to the Gaelic language.[1]

The value of any language that was actually in use was undeniable but its prescriptive use as a nationalist statement seemed to Graham at best unnecessary and at worst ridiculously artificial. His failure to support the politically aligned literary movement may be one of the reasons for his poetry being unreasonably neglected in Scotland for some time, but it was characteristic of the generous natures of both Graham and MacDiarmid that, despite their different opinions about Synthetic Scots, they retained a friendship and a warm respect for each other's work in later years.[2] Cornwall provided Graham with peace in which to work but he was far away from most literary opportunities, including Scottish ones. However his work was attracting increased attention and his poems appeared more frequently in magazines.

There were also numerous visitors during 1946, amongst them the young poet Burns Singer, a great admirer of Graham's work who seems to have arrived uninvited and camped close by for several weeks during the summer. He was not very popular with other visitors. David Wright, for example, referred to him in the *Edinburgh Review* 75 as 'a fanatical disciple of Sydney's, equipped with portable typewriter and insupportable ego'. Though eventually exasperated by Singer's rather frequent interruptions to his concentration, Graham continued to be friendly towards him whenever they met in later years. The Glasgow painter Bet Low (with whom Singer stayed for some time straight after his visit to Cornwall) remarked that Singer always spoke to her of Graham and his poetry with the utmost respect.[3]

Graham's 'Notes on a Poetry of Release' was published in *Poetry Scotland* in July 1946, and reprinted in the American *Quarterly Review of Literature* in 1947. Between the autumn of 1946 and the winter of 1950 the American critic Vivienne Koch published three penetrating and encouraging reviews of Graham's work in the *Sewanee Review* and another one in *Poetry Quarterly*.[4] She arranged to meet the Grahams in London, visited Mevagissey, and became Sydney's close friend. When he obtained a Rockefeller grant to visit the USA he was able to stay with her in New York and later also in London when she was researching her book on W.B. Yeats. While in New York he gave lectures on 'Forces in Contemporary British Literature' for New York University and appears to have stayed for about nine months, returning late in the summer of 1948. He first met Moncrieff Williamson in New York and later said that he had enjoyed the city, especially the Jewish theatre, but would never have written another line if he had stayed there.

Early in 1947 Frank Baker lent Graham and Nessie Dunsmuir his house in Mevagissey for six months, bringing to a close the period of caravan life, and after this they were able to rent another cottage cheaply. Graham became friendly with a local fisherman singing in the pub and was invited to go out as a working member of the fishing boat crew. Somewhat to local surprise (as they were unaware of his Clydeside sea-legs) he acquitted himself well and went out with them on several other occasions. The experiences no doubt contributed later to his best known poem, 'The Nightfishing'. This must have been started in 1948 as it is referred to as 'finished' in January 1949 and also in November 1949. In May 1950 it was being revised and he was asking for an objective opinion on it from Edwin Morgan. In October 1950 Graham said 'I'll be giving The Nightfishing a final revision and sending it in before the year is out'.

By the autumn of 1947 he and Nessie Dunsmuir had agreed to separate for a time. She was thinking of going to work in Paris but had first to spend a period in London undergoing medical treatment. He considered basing himself in London. By May 1949 Nessie Dunsmuir was working in Italy, *en route* to her job with the Berlitz School in Paris. They were not to meet again until 1953.

While in America Graham had received news that T.S. Eliot had accepted his collection *The White Threshold* for Faber and Faber. This was an important step in his career as the firm became his major publisher. The book appeared in 1949.

1 'The entire Scottish contribution to English poetry could be excised without noticeable detriment to the latter. In these circumstances it has simply been my contention that it would be better for Scottish poets to cease using a medium in which time has shown they have an irremediable inferiority and see if they cannot do better in the very different Scottish tradition, first of all in the "halfway

house" of Scots, and ultimately in a resumption of Gaelic.' *The Letters of Hugh MacDiarmid*, ed. Alan Bold (London, 1984), p. 788.

2 See Alan Bold, *MacDiarmid* (London, 1988), p. 277.

3 Conversation with the Editors in 1999.

4 In an unpublished article Moncrieff Williamson described Vivienne Koch as coming from a cultured Hungarian Jewish New Yorker background. Her sister Adrienne became a Professor of Political Science at Berkeley, her brother Sigmund retired as Vice-President of Boston University. Vivienne herself was lecturing in Columbia University in 1948 and published studies of William Carlos Williams, W.B. Yeats, and a novel, *Change of Love*. She reviewed *Cage Without Grievance* in the *Sewanee Review* (Autumn 1946), and *The White Threshold* (*Sewanee Review*, October/December 1950), as well as writing two articles on Graham: 'The Technique of Morality' (*Poetry Quarterly*, Winter 1947) and 'A Note on W.S.Graham' (*Sewanee Review*, Autumn 1948).

41. *To J.F. Hendry*

26 May 1946 — Germoe

Dear J F Hendry,

Ian Finlay writes to me that you are making up an anthology and that you would like to see some of our work. Do the poems have to be new or can they have appeared somewhere before? At the moment neither of us has much new work. Will the anthology be likely to pay its contributors? It is hopeful to hear of an anthology being edited by you.

What a poor sad bundle of pages to come from Scotland under the responsible name of SCOTTISH ART AND LETTERS. Though I am not a nationalist in any political sense it did put me down a wee bit. I didn't expect it to be so bad. It isn't that it is just 'playing safe'. It's corny. And just bad. I wonder fearfully what PS3 [*Poetry Scotland* No. 3] will be like.

I would like to meet you sometime we are in Scotland at the same time, or South. Are you ever near here?

Yours sincerely
W S Graham
and for Nessie Dunsmuir.

42. *To J.F. Hendry*

26 June 1946 — Cornwall

Dear J F Hendry,

You might like to see Nessie Dunsmuir. She's gone to London for a holiday from the country and for a long time she's not been seeing anyone new. She's staying with McBryde and Colquhoun - Studio 1, 77 Bedford Gdns. London W 8 (nr Nottinghill Gate Tube) (Park 9003) I think she would like to meet you sometime. If you think its a good thing to do *you* might ring her up and arrange to see her some day or night. She'll be sending some of her work very soon. And me too.

Sincerely – W S Graham

43. *To William Montgomerie*

21 August 1946 Cornwall

Dear Bill,

It's good to hear from you and the lovely copy of Donne. I write first this time to ask. Can you lend me five pounds from the 15th September till the 30th September. The thing is this. I want to go to Tring for a fortnight. I'll start off on the 16th of September. On the 15th I finish a BBC Survey (in Nessie Dunsmuir's name) but I won't be paid for almost a fortnight. Nessie would be here at the caravans and send it straight on to you. I enclose the 'Offer of Assignment' so you'll know what kind of thing it is. It is just that I want the money to go off with. Try to let me know by return so that I can make arrangements. But if you will, don't send the money till the 15th September. Anyhow let me know.

No, no South America though not my fault by a long chock. It might just as well be Labrador, Rimbaud's ILLUMINATIONS, Thel's countryside, or the pacing whitehaired kingdoms of the sea. Today the mist and a visit from David Wright, a nice gentle poet, my goats grueing at the sloe and the rooks at their black concert. Me at my long poem to be called THE WHITE THRESHOLD and playing my gramophone, a gift with two records. I know the records backwards.

It's a lovely copy of Donne. Well printed and some prose too. I'm pleased to have it. Recently I've been reading good poetry by the Irishman [W.R.] Rodgers. Do you know his good poem about Christ on the waters? And exciting poetry by an American, Dunstan Thompson.[1] And at last I was able to read TROPIC OF CANCER. Miller. It's great. Christ so full of life the man is I'm ashamed at not having gone over the Victoria Falls with my love in a barrel. You must try to read it if not already. My 3RD POEMS will be finished when my long poem is finished. I'm fearfully waiting the PS3. I bet it's a WOW. Hendry's starting a new magazine called LIVING. Maybe you know. But Maclellan's doing it. It's a pity. It doesn't give it a chance.

Bill please try to let me know about the loan by return so's I'll know. Cheerio. Yours sincerely, Sydney

Please return the Assignment thing. Julian's done some very good poems.

1 Thompson's first collection, *Poems*, was published by Secker and Warburg in 1946

44. *To William Montgomerie*

undated [Autumn 1946] Again Cornwall

My dear Bill,

Nessie got your letter all right and I'm back again and working well and full of a great anger now I've seen the Faber MODERN SCOTTISH POETRY [*An Anthology of the Scottish Renaissance 1920–1945*. (1946)]. I'm so angry at Lindsay so obviously going to town on the Scottish wagon.[1] The allotment of space is incredible, even mysterious in a way, but that is not the worst cheek. It is the Joy dedication. What right had he at all to dedicate the representative selection of contemporary Scotland 'to Joy'. Who's Joy? Fuck Joy. Christ, the smug insensitive cheek of it. I've written Lindsay a letter something like this to help get my anger out. I've sent a copy of it to Grieve and MacLellan just so that I'm in the open and everyone knows what I've said. Well anyhow Bill enough I suppose.

Your book is very good and I've been picking it up at all odd moments for there are so many I've never heard and some I half-know and it's good to get the right words. I'm glad the book has gone so well. I hope you have a new edition out soon and away. Your talk of the mountains makes me homesick for the glens. And that eagle. O Christ it sounds good. Here we have winter upon us at a blow and the trees already shivering in their black bones. I've finished my new long poem THE WHITE THRESHOLD and I'm pleased about it. The most sea poem for a while I've seen. And more 'human' than anything I've ever made. To do with the changing intricate heart and yet to do with the possibility of a creative love relationship.

'They are the others with my likeness enhungered.'

It was good of you to lend me the 5 and to send me the book. Can you find time to tell me what you're doing about your own story essay and poetry work. Your wee foreword is charming and more. I don't know which rhyme I might say I like best. I'm out of paper at the moment that's why on this. My love to Norah and children and yourself.

'The bush I burn in gives me room enough'. Maybe THE WHITE THRESHOLD will be coming out in WINDMILL. Do you ever see it?

1 Maurice Lindsay, poet, literary historian and anthologist was born in 1918. Trained as a musician, he worked as a critic and broadcaster.

I've poems in the next two numbers.
Sydney

45. *To William Montgomerie*

17 November 1946 Cornwall

Dear Bill,

I've been daft about this Maurice Lindsay business. I was wrong. By precedent he was entitled to act as he did. I apologised to him and said I would let you know I had. The thing is it is not a personal matter at all. I really got angry when I saw the Faber Anthology and I suppose I was a bit quick and thoughtless. What's happening? Are you writing? Try to spare a moment and let me know how you are and what you are doing this weather. I wonder how PS4 will be.
Regards, Sydney

I've been lending your Scottish Nursery Rhymes to a friend called Frank Baker, (novelist – BEFORE I GO HENCE) and he thinks they're great.

46. *To William Montgomerie*

9 December 1946 Cornwall

Dear Bill,

Thanks for your letter all about yourself as you say and the good news of such good sales for the Rimes. I can't think of Lindsay much without anger and indignation. [...] But I musn't dwell on it. I see PS3 out. I fairly get a beating up in the review section but I suppose I have to expect that now. It was nice to have my article[1] (which, if anything, is enthusiastic and lively) in the same number with the reviews. It helps to balance things. It isn't a very good number at all. Lindsay's poem with the line 'where lumbering tramcars squeal as they take sharp corners' doesn't help much. Drinan's work here is not as good as usual. I like very much the wee poem HAMEWITH. Bruce is nice but at times a wee bit safe and thin. The poem McAlister is a horror. The Muir poems are so good and dignified beside most here. God isn't MacDiarmid's notebook dry.

1 'Notes on a Poetry of Release'; see p. 62 above.

I wish I had heard the Gibbon talk but we've no radio and it's difficult. I'll look out for your story if there's a radio near when it's on. We have been invited up to London to Christmas and Hogmanay with MacBryde and Colquhoun. We were not expecting to be away from here this time and we are excited and looking forward to our jaunt into civilisation again. I think we'll be hitchhiking up and we pray for the weather to ease.

I'm off writing since finishing THE WHITE THRESHOLD and I want to make some commotion in my life before I start on my next 4TH POEMS. I've been reading a lot, mostly poetry and philosophy. I don't suppose you know a captain of a whaling vessel or a pearler square-rigged? Tibet. Peking. Nantucket. The Amazons. The Ohio the Orinoco the Brahmaputra. No wonder one is driving to sailing on imagined deltas. Yes it must be difficult in a small Broughty-Ferry-sized town. Can you not get any other kind of job which would allow you more freedom to move about? How about a novel of Glasgow, a real Montgomerie children's Glasgow? Or a book of criticism? Or a second book of rarer rimes? I don't mean journalism but is it impossible to live by writing something you want to write. I'm no good at telling a story or I would be writing a novel about something.

I also in my place here feel lonely and that I should be in touch with alive people to talk to and sing with, people who give out some joy and are not spiteful and small with fear. I know how you feel. Scotland (and I'm often homesick to be there) seems so empty of alive people. If I lived in Glasgow and wanted to go out to the pub one night I can't think of anyone I could ring up. Well write soon again please Bill.

Love to you and Norah, Sydney

47. *To Sven Berlin*

12 February 1947 26 Cliff St. Mevagissey

Dear Sven,

Well here this cold gullmewing morning and I come down to find your greekEed letter and news of the yelloweyed hawk of the wind or mind and mushroom debts and having flu in the tower. What a time Sven. The Spring and some money is all we want. We would have been over to see you of course if we had been still at the Wheelhouse but now for about a month we've been here and out of the bitter cold weather with good stone around us for a change and room to stretch. Christ the weather. The knife winds and the nettling spray and the high tides with the horns of the harbour dipping like bows. You must come and stay a few days with us while we're here. With luck we're here till the end of April. I haven't asked you yet thinking each day might bring some money so that we'll have some when you come. I've had no word yet about the Atlantic Awards and I try not to hope too hard. But anyhow if nothing comes I'll fix a date with you to come here and we'll be merry some way. Bryan [Wynter] too. I'd like fine to see him.

The hawk sounds to do with the second sight, stony and druidical. The pineal eye. And a wee bit like the feeling of my Sixth Journey.

A hundred heavens and West on every pinnacle
Tent with a geography of gannets my trinket skerry – – –

Yeats is specially strong to read in Cornwall. I'd like fine to see the carvings. Are you doing any illustrating at all. I see notices of a Moby Dick out. Does that mean the one you mentioned is off. I suppose you're trying hard to get as much of that kind of work as you can. Look, Sven m'lover, if you get too fedup come over money or not. It's an easy hitchhike from Hayle. That's if you think we could manage without the pub. We could work a bit and explore about the coast and get real healthy. O what a carryon.

I've begun work at last again and strangely a love poem after not a love poem for nearly 3 years. It begins like this though it probably will be changed and chiselled a bit. Well e' begins like this -

Since once (livelong the day) my prayer measured
A love along your face, I've raged and variously
Had all smiles and butchery daily acquainting
You of the springing bloodshot and the tear.
Since there (spun into a sudden place to discover)
We first lay down in the nightly body of the year,
Fast wakened up new midnights from our bed,
Moved off to other sweet opposites; I've bled
My look along your heart, my thorns about your head.

A U.S. magazine[1] which is running a number giving me 'more

1 *Quarterly Review of Literature* (vol. 3 no. 4, 1947).

solid representation in America' has also taken my essay NOTES ON A POETRY OF RELEASE to print it with the poems because it 'goes so amiably' with them. That's something and should help a lot. I see my American book FIRST POEMS advertised as out soon.[1] I haven't seen proofs or cover or anything and pray it's not too 'Progressive'. I might try to work on a series of love poems. I've so much to say about man-woman and up till now I've not attempted it because it's so difficult and complex. We'll see.

Here it's a good place. A harbour's arms round the boats. Three pubs. At the moment plenty drink all kinds. Coves, beaches and high gullwhite rocks. The fishermen are good and we feel happy being accepted well and not too obviously like visitors and thank Christ not as writers. Nessie sits at breakfast and reads about the parson-bigamist and sends her love. I said to Bryan in the Wheatsheaf 'I wish we had Sven here to talk about the "patin"' (Scot. patterrn). Not a thing more to say except that 'circumnavigation' is certainly a big word almost as good as '—— hochmagandy'. See any glossary of a complete Burns.

'A host of years a tithe of troubles and is there one who understands me. One in a thousand of years of the nights.' Joyce, but I'm not sure of 'host'.

Love, Jock

48. *To W.R. Rodgers*

7 October 1947 Mevagissey

Dear Mr Rodgers,

Here's the copy of my poem I mentioned, THE WHITE THRESHOLD. Though now I remember you've probably seen it before. I like the fourth part best.

Thanks for the advice you gave me. If anything else crops up you can think of will you let me know. I want to drive hard at getting as many letters or documents together as I can before applying for my visa etc. I've just written Allardyce Nicholl of the Awards Committee and also a note to see if Herbert Read can help me. I hope to see you for a drink when I come up again.

Yours sincerely, W S Graham

1 We have not traced this book; it was probably never published.

49. *To J.F. Hendry*

8 October 1947 Mevagissey

Dear J F Hendry,

How are you? Are you back from Vienna yet? I write first to ask for any advice you might be able to give me on getting out of the country for about three months. As you know I was granted an Atlantic Award. Now part of the condition is that I should not take any regular employment during that year. Also it has something to do with the Rockefeller people. So I'm trying to get out on the grounds of having a student grant my reason being that I want to meet American writers and study new American poetry. A critic over there, a member of the Faculty of Columbia University has invited me and is willing to put me up so that should help. Now can you advise me in any way before I attempt the American visa? I want as imposing a battery of letters and documents as I can amount. I've already just written the chairman of the Awards Committee and Herbert Read. If you can let me know soon about this it would help me to make arrangements more quickly.

Are you writing just now? Nessie says you were turning more to prose lately. Will that old LIVING ever come out? Maclellan is slow.

We both send our regards, W S Graham

50. *To J.F. Hendry*

23 January 1948 c/o Dr Ralph Ross, Division of General Education, New York University, Washington Square, New York. NY, USA

Dear J F Hendry,

I'm sorry to have kept off writing to you for so long. Thanks for your letter, It was a great help. As you see I'm here now and have been here about 5 weeks. It was all much easier than I thought. Also I am a lucky person it seems (I touch wood).

No difficulty came up about me leaving the country from the British. The only touch-and-go moment was talking to the American Consul in London when I got my visa. I was definite about not wanting to stay more than six months and showed my letters from the Rockefeller People and told him I was a 'poet' you know in the kind of naive way that occasionally just lets an American think you're daft and let you through. The passport I got for the asking. I got my passage by a cancellation just coming at the right time. They didn't ask for any bonds or anything. I just said I was going to be kept there during my visit by a friend who was a critic in New York and gave the name and address. The only money question they asked was was I taking more than £5. I said no and that was alright. I go over this for you in case you might want the information. Ask anything about it.

I am interested to see what like your new poems will be. Also the novel about a childhood in Glasgow as listed by Maclellan. What are you writing at the moment? Myself, I've written one poem since arriving, trying to be more simple without confusing simplicity in art with threadbareness. I'll type it on the other side.[1] I had word not long ago that Faber & Faber are putting out my 3RD POEMS. Eliot wrote me saying he was 'considerably' impressed with my work which is a happy surprise and will certainly help in England I mean Britain. I feel quite good about writing this weather and have begun a good solid book of poems. I mean that my usual way has been that at one point after writing about 30 poems I've collected them and said a book finished. This time I want to plan the whole book, something like twelve poems having certain subjects and maybe all the same metric structure. I feel the need to make some kind of (even structural) formality. What's happened to LIVING? Do you think it will ever appear? Nessie's in Cornwall getting over an operation. She's living alone and writing and I expect to get back to Cornwall. The drink here is fantastic. What strange people. It's difficult not to feel more grown up and more 'sensitive' than the intellectuals here and yet I can't help thinking there must be more to it which I'll get when I know them better. I didn't start with the usual English traditional snobbism about all the Americans being adolescent and ourselves being attached to a great and deep literary tradition. I would like if you could spare me a wee note about how you are getting on. Is there anyone here I could see for you or any messages or things I could do for you. Best Wishes, A Happy New Year,

N. would appreciate a letter if you feel like it. W S Graham

1 The poem was 'For My Brother', later retitled 'To My Brother'.

51. *To David Wright*

25 April [1948?] New York

My Dear David,

Typewriter's broken. Certainly a fine thing to hear from you and living the quiet life too, not that I can say it for my sodden self. At another anthology? Are you serious about your autobiography? Is the long poem finished? (myself – lately I've been studying the long poem – how to make a long poem which is not 'green hill to wander on', but a long poem with a real single whole poetic impact.) I've written three short poems – each 30 lines – 3 foot iambic – rimed strictly in form – the verse tight, a poem to my brother, my father and my mother. Simple I hope. I'm impatient to see your book of poems. When now? I teach at the University and energy goes well. At the moment I'm teaching Lawrence and Joyce's Finnegans Wake. My book, The White Threshold comes out in the summer from Faber. Eliot says he's 'considerably impressed' – whatever that means in the Eliot manner! It shouldn't get hit for just as big a six as the others. That is the way people are, a pity. I like your quotation – the broadsheet ballad. I'll be home- late summer. Give my love to the people. I would like to know what kind of poems you're writing now. Are they still as influenced by the Darley poets? I work at looking into the works of the Wake and W B Yeats. Also my dear friend Blake. What a good thing to have left such objects upon the earth, The Prophetic Books – also that great poem – The Mental Traveller. I'll see you all when I get back. And Fred Marnau.[1] I'll always seem to just miss him. And after having a reading of his poems here in a house to about 20 people – with a German lad saying the German and me the English – I really must see him next time. You might tell him that this German lad, quite a good poet in English, thought the poems wonderful and the translations specially revealing to him in his own work translating. I talk about The Death of the Cathedral. [One of Marnau's books] If you see Jimmy Singer again tell him good luck from me – also my regards to Heath Stubbs – I hope we may get on well some time.[2] cheerio for just now – Please write me again soon and tell me what goes on and on with you. Ask Archer to write. Love, Sydney.

1 Fred Marnau (1918–99), Austrian writer settled in England, wrote novels and poems in German, some of which were translated into English by Ernst Sigler. Others were written in English.

2 See Marie Singer in list of correspondents.

52. *To Mary Harris*

17 July 1948 Yaddo, Saratoga Springs, N.Y.,U.S.A.

My dear Mary, how nice it is to hear from you. So much water below so many bridges. What a lot there is to tell you. In your letter you don't tell me enough about yourself. Are you happy? Writing? Love? Health? It's good Rosalind's so bright. O I would love to see you both. I get back to England about the end of September. Could we arrange it? My latest book is due out with Faber & Faber this Autumn. Eliot himself wrote me that he was 'considerably impressed' by my work. A fine encouragement, eh? I think you will like the poems better too. They are more simple and yet I think as lyrical. The snob stamp of Faber will help my work. How silly that it should be so. What are you writing? Any new stories? How did I get here. An American critic (Vivienne Koch, article in last PQ called W S GRAHAM – THE TECHNIQUE OF MORALITY. O no, I mean the Winter 47–48 number.) said she was in London and would like to meet me. She had reviewed me very favourably and shrewdly in an American mag. I met her there and we got on well and went around together. She left for USA in August and arranged I give a season of lectures at New York University. She is a professor there (34). Also I had my fare left out of the Atlantic Award. I had a job getting the passport and visa but eventually made it. I arrived here last November. The lectures went wonderfully and I found out I could 'think on my feet' and lecture articulately without nervousness. I lectured on – UNDERSTANDING GREAT BOOKS (I chose DUBLINERS, TESS, MOLL FLANDERS, WUTHERING HEIGHTS and SONS & LOVERS) and CONTEMPORARY BRITISH LITERATURE, from Lawrence to the most recent prose and poetry. It went very well and they wanted me to stay another year. Also while I was given a short term fellowship from the Rockefeller Foundation here. That helped for living is impossibly expensive here (5/-haircut. Butter 5/-lb. Meat 6/-lb. and so on. Rent (cheap) is 72 dollars a month – about £18). Fantastic. But I'm coming back in September. It's too difficult to try to get an extension I've found. Also I want back to the sea and home. While I've been here I've written a long poem of 500 lines and several shorter pieces.

I'm healthy though I've been on the drink quite a bit. What cocktails here, Manhattans, Martinis, Tom Collins, and all calculated to 'disarrange the senses'. Now I'm at a place here for artists which the

Rockefeller people sent me to. It's a large mansion and they keep one for 2 months and feed and give quiet for work. Here there are 27 guests, writers and painters, some quite famous in U.S. The writers are either short stories or novels. I'm the only poet. It helps. I've been playing a lot of tennis here with the temp around 95 and feel very well. Not the suggestion yet of a pot and eyes maybe as blue as Ros's. Just a noticeable greying at the poetic temples. Why? I suppose I worry less than most. I won't advise you about USA. My first reaction to your idea to lecture here is Don't. You won't like it. It is really poorly paid compared with the price of surviving. It's just incredible. Also New York (I can't speak for the west) is the most vulgar easily city I could have imagined. I am even homesick for *England*. I would like to see you soon when I get back and have some good talks. We're both maybe a bit more (what a word) 'integrated' and should get on better and see each other's values more sympathetically. What age exactly is Rosalind? I showed her picture here to some of the people I like and they thought definitely she 'stood out' as a personality and had something more than the other kids. You certainly did a good job. Might you have room in your cottage sometime for me to have a week there. And would it be all right with Tony?

my love to you and Rosalind, WSGraham

53. *To Moncrieff Williamson*

undated [January 1949?] Mevagissey. 23 Cliff St. The Wind Dropped.

My dear Crieff,

Here I sit in my lane (I mean 'I sit my lane') and this is not me really begun to write you properly at all because I sit by the fire and enjoying the lack of that continual blowing (that wind honing the gable ends) and what a wonderful violin concerto – no. 5 in A Mozart? So there you are, I'm only writing at the moment thinking how good to hear from you and that your (half) creation comes out in March and what a kind invitation to use the jungle of language invite (*in*vite). A great stimulating book, THE WHITE GODDESS (Graves). Impossible to describe in nutshell – myth ancient history – bards – Celt – prophecy – language. A more creative, less academic, 'branch' from the Golden Bough by Frazer. 30/- but indispensable to a Celt and an aware 'makar'. If Pam had to have a new (a specially bought book's always doubly rich) book for an amusement in her abed days, it's a good one. Either to be swum from cover to cover or dipped into. ——The violinist in this is so very exact and 'clean' in his playing. He makes almost a visual line in the air – I think of Klee's phrase – 'taking a line for a walk', of course about drawing. Christ! what a literary letter – not meant – it's the music makes me reflective. I try as much as possible to keep in my little igloo of either – 1. making poetry – 2. listening to music or reading. I'm afraid I'm at a lonely low wretched ebb. Though I suppose I'm fundamentally an ascending and happy person. I'll soon be up. Your letter was nice. I seem to be in that awful stage which is I suppose, the first mild potentials of a persecution complex – an urge to 'suffer alone' – keep off from my friends – magnify or imagine slights – a kind of Jock agin the world. So there you are Criefy. I don't think at all serious and a situation I can see as comic and in its ridiculous perspective. I haven't seen a soul over Christmas and new year – 1 XM card from V., not a drink, ulcer resurrecting furiously in m'guts, no financial future even in pennies, lots of good work done in poetry and I feel I've developed (maybe in 'spiritual integration' – what a phrase – as well) as a poet a great step from pre USA days. The whole American descent into the labyrinth or whatever it was has certainly been a considerable enrichment though in many ways I haven't got round to finding it all out. Vivienne, in every way, has helped me so much. What a wonderful person of energy, generous energy, she is. Crieff, how good to hear from you and that you are more settled and happy in your sun cottage (son cottage?) and going on with the writing. It will be good seeing both you and Pam and hearing about what you're doing and to compare our notes of that land which certainly seems like a nightmare or daymare or mare of some galloping sort. Do you ever have word from that poor near mad family living away out yonder with the neon-lit tavern and the drinks and the fight – Christ! what hopelessness was around there? Remember the long journey in the underground under rivers and shuttles and changing and everything. Mozart stopped and for the moment I get on making tea and putting a sheep's head on the hob to simmer – the beginning of a good graham broth.

A Sunday later

Dear Crieff I really am ashamed, taking all this time to write you. I could have dropped you a note by return but I thought each day I would be in a position to say when I'll be up. As it is, I'm still unsure. It's a long kind of mixture of events and reasons concerning rent and me almost ready to let go completely of that monster, my long poem and, really the decisive reason, my ulcer's been on one long riot and I've hardly eaten so my weight's dropped to 9-6 which frightens me a bit and I lie back in a semi horizontal position which seems to ease the pain and I clip paper to a drawing board and use a pencil thus. Yesterday and today I've begun to eat better and a sweet harrassed fisherman's wife who lives near sends me up some potato soup and says 'that'l stick t'your ribs'. I would like nothing better than to jump on the train right away and come up and see you but I won't be able to leave here for a fortnight or 3 weeks yet. I'm crazy enough looking at the house and without thinking maybe I go to read out an altered passage in my poem and what a voice struggles up and I realise I've not said hello or rain again for a few days. As they say on the Bramaputra Delta – 'It ain't right'. So it would be wonderful to have a few days away and to see what you're doing and meet Pamela and maybe show you some of my poem for I'm excited about it and sit down at a table, passing the salt, raising a sly eyebrow, and conversing on the state of Scottish culture or what a racket getting published is (as it certainly is). See what a blether – even in a letter.

Now, Crieff, the thing is this. March is the 'big' month, as you say and the sooner I make my visit the better. How late could it comfortably be? If *now* is really the only time which is suitable, then it can't be helped Crieff and I'll certainly be seeing you both before much time goes by. Don't try to stretch things for me and let me know about how late a date it can be with plenty margin. You must feel good about things and I suppose a bit anxious.

Your letter and invitation has really made me feel good and I look forward to seeing you both very much and I'm curious to see what kind of animal your book is turning out and we can list everyone we remotely claim as a friend who is also remotely to do with writers editors publishers, because to not use those awful rackety helps, would certainly be glaikit.

My long poem's called THE NIGHTFISHING and it's about 330 lines long and looks helluva long to me. I still go over it changing lines and phrases but it's almost come to the point where alterations don't seem to make it (to my measurements) 'better' but only make it say another thing, different. In making notes and experiments during the writing of it I seem to have amassed, like shale, a considerable amount of material I couldn't use and so those ideas, information, words already form a direction and a project for after The Nightfishing. Do you already have names for it boy or girl? What a king o' the roost then you'll be with your pipe over the beer. Now I skip quick over your letter and see if I've to answer anything more. O I forgot to say I'm afraid Crieff I'll have to accept your help with fare money. I just won't have it and probably won't be in condition for hitching although I like it. Use all your willpower and self-trickery to keep at the book. You'll be aiming at completing it before The Date? There's no easy way, only to plow on till you get to what you decide is the end and don't let yourself get stuck. You can fill in something as a kind of note to remind you just what you were after at that part and when you get to the end that will come with the trimming it up – because then the strain of unfinished movement is gone and it's maybe just a cool job of intelligence to work it right.

One of the things I've always been naturally bad at (besides spelling) is reading handwriting the slightest bit erratic. I hope you get a new ribbon soon. Was it the ribbon? No I haven't seen THE GALLIARD. What's it mean? Editor? Who's in it? Published where? Do you think it's any good? I now consider myself as banished, more or less, from the Scottish Lit Scene, which I don't hold with and seems to get more embarrassing with its playing bards glumerin lufts keekin wi sna. The final wow was reading an intimation of a ceremonious dinner for presenting The Bard (McD.) with his portrait and it was written in this Plastic Scots (which all the Bards have a different idea of) and ended by giving the address of some office where tickets could be had and the *telephone* number, and, dodging the leprous word he ends with –

Farspeak 7638.

I don't know. That did it. Faber proofs corrected and the poems revised considerably in proof and they promise 'late winter' or 'early spring', whatever that means. How did you know I was appearing in V.B's Corny Review? [D. Val Baker's *Cornish Review*] Curious. Please, not like me, write soon and say what's doing. Best Wishes. Keep hard at the B.B. Jock

54. *To David Wright*

11 January 1949 Mevagissey

Dear David,

Just a wee note to tell you how pleased I am to see that your book's out at last. I saw it mentioned in The Sunday Times. It deserves to get a good reception. It should be one of the few books of verse around where the poems are seriously made from a study of how the action of 'poetry' is brought about. Best wishes for it.

Nessie's in London. May be returning for a month before the final nipping of the cord. I'm at my most unsocial and broke and live in my little igloo of working at poetry and listening to music. If I poke my nose out the door I'm done for. My long poem THE NIGHTFISHING is finished, except for changes here and there as it recedes into a more clear perspective. It's, as it stands, about 330 lines. I'm quite overwhelmed with it and I think it has good poetry in it. I hope it is a good poem, I mean – valid as one object. Where are you? Cornwall or London? What are you working on at the moment? What happened about the Zennor Mermaid poem? I think, as a subject, almost an impossible handicap. After this, for me, monster I'm thinking about a cycle of love poems (as at present I'm less caught up that way than usual). Again, the book out's good. Love. Sydney

55. *To Sven Berlin*

7 March 1949 The Green Steps, Mevagissey

My Dear Sven,

I'm back again here and have managed in the last few days to attach myself to 'The Poem' and I think it should be something. It's a little late tonight for the typing but I shall certainly be wanting a stanza or two pinned on the Berlin Walls.

Thanks for the white friends, certainly a Godsend or St Svensend. Here's 10/- for anything you can do further in the matter. They go quickly. I've watched, as you advise, and haven't rushed them too much. They are a great help in putting in a really long stretch of time on the work – when that is specially needed.

It is a long time since I've seen you, Sven, and there seems to be so much happened to me. It should be good to talk and have a few walks around and on the drink. I've had about three drunky nights since Christmas. At the moment affairs are at their lowest and it is rather a hopeless horizon. I'm never out at the pubs and I don't mind at all. But I would want to be on the drink coming to St.Ives, so I think I should wait a little. Something sometimes turns up unexpectedly – remember our sudden descents on St.Ives from the caravans. I'm impatient to see your drawings and carving. Everything you've done for a long time will be new to me. You've mentioned writing. What's it about, Sven? Is it fiction of some kind or didactic and about Cornwall and painting?

I saw the first review of the Wallis (which I've seen anyhow) which is so ridiculous in its spite that I wonder – 'well, did you steal this man's woman or what' for the feeling of personal temper in the review rather capsizes any conviction it might carry. I hope you're not bothering about it in any way. Because it's in The Listener and read a lot, it's a nuisance – that's all. I don't see many of the current periodicals – what like are any other reviews out? Tell me, how many copies were printed? Has it been distributed in U.S.? All the bookshops in the principal town in Cornwall should have it displayed specially with notices giving information like – Alfred Wallis – Cornish Fisherman Painter etc, to get all the Cornish-conscious crowd eh? And is it being reviewed in Val Baker's Cornish Review? Have you any friends having to do with the libraries in Cornwall? I think Wallis is the most perfect primitive painter – and sprouting from Cornwall – it's something. And there is so much to be said (and found out) about all this from a regarding it as Celtic – taking care too to shoo the'twilicht' awa. Do you know if it's selling well? It should. Bang away at Nicholson & Watson to get it around well – and Sven, America should snap it up if it can be got to the main N.Y. shops. Get N & W on this.

I like the text. There are so many ways to write the text to the first presentation of those reproductions. So, as you choose this way, this is it, and successful. It should create an interest in Wallis as the man who made those paintings. As this kind of statement it is successful. The Listener reviewer obviously wants another kind of book. So do I, now. But not instead of this one. I think this kind of book the kind best for its purpose, the introduction of Alfred Wallis. Now I would like to read a book about 'primitive painting' and Alfred Wallis. Talking about the paintings and 'primitiveness' as coldly and clearly and exactly as possible and, if it could be done, not relating it to W's life at all. I haven't read much aesthetics on art and primitives, so I don't know if there is much theory on the aesthetics of primitive Art or even if it's treated specially anywhere. I imagine it should be? I mean writing of the intellectual texture of Klee which I came across in some passages from his notebooks somewhere. I would like to be helped more towards an appreciation of Wallis' paintings as formal organisms working and sustaining themselves as a life not at all depending on the literary values of the subject they are symbol of. I now would like to read about W's paintings with the accent on this side – remembering that the magnitude of the whole painting is the outcome of both the formal abstract and the 'seayness' or whatever the subject is. Well, how about that? Do you feel at all interested in such a book on Wallis? Do you think it would help? You asked me what I thought about the text. That's it. Also one other thing, Sven. I think it comes through your writing that you want to write – I mean 'write', – create. Of course I think any kind of writing is creative. Well, anyhow, I'm not quite sure what does come through but it's something like a feeling that the writer would rather be writing about some world made up from his head and not have to stick to those facts which have to be given over the pages to the people. – It's like me when I'm writing a letter. I hate having to say anything which needs saying. I would rather write to someone I like when I've nothing to say (which I'm aware of) and just want to let them hear my sweet voice – like – 'There is the whole east leaned at last to us.' Christ the great vanity. I could write me till doomsday. I've just had a walk out to the quay-heads. The sea's rough and noisy tonight. This coast has not the same mystic feeling as the coast from Penzance round Land's End to St Ives. I must get down there some time again to stay a while. Though I've been thinking a lot of the Western Isles recently. You would like them, Sven. They would, without a doubt, send you daft.

The Kyle of Lochalsh
The Pass of Brander
Rannoch Moor
The Sands of Morar.

In spells of the poetry I've been trying some drawing. Only to help me to see better. Some strange faces appeared. A few allegorical drawings though Christ knows what they say. One automatic drawing of 2 figures. I've had it on the wall for a few days and find I have a wee affection for it. Strange. It was really automatic – fast, calligraphic and I didn't seem to be thinking of anything. I must keep it from the psychoanalysts. Also some fish and birds influenced by some early Art via friend Braque – -[drawing of fish in text] – - you know. They look nice and make the wall different for a day or two. Some fierce faces appear from my pen.

I would like to write something in some way to do with Wallis and his world. What a vague 'like' it sounds, yet I mean it and I've thought about it before. Thinking of him, he becomes for me more and more a symbol of that energy which manifests itself in all kinds of places, so often when it is shouted for and encouraged by all the gear and disguise of 'rolling eye' etc. – not appearing – and at times appearing, as in Wallis, seemingly 'in spite of'. The poem, is one of my less cluttered & pretensious pretenteous (O Christ take your pick Sven) and I'm glad of that but now it's so inadequate when I'm this far along the road.

I love Susan Agland.[1] The Schooner at Night is a very fine one. I am cutting them out, one at a time and having them on the wall for a few days then sticking them back neatly with tape – the best way to get to know them. Here's the last line or two I've written on The Nightfishing

'——, and has
The iron sea engraved to our faintest breath,
The spray fretted and fixed at a high temper,
A script of light.'

Try to round up a good team of whites. Important to me at the moment. Also I would like to hear about what you're writing and how the W. book progresses. Also to hear from you. Love, Jock

To read – THE WHITE GODDESS by GRAVES – the most stimulating book I've come across for years.

56. To Sven Berlin

[12 March 1949]

Mevagissey – Saturday – Something to read – This makes a spell off my poem here for a moment. Dear Sven, hello. Thanks for your letter.

1 This refers to a photograph of Wallis's wife in Berlin's study; see above, p. 82.

There's a nice wee bit in this week's Listener on the Japanese painter, Hokusai by someone, Wilfrid Blunt, a good article and I found it moving and with reproductions. You'll probably have seen it. I have the 'Fuji above the Lightning' on the wall. In the last 1/2 year I find myself waking up more towards painting and, in fact, more awake visually, generally. Of course the bad thing is being in somewhere like this with no chance to see pictures. I must find some good reproductions to look at, not just of 'new' painting.

I'll see if there are any books worth reading I can send you. I'm sorry, no, Sven, no White Goddess. I get it from the library when someone sends it back. There seems to be a busy run on it. I know you will find it very exciting. Try to get it from your St.Ives library.

I'm still doing a few drawings. Though I've never felt more rich with ideas for poems and experiments about poetry in my life. This 'Nightfishing', because of its size, is a bit of a monster to finish off. So often I feel lost in the middle of it not able to get out and back from it to see it as *one object*. But the bugger shall be fucked into an organic whole all the same. Christ it will be good to get it finished. I'll type you something for the wall – Nightfishing? Or something about flowers or rolled trousers or clattering clitori?

I can fill this line with – The streaming morning in its tensile light – – – –

Can you say anything about 'automatic drawing'? Have any established artists done it? Yourself? Results?

An idea I had. To write a poem about some object in the kitchen here (which I'm in always except sleeping), maybe the sideboard, or the jug I have catkins in, or a funny low chair. The poem to be fairly short and fairly descriptive and needn't be very good. And to see how the writing of the poem changes the object so that a week after writing it maybe the object will be related to me in a significance out of all proportion to the significance of the other objects in the room. (Christ how long winded that sounds) – but – see what I mean? It's not important but a nice thing to do. It would even be more interesting if I lived in a cottage like Bryan's. I could write something about the cromlech – which one can see from the cottage all the time – and see how it changed. I can see me writing on all the rocks and 'druid rocks' around there and and be frightened to go out. I would like to stay for a week or two there, writing, sometime this summer. Though it's almost overfar from the sea. A wee bit out of a more abstract, less visual part of T.N.F. –

This instant, bounded by non-silence moving
Towards the terrible novelty of light
Masters me into measurement so that
My ghostly constant is articulated.

It's something, an idea, in my mind a lot this weather. The identity of 'the ghostly constant'. If there is such a thing imaginable to any concrete degree. And its relation to all that flows over it. I am a river flowing past a point, not the man I was a second ago, but what is the point? What is the one me? – A great carry on it all is.

Today is a Monday, March 21st. A year or two from that Saturday I began this letter. It's 4 a.m. I sit here by the fire and Nessie has gone to her gentle sleep. Some tea in the pot keeps hot on the hob and I suppose stews, by the smell of it. Outside it's thick and pitch, no fishermen moving yet, the gulls not roused yet. One faint-strained cock a few fields above the village. The clock on the wall. Nessie's mother calls it 'the knock', a strange Scotsism. But then some old people in Scotland still say 'sclim' for 'climb' and 'lether' for 'ladder'. There's a children's rime like this -

Sclim the lether, sclim the lether, High high high
Up to the top of the bonnie blue sky.
Dr Brown's a very good man.
He teaches children all he can.
First to read and then to write
Then eery airy ory.

At last Nessie is ready to go to Italy. People who run the thing she is to have a job in are now in London and will be driving her to the north of Italy by car – via France. She leaves here on Monday and London 3 days later. A serious change in both our lives. What a strange world it will be, having no gentle Nessie to make it a little sweeter. Yet we've realised for a few years now that it is the thing to do. There was really no choice. Things are at their worst ever financially and it will be a fight to keep out of a job of some kind. But if I can I must work hard and solidly for a good 3 or 4 months. I'm working so well and, I think, profitably. When Nessie goes I'll have to live *in* my poem more than ever. Thank Christ the days get a little softer and the birdies singen.

And the 50 were a great help and faded fast and I must, next time, remember to put those tiger glands on shorter rations. Do what you can, Sven, for at the moment they are a spare engine in this bull-shouldering sea. Again I've resorted to sniffing those bloody B.H.s [benzedrine inhalers] and got my nostrils really buggered up and bleeding. What a mad business. Still, it is the right thing for this time. The work gets down on the paper. After this letter I write to London to try to borrow £10 to pay the back rent here. It's only 5/- a week but it's got to that and I avoid looking the landlord in the eye.

I'll try to borrow on the first royalties of T.W.T. which should be out in a week or two. I saw it listed in the Times Lit. Sup. 'One of the most promising of the younger Scottish poets.' Not much help I suppose but I like them putting in Scottish – though, the Scottish Bards will be livid, having (in reviews) exiled my work from any claim to Scottishness and me from being a 'bard' at all. Though the poems are 2 1/2 years old I'll be a wee bit excited to see the book out by the first professional-poetry-list firm for me yet. It should be solider to handle than the 2ND Poems. The three last poems (written in US last year) added like an epilogue are a wee bit kinna mature. (Christ the tea's stewed to soup). I've had no advance on the book. I'm hoping it makes maybe £20 at 1st payment of royalties. But I don't know what poetry books usually do. So, Sven, my dear, here I am. Stewed tea, the gulls not started up yet, the clock engrossed in a Bartok equivalent of a Nicholson [sketch of a Ben Nicholson Relief inserted], a leaky pipe somewhere outside in the fisherman's yard whispering on and on, my nose fucked, my jersey steeping in its navyblue water, the fire a ruin of paling embers and seeing before me my summer life lived in here seeing no people and working hard and keeping off 'regular employment' if I'm lucky. I'm hoping this monster of a poem should open its portcullis jaws and drop me in about another 3 weeks. Then I have a series of 12 poems with their subjects (how valid?) decided. Then another long bugger, a companion for N.F.

One day there [David] Lewis and Billy Barns Graham stood in the bright doorway when I had opened the door at a knock. We drank tea and talked. He should be able to put over something on Wallis with the correct accent and be interesting. He seemed very nice and young? He asked us out to his cottage at Zennor to stay a few days. It would be maybe a good thing to do soon, taking my work along and working a few days there for a change. But I don't know. I find it difficult even to go out for a walk and stay out for an hour. I'm much better and put on weight every day. I was down to 9 – 6. A bad thing – with the Elijah-catchingup gales of the west. Willie seemed enthusiastic about the new organisation[1] and looked prettier than I had remembered her, [...] She was nice and we talked about the 'ART' and she promises to send me a loan of her Cahier D'art' – because I said I was famished for a sight at painting or good reproduction. If you see her around, Sven, would you remind her. So off they went and Lewis had a wee talk with Derek Savage (Critic of Lit. – THE PERSONAL PRINCIPLE).

'Disturbance in the West' sounds interesting, Sven. I think the title a wee bit not good – I'm sorry, Sven, but when I read your letter I read the title and involuntary react – not liking it. And I think I should tell you. 2 main reasons. – 1. it falls into the group of those titles, usually of over-boosting of semi parochial activity – Promise in Portsmouth – Deep notes in —— Rare songsters in — — *Reason* – immediate recollection of Decline of the West – hence (and also) 'West' suggestion – the Western World in some political or sociological way. So it seems unfunctional. But that's what *I* think. Have you tried it around any *reliable* people yet? Look, Sven, — IMPORTANT! — after seeing here in your letter what you will be dealing with in this book you *must* get that book from some library or somewhere, – THE WHITE GODDESS, to be talking about those things without having read the Graves book (which is always mainly exploring the Celtic and Druidical side of the subject) will be working under a great handicap. Get it somewhere. I'd like to see your notes in Facet. If you can spare your copy a few days I promise prompt return. I suppose I'll see the Cornish Review when it appears. Any new Wallis Book reviews?

About a letter to The Listener regarding the W[allis] Review. It's no good, Sven. That is not the way. It wouldn't be good for either of us. The only time one can get in a return blow which works is when the reviewer has made a factual error. Then that's something. Otherwise you are definitely turning the other cheek and giving the reviewer another chance to use more space on you and really slay you. We don't pretend that reviews are fair in any way. A nasty reviewer with the least intelligence can make the best book appear silly for a wee while. But it usually, in time, (I mean the book) stands before the review reading public in fairly general proportions. I would advise you not to write in against any reviews or to suggest

1 The Penwith Society of Arts in Cornwall, founded on 8 February 1949.

that any else do so. If an *anti* reviewer makes an error – maybe the thing to do is to write in correcting it 'quietly' and suggesting general casualness and incompetence. I think one must mind one's mouth when turned to the review mic. Remember too – most of the reviewers are professionals – they can know a smattering, only, about the subject, and yet gut you in one movement like the pilchard girls here at the troughs. As my friend Charlie Ball says with a wink over the pint – 'speak easy'. In N.Y. instead of cheerio it's – 'Take it easy.' And so in N.Y. one hears 'take it easy' going between everybody as they kill themselves riding the galloping skedjul of progress.

My Dear Sven (hand tired writing and top of a drawing pin came through into my thumb the other day and I was almost in a flash out of the Graham skin) I am happy as you write me that Jacque is getting better and that you are emerging slowly towards the house with ye're ain fireside – which is a great strength to any kind of artist – whether the extreme of the tranquilly recollecting or of the pouring-forther. The sea to sail and storm and suffer on and a good, (FOR ME), kitchen with a fire and tea and a scrubbed wood table to make something from it all, in. The landlord here seems very pleasant – but houses are scarce and I hate owing him – and if he took the house away now Christ knows what there is to do or where (as through those words the thunder waters move) to go, with that grey swell running heavy and moving down on us.

Sven, – I've always written you recently 'after typing hours' and so – no extract. I promise you it will be coming all right. This Night Fishing – whether a successful whole poem or not – is the most definite *sea* poem in the language since 'The Wreck of the Deutschland' and I think it is seaier than it is – whatever seaier may 'bring up' or to the nostrils with all possible jokes of being taken with a pinch of salt and so on. The thing is a sea monster with poetic licences by the dozen.

Sven – this selling your books to the 2nd hand man is daft. Especially a book like the collected Yeats. It would fetch so little it's not worth it. You said you read so little. Maybe you should read more – as you're writing. I've some books you may find something in, which I'm finished with.

Yes – we'll get into the drink and Christ it's so much better talking than writing so slowly the words out. I can't say when as you'll realise. The first money I get to spare I'll be hitchhiking down. I can't help making guesses in image about the wonderful – 'head with the eyes inlaid with lead'. It sounds fine and barbaric.

So it looks like I've worked my way through your letter and most things answered.

I'm on the heavy side now and the pale blue light stares in the window. The gulls are at their wailing now And the black hags going low over the sea and the fishermen's boots clump down the cobbles. Now for a few bloody sniffs at this awful contrivance to help me 'up' and a wash and shave and to start the day well on the monster. Do you know, Sven, I miss Leah. Leah – our nice white and fawn goat at the caravans. The most beautiful of them all. *Try about the B's to save my wee nose before it drops off and it's wee enough as it is. The sooner the better.* Nessie wants to be reminded to you and we talked rather a lot lately about you and been a little concerned. But it's good J is improving and plans are going ahead. I hope the Wallis book makes a difference. Nessie sends her love. She is all excitement and the mixed emotions of such a venture. Please see White Goddess.

Take it easy, Love, Jock

57. *To Moncrieff and Pamela Williamson* (extract)

23 March 1949 Mevagissey

I go through the days here working hard at my monster and as the weather grows milder getting out for a dauner on the quay. The boats get ready for a new season of Longlining because now the Dogfish season's finished. The men are busy fixing lines and getting the boats ready for their deepersea work. The primo roses are out and this morning I found a bluebell on the cliffs. Soon I'll be able to get seagulls' eggs, wonderful for omelettes.

58. *To Moncrieff Williamson*

25 March 1949 Mevagissey

Dear Crieff,

I think The Vertical Distance is ahead from The Fluid Idol poems. For it, – I can say the language is sharper in texture, no sentimentalisms. Against it – a lack of definite rhythmical movement – an obscurity which might awe some who don't know anything about poetry and irritate others. I think you should try to write in definite metres. This 'free verse' with lines all prose in rhythm is the most difficult kind of verse to make successful. Even Eliot's 'free verse' is no 'free' but ordered into a pattern. I like – 'the low-scale flats of the earth'

and

'the clipper wings are christened constellations'.

I miss what you are saying. Remember that your 'message' might be quite clear to you but you've got to watch that the terms you use are the currency you think they are to other people. I can't get the significance of the small 'j' in 'jew'. I think you should tidy it up a bit and send it the rounds. And, Crieff, do keep sending out. You've got to get used to them coming home. They always do for quite a while especially this weather. More mags herewith. Look to Pam – cheerio for now – Jock.

59. *To Edwin Morgan*

14 April 1949 Mevagissey

My Dear Edwin,

Here are some notes, some kind of reply, to your good letters which I have here. And I'll go through them putting down answer to questions or questions implied.

Your letters are always so very live and civilised and sensitive. Though I have hardly replied I have often thought about you and what you've said about my poetry and what is in the letters, 'The Morgan Letters'.

Here I begin on the June 48 one. This must have reached me in America. You'll hardly have remembered what you've said. Still, I'll try to be clear.

I can't remember very well your 'Egypt Letter' which you say was 'carping' and which I defended. Probably I would now agree to most of it but say that it was a necessary and wholesome display of energy (to a degree which let it become valid, at times, as poetry) and point out its signs of a rich potential. I remember you using the word – 'stevedoring', about how I was manhandling and twisting words. It was so true. The 'distortion' is legitimate but in those early poems it was so often done rudely and not 'with grace'. The paper's bad. Forgive the pencil from now on.

I'm pleased you like what you like in Cage Without Grievance. You mention what I think are the best – 'Gentle Queen', 'I, no More Real', and 'Here Next the Chair I was'. And even that line you mention is, I have always thought, particularly successful with its choice of the word 'trundle'. Though many of the poems are unsuccessful as whole poems they display a variety and richness of ingredients.

1. 'Who longingly for violet-cells prospect the meads.'

2. 'Look there O where tear has never told.'

3. 'That puts God mildly to the heart I own.'

4. 'Conceal the hollow in the core of love
For fear will fast after it move.' Etc...

Breaking the metrical framework then (C.W.G.) was, I thought, to preserve some feeling of rhetorical inevitability which had been got rather by accident than intention. Now, of course, I am more the 'master of things' – or, at least, am more within the illusion of the artificer. I am for order, for the selection of PROPORTION.

So many of those early poems are 'difficult' – but as well as 'difficult' they are often lazy offerings, with the 'suggestive' serving as that dazzling stroke of communication which they should be. There is obscure poetry and lazy poetry and, of course, often a poem is both but is more often more lazy than obscure. I am, I think, specially supplied with a facility for the lyrical and memorable phrase and I've exploited it, as sole power in the poem, overmuch.

The 'Threnody for a Ruined Landscape' wasn't mine. And I didn't like it much. It would, for me, have been 'back'. (In other letters, Edwin, would you write bigger with lines further apart. I don't seem to be good at reading other people's handwriting at all.)

The sea in The White Threshold is a changing symbol. It is variously – the Continual Arrival from 'otherness' – the element through which we all move and with the urge to really contact and share with the other 'inner sea' of other people and break the centre aloneness. Yet the centre aloneness is the greatest joy and gift from Him. If sharing it were easy it would be nothing. – the mingling, always moving, spontaneous morality of the 'heart' as opposed to the outside constructions of order because we are a world and live together. —- and the sea with no exactness but with nonetheless intensity and positivity – moving mingling with a storm 1000's of miles away having effects and movements at our door — Edwin, I really love being on the sea. There I have feeling of freedom and cleanness and being part of a great energy which has nothing to do with any morality and is completely unhuman.

As I read on I begin to think how it would be so much easier to talk. Maybe you could somehow have a wee holiday down this way. I mention it later in this letter. It might be a good idea?

I am expecting my 6 author's copies of T.W.T. any day and I will be sending you a copy. I have been pleased at you reading my poems so seriously and you've certainly contributed to a greater feeling of responsibility which I think I have now. So I'm not writing anymore in answer to your remarks about T.W.T. excerpt which appeared in P.L. because you'll have it all then.

About the difficulty of my poetry, for example that T.W.T section. I do agree 'that the attempt to fathom the bottomless is not misplaced'. As to what indications I might expect to experience at those depths, I might differ. Let me say generally that – I think of my poetry as 'intellectual poetry' because it is intellectual in texture always whether it could be called intellectual in its whole statement in the one poem. But that is more from the T.W.T. volume on. For example this from 2NP's [2ND *Poems*] has it –

'I am my womb or man for woman fetched
By strict ambition. I my shepherd am
And feed a million harmonies.
The roar they fall in is my home
And all the serving distance is my room.'

or

'I no more real than evil in my roof'

or, from the long present poem I'm working on –

'What measures gently

Cross in the air to us to fix us so still
In this still brightness by knowledge of
The quick proportions of our intricacies?
What sudden perfection is this the measurement of?
And speaks us thoroughly to the bone, and has
The iron sea engraved to our faintest breath,
The spray fretted and fixed at a high temper.
A script of light.'

A Few Remarks about the poems which I hope to write about more fully later on. I would like if we could establish some come and go of opinions about poetry and things. Don't laugh, that *I* should say this with my neveranswering letters. —

First let me say, there are no editors I know of that I respect at all as people of any real taste in poetry. Why they reject and accept is not important. The only ones whose sympathy to my poetry I respect are those who write poetry also and in whose poems there is evidence of that relation to language as a dialogue taken part in, going on in the very centre loneliness. I quickly think who I might care about liking or disliking my work. About half a dozen. And I know that if I become well known and at all 'famous' in my lifetime it will not be at all important but will just mean that that larger public, who draw a certain selfconscious and nostalgic excitement from running their eyes along the words in my poems, believe I am a poet of some magnitude because 'the few' believe so (from Eliot down to say, Read), and can read my work knowing they are not being 'taken in' whatever that may mean. Art can not be fake. It either unites with us to our advantage or doesn't unite with us at all. By 'to our advantage' I mean to our enlargement of spirit. So, more and more, I realise the aloneness is a joy to live in and talk there to the most marvellous listener which is within my imagination and the limitations of that listener are the limitations of my poetry. So certainly now I think – if I hadn't poetry – that place to be in in the act of making poetry – what would I do? Where would there be the least peace in my life?

My dear Edwin – hello I didn't mean to go on about that. The main thing I wanted to say – don't be affected, either way, by editors. It's good to be published, of course, and good for one's attitude to writing. But O the few who will really get the subtle heartbreaking gestures of speech woven and positioned so exactly in a poem – a very very few. And the striving to communicate the merest wink of torment or sudden drench of sweetness is as though one were talking to God. – The Poems – The DIES IRAE is like nothing in contemporary poetry. As a whole poem for me it is not successful. The listing and cataloguing goes on too long. Phrases lines and some parts are very moving. In fact, Edwin, I find it very moving anyhow as a whole poem though I think it isn't successful. You would know I would like the strong physical action language which seems to be kept out of contemporary poetry as much as possible, maybe thought as a sign of naivety. As you would notice in the T.W.T. excerpt I, like you, am drawn to very much to Anglo-Saxon words and language with that basic strong feel about it and recently in this poem I'm working on I've been going through all the Anglo-Saxon poems and earlier. A coincidence your translations coming – I had then a book – Eng. Lit. from the beginning to the Norman Conquest by Stopford A. Brooke. Very good with good translations. But I want a certain kind of strength in my work from the Anglo-Saxon poetry and even a certain faint echo but I must speak in the idiom of the language at its present point. To use archaicisms (and you have) they must be used very selfconsciously so that the knowledge that they are used by the poet to carry all their archaic associations in itself goes towards the success of the poem. It is usually as a montage value in a poem that archaicism occurs. Exception Pound. And Yeats is a curious instance and very special. Here, Edwin, it would have to be successful in the Pound way of The Seafarer or an earlier 'troubador poem'. So then, in some ways this would be like the best kind of translation of A.S., yet would be original? But there are phrases and words which have by now taken on too tarnished a poetic diction to be very often used freshly and I am apparent of them fairly soon. – God's *Wrath* – sea of time – groaning shores of wrath – faced the blast – poor coat threadbare. Now – no matter how thought out the reason – or how cunningly constructed into the organic of a poem, it's almost impossible to carry the weight of this worn out stuff. And that is the first thing which I think is bad about this poem. Next – the verse lets me down a lot. I take it that at the beginning, at least the first 30 lines or so, are roughly blank verse lines. But after the first 2 opening lines the 3rd. 6 syllabled line comes with a jolt. Generally I would like the verse constructed more tautly and not so galloping as it is apt to do with so many 'ands' in it and 'of's'. And so it's apt to race a bit. (I know that we may differ quite a bit in our ideals of good verse but I try to measure this to fairly common standards which we'd both agree about I think) line 3, when I read it out in its place is difficult to fit in, line 4 read as a 5 stress line is very good with its acre and burgh 'chime'. Then we go on and down all the 'My' phrases and I long for some relief and distortion in the rhythm. They even all end u -. So I don't understand why that should be. Why not even the slightest little skip – even 'My clothes were sodden, rotting with the wet' could so easily have been – 'My clothes were sodden, They rotted with the wet'. and a line like – 'My eyes half blinded by the harsh salt spray', when run out smooth like that, is not good verse, and 'blinded by the harsh salt spray' has a 'fitted-in' feeling when read aloud and an infirmity. Not that lines should not occur which are exact in their iambics, but that one shouldn't be, rolled out on the tongue in the exact metre shows it up as thin. Better more like 'My eyes half blinded, blocked by the harsh salt spray'. Yet a line like – 'And sheets of freezing grey lay all his world' is wonderful and a great line and would be spoiled with any extra skip of rhythm. I don't get the rhythm of the second last 2 lines of that first section. And apart from its movement the word 'boomerang'is completely out of its element and is not organic here. Also to a slightly lesser degree 'drumroll' is too. An incidental fiction is created behind every poem and automatically it has its words which are native to it and then less native to it, as the words become less organic to it, till at the extreme is the stranger – which can be fitted in as a 'shock word' only at very special occasions – (what a nice wee story).

Parts at the beginning I like are – first 6 lines except 'mortal voyager,' 'raw haul of the waves,' the inversion of 'Cower among the pebbles, I could not for the cold,' 'sea birds with stiff starlike feet' – though the other adjective 'stiff' so weakens the fine 'star-like' applied to feet of the birds. Sometimes withstanding the temptation to govern the object to a greater exactness results in it being left more fresh and vivid. Here 'stiff' spoils it. Edwin – watch too many adjectives – and especially you ask for disaster with so many double adjectives. Here you have 3 lines following [each] other with 'and's becoming hypnotising almost -

He was that *blaze and meditation* in the sky.
That *pierced and scoured* the spaces of the air
And *showered and shook* those lightnings quiet & keen

Too much, Edwin.

Another weakness, for me, in a poem of this length – there is too much shouting. To start off at such a high pitch of rhetoric (and I mean good rhetoric) is imprudent. It is like a singer singing full blast and then finding that when he wants to interpret a special glory or elation and that he's going as loud as he can already and can't make it a bit louder, there are too many highly associated words in too short a space. Talking about words in a poem of any length, Eliot says – 'The poet should dispose the poorer among the richer. He cannot afford to overweigh the poem with the richer for it is only at certain moments that a word can be made to insinuate the whole history of the language – 'The Music of Poetry'.

I just can't understand your intention in the construction of the verse. You go down line after line exact and too flat in rhythm, then you suddenly have a line -

'A lee of stone I'll have, mussels and limpets eat'

of 6ft. And it's difficult to read as 6 because it's so isolated in that metre. It is a strange poem, moving and has a certain massiveness but in its apparent lack of verse construction, heavy to get through.

Dear Edwin I must stop now — thumb sore with writing and 4 a.m. but I'm posting this because I know myself and don't be hard on this letter.

Is there any chance of you getting down here to Mevagissey for a week maybe if I found some land-lady would take you a week cheaply? Myself, I can't and am broke so can't move but would be happy to see you and we could talk and write and get the sun. (I know bits of your Horizon trans. very well.)

best wishes – let me hear from you soon, I'll go on with this letter soon, Sydney

I've been listening a lot to the Beethoven concertos and sonatas

60. *To William Montgomerie*

10 May 1949 Mevagissey

Dear Bill,

Here's the next one. I hope you find it an advance and don't mind the blurb. It's inaccurate and a bit of a boast. Anyhow there it is Bill and how are you? I hope your life's going well and Norah and Dian and Ian are hale and happy. How's the Hamlet work going? And any poems? The more I go on in my work the more Scotch I find I am and just lately too I've been reading Burns extensively and find I react to so many words my parents must have used which I didn't know I had. Some of the less known songs are real heartbreakers. I would like to write some love-songs but working with a composer and I mean a composer 'of his time' and composing in contemporary idiom. And though I would be influenced very much by the Burns songs I wouldn't be writing in the 'Plastic'. I'll see. I suppose the twt [*The White Threshold*] will have an easier time than the other three, having the snob-value of the Faber seal and also the poems are, generally speaking, easier. The critics with no real measurements of their own will be helped a wee bit. And a wee so-slight poem like Gigha will let people see 'he really can write poetry'. (I hope). It is a pity and sad that it really works this way. I hope you find some feeling of Lanarkshire landscape in THE CHILDREN OF LANARKSHIRE. It is your airt? THE LOST OTHER too has a wee bit Lanarkshire feeling in it and somewhere ' the dog's away to Hamilton'. Your Nursery Rimes is a great book and I know it so well. Any chance of bringing out another volume?? How did the Burns book go, I mean sell, was it a help for you?

Myself I've been broker than ever I've been in my life and also pretty ill and I've lost 2 stones from my usual 'stolidity' and now down to 9– 3lbs. For now, cheerio. I hope you will like the last three 'Letters'. There's a great distance between the man who wrote them and the man who wrote the rest. What a way to put it but there it is. Regards to all. Sydney

61. *To William Montgomerie*

[undated, 1949?] Mevagissey. Sunday

Hello Bill again, just a note. Tell me, is there any good writing on Burns? I mean principally his work, verse, how he wrote, what he thought about how he wrote, technical self-consciousness etc. Is there anything on that. I know there's plenty on his life and the 'myth' of him but has any Scottish writer gone into the analysis of his art and said anything valuable about it. I suppose it is generally agreed he wasn't a naive artist. Can you drop a wee note and give me the name of a book I can try for in the Library here. Better still if you can lend me anything you consider valuable on Burns. I seem to remember that volumes of Burns were fairly easy to get around barrows in Glasgow. If you can pick me up one for say a couple of shillings I would be pleased. I haven't a book of my own with Burns poems at all. I can 'reimburse', what a wow of a word, you by return.

How strong so many of those poems are. And yet I know it is because my childhood was full of Scotch and Irish songs. My father was the leader of a concert party and they were always up rehearsing and my father was the accompanist, so that at an early age I was greetin to the strains of 'My Nannie Awa' and 'Flow Gently' and 'O Open the Door'. I mean that is a good bit the reason. How fond he is of the winter and the blast and gathering gloom and storm. Even at the end of 'Nannie' he so strangely says -

The dark, dreary winter, and wild-driving snaw
Alane can delight me – noo Nannie's awa.

Reading Burns makes me quite certain that after my wandering Willie-ing I'll be back to stay in Scotland somewhere and, in fact, puts me into such a great homesickness for the accent and the hills. Yet what a disappointment it always is. But I'll be there 'In spite o' them a'.' A strange thing, so many poems begin so well (I mean the epistles and longer things. Not the songs.) and thin down to that stylised diction of the time. Have you any theory about that? You know his work. I don't.

I'm sorry about the wee scraps of paper. It is 'a note'. But got longer than I intended.

cheerio now, Sydney

Funny the energy put out in Scotland in the showing of how unprovincial it is and which, of course, results in a special kind of provincialism which retards the organic growth of any true culture. Maybe doubletalk?

the only envelope I could get this Sunday

62. *To David Wright*

15 May 1949 Mevagissey

My dear David how pleasant it is to hear from you.

And, too, how pleased I am that you think the book is something. And that you like the 'LETTERS'. They are, I think, the most successful whole poems I have written,and the most mature. Not that parts of other poems in the collection do not contain more exciting 'peaks' for me. Yes I think this book should not be quite so torn to pieces. And there is a great variety of kinds of articulation. I could never before have written –

I've met you across a look
In a quick room cropped up
Out of the law I break.

That, personally, I look upon as a success. I mean the being able to speak at such an *un*tense, casual level of idiom and yet be (I hope) exciting poetically. I still get a good feeling of 'pastoralness' from those long, shortline poems. I mean THE LOST OTHER, THE SEARCH BY A TOWN and THE CHILDREN OF LANARKSHIRE. Parts are a wee bit like 'pure' poetry, serenely other-world-creating poetry. THE CHILDREN OF GREENOCK is a strange poem and I think it has a range of harmonies and tones which is fairly 'original' and not very immediately sprung from any other poetry I know. A strange business; when I was checking the proofs of the book, in February it suddenly came through to me to me strongly how like a nativity poem it was. Nativity but barbaric. I'll be interested to know how the TWO LOVE POEMS strike you. If you can spare time for a note, let me know. I'm sorry I couldn't spare you a book but the 6 went out as almost 'business' gifts. And I've never been broker in all my life, ridiculously so. And never been ill for so long and what an angering thing it is I hate illness and when someone's ill and I love having the energy in me and showing it off. What a carry-on it certainly is. Yet I've made some good poetry I think and miles ahead from the THRESHOLD, however we always think that, eh? David it's good to hear from you and to have praise from someone I know is aware of the whole orchestra of a poem, the whole intricate organism which the poet has made. Or to say it with a more profound turn of the tongue – I'm glad you, a good responsible poet, like it. Enough o that kinna stuff o poesy.

I still haven't seen your book David and if you can lend me a copy for a few days I'll return never fear. I would not expect it to be tremendous and with all its poems at the level of your best I've seen, but I'm curious to see it and it is a good thing it's out though what on earth is all this carry-on about being a South African poet for. I mean WHY? It does no good. The information is no help whatever in fact why take on this handicap for your first book. It's a struggle enough. I saw the review in T.L.S. which was bad and against and lumped you with other 2 or 3 South African poets and you were the only one worth considering and it put you last and it was the writing of a reviewer who knew just nothing about poetry. I'm all for South Africa but can't see its use here.

I'm sorry you didn't enjoy France so much. One day I will go myself. Nessie's in Italy, the northern plain, at a job with plenty leisure and loves it and is there indefinitely. She is the sweet one, I miss her.

Her happy stillness. And the sweet courtesy of her mouth.

I thought of you and Bryan [Wynter] going your respective miles throughout France and with wine and fems and filleys and the acrobatic brothels and Arles and Van Goh and the continual blowing of the Minstral. The Minstral Flow. Well anyhow what a pity it wasn't so good. I didn't know you were ill in Cornwall. What was it? Hospital christ almighty what a terrible thing what on earth was wrong?? I can't see me up in London any soon but if I'll look you up. In fact, if I am, I might be asking can you let me sleep there a few o nights.

Poor Tambi. A good thing though. He was useful and did some good things at the beginning. Now I'm afraid he is, in his late position, a retarding force and I don't know if he ever had any critical standard of his own which he has no longer alas.

I am curious to know what you are writing now and what kind of writing it is. If you can send a line or two to show me? Myself – the NIGHTFISHING goes on and for that I lack no enthusiasm. Good or bad it will be very different from any other long poem in English. Because, for one thing, no one else has been interested in trying to do this kind of thing. So far it's about 600 and I try very hard to get it complete under 1000. When it's nearly finished I'll send you a few bits to let you see it if you're interested.

You probably will not be able to help me but if you happen to have any books touching on Celtic mythology, Scottish Celtic Mythology or Welsh or Irish or any translations of prose or poetry from Gaelic I would like to borrow them for a week or so and would be very careful with them and return them so pure as they came unspotted or blood-or-beer-stained. You've probably nothing. Just a thought.

Well now love to you and work well and hard, Sydney

63. *To Edwin Morgan*

23 November 1949 — 3, Warwick Gardens, London W 14

Dear Edwin,

Here I write just a wee note to answer ever yet your good letter but to say hello and give you a little news about myself. Though I write to you so little I think you would be surprised if you knew

how often I think of you and your good seriousness in the middle of this frantic place. Also (if I can suppose that I write for some serious audience), in the temptation of the weak moment, when I am tempted to say the easier more attractive thing instead of trying harder to say the more difficult thing; you are one of a halfdozen people I might think of who would see it as a lesser statement. So hello there, and how are you and is at all there a chance of you being near London in the next three months or so? It would be nice to see you and talk. What a strange thing, to have met that twice (or was it only once?), and you are one of the people I would want to write for.

A nice thing. I have been seeing Eliot quite a lot and what a real comfort (strengthening) it has been. We have talked mostly about verse and what he remarked about my own was cheering. Again, it is good to realise that, if one had been lazy or deceitful (though I am guilty enough and should try harder) in one's verse he would have known. We talked a lot about the structure of the long poem (I've just finished mine) and 'the purity of criticism' which I am almost a crank about. I mean that the criticism of poetry in Britain today is so bad and trite often through the 'critic' not bringing pure critical canons to bear on the object, but bringing in outside values (which I admit have to do with values in the 'poem' but which are incidental) of morality, ethics or even politics. Or they write so, what they call 'impressionisticly' that there is no need for them to think. Or they write about everything but the object because they have no elementary knowledge of what such an object is made of or how it works. I am not pleading for a dead, mechanistic criticism, but for a criticism which will enable the reader to understand the new special language of the new poet and which will more or less leave the reader to weigh and value and use the statement without the critic saying what he imagines the statement is (in paraphrase) and telling the reader it is good or bad accordingly. What cheered me was, he said that I had 'a good sense of form and a wonderful sense of rhythm'. He suggested that my poetry was 'intellectual' poetry and would go slow because people just were lazy about thinking. He thought no young poet had produced a long poem with any formal structure, which he thought was necessary. My poem's been finished a month and though I made about 11 drafts before then I've been changing words and lines a little till yesterday and now I really think it's finished. I'll try to get it on the BBC and published in some periodical, though it is 520 lines, and when it's ready to go in the next book for Faber I'll be able to see it better from the greater distance. If I can whip up any money to get it typed with 6 copies I'll send you one. I would like to know what you think about it. It's called THE NIGHTFISHING. The longest section is 300 lines and consists of a voyage at night and fishing with the nets and is also metaphor of a search in the mingling darkness of the memory (a place of mingling dead continually changing and being added to by our own death) for a 'home', or for a conception of one's self as one identity. The shortest section is .... but here I'll type it for you. [Here follows section 2 of *The Nightfishing*.]

There you are. Remember it is a lyric and will be in its position after the 1st. part which is rather abstract and nonvisual, and before the long moving physical voyage. But this is just a taste and not necessarily for critical comment. But I always like to have a word from you.

Some news – I've been pretty ill and out and in hospital here having Xrays and treatment. I feel a little better and must scurry round for a job. I don't want to go back to Mevagissey. I've had enough of the country for a long time. I feel that me always living in the country has in some ways been an evasion for certain personal social problems in my relation to people generally. So now I'm going all out to get a job here and stick here a year or two or, if I get any money anywhere, I would like to go to Europe. Your letter was good and what you said about my verse was useful as always. I liked you giving me a check-up on what you liked best. Small reaction comments like that are so useful. I have never met anyone (maybe [Dylan] Thomas and to a certain extent [George] Barker) whose comments on my work really interested me.

What are you writing? Have you any more Anglo-Saxon translations I might see. Do you know of any good translations of Early Gaelic poetry, Scots or Irish? I've been reading the Book of the Dean of Lismore and the translation is so bad even I can see. And yet I get the feeling it is wonderful poetry underneath in the original. If I could get in touch with a Gaelic scholar capable and excited about making the early gaelic poetry into 'good English poetry' (like some of the Pound Chinese poems) I would like to work at making them at least into good English verse with no poetic diction. Do you know anyone who might be interested?

What is going on in Glasgow in the literary world? I hear the Scottish BBC has some good poetry programs. Is that so? I would like fine if you wrote.

love, Sydney

Worldhauled, he's grounded on God's great bank,
Keelheaved to Heaven, waved into boatfilled arms,
Falls his homecoming leaving that old sea testament,
Watching the restless land sail rigged alongside
Townful of shallows, gulls on the sailing roofs.
And he's heaved once and for all a high dry packet
Pecked wide by curious years of a ferreting sea,
His poor house blessed by very poverty's religious
Breakwater, his past house hung in foreign galleries.
He's that stone sailor towering out of the cupboarding sea
To watch the black boats rigged by a question quietly
Ghost home and ask right out the jackets of oil
And standing white of the crew 'what hellward harbour
Bows down her seawalls to arriving home at last?'

Falls into home his prayerspray. He's there to lie
Seagreat and small, contrary and rare as sand.
Oils overcome and keep his inward voyage.
An Ararat shore, loud limpet stuck to its terror,
Drags home the bible keel from a returning sea
And four black shouting steerers stationed on movement
Call out arrival over the landgreat houseboat.
The ship of land with birds on seven trees
Calls out farewell like Melville talking down on
Nightfall's devoted barque and the parable whale.
What shipcry falls? The holy families of foam
Fall into wilderness and 'over the jasper sea'.
The gulls wade into silence. What deep seasaint
Whispered this keel out of its element?

Three

THE NIGHTFISHING
1950–1955

from THE NIGHTFISHING

Far out, faintly rocked,
Struck the sea bell.

Home becomes this place,
A bitter night, ill
To labour at dead of.
Within all the dead of
All my life I hear
My name spoken out
On the break of the surf.
I, in Time's grace,
The grace of change, am
Cast into memory.
What a restless grace
To trace stillness on.

Now this place about me
Wakes the night's twin shafts
And sheds the quay slowly.
Very gently the keel
Walks its waters again.
The sea awakes its fires.
White water stares in
From the harbour-mouth.
And we run through well
Held off the black land
Out into the waving
Nerves of the open sea.

My dead in the crew
Have mixed all qualities
That I have been and,
Though ghosted behind
My sides spurred by the spray,
Endure by a further gaze

Pearled behind my eyes.
Far out faintly calls
The mingling sea.

Now again blindfold
With the hemisphere
Unprised and bright
Ancient overhead,

This present place is
Become made into
A breathless still place
Unrolled on a scroll
And turned to face this light.

And so I spoke and died.
So within the dead
Of night and the dead
Of all my life those
Words died and awoke.

During the latter part of 1949 and the first half of 1950 Graham had several more conversations with T.S. Eliot. Living in London with no regular income became increasingly difficult and in April 1950 he was introduced to Messrs. Foote, Cone, and Belding, by Julian Orde, and began work as a writer of advertising copy. He had written no poetry for three months and drink was causing a recurrence of his ulcer. After treatment he left his job at the end of June or beginning of July and, with help and advice from Eliot, returned to what was intended to be a quieter life in Cornwall. Bryan Wynter lent him his cottage near Zennor. In mid-September he went to a birthday party in St Ives and was later taken to hospital in Truro with a broken knee and concussion, having fallen from a roof onto a concrete yard. In hospital for three months, he made an excellent recovery and later walked without a trace of a limp. At Eliot's suggestion Ronald Duncan visited the hospital. Graham mischievously watched him talking to the wrong patient for five minutes before introducing himself to him but they seem to have got on well afterwards!

In January 1951 he travelled back to London, staying with Sidney Whitcomb in Richmond. Another friend, Elizabeth Smart, to whom he was greatly attracted, gave him space in her flat in Chelsea. She lost her flat when the landlord found four young children could make rather a mess and moved to Tilty Mill House in Suffolk. The Roberts Colquhoun and MacBryde were evicted from Bedford Gardens and also went to Tilty Mill to help look after the family while Elizabeth worked in London. Graham had been a frequent visitor to 'the Roberts' and remained so at Tilty Mill. In May and June he was a guest at Rainthorpe Hall near Norwich and it was probably during this period that he went to Aldeburgh and met Benjamin Britten, Eric Crozier and Peter Pears. Later in the year he was invited to return to America with David Gascoyne and Kathleen Raine on a reading tour organised by Malcolm Brinnin. He seems to have been a little apprehensive about his companions.[1]

During this visit he mentioned two interesting meetings with Ezra Pound. His friendship with Vivienne Koch, often stormy, had ended acrimoniously and the financial arrangements for the tour appeared mysteriously inadequate, leaving Graham effectively stranded. He had made recordings for the Library of Congress in December and in August 1952 he wrote a card to Elizabeth Smart from the island of Procida in the Bay of Naples, Italy, probably having gone there with assistance from Princess Margherita Caetani (who admired his work and had published it in the literary magazine *Botteghe Oscure*). He stayed some months at Sermoneta, her residence thirty miles south-east of Rome.

In January 1953 Graham visited Nessie Dunsmuir, who was working at the Berlitz School in Paris. They had communicated very little during their separation but were instantly able to re-establish their interrupted rapport (though Nessie had been seriously considering marrying a wealthy Frenchman). Graham also taught for a short time at the Berlitz School but they returned to England in August and stayed in a number of places, including Elizabeth Smart's house, at Castle Eaton in a cottage belonging to David Archer's parents, with Biddy Crozier in London, and with Graham's half-sister Nettie, also in London. Robert Frame was best man when Sydney Graham and Nessie Dunsmuir were married at the Registry Office in Higher Blantyre in October 1954 (see below, p. 138).

The Nightfishing was published in 1955 when Graham was 36 years of age. It was well received and remained for some years the poem by which he was best known.

1 Dylan Thomas (writing to Malcolm Brinnin) asked, 'How goes Sydney G.? He was moaning for weeks about his companions, Raine and Gascoyne. "Och, there'll be wee orgies with those two sparochs!"' David Gascoyne, quoting this letter when writing to Chris Stephens in 1989 said, 'I'm not too sure what a sparoch is, but can easily guess'. He added, 'It certainly was not the case that I failed to recognise the value of Sydney's unique voice as a poet. From the start I have always thought of "The Nightfishing" as a great poem, – essentially a meditation on Being (as is, in an entirely different way, Virginia Woolf's "The Waves"). I am grateful to have had so many opportunities in those days of hearing Sydney read from it.'

64. *To Moncrieff Williamson* (extract)

24 April 1950 at the office

Unfinished letter

Dear Crieff how good to hear from you and what a nuisance about the Elms [Press] people. First, before anything, let me say I've been worrying about not sending you anything recently and you'll have to let me off another few weeks because V.[Vivienne Koch] goes tomorrow and she made things easier by paying more than her half of everything. So in a few weeks I'll be out of the wood and even down to see you I hope in Fludger's Wood. Too wid too wood, as the aul owl says. [...]

I see Eliot for lunch on Thursday first. I said I knew he was such a busy man but I would like to see him and he said 'It's about time'. It bucked me up grrrand. And he's going to read my Nightfucking too. The dearrr kind crrater. [...]

65. *To Edwin Morgan*

4 May 1950 3, Warwick Gardens, London W 14

My dear Edwin

I got your wonderful letter and here I am in a hurry asking you to do a difficult thing. I send a copy of THE NIGHTFISHING which I would like you to see and say 'something' about and send me back within a week from now. I shall be typing it again with a few revisions and I'll let you have a copy then. I know it's a lot to ask. But I want some kind of objective check-up (I've been so near it so long) to put alongside Eliot's remarks about it. If there is any one thing I want your opinion on it is, Does it hold together as *one object*. I don't want it to be a stream of verses. Other than that say anything good or bad about it. You would know that I would not expect a long thoroughly thought-out criticism. O must rush – I'm in the office and the post's going. I'll be writing about your letter and poems. Nice about the article.

I had another injection of 'life' or 'THE REAL' last Thursday by having a lunch with Eliot which lasted three hours and the talk being all about poetry, Scottish Renais. (which he's agin for right reasons), fishing, publishing, drinking, Fry (Christopher Fry – against him for his backward step) . . how bad I'm writing. sorry! I mean in this letter. Anyhow he was very very encouraging and how good it is to know that there really are some people in the world (yourself too) who take the word seriously. I'm impatient to see your NINE article. I keep reading your good letter.

how good to have you to write even so infrequently too, Sydney.

66. *To Moncrieff Williamson*

[undated, probably late May or early June 1950]

friday dear crieff hows things for here i am
working away and writing great and enduring
copy about soap furcoats airoengines chanelle
et cetera and the rain kettledrums the pane and
with clouds low over london and here's the first
pound of the ten which will follow regularly
each week after this what a funny thing to
see you suddenly out of my igloo of droonk
and you astanding there with ane beardy loon
and how did you get on with barker hes worse
than his bite and hows wee carowayline and
her mamy Pam the only capital letter ive put
down in the bunch write soon and say hoots
and about your book vivys yeats book accepted
heartily and speedily by reed for routlege
and her as pleased as a rumshydumsher your
old freen wullie dookpiece hoody hoody doo

67. *To Bryan and Susan Wynter*

[undated, probably 1950] The Carn Cottage, Zennor

Dear Bryan and Susan,

'Hello so! What is to do?' as that good man Jankel [Adler] used to say. Here it is, then, The Carn, at 3-30 a.m. on Wednesday morning. A 3/4 moon showing, rather pearled by light nimbus ranges of cloud. (But I write too too bloody big. That, then, must stop.)

It is wonderful for me to be here at the moment. The very persistent ghost of Vivienne around London was alone reason enough to make me lose my reason. And the drink which made me ill and the advertising which had to be stopped and, above all, the no writing. Why should I go over all the reasons I've left London when I've left? I don't know and I don't think it is to justify my decision because I'm happy about it.

I sit here in the wee room. Not a word from the Alladin. Not one waft of wind and it is so quiet a daddylonglegs bangs furiously against the window. Now let me see if I have any nice sweet little pieces of poesy for you, you sensitive people you.

1. – I look the wide night's garment from my eyes.
(to be read aloud with the grand Marlow cadence)

2. Yet you who cry 'be saved'
Can murder in that name.
(A strange couplet. I don't think I'll ever use it yet it's got a curious memorability about it.)

3. O what a fine upstander
I was for the cause of love.
I could sing a tear out of
The drunk or sober or deaf,
My far my vanished dears
All in your bowers.
(amusing in a kind of song way)

68. *To Edwin Morgan*

31 July 1950 Zennor

Well, to your good northern self here I am beginning to write some kind of a letter, Edwin, and let it write itself a good deal as it wants to as long as some communication is achieved for I've a lot to say ranging from just straightforward news of my leaving London to the best things I can say which I always anyhow hope go into my poetry. First, how fine to have your letter. I thought 'surely there's some word from you on the way'.

Let this letter be anything that comes up to the light in whatever order it may appear. It may even approach some kind of verse occasionally. But thanks for THE WANDERER and THE SEAFARER. How vulnerable I am to such subjects! Your letter arrived today here among this almost-druidical moor of rocks where this cottage is the only one for a long way. I sit almost surrounded by 'standing stones', cromlechs, and grey piles of rock and grey 'drystane dykes' and (I do think I'm the last person to believe in a whymsy way about druid feeling about the landscape) do you know, Edwin, it feels early and Celtic and definitely Unenglish. I say this because, reading your letter this morning, I was very conscious that I was up on this moor (where Christ knows what has been done in the name of Magic and Worship) which is hard and unluscious, that your letter was hard and so extremely not English, and that my own work tries more and more to break from the oversweet exhibition of sensitivity which is so much the mainstream of contemporary English poetry (apart from Eliot and to a large extent Dylan Thomas – I can't help feeling that some of his later poems are a wee bit over-sweet and easy – and maybe to some extent Barker and Watkins).

I suppose I don't like writing letters because one goes on in this rather long-winded way and it always makes me impatient and feel how clumsy and slow and laborious it all is. Now I've a lot to tell you but I'll try not to get into big slow bogs like that last paragraph. If it makes the prose or verse seem needlessly tortured it does not matter. I must talk to you quicker with more immediacy. OK?

What happened to me between that drinking night and this last second? Ill again and in the hospital for four days. Increasingly depressed at not writing. In one quick decision left my job. Saw T.S.E. Advised to go into the country again. Was offered this cottage to the end of August. Can just make out till then here if I watch eating. Till then must hunt for some 5/- weekly cottage. So far – nothing. TSE cautiously said he would try to get me some small grant. He knows I can't last much longer than the end of August anyhow. Arrived here a fortnight ago. I've read a lot, written a lot of notebook poetry-parts, tried not to go crazy and to feel at peace again (which I've not felt for a long time) and written some simple words which might be set to music and begun something which I am still unsure of as a project (I mean a poem). And what do I want at the moment? To be secure enough financially that I can see a sure year stretching ahead where I won't have to worry about what's going to happen the next month so that I can be at peace enough and feel 'stopped' enough to live days of writing whatever poetry I'm at.

The words which might be good for making a song –

Then what a fine upstander
I was for the cause of Love
And what a great woman's
Man I went sauntering as.

I could sing a tear out of
The drunk or sober or deaf.
My love would lie down pleasanter
Than any love before.

She who once younger lay
Lies lost in the husk of night
(My far my vanished dears
All in your bowers).

So there it is. Nothing great and not good enough for bringing out in my next book. But there it is. [...]

For the last let me say 'Edwin, you are one
Of the few people I love.' Let it go on,
That we each try our utmost towards helping
Each other in the facts of even our existence
And each other to go into the farthest silences
With vessel and art to break them into words,
I sit here quiet. The moor and rocks are darker
And I haven't spoken to a human soul for a week.

Now that's that said in the way it is said. I
see your letter must have been buzzing around for
a month. Everything in my life's unorganised at
the moment. That is how it is. I have the late
Yeats poems beside me. A great original voice.

'Things thought too long can be no longer thought'

Edwin, keep writing when you can. It is always good for me to hear from you. Any poems or Anglo-Saxon translations please send. I'm still thinking about beginning the Epistle. I put down a lot of words to do with it. If you're passing within a hundred miles of here (5 miles from St. Ives) look in on the Moorfarer. Love. Sydney

69. *To Edwin Morgan*

[undated]

Higher Carn Cottage, Zennor. A grey evening not long till dark and low long wisps of cloud blowing past the windows. Dear Edwin hello. You'll just have to read this anyhow And I have just got to write about how I feel at the moment or go quite mad. So I am writing you though I've all kinds of letters I owe but somehow I think I'll feel better after I say how 'No worse' this time seems to be. And I might not even send it when I finish.

A letter from Joke Grim, the desert of a laugh. Forgive this using you. I sit here with all my pieces of started poetry on the table by me and with the mist thick at the window and the light rapidly going. What do I write to say? I don't know. I haven't spoken to anyone for five days. I've been working hard, notes and beginnings etc. yet I haven't begun a poem yet in all this time. The kind of poem I want to write is very far away from even T.N.F. I know more about poetry than I've ever done before. Maybe that is what is wrong but I don't believe that. No amount of selfconsciousness to his craft should harm the poet, though, in some ways it is to be expected that it will be more difficult. But, then, if successful at all the poetry should be so much more mature and 'new'. If I could write more poems of the intellectual and language texture of the White Threshold poems I wouldn't. It's an ironic business. If (I mean 'when') I succeed in producing any work which is anywhere near my intention at the moment so many people will see it as not so 'experimental' as the W.T. poems.

I have been shaken up in the last three years by my study of Pound and Eliot, analysing the structure of their verse and form. I know that as types of poets they are at the opposite extreme from me (poets who use in their poems a literary sophistication) and that the subjects of their work could never be very near any subject I would be concerned with, but the way they have used different textures of thought and idiom in the same poem (like montage) is new, an addition, a widening of the possibilities of what a poet may say. Also I find more and more that the breathless almost hysterical rhetoric of Barker in so many of his poems is for me rather thin and is not really very 'experimental' at all and is at times far too sweet and easy. Even I have found that I want more from Thomas than that rich clutter of language gives me. I want to write 'harder', the poems having more shape, being more abstract, the verse not so brow-beaten still by the Shakespearean iambic line. And yet I want my poems to be more than ever a valid extension of the possibilities of the language. I mean don't think I have stopped wanting to invent. It is the opposite. And I suppose all this is to persuade you and myself that this break in writing will finish soon and that then my work will be miles ahead. Enough of that. Just some words to keep sane.

A 'Beginning' which only begun –

Offered this grudging element, the sea, a way
Over that dark dread to you, I am again
Moved off land, faced out from any least
Rest I had. And with so endured a loss.
There is no voice walks here within earshot.
This I've inherited.

All things drag one down at once. Or – It never rains but. Stomach fucked. Not a soul, not even in St. Ives, that is (apart from knowing anything about poetry) able to talk with a brain humbly and seriously about anything. Christ! Hardly a soul that can talk straightforwardly with a humble enthusiasm. So many can't talk for thinking about what kind of impression they're making and if they're 'winning' or not. And at the same time Eliot hasn't started any negotiations for a possible grant because my doctor hasn't sent the report yet and I've written the doctor three times and no reply and I just don't know what is going on maybe he's on holiday and so I try to borrow five-shillings's for paraffin and try and try hard not to feel bitter or persecuted when I see the people in St.Ives who don't want to do anything much getting money for nothing. What a place this is we are all living in (This is a list of complaints, Edwin, let it be and don't mind me having a revel in them) And I haven't found a cottage because I can't go ahead and say I'll take it because I might have not received the grant and I'm supposed to have this to the end of August. This is, I suppose, at the moment the NO to life. Down down down. I can't remember ever having been so deep. This surely must be the lowest before the ascension again. I don't know but writing it is like talking it and talking it must surely help. Poor target.

I have procured a new battery for my radio 'on tick' and so I am able to sit here between sentences to you and listen to a woman talking in French, the cadences very sad and falling, and I don't know the slightest school French. Yet what a complication of emotions she arouses. Christknows what she's talking about. Maybe a cookery talk.

'When with his hunting dog I see a cloud' – the beginning of a Canto by E[zra] P[ound]. So authentically poetic.

A joke or jock among the talking empties. Now on the radio –
The harp that once through Tara's halls
The soul of music shed
Now hangs as mute............

A great song. It has always affected strongly. When I served my apprenticeship as an engineer I used to have to get up at 6-30 to catch the early train to Glasgow and I remember those dark cold mornings and me with no more wish to be in that screeching bedlam of tortured metal than die but strangely Radio Eire started gramophone records early and they always started with [John] McCormick singing The Harp That Once and he was so good I never tired of it. What a story to tell. Don't mind much. Let it be. Let me go on for it's easing to talk at the moment. I've had my mind so steadily at verse day after day from 10 to around 7 at night that I just don't seem to know anything about it any more. I looked at the poems in C.W.G. today and I hadn't looked at them for years. I wondered how I could ever have written them. No, not that they are so much not what I want to do now, but I was struck by the fact that I couldn't write any more poems like that if I tried. And, of course, it's probably always that way. One is another person with a different voice to say different things. O and also I was reading your SLEIGHTS OF DARKNESS.

I liked it. It is strong and immediate, real 'word poetry'. And it is perfectly professional poetry. And I hardly ever see a poem even by the older poets which I think is really professional. By professional I mean not whimsical or fey technically. For example – Lewis or even McNeice don't often produce a professional poem now. I don't think Spender has ever. Watkins used to and recently has gone off I think. What's this for? All just to try to tell you what I mean by the word 'professional' and to let you know that I think the poem a very good poem. I suddenly realise I go on a lot using words like precious, whimsy, sweet, soft, easy etc and that they are my chief words for the qualities which make (for me) bad poetry. I don't think there has been any great change in the heart or head. It is something to do with being able to see more clearly now what is a real and honest statement of the imagination and what is a Narcissistic whimsical statement. I don't say it well but I hope you see it. It begins so richly and inevitably, the movement of the words is perfect reading it aloud. I'll just go on and ask some things as I go and tell you how some parts strike me.

(Though I compare you to people like Lewis, Louis MacNeice, etc you know I don't think verse is a competition in any way. I just wanted to suggest some scale of merit though those names don't help much.)

Tell me, the first stanza suggests a dream. It's not important but is it? 'Cinderfall' is a lovely word. If you meant something exactly by it what did you mean? The line – 'To see my friend in his golden fell' is a real pip of a line. Tell me what you meant by 'golden fell'. (Forgive me asking for so many meanings of phrases. As it is they work for me in the poem. I only want to know what the most exact meaning was for you.) I go on reading and want to list every line and say it's specially good but they can't all be specially good. I like so much – 'to mingle loneliness.' The word 'understanding' in the 14th line comes as such a transparent almost-abstract pleasure after the more physical opaque words. 'The mavis drowses on its fable' is the kind of line I feel good about writing when I can. In the last stanza I'm suddenly stopped by the word 'valid'. First, I can't get what it means. 2nd, the word seems inorganic in its surroundings, it seems on a different level of statement. It's a difficult word to use, I think, in a poem. The ending's good and the whole poem is a shape. I wonder if it is a Scots characteristic in poetry but I find myself writing so many poems that begin in that form of starting to tell a tale like your beginning – 'One nightmare after cinderfall' With me I think of 'Local I'll bright my tale on' and 'To put it springtime the green shepherd'. I mean that beginning which is a definite beginning like 'It fell upon the Lamastide' if that is a real line or not, I don't remember. Forgive this negative statement but this is so beautifully different from the usual English poetry one sees. If it appeared in P.Q. it would seem like some completely different kind of object made for another reason. And so it is. Though I think Barker's piece in P.L. is him at a less hysterical moment I think your poem is better. Of course his poem is part of a long one and this piece is fairly long. The other poems are impossible. The long Donne-ish one is a bore. I hope you work hard and produce enough soon for a short book. I think a first book is better short. It's a pity that this time is the worst ever for getting published. Do you send them around the magazines? Keep trying NINE. Though it's not too bad they've printed their quota of gowks. There are so few magazines. Please send me any new work if you've time to type me a copy. The other two SLEIGHTS I find difficult. But I would like to talk about them [in] some letter. The translation I like and have read often and know well. I mean WEM LEBEN LEIDEN IST. (Christ what good things people have written and what a horizon stretching of different things to make poetry about and here I'm whining and wailing about. A poor lout.) The Anglo-saxon translations have been a great help and I mean to write you about them re Pound. I see in the Editorial of NINE my poetry is described as 'Elliptical and exploratory'. Whatever that may mean. Surely all poetry tries to be. How about trying yourself to write a short letter to me in verse. If it rises to poetry in parts so much the better. I am curious to see what would come forth.

A man called Whichcoat has an aphorism which goes –

We naturalize ourselves to the employment of eternity.

I'm crossed with light in this immortal space.
Maybe I shall encounter my own corruption,
Crossed with the scorch of The Iron and The Fire.

Position itself is a language, like selection
Whose pandemonium medium creates the tyrant.

That was two bits of verse from an old notebook I kept in Mevagissey. And naturally this quotation appeals to me –

The wan moon is setting behind the white wave
And time is setting for me oh.

Yes what a pass for me, the hawk-heart braced in the epic's hero, to come to. Better – The hick-heart based in the comic's peeriot. And I see that's not the spelling of a Canio but I've did my laughal best. Here's twelve madnight. It's some poor hurt but ever rejoyces. Morgan the Mighty or McMorgan the Michty. A lament on the moothiamonium. Or, to spoke police-lightly, a sonnetear of Soong will noby had from Muster Edinbro Moomorgan. Play jest yin metrefor o' muse-hicks for Jocky Gramfunny, Juke Grumf, Wullie Grum, Troubleyouas Greyhim. Sadknee Graham, Willheyum? Groom and Ankle Bum Kidney and all. Rejoyce in the word. In the begrinning wiss the worried. An wan o'cluck o' moornin soughs roon awe. Gret but still grey gusts lowed an daunert abane the gabble. Way nay lea-rug or eestrung ster,

Moan kine drear hurrah.

Thus Tom Mick a Muse-meant for yews elf use Jams Joss – BUST IN HELL WARLID. Thus double in boy mucks goo. Ruskin wee day illso. O mush as end glims nigh so snorely noire arain the chummies' gabbles sloopin bemoth an a'sternlauft. Lay mint. Sick cloth to Waly Greymoo. Nare doed tae deid. Wi sear a stormache it he hid he laugh would turn his fuss tae the leal. A's hour an din o triprighter lits ruts drum nslumber sae slopy fell ma shudders than that Blackmanned Mirtheus appreached see siftly lully tongued. An hour me blent so sablebodied big booth disindid drown tae tar me oot. Me Fah Lah Fah So Fah dinty floure. Doonfle aslap to luck's lap. An ss leapt and ss leapt sweat lay wrathin a dram dram oh fear wozzem no no entercoarse jest plandaft.

Thus entertuned to purefact pitch by instant Aeneas lie tupping erotter godybaby Awaya. Bony Churlie's noa byby. Illtaegather gatruddy. Lest and last lay if all tae haunchache still taegather Men laudies liedies maysons frownds fumen chilldears rushouters dourshitters darecapers munswiwimens munswayoot glumfers and a' skittish barbs tae dull by Doric Ontwaddle. An yore silf Sadneigh listed a bit not least. Yawn vice rift up encore us. Tinderly armagirlo an besad or stunned say lavingly carrousing whore hair or heehaw seeks zone hairs a lust tae stir by. That wade myth an partied laps read ruin canny sham. The knack hair sulky a wee uncome nape weasely mad hypnoteased. Bit of coarse spute out the papple pips. There you'll rose badlimbs you'll pant the teen red. And on to ither ethers. Whit? Noosing noo. She-dolled a quintense beaf or get

Handover brute amend

Write soon, Edwin, and say what you're doing and send any new poems. Is there anything going on in literary Glasgow?

as ever, Sydney

70. *To Moncrieff Williamson*

11 October 1950 ORTHO WARD, R.C.I., TRURO, Cornwall

Dear Crieff,

Yes it is myself. It is a long time since we spoke or wrote. I hope the three of you are well and that things have been good for you since I saw you last.

Now the best thing is for me to try to give you as factual and concise a report as possible. Here goes. I left F.C.& B. I think about the end of June or beginning of July. I made up my mind quickly and they kindly let me go without giving a week's notice. I had to do it quickly and in a rush or I wouldn't have done it at all and it would have dragged on. A nice thing, I took my leave quite honourably and not under a cloud or anything. But I just had to get away. I missed V. fantastically. I wasn't writing. And physically I felt bad, stomach and nerves. So that was that. I left.

I had another X ray, result positive. I saw Eliot again and he promised to get me a small grant and advised me to stay in the country a year or two and I left for Cornwall with £20 he gave me and have been staying at Bryan Wynter's cottage which is isolated and right up on the high moor above Zennor. I saw few people, worked hard, tried my best to beat the damp and on a wild rainy night 3 weeks ago I walked 5 miles into St Ives to attend a birthday party and coming home I managed (don't ask me how) to fall off a roof 30 feet and land on concrete.

Well being as I have angels galore awatching over me and being the luckiest man in the world I only collected – 1) A smashed patella (kneecap), 2) A split forehead (5 stitches) and 3) concussion. I was taken to the hospital here. I've had two operations and my kneecap's been removed and during the last few days I've been ascending out of the aftermath of the operations and I don't need to be doped to sleep and I could read and almost do some work on poetry. For a fortnight after the operations it's been painful but now it's good to feel easier.

My plans when I'm discharged from here are to get a cottage somewhere in Cornwall or Devon and pay down a year's rent (if it's 10/- a week) and that will leave me £30 and I will try some way to keep going for a year and get some good new poems done. I don't know how long they'll keep me here. The thing is they send other people out to their homes but I'll have to be well enough to be able to get around and take care of myself. I'll be giving The Nightfishing a final revision and sending it in before the year is out, though I don't feel optimistic about its chances.

It is all a great carry on. The last few years of my life seem one difficulty after another. My luck must be due to even things up a bit by now. Now I'm tired. This is the first real-sized letter since leaving London. What are you doing? Still at the gallery? Whatever, surely you know you must get that novel, no matter how rough or sketchy, in front of some publishers. I hope Pam is back to full health again. And how's wee Carolyn? Love to the 3 of you, best wishes to your Aunt, Jock.

71. *To Sven Berlin* (extract)

25 October 1950 Truro

– I work hard at finding my 'spiritual sustenance' inside my work and try hard to live in the thoughts of writing my poetry. For the environment is deadly in every way with a radio bellowing bad jazz from 8 to 10 (14 hrs). Christ I'll be glad to get out. I hate this horizontal position.

When are you coming to see me? I know this war of the Council must be trying, so don't hurry. But it would be nice to see you sometime.

Have you any Benz.s? Sven, try to send me 50. The leg's healed and its just a case of doing exercises to get it working again. The Benz.s will help the getting into the work. They act like a metaphorical cotton-wooling the ears and the outside stays outside for the time of writing. I'm in the middle of that song cycle I mentioned and it has to be sent up in 2 weeks from now. I must send you copies of some of the songs. How's your sweet Juanita? Try to send the B's soon. Try to write soon. Try to come over soon. Think of me over a rum.

love, Jock

72. *To Ronald and Rosemary Duncan*

[December 1950]

In the train speeding Hogmanaywards at 6 oclock and feeling already the even colder weather in my 'bare bane'

Dear Ronnie and Rosemary,

It was a pleasant time for me there those few days and such sympathetic talking about the mechanics of verse with you, Ronnie, has got me ready and impatient to get going and work out some projects I have in mind. How good it is to meet someone and, in talk of verse, to agree so much – for a change. Already I have things in my mind I should have asked you about but they'll keep till the first real letter. I still hear snippets of the urgent music of Lucrecia in my head and remember the general rich vivid texture of the words. – By the way – sometime I would like a copy of your Pound essay. It's a 'smasher'. – It was good for me there and remember that the Scots are a dour-faced race and me especially and I look like Joke Grimm even when I'm enjoying myself. It will be nice to meet again when I'm all of a piece. That 'Only man in the World' story could be a smashhit and of quality too, R. best wish to Both and Roger and Bryony. Jock

P.S. Rosemary! Buggerit! You didn't draw me after all. Did my natural shyness-dourness put you off?

73. *To Elizabeth Smart*

[undated]

'On the bustops sat she smiling
On big bustops said she Haha.'
(Longfellow's LIZIHAHA)

Well what is to do other than say My Sweet or Dear or best in the wholest girlaxy of all the Elns and Clapatras how is your brave Siouxsioux life? Yes I certainly do find you wandering the corridors of my mighty most Elizabethan brain of all the thorpes. Say to me some fine fond thing out of your hertzen or yellowhaired brain. Here the quick fidgiting goldfinch tweeks the air. The blackbird, Glossy Gilt-beak startles charmingly the leafy air. Larks mount the invisible elevators of May coloraturawise. Stones chat. Wagtails tell. The Wren she lies in Care's bed. The man-bewailing gull lost inland dies, falls and is gathered into the leaves of an indifferent book. Pigeons, having been declared redundant as symbols now the war's over, stand pecking aimlessly at terrace corners. Angels are just all over and twoapenny lucifiring the branches that roar above the gabriel glades. That naughtigale (the loverwaking sonnetear) trills out his rather english best. Those birds that are more for me for what I am are not here. Kestrel gannet shearwater sheldrake teal shag tern ptarmigan blackcock buzzard kittiwake skua barnaclegoose and all their oceanmates.

Christ what are all those bloody birds doing around this part of the letter anyhow. Its my tw and my paper etc.

The more I read your book the more different I feel we are (whatever that means) and that's maybe good and that's maybe bad. A strange thing, which I've never felt about any woman before – I *WANT* not to stop being in love with you. More than that – I feel occasionally frightened that it will soon be over for us and I don't want that. I want to feel the way I do endlessly on and on. You mustn't think I'm unhappy about the present thinking of the future. It isn't that. I think I earlily learned that. What wonderful complex people we all are, always with our merging vasts of darknesses and lights. Hoho for the rhetoric. Hand me the cymbols, please. Not the tremblbone. O, yes, and corn it. I'll give my french horn when I run into you on the playform. Now steady, wait for the first villains to reach the fifth bar, that's the Tremolo. Steady, there's no resin for that. See, he's raising his button. Not long now. He's so highly thought off and a lightning ducter. And there. See what I go through just to have you sitting down by some obscure station where I am not and smiling foolishly. Howthehell dyousualy smile anyway. With burnished alertness? No. You do not. How DO you look? Who am I to say? Who am eye to see like God? I am myself a sample shepherd from the Firth of Clyde. My mother (Him blesser.) was early on from Galway and a head for business which soon saw her rising to manageress of three shops in Greenock for the Buttercup Dairy company. She might have married a professional golfer but was more or less lochinvared from the scene by my father, then blacurlyhaired, soft bigbrown eyed, who could play the fiddle piano melodeon and the mandoline and sing and paint in oils. (and what on earth am I writing about anyway for that's true, curiously enough, and I'd rather make up things 'out of my head' for all the true things go into it somehow and in that form probably truer things than we know go in.) Well as I was saying I'm only a simple father's simple son born to fall down my steep life.

Here's a quotation I know almost by heart from Finnegans Wake –

I throw this ended shadow from me,
manshape ineluctable, call it back.
Endless, would it be mine, form of
my form? Who watches me there?
Who ever anywhere will read these
written words?

This, because I am whoever I am, is wonderful, good, unwhining, courageous and, as well, human.

Night, Elizabeth, now so now goodnight. Those words must stop. This typesinging must swan its end. My whymsy hymn shall nightingale no more. What's here for me? Only Narcissis (Is that his spell?) that I know less and less (though I can claim no real connection with that old onanistic family) and rather I'd feel my seamen sail better seas. Bjuices it's Souterday night. Certainly a frrriend or two of mine will be abroad. MacBryde and groom (they do make anansome scruple, Miss Smirtch), and happier may they stravaig in London's publicked and bartended thoroughfars, and look, Elizabeth. Elizabeth, who is leans towards us there from see the gold bar of Heaven. Let's have one more here eh then we'll go. Oh look. Anemone. (Who shall I say it is, sweety?) It's big Bassy Belly. Let's go for he's that lessertufted pintcatcher. Ah mooneys of my delight that knowest not mine. Good, see, here have they wended to this hopy bower. Whitlyhuv? A draught bus but it takes you a long dizdance. Well just look at the hurtist in'm coming out. It's queer, so many suddenists here, one was jeweled for suddeny the other day. But there a good one as Godlooking as he breaks them. One wanders who's been in that Cocoon. Queerly, not many, I think. Come on Elizabeth. How sweet you look tonight. Yes, sweet, the hairup is lovely. It makes my heart to very break when carelessly I turn my drinksinging head in a pub of crowd and

encounter you before my knowledgable eyes are ready to
make of you what they halfexpect. In an instant I'm
struck by that doubleurged sword, that flushing blade,
that sweet hurt into the tinder heart. Yes luvit I
do. Be maybe the rare her hair of my Love put up at
the back / O be at my beck and very kill /? And iris
coat. I mean the purple one. And that nice very-
close-check bluegray dress on of some shiny material.
And be there be therrre be. Be

There in the square where, not the nightingale
But love chimes six oclock from my steep fall.
(tis poesy)

An kid, yawunt stand me up? Get the date
down can't you. See, write it here. No,
you'll get your notebook ruined. The bar's
swimming, even though it is Mooney's best.
See, I'll write it. And remember to read it
for Christ your as drunk as a fuggy, yes FUGGY.

Meet Suddenly Graham in the square outside my house and garden at sex o'clock on the first Friday evening from now, the 32nd of May. Don't forget. Wear hair up neatly and unstraggled. Smile my most foolishly becoming lovesmile as I cross from the door to the square proper where he will be lounging against a breadfruit tree with a toothpick in his sneeringly handsome mouth. Try to seem collected and a loaf for he will be watching keenly through great big window-open shepherd eyes which notice the least whore out of plays. Be babysexy even to the ex-stunt of brashing up against him in the street. Remove narcotic stains from handypandies so that they're worthy to be for him fairskin lilypetals of delight. Smile ascent to all he says. That'l gut him and you'll have him under you spill foriver alm. Check up by litter to say 'off curse I'll be very hippy whory to see you'.

Christ, Elizabeth, come on, try it. If it
doesn't sober you up it'll make you spew.
Robert, jesus is that all you can do, sing
The Canadian Boat song? No. And not The
Nipple Laugh Forever either. Nor My Mother
Drives The Royal Scot. Feeling better, sweet?
That's it. Chin up. You're one of the best that
come. What, dear? Yes I said COME. Yes I
know, you're plum nickered out. But don't pissout.
Actually you're beheaving tremendously well old
gell. On a wet workout too. Goodshow, I knew
it. A Sioux through and through. But you come
from an old wigwam. Take my arm. Stopped raining
well almost, only kittens and puppies now he he.

Sweet, now reading this over I can't help thinking it's not bad –

and honestly I've not been trying and just went ahead as quick as I type. Tell me. Is there any marketable kind of thing that could be done in this style, cutting out all of the toocorny or involved puns and telescoped grammar and having a subject. What do you think? Reading it I find that parts of it work very strongly for me. I think I've a richness of impressions, visual and auditory stored somewhere. I think I'll be good at real live organic dialogue. The nice thing about writing to, you is that I satisfy more than one urge. Firstly I write to talk to you, to have you with me in a life I make up. Then I write because writing to you is writing to a sensitive wordinformed mind which makes it not a bore but a performance for the best. So here I write longer than I ever write letters and, as you see I clown in them and try any tricks that the language leads me into and maybe in one page I be a dozen different speakers one after the other as they crop up. Now tell me. And because I know (I do not.) you I have the carelessness and ease and can try anything which occurs to me. Now tell me. And this time it's *your* trade. You are the prose writer. And don't let's argue about that and be some help to me and not so cautious. What do I want to know? From this letter do you think I could write anything in prose which would be really good and I mean better than most living prosewriters I know of except Henry Green and Ivy Competant Burnett? I know that you have no means of guessing if I can write a 'story' or create drama.[1] That hunch I don't ask you for. I mean as far as texture, sense of mood, visual scene, weight of meaning in each word etc., are concerned? Darling I've read back from the top of the page an jesus how pompous and conceited and be a good Elizabeth and try to see what I mean. I don't think I'm as good as it sounds I think I am. What I want is this – do you think I could write something in prose which would sell and yet be good as well. I was trying to indicate how good it would have to be. I don't want to put out something in prose just better than most people. I would have to have it a lot better. For otherwise it would not help my poetry public, you know the five of them. That's all. Try to have time to think about it before the 32nd. By the way, Sweety Busmiler, can you not have to go back to Flood St. at six. Be all ready to go and aroarin we'll happy together be.

1 Graham had already published 'A Letter To Norman' in *Tempest* magazine in October 1943, a prose piece of approximately 1100 words in Joycean style.

Darlingly lie you down.
Come at my beck and call
As we ride the whole town down. (it's easy)

It's good to think of at last her dearly by my side and how sweet a pleasure to walk not turning to look too often yet knowing and feeling exactly how she walks at my side and knowing I have her here and I can turn and hold her to me (as closely as my natural prespiteryan modesty will allow) and say, as Grim the poet used to whisper poetically, hello Sweetipie. Send my jacket. The notebook. Tide. Any socks you see. Some love. Ten shillings please. And O please stay my best prize till as long as I become your third. When I'm rich I'll buy you a writing pad big and lintwhite and a pen that writes as black as night. Have you seen George? How's Rosemary I really liked her are you sure? Some naughty nightthoughts must take place surely if not in her giglbrain, in her own little vestival hall. Put in a good word for me I know you will. Or shall time soon unvirgin her? How lucky you are with such a fine long letter.

I could slip it into the slot mesel. lovemewell. Sydney

74. *To Elizabeth Smart*

8 June 1951 Rainthorpe Hall, Norwich

Hello Elizabeth sweet,

on this sunwended and greenwooded day, how is it all with you for I myself have sorely the want of your sweet presence in me like a persisting thorn in every breath and I look here and I look there and I say for chrisake and thread the minutes of each letterless day. Who knows? Not me. What is it at all happening and what fucking sly bolt struck down from somewhere between you and I? Christknows, and not a fucking murmur from him. What is going on? What is this litmus test of yours for 'imitation'? I don't get it. As well as that that certain kind of caution is not like the person you are and it's not good. Knowing how we feel towards each other is difficult enough without that. Christ what a waste of time. The stations flash by so fast. The beer flows under the bridge and quicker than I know 'time' will be called (and not a sip after time). I love you sweet and you're a good one. I don't want 'to win'. Do you? I think we must completely misunderstand everything we try to say to each other. Also I think we're probably very different. You say

I don't know about women. Maybe that's it. Anyhow,you fondly difficult dearest Elizabeth on this sungazed day wherever you are with the speedwell eyes and the look that can gut me like a herring, what if you came walking over the field there and said hello there sweet. Women? The muse too seems frightened away this weather which should be just her weather for my poetry's buggered and I can't put down a word that's right. What's cooking with your own works? I want to know. Tell me I want to know. And get on with some writing or it's a great skelp on the ear you'll get. Then, scratching a lobe of his shell-like, and nonshallontly gazing from the flying buttress bow-slot, he asked in his peculiarly clyde-firth voice – 'then shall we two everrr meet again?' and, thinking better of it, fell flat on his funface with a loud sleevelaugh to the crimson astonishment of the young lady concerned.

Mrs H. is off for 10 days to the Aldeburgh festival today and here I am. I had lunch, head of the long table as long as the Mauritania. What? A slice of cod – salad – a bottle of beer. And so this life today reminds me of that grimmest of all clowns – Rimbaud, saying – 'I expect to become a very spiteful madman.' Though, and it is still the greatest thing I am thankful for (to who as well as you?), I love.

I wish my poetry went better. At times I feel I'm absolutely untalented and that I've been kidding myself and Christ that's terrible. I get down (though indeed it might be some internal sex-important gland) right into the hopeless fathoms.

Sweet, be well. Never fear. And if it's not an unrewarding trouble – love me. Sydney

my love to my dear friend, Big Davie, who(m) I am writing this verry nicht.

And Bill and Peggy.

And Georgina and Chris and Bash and Rosie.

75. *To Elizabeth Smart*

26 November 1951 c/o Poetry Centre 92nd & Lexington N.Y.C.

My dear Elizabeth,

It is all so much worse than I thought, being without you. I keep wondering – 'why am I here?' It is all a continual missing you. The first week of parties and drink had me with the beginning of the DTs and even seeing a doctor and in bed 3 days. I found some benzedrines and that and the drink murdered me.

It is all so much worse than I thought, my sweet Elizabeth, not having you with me to light up everything. Christ, sweety pie, it's no good without you. I didn't know it would be like this. There's just no meaning to anything without having you around.

I've met Jane [Elizabeth's sister] and she's been sweet and kind and helpful. I still have no place to stay and keep going from place to place spending about three days in each. I've had a terrible carry-on with Vivienne who wanted me to stay there and have things go on as they were.

Jane asked us both to a party and V suddenly made a scene and began hitting me and insulting Jane, insisting that J. and I had slept together and rang her up threatening all the next day and J. said she was a dangerous woman and now I haven't seen poor V since.

It is all even better than I thought. That is – the publicity and reading and admiration. O if it was just my vanity at the moment that certainly is surfeited. I lap it up. But sweet, I want you all the time. I keep seeing your terribly sweet look and the sickness and longing comes on me so strongly I could kill them all here, all the zombies and dopes and dishonest talentless bastards. Yet – everything I came for is happening. We've done 2 readings and I was good. J. came to the first but not the second after V's onslaught. Invitations to read and to partygo shower us. I write here in Washington where we are for the weekend, to read on Monday night, staying with Sir somebody Ricket who's a dull man and this afternoon I go with Mrs Pound to see Ezra. That is an exciting thing for me. Other readings have been arranged – Mount Hollyhock, Bard College Harvard NYU and one or 2 for me alone. Others are being arranged and we may be going to California. So far the latest reading is in January. I certainly won't let it go much past that. I'll do as much good (or bad?) as I can for WSG here and then head to my (please!) true love as fast as I can hie.

The insecurity is trying. No place to feel 'stopped' in. My bag not really unpacked or poems looked at. And money very difficult. Brinnin (apart from securing so many readings) has arranged things rather precariously. Tomorrow I'll be a fortnight here and I've had exactly $41 which is nothing at all. If the people I stayed with hadn't given me some meals I wouldn't be eating much. A publisher called Dutton wrote me asking could they consider The White Threshold for publication. Now that could be a help. I wish it was over and I was wading through the Tiltymud to see you with your sweet flushed face.

Now that I feel better I'll write oftener. How are you my sweet? Write and say something. my dear. Sydney

76. *To Elizabeth Smart*

17 January 1952 c/o Joudin 73 – 12 35th Av. Jackson Heights N.Y.C.

My dear sweet Elizabeth,

Here I am awake at 4 in the morning having been given at last this apartment to myself for at least 10 days. O my dear if you were here with me tonight. I want you beside me. I've had enough of being away from you. I've had my fill of the parties and drink and I've lapped up enough flattery to do me for a long time. Now I work at getting back, and getting enough money to eat with while I'm doing it. I've come in here with 5 dollars and bought a few things to put in the ice-box and have a dollar left which I'll use for phonecalls and fares. Kathleen [Raine] sold some poems to the N Yorker and an article on the difference between English and U.S. poetry to the New York Times and got her fare out of it and she's leaving soon. I should have word from the Princess [Caetani] any day and maybe she'll suggest sending something. My sweet – again what a dismal letter – forgive me. I'll go over your letter and reply reply reply.

I'm glad to hear you miss me – you sweet torment when I'm with you. No – no new work done though some notes which may blaze up a bit. By the way – the reading of parts of T.N.F. has been very very successful. (O sweet, so many things to say to you. To make the world good the only thing for me is to be with you.) 2 visits to Ezra Pound were lovely. Mrs P. said she hadn't heard him talking so 'happily and serenely' for a long time. We got on well and talked fairly technically, which he seemed to love.

My dear, what an idea – for you to be sleeping alone in that huge bed. Are the Roberts coming back to T.M.? Eliz. don't please establish some younger 'young lyrical poet' in my stead. *I want you.*

Elizabeth, why is it I keep putting off writing you? I somehow think I can't bear the misery of thinking and talking to you like this and yet not really having you here. Yet, when I write, like now, I feel suddenly better and nearer you and that I'll really see you again. Sweet, be patient of my not writing, and anyhow please write me. Don't say – I don't deserve to be written to. It's late and I stop and seal this so that I really send it. I wish I were phoning you from London now saying I'm here. I want you. It gets harder doing without you.

you sweet girl. Sydney

77. *To Elizabeth Smart*

28 March [1952] c/o Len Lye, 737, Washington St. NYC.

Elizabeth, hello my sweet at last things are really moving towards an escape from this Elizabethless place. Don't say to anyone *but*: I'll either be working my passage back (via the gigantic kindness of Rockefeller's arrangement with Cunard -which I'm not sure is a good thing 'politically' for me in England!) or being shipped back by the British Consul (I don't like that either) or the Sewanee Review may take my N.F. and that would be the best of all. I should know in a week. Money's too scarce in England for us to use the BBC money (surely I owe most of it to you anyhow) and I would rather use/have it there with you or let it take us a wee trip to somewhere or pay something of your own. Sweet I want to get there early in the spring and I must see your sweet face soon.

I got your letter and enclosures. This must be finished in 5 minutes. I'm at the Lye's and we're going to hear a concert – Beethoven and excerpts from Wozzek. You really liked how the N.F. sounded? If – in the next week or so – everything proves impossible about getting back – I'll ask you to try to get me a passage there eh? Nice for you to have seen Alastair. I haven't seen him for about 10 years. Is he really like me? My dear write even though I've been so bad with my letters. I want to hear from you. Let me know if any comments are made about the N.F. I'll see you soon.

love, Sydney

78. *To Frank Baker*

25 November 1953 Coombe Cottage, Shoreham, Kent

My dear Frank there you are I see as full of the joy and rant as ever and that's certainly a happy bit of news and we must arrange something soon. Nessie and I are here for the moment not the most satisfactory housemates (we have) but I'm working well at the moment and producing 6'-3' poetry a day or 5 -2 1/2 (riming). But, wait! – system, –

I've never written better. 5 pages of poems in the Jan 1st. Encounter (asked for by Spender). My book published in the USA. Good reviews. 600 line poem off to the BBC (requested). Poems in US mags. Book almost ready for Faber. Yes, Frank, everything's coming out 'right' at last and it looks as though I'm going to 'get on'. 'The Nightfishing' was published in an Italian (international circulation) mag called Botteghe Oscure. I got £100 and a year in Italy in a castle. Also I read it on the 3rd [Programme] and that was a fine thing. OK.

Great news you're doing a musical play – what that means I don't know. I must unbushalise my light I'm afraid and admit I've written several songs myself. I offer them here and you may have them for a small consideration. Of course they're influenced. They're yours for a song –

The Nostril Boy
Cheery Rape
It's a Long Way to Tip her Hairy
The Girl I cleft behind me
Down By the Silly Gardens
Is the Old Fogey Due?
The Lust Chord
My Tiny Puccini is Frozen
The Mating of the Trotters
Who is Saliva?
Let Air in, Remember
In a Minestrone Garden
Somewhere a Vice is Calling
Pop Goes the Wee Soul
Dae ye Ken John Weel?
Silly Me O
Little Brain Jag
Jaunty Jesus Make and Mend
The Pullman was Racing
God Sieve the Queen.

And I'm afraid that's all I can muster for you at the moment! Yes

Brigadoon was a fine night and I do remember it very well. Well I must come to, see you and Katie and the children when the times are better. And Gilbert? How is he? What story do you have? From your address I can't tell if you're far out or not. I should be coming up soon to see the BBC people soon (I hope) and maybe a pub would be the best arrangement. Any how I'll let you know. My love to you all.

Great to hear you're there! – Sydney. [...]

79. *To J.F. Hendry*

6 April 1954 c/o Swift, 30, South Hill Bank, London NW3

Dear J.F. Hendry,

I have never met you but, of course, I know your work and you have met Nessie Dunsmuir. I heard last night that you were in Oban and maybe you could help me. It is this.

Nessie and I want to come to live in Scotland. And not for just a holiday, for a year at least. I want a cottage somewhere high up on the West Coast or on one of the Western Isles. The thing is that it should be right by the sea. Also it would have to be cheap. I suppose an unfurnished one would be best. It wouldn't matter in what state it was in. I could fix it up. Now I know it's almost impossible to find but maybe you know of a place or maybe you could advise me about writing to someone who might know. I would be very grateful if you could help.

I hope to hear you are writing a lot and some work is coming out for I see your poetry too seldomly. My new book of poems called THE NIGHTFISHING has been accepted by Faber and should appear within a year and I am in the middle of new work. Are you right in Oban or outside a bit? How do you like living there? Nessie sends her regards. Yours sincerely, W S Graham

80. *To David Wright*

8 November 1954 2, Morley Rd. London, S.E.13

My dear David,

Christ! It's a real book of poetry, made up of the authentic material that makes the heart (or the head) turn over in that way which is poetic experience for me. There are so many books of 'poetry' around which carry some different kind of material, about as far from the object a poem is as a fart from a whale's ear. David it's a good book. And, of course, it's better than your last. I must see you sometime soon but can't make any move at the moment for lack of money. I'm married I suppose you know. – That girl I knew slightly Nessie Dunsmuir.[1] I feel I've been rushed into it. O what a drouth!

— — — — — — — I write
This thirst upon the parchment of my tongue.

For The MORAL STORIES thanks, David
love, Sydney

81. *To Alan Clodd*

16 November 1954 2, Morley Rd, London, SE13

Dear Mr. Clodd,

Thanks for your letter. It's always a nice thing to be reminded one's poems do go somewhere and are occasionally exciting to some readers.

I haven't even a copy of C.W.G. myself at the moment but I think maybe I can procure two copies from Glasgow and if there is a numbered edition available I'll send it on to you.

Yes I have a new collection of poems coming out with Faber in the Spring, March I think, and it's called THE NIGHTFISHING .

'Baldy Bane', compared with most of my poems that went before it, probably seems suddenly relaxed and more 'traditional'. The thing is that that ballad and another (The Ballad of the Broad Close) were certainly not (by intention at least) imitations of the old authentic ballads. They constantly address the reader on what part he is likely to play here or there at different parts in the main narrative and even remind him that he is as necessarily present in the

1 An account of Graham's unusual proposal of marriage is given by Tom Scott (*Edinburgh Review* 75, p. 58). It is confirmed in essence by the painter Bet Low. Sydney was staying in Glasgow with her and her husband Tom Macdonald at the time. Unable to contact Nessie, as there was no telephone at the house she was in, he rang up the local policeman and asked him to go and bring her to the police-station telephone. When asked if it was urgent he replied, 'Yes, it's very urgent. Tell her I want to marry her.'

action as the writer and that he is just as responsible as the writer for the outcome of the action.[1] Forgive me! What a mouthful that is! Anyhow,these two ballads are, for me, the most technically sophisticated poems I have attempted. I'm glad you find it exciting for I am curious how they will be taken by readers knowing my earlier work.

A '*hoodie*' – hooded crow or carrion crow, common in Scotland.

'*yella-yite*' – insulting expression meaning cowardly.

'*bowbender*'- old wooden roof beams used to be 'bowbent' – bent in the shape of a bow . . . . Here the immediate connotations are – I am the man who can bend the big bow – The Ulysses who can manage to bend the woman like a bow. And others, for all of us differing more and more as they reach the more outside rings of the 'splash', continue.

Robin Black's magazine was THE FREEMAN. I can't remember the number the McD review appeared. It wasn't long and rather spiteful.

And that's about all. I'll send the C.W.G. when it arrives.

Yours sincerely, WSGraham

82. *To Alan Clodd*

8 December 1954 2, Morley Road, S.E.13

Dear Mr. Clodd,

I've managed to find you a copy and here it is and I have written 'something, anything' in it and I managed to get the artists to colour it. It was printed in 1942 to sell at a guinea and I've no idea now what people may have them.

The narrative in Baldy Bane, as far as it is a succession of physical events, is – The host welcomes guests he has invited to some gathering. He explains he can't get up because he is superstitious

1 The Alan Clodd Collection contains a typescript copy of 'The Ballad Of The Broad Close' with Graham's handwritten notes. The first reads: 'Dear Bill Troy [American academic], This kind of poem will be maybe a surprise, coming from me. On the other hand you may find it quite consistent (and that is what I hope) with the more tentative attempts at introducing an extreme self-consciousness of both the poet's and the reader's responsibility which function in the 7 Letters (and to a very slight extent in The Nightfishing).

'I have tried to keep the person who reads and shares the poem continually aware that it is as much his responsibility as mine to create the outcome of the poem, and create it in as cathartic a way as possible.'

about a crow he has seen on the gatepost, but that they should go ahead with the singing and dancing (let us communicate) he will see it from his bed where he lies with his wife (who is also the muse). And so the night proceeds and they all get drunk and he (who, after all, feels he is 'writing' or 'speaking' them alive to each other and also to who he is speaking to) alternates between power and aggression and self pity and quarrels more and more with the reader, and the poem ends with his final encounter with the muse (or his wife) and he steps out of the poem leaving it at an end (or he makes love to his wife and then falls asleep). Now I know this is all rather loose but the stream of narrative here is a broad complicated stream woven of different strands to do with – the poet, the I, the man in bed, the man who is speaking to the one who is listening and also the muse, the wife and various characters at the party like – Kate Dalrymple and the tall man drunk as a wheelbarrow. I hope that helps a little.

The Ballad of the Broad Close was published in the last number of Botteghe Oscure in Rome. It's an international literary magazine in four languages. Also there's a new poem of mine coming out in Encounter in February. It's called Letter VII and it is the last 'letter' of seven.

Yes there is a study of my work in Poetry Quarterly. I haven't a copy. I wrote a prose piece called Notes on a Poetry of Release when I was 'very young'. It was printed in a number of Poetry Scotland, Quarterly Review of Literature (Bard College, Allendale on Hudson, N.Y, State, U.S.A.), and a number of Sewanee Review. There was a long review of THE WHITE THRESHOLD in Poetry, Chicago, by Leonie Adams. And aslong review in a number of NINE.

Yes Vivienne Koch's book is very good even for the energy it somehow suggests. Well, may you find something you can make something of in the cage.

Yours sincerely, W S Graham

83. *To Alan Clodd*

9 February 1955 Castle Eaton, Swindon, Wiltshire

Dear Alan Clodd,

about not writing to you – nothing is best. I am here in the country for a while, I hope maybe throughout the summer, but I will be coming up to London occasionally and I hope still we can arrange to meet somewhere. I write this sitting in the cottage here (my wife has gone to London for the weekend) with the logs hissing and cracking in the grate too much like a Christmas card to be true. I've always been frightened of the insidious anaesthetic of comfort and although I am far from an ascetic by nature I've rather welcomed conditions in which I could not entirely forget the weather. But it's terrible sometimes having the winter approaching. It's a great thing to have a house and a warm bed. I'm not trying to be 'simple' and 'down-to-earth'. Of course this is always true, in its relative way, but it is just that at the moment, being more or less secure here for a while, it occurs to me. I remember poor Purcell being locked out and Rimbaud under the bridges of Paris or have you read Nansen about crossing Greenland? But anyhow here I am and the logs do crack and it is easier to work.

Well my book will be out on the 11th and I find myself being more excited about it than I had expected to be. The Nightfishing is already a poem I did not write and I can see it and be curious about its eccentricities and the various strands which suddenly emerge to the surface to become for a moment an ephemeral objective correlative before they sound again. With all its mistakes and blemishes I think it is a knit object, an obstacle of communication, if you like, which has to be climbed over or gone round but not walked through. I think it just might make its wee disturbance in the language. I think (in a dramatic way) it makes a place, organic and believable, within its lines. What it will be to others I have no idea. What I meant when I wrote it is in it but for me its validity is already because of something else. If it made somebody seasick (a good unliterary measurement) I would be pleased. Anyhow, hello! From where we are it is not us we see.

Just one other thing about the book. I'm curious about what might be said about the difference between T.N.F., the Letters & the Ballads. I think T.N.F. will probably be easier to like and its innovations of prosody more obvious than 'The Letters' and its innovations. And I wonder what any reviewers , knowing my earlier work, will make of The Ballads.

And since 'will make of The Ballads' I have been out at the pub and that was an hour ago and I've got the fire up again and I resume this letter wondering what kind of man you are and noticing that my handwriting has loosened and my thoughts become more fluid. Christ what a selfconscious man I sound and yet to become an artist of any singleness of purpose seems to make this inevitable. Sometimes when I've been a bit drunk in some pub in some place where I've known nobody I've turned to some man standing near and said – 'and what kind of a man are you' and that is, I think, one of the main reasons I am a 'poet'(forgive me but you'll just have to believe I am not a person completely without humility, because I can't govern everything I say with 'to my own measurements'). Whatever intelligence made us (He, She, It) made us so beautifully and so well knit with the paradoxical hunger –

1 – To be one, in one's identity and indestructible in anything or anyone else. To have been given one's own unique gesture of consciousness.

2 – To always want to share the aloneness, to share what happens within one's own lonely room, to wonder how alike or unalike one is from someone else. So we have those two things, not necessarily contraries. The responsibility of aloneness without which life would be nothing and the hunger for love, to be recognised as what we *think* we are and loved for that. Art is one of the ways we achieve this to a certain extent. Listening to a quartet of Mozart I have a love for what intelligence made it and I don't mean in an inhuman way. The effort to speak honestly and be heard is difficult, communication is difficult. To speak to one's self honestly is difficult. I have the beginning of a new poem which, I think, will be a long poem. I mean over 500 lines but, more importantly, have the structure of a long poem. I'll quote this and then I'll post it out there in the wee post box in the dark in the frozen wall with its icicles dripping down from the postoffice roof -

'Meanwhile surely there must be something to say
Maybe not even suitable but at least happy
In a sense here between us two whoever
We are. Anyhow here we are and never
Before have we two faced each other who face
Each other here across this abstract scene
Stretching between us. This is a public place
Achieved against subjective odds and then
Still mainly an obstacle to what I mean.

It is like that, remember. It is like that
Very often yet sometimes we are singled out
By some intention risen up out of nothing,

And even then we know what we are saying
Only when it is said and fixed and dead,
Or maybe, of course, surely we never know
What we have said, what lonely meanings are read
Into the space we make. Therefore I say
This silence here for in it I might hear you.'

This section will have a third stanza ending -

'– – – – – – – – – – – – – – and so I am
More truly now this abstract act become.'

Don't be frightened at the bareness and prosaicness of this section. It is meant to be as 'abstract' as I can make it, unvisual in its images and suggesting no place or atmosphere.

Now without reading this over (or I might never post it) I send it off wishing you well Sincerely

W S Graham

P.S. when I sort my papers out I'll be sending some things

Dear A., I'd better post this off. Writing soon W S G

84. *To Charles Causley* (extract)

23 June 1955 Castle Eaton, Swindon, Wiltshire.

THE NIGHTFISHING is a long poem, at least as poems go nowadays, about 500 lines and a long poem is not just a short poem extended to the length where we agree to call it 'long'. No. A long poem is a different thing with its own particular laws and behaviour and does not just 'come about' in the way one might say some shorter ones do. Well I decided to write a long poem, a poem of not less than seven pages. There are probably all sorts of reasons why at this time in my life I felt it inevitable that I should try to do this but there are certainly two reasons which I am aware of more or less objectively. The first is –

I had never written a long poem and the technical problems involved in writing one today were exciting and new and an artist is always curious to see what the technical *intelligence* or principles he chooses will lead him to say. So that is the first. Let us say – THE TECHNICAL CHALLENGE.

The other reason I decided to try to write a long poem is –

It seemed to me that what I had to say needed the vehicle of a long poem. I needed the dimensions in which I could be to a certain extent DRAMATIC, and I mean 'dramatic' not so much in the sense of creating other spokesmen to speak for me but dramatic in the sudden shocking bringing together of different and seeming incompatible textures of narrative and gestures of language. As in Beethoven's Moonlight sonata where the very sheer and (excuse me this word) magic opening movement is followed by a careless and jaunty scherzo. A long poem allows space for an accumulative representation of a scene which is organically valid and which creates the reader's involuntary belief. Where, in a short poem, the poetic shock usually has to occur in an immediate way, in the very texture of the verse, the long poem can also create the massive montage of one such theme upon another, one age on another as in T.S. Eliot's THE WASTE LAND where, in the section – A GAME OF CHESS, a lusciously worded almost-Keatsean scene is followed with hardly a pause and with no warning by –

'My nerves are bad tonight. Yes, bad. Stay with me.
Speak to me. Why do you never speak. Speak.'

I wanted to write about the sea and make it a grey green sea, not a chocolate box sea. I wanted to speak about the boat maintained on its strange element and sailing out, dividing the water with its bow and keel, lifting up by the water rushing in underneath as the used bow-cut water rushes to meet the rest, the screws twisting the water to spirals like twists from drills. Leonardo da Vinci has curious drawings in his notebooks of poured water and its currents and momentums and storms and driven tides and in a way I wanted to use those kinds of very physical phenomena in whatever real action was represented. Because although I wanted to write about the sea it was not the sea only as an objective adventure (if there is such a thing) but as experience surrounding a deeper problem which everybody is concerned with.

I mean the essential isolation of man and the difficulty of communication. To speak much about what I have tried to say in THE NIGHTFISHING and discuss those ideas which are, you might say, take-away-able would be to curtail what the poem says to you and that, after all, is maybe greater or less than I had in mind but is certainly not exactly the same and it is certainly unique.

W S Graham

I LEAVE THIS AT YOUR EAR

For Nessie Dunsmuir

I leave this at your ear for when you wake,
A creature in its abstract cage asleep.
Your dreams blindfold you by the light they make.

The owl called from the naked-woman tree
As I came down by the Kyle farm to hear
Your house silent by the speaking sea.

I have come late but I have come before
Later with slaked steps from stone to stone
To hope to find you listening for the door.

I stand in the ticking room. My dear, I take
A moth kiss from your breath. The shore gulls cry.
I leave this at your ear for when you wake.

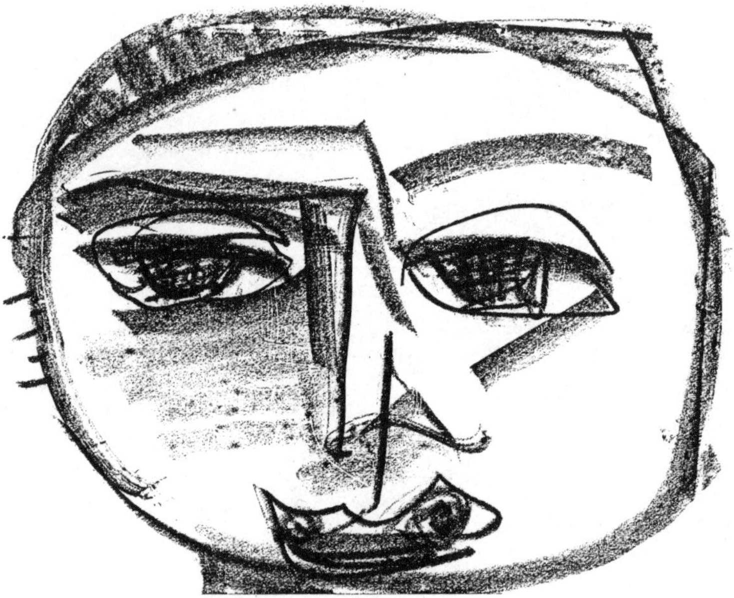

Four

THE DARK DIALOGUES
1956–1960

from THE DARK DIALOGUES

I speak across the vast
Dialogues in which we go
To clench my words against
Time or the lack of time
Hoping that for a moment
They will become for me
A place I can think in
And think anything in,
An aside from the monstrous.

And this is no other
Place than where I am,
Here turning between
This word and the next.
Yet somewhere the stones
Are wagging in the dark
And you, whoever you are,
That I am other to,
Stand still by the glint
Of the dyke's sparstone,
Because always language
Is where the people are.

*

This is no other place
Than where I am, between
This word and the next.
Maybe I should expect
To find myself only
Saying that again
Here now at the end.
Yet over the great
Gantries and cantilevers
Of love, a sky, real and
Particular is slowly
Startled into light.

The Grahams were seeking a more permanent base. During 1956 they had visited Alan and Valerie Lowndes, Bryan Wynter had tried to find them a cottage and Sven Berlin had lent them his old house, Penderleath, at Cripplesease outside St Ives. In March they were able to rent one of the old Coastguard houses on the cliffs overlooking Gurnard's Head, midway between Morvah and Zennor on the north Penwith coast. Graham was sometimes employed as an auxiliary coastguard on bad weather watch in the small exposed lookout post (now demolished) high on the seaward face of Gurnard's Head itself. The small Gurnard's Head Hotel on the coast road was very convenient and had a generator but the old coastguard house had no electricity supply and could not at that time be easily reached by road. All supplies were carried by hand down a long rough field path. For the visitors attracted by his poem *The Nightfishing* this solid but rather bare house very close to the sea became something of a symbol, the setting, like the work, having a dangerous austerity and grandeur of scale outside their everyday experience.

Almost all of Graham's poems were composed at the typewriter and, although some notes existed in manuscript, handwritten copies of completed poems were usually specially transcribed. He enjoyed decorating some of his letters and manuscripts with colour, drawings in pen and ink or watercolour. Postcards or old book illustrations were sometimes inventively worked over too.

For some of his early readings at Sandyford Place in Glasgow Graham had improvised screens and patches of colour in the room using string, bits of cardboard and drapery. This created different settings for different poems. Occasionally the rooms at Gurnard's Head also were constructively 'changed' as paint, cardboard cartons or debris from the shore came to hand. Pinned to the wall or stuck down on old sheets of cardboard there were drafts of the current poem, or fragments that might turn into something, and when these had served their turn they were often spontaneously given to visitors as souvenirs of their visit or as reciprocal gifts. Between 1956 and 1958 much of the working wall contained materials for what was to become 'The Dark Dialogues', a poem completed by September 1958. It was published in *Botteghe Oscure* in Spring 1959 when Graham was forty. In later years he sometimes thought that this poem was the most consistent and unified of all his longer works. Together with 'The Beast In The Space' and 'The Constructed Space' written during the same period, it can be seen to confirm a developing emphasis on the nature of the language itself and his own position as simultaneously maker and observer of it. The physicality and strongly visual imagery of *The Nightfishing* was to a degree relinquished in favour of a quieter, no less intense, more interior landscape. This enhanced consciousness of speech as forming a real part of his living environment ('This is no other place / Than where I am, between / This word and the next.') in no way diminished the sensitivity with which he explored his sensation of the material world and the consciousness of the imagined reader. Another of his notes to David Wright explains:

> No matter what illusion you hold or what conscious intention you have as to who you are writing for, the poet is always talking to the best ingredients of 'truth' in himself. He himself contains the measurement of the greatest 'other' sympathy he can imagine. It should always be very much talking to one's self. That is how the most universal poetry comes about.[1]

Sydney Graham had a fortunate ability to endure and even derive great pleasure from very simple surroundings and was fairly indifferent to ordinary domestic comforts.[2] Nessie was just able to support them both by seasonal work in St Ives, and there were the widely separated cheques for poems, but most of the time they were extremely poor.[3] He seemed determined to avoid temptation, to avoid becoming hostage to a more regular lifestyle which could be supported only by him giving up his true work in order to earn more money. His need for freedom of movement, association, and experiment took precedence over any need for everyday security.

Roger Hilton had sought out Sydney Graham at Gurnard's Head in 1956 and the two men formed a close friendship. Roger Hilton had begun his own heavy drinking in 1948 and was already noted for episodes of outstandingly rude behaviour but he could also be both generous and perceptive.[4] Robin Skelton was introduced to Graham by Michael Snow in 1956 and the Peterloo Group, which Skelton, Snow, and Tony Connor had founded in Manchester, was able to mobilise some small support for the Grahams at this time. Ronnie Duncan was introduced to Graham by Terry Frost and Trevor Bell in 1958. Bryan and Monica Wynter, Ruth and Roger Hilton, Jimmy and Daphne Goodman (Gurnard's Head Hotel), Patrick Dolan, Alan and Valerie Lowndes, Robert Brennan, and Nancy Wynne-Jones were among many friends who saw them fairly regularly. Whether they had brought a drink with them or not his visitors were soon pressed into listening or reading aloud, writing alternate lines of extempore doggerel, inventing and acting dramas. They were exhorted to speak about themselves and their own work while having their attention continually drawn to the way in which they were using (or, in Sydney's view, not using) the language. Back in the Gurnard's Head Hotel even passing tourists might find themselves invited to provide sound effects for imaginary storms, 'Make sound of wind'. One morning the painter Alan Wood was drinking quietly at the bar with the landlord and a stranger when Sydney threw open the door and looked around. 'He suggested that he should make his entrance again, but as though it were a stormy night. The others were to make suitable storm noises. When they all, including the innocent stranger, were howling and shooshing satisfactorily Sydney went outside again, presumably to make a dramatic re-entrance. The three blew and howled. Sydney did not come back.'[5]

1 *Edinburgh Review* 75, p. 54.
2 See letter to Alan Clodd, 29 February 1955.
3 Patrick and Wendy Oliver stayed with the Grahams for a time during 1957 and Wendy recalled that 'We lived on flour-and-water pancakes cooked on a primus stove, and, when the paraffin was finished, over a driftwood fire. Sydney and Nessie also used to collect limpets [mussels?] off the rocks and cook them, but only the cat would eat them, and even then not always' (letter to the Editors, 1995).
4 Adrian Lewis, *Roger Hilton*, Exhibition Catalogue (Leicester, 1984).
5 From an unpublished article by Don Brown.

85. *To Juanita and Sven Berlin* (extract)

7 February 1956 Little Penderleath, Cripple's Ease, Nancledra, Penzance

Hello, Juanita, Hello Sven

Yes, what a lifesaving device you have turned out to be at this time. It's a strange thing that although my position as a serious poet becomes more consolidated every day and although I wait patiently for signs that the 'fight' is easing, it has never been more difficult than it is now. And the sad thing is that now I need a sense of at least an ephemeral security stretching ahead for at least a month or two because I'm working at a long poem which (let us hope, Sven) will knock them all into a half-cocked hat. I mean I don't want to just write occasional poems at the moment but complete good big long poems that will cover the experience of whatever technical field was uncovered by my last poem.

Sven Nessie is here, sitting here in Michael's Castle [Inn], beside my rucksack filled with candles flour monkfish tripe potatoes (the rucksack not Ness) and this is my first day up since getting into Penderleath.

86. *To Roger Hilton*

13 December 1956 Gurnard's Head

My Dear Roger,

you would not have wanted to hear from me in the strains which surely would have been mine if I had written you before now. Profound melancholy was my lot and not inconsiderate upheavals of a domestic nature. Yes, Roger, everything was buggered and I seemed to have entered a real hopelessness. First of all – we've never had such a long period with so little money so that living mainly on bread and potatoes and some fish and mussels and not having enough paraffin for cooking got us down and a wee bit undernourished and Nessie's had flu twice in the last 2 months and wood seems harder to find and takes more energy to work at getting each day. But that is that. Fear no more. I've said my say of complaints. Ruth was so very good sending something down and the provisions. Our greatest worry was that the rent being let go so long might lose us our house.

Curiously enough I've been 'creating wildly in all directions' and

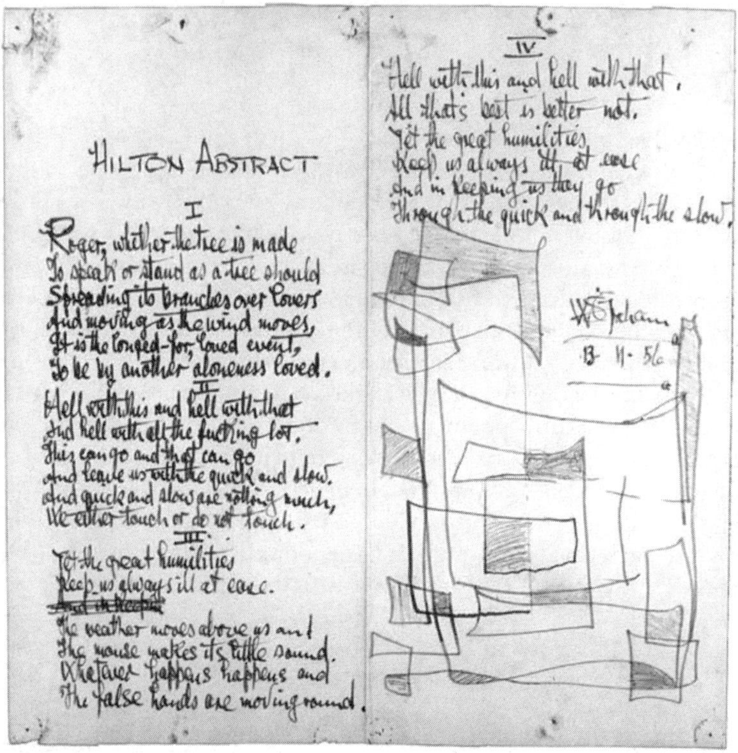

I've finished two new poems which I think will stand. Its like making some construction and being so close up to it that you can't see it, like picnicking on the nostril of the Sphinx, and having to pack up and trudge 10 miles away and look back to see it and just how it is.

Now, Roger, if you can manage to turn aside from those moans of unbearable ecstasy, what is going on with you? How's the work? Are you pleased with any recent things you've done? The strange thing is this, Roger, I found when I returned here that your pictures and 'timbre of voice' of your painting had affected me more strongly than I had realised. In the same way as one sees influences of contemporary abstract painting in Landscape and in News photographs in newspapers lying upside down etc., that particular kind of graphic disturbance which is your 'voice' in painting suggested itself more and more in things. You must both forgive me not writing when I got back here but I just felt that a letter from me out of the depression I've had recently would be just disturbingly dreary and I kept thinking 'well I'll wait till I'm through this depressing week' and it just stretched on and on. Not that I'm the cat's pyjamas (if that is how one uses that term) at the moment but I'm here sitting up in this wee cabin and the wind shrieking my ears off and I just got to thinking, 'Whatever will Ruth and Roger think of me'. For you see I did enjoy very much being up in London and staying there. Me being in a money crisis was a nuisance but that was my business and I'm sorry if I kind of put you on the spot and I do feel badly about not being able to pay back the money I got from you yet.

So, Roger, my love-chasing abstract boy, my hero of the graphic plain, my boy alone and lost in the disguising angers and rudenesses and precipitations of catastrophe, my touchy switherer and butteryfingered bearer of your self-esteem, artist of the astringent, the uncharming, the unkitchened, the unpotted and panned regions of the great proportions and intercoursing areas of light trying the eye, hurry up and come down soon. We look forward to seeing you and I really missed you when I got back here. I've been thinking you were arriving before this somehow. Shall I compare thee to a day of storms. Batter my Gurnard's Head. The wind roars and the waves rumble in (remember I mentioned that a man who is dead now called Norman Cameron had translated Rimbaud's 'Bateau Ivre' and that one of his specially successful lines, when he is describing waves coming in on the shore, is 'Those famed old trundlers of the dead'.)

87. *To Marie Singer*

27 January 1958 — Gurnard's Head

My dear Marie,

what a sweet good letter from you. I'm glad you wrote. Our last leavetaking worried me, of course, and I felt guilty letting you in for all that histrionic nonsense. Yes, my dear, I hope sometime we can have an easy meal together. The great thing is not to be a freud chicken but to eat it or is all this just wishbone-thinking to a three-speed trick cyclist like yourself? My apple edges! No more! A pun my word of myth.

The news of the sweet shirt and the bonny jeans is great for the ones I have (my only trousers) are worn thin as pyjamas and anyway were always at halfmast. It really will be lovely to have them. Now please forgive me asking a gift horse for another but I may as well ask you this in case you know of someone. I'm terribly desperate for a pair of shoes or boots and when I've been writing my friends I've been asking them if they have any old pair which they have finished with and which, although not wearable in town, would keep my poor iambic feet off the flint of Cornwall. I keep thinking there must be lots of men with old army boots they'll never use. And this request, Marie, is just a stock one at the moment and you'll probably not know anyone, but I had to ask in case. About this don't bother writing specially and by that I don't mean that I would not like hearing from you soon again. O what a dismal unclear meandering apologising prose. My metres are rifled, my sin tax unpaid and what is really a meta for?

Nessie's been 'sent for' because her mother's dying and she went off to Scotland two weeks ago. It's sad, of course, but after a series of cerebral shocks it was expected and she is 87. Nessie was always very close to her mother who was a very wise old peasant woman. I say 'peasant' because she could neither read nor write and had come over from the west coast of Ireland when she was a young Annalivia Plurabelle rejoyce. So alas I'm alone with my lamp lit and my house about me and Janwer snell and loud at the window. Hand me my book of storms there and I'll look up gaelfarce nine. Wedge up the sashes that me father wore and putty the started astragals. Forgive me how I go on for company otherwise only hearing a wild pin drop. Your ears I'll soon backhand you back, never fear.

I hope you are both defying the fogs of the capital. I'm a country boy myself. The main trouble's keeping warm. I measure out my life in paraffin gallons. I hope Jimmy's in with the muse this weather. Myself, I'm on the sweet home stretch on a poem that's nobody's business. When I'm in town again I'll get in touch with you both and hope that Jimmy is less conscious of the writing of poetry as a competition. Again, my dear, thanks for the jeans and shirt.

love, Sydney

88 *To Robin Skelton* (extract)

31 January 1958 Gurnard's Head

A nice thing to hear about your ballads and I am excited and curious to see them. To write a contemporary poem consciously using the nostalgia of a form which is not possible now to use in the way for which the form came about is exciting. I think there is quite an extensive technical area to be explored in that direction. Pound, Eliot and, of course, Joyce (in prose) have exercised there in their different ways. But remember, Robin, (and forgive me saying this for, of course, you know it already) it must be more than just your own contemporary poetic experience expressed in the characteristic ballad 'voice'. The performer playing the Green King of the Wood must never for an instant let the audience get the idea that he thinks he really is the king. The disguise he uses to play the king must just be merely held before him, formal and apparent. In my own ballads one of the ways I attempted this was to lean round the disguise and grimace and speak 'personally' to the reader so that we became two intelligences or characters taking part in the action of the ballad. And as a device that is as contrary as it could be to that particular gesture the ballad originally evolved for. I wish you would let me see them. I promise not to write back starting a lot of doubts in your head about them. An' gosh, man, I'd sure be right proud to have one o' them doggone ballad critters dedicated to me. I'll carry it around in ma' saddle bag an read it to the boys when 'am on roundup.

Sydney

89. *To Alan Clodd*

8 February 1958 Gurnard's Head

My dear Alan,

forgive me not having replied to your letter sooner. There is really no excuse but the usual untidiness of my life and recently I've been feeling specially exasperated over this long poem I'm working on which is certainly proving the toughest poetic nut my blue-eyed brain has ever set out to crack. I think I mentioned the poem to you. It's the one beginning

I always meant to only
Language swings away
Further before me.

Language swings away

Before me as I go
With again the night rising
Up to accompany me
And that other fond
Metaphor, the sea.

Images of night
And the sea changing
Should know me well enough.
Grieve me the great midnight.

And who are you and by
What right do I waylay
You where you go there
Happy enough striking
Your hobnail in the dark?
Believe me I would ask
Forgiveness but who
Would I ask forgiveness from?

Wanton with riding lights
And staring eyes, Europa
And her – – – – – – – – – –

In no other poem have I 'lived' so long for so little. I feel I'm at last on the sweet home stretch and I believe, somehow, that when it's finished and receded a little in time so that I can see it better as a whole, it will be something of some magnitude.

It was fine, you taking all the MSS and, of course, the £2 a week is a nice arrangement for weakwilled poets. About information re publication of The Seven Journeys, the best thing is, I think, to write to Bill Maclellan himself – 240 Hope St., Glasgow. Tell him what you're doing in such a way that he sees it also as possible future publicity in the mention of Wm Maclellan.

I'm writing this in the pub, waiting for a bus to go into St Ives for my paraffin to keep the Arctic weather at bay. So I havn't your letters at hand at the moment Alan, but I'll answer any other questions you may have asked later. The syntax of those last two sentences is not of the best and I reckon it's because I havn't paid my sin tax for the year yet. I'm afraid I'm afraid in this letter I'm not at my best but another time another letter another me. Wow what a howl of wind and sleet! How goes the Winter with you there

Gurnard's Head
Cornwall. 8-2-58

My dear Alan, forgive me not having replied to your letters sooner. There is really no excuse but the usual untidiness of my life and recently I've been feeling specially exasperated over this long poem I'm working on which is certainly proving the toughest poetic nut my blue-eyed brain has ever set out to crack. I think I mentioned the poem to you. It's the one beginning—

I always meant to only
Language swings away
Further before me.

Language swings away
Before me as I go
With again the nightrising
Up to accompany me
And that other, found
Metaphor, the sea.

Images of night
And the sea changing
Should know me well enough.
Grieve me the great midnight.

And who are you and by
What right do I waylay
You where you go there
Happy enough striking
Your hobnail in the dark?
Believe me I would ask
Forgiveness but who
Would I ask forgiveness from?

Wanton with riding lights
And staring eyes, Europa
And her - - - - - - - - -

In no other poem have I lived so long for so little. I feel I'm at last on the sweet home stretch and I believe, somehow, that when it's finished and receded a little in time so that I can see it better as a whole, it will be something of some magnitude.

It was fine, you taking all the mss and, of course, the £2 a week is a nice arrangement for weakwilled poets. About information re publication of The Seven Journeys, the best thing is, I think, to write to Bill MacLellan himself – 240 Hope St., Glasgow. Tell him what you're doing in such a way that he sees it also as possible future publicity in the mention of Wm MacLellan.

I'm writing this in the pub, waiting for a bus to go into St Ives for my paraffin to keep the arctic weather at bay. So I haven't your letters at hand at the moment, Alan, but I'll answer any other questions you may have asked later. The syntax of those last two sentences is not of the best and I reckon it's because I haven't paid my sin tax for the year yet. I'm afraid I'm afraid in this letter I'm not at my best but another time another letter, another me. Wow what a howl of wind and sleet! How goes the winter with you there around the gloomy hills of London? —— regards – Sydney.

around the 'gloomy hills of London'?[1]

Regards – Sydney.

90. *To Robin Skelton*

25 February 1958 CORNWALL

Dear Redbreast,

I am sorry again ('shall I say it again?') for the long time no write and do let me now make no other excuse but say it is the tryingness of the time and also I think I should say that in any future letters to come I will never go on at lengths of apologies for not replying sooner. Otherwise my letters will always be beginning with nonsense and black sheepishness. Allow me not the guilt piling up from a letter long unreplied to and I am a better man. A letter the longer to leave the less to love.

Robin, thanks for the money for the mss and the two to Nessie. Believe me, it was never more necessary. But there we are. We choose our way for what we get. The photograph of spouse and son makes me as jealous as hell or nearly not really but gives me the old longing for children. My love and congratulations to Sylvia. And, of course, yourself. Proper job!

THE BALLAD OF THE MUSE and maybe this is why I've put off writing, when I come to think of it. Now, Robin, if we've to go on communicating and having any live relationship we should be able to speak like this as I speak now without disturbing our essential vanities or harming our belief in what we know technically about poetry. I think you are a poet. And, having said that, let me now talk about the ballad knowing I won't blight you. And, believe me, I wouldn't bother with most.

I'll try just to make some points. I won't try to say too much. I wish I had you here down beside me tonight to talk about it and go over it and, not being able to do that, it is very difficult and I don't want you to get the wrong idea. To my mind, what you attempt technically is more ambitious than your previous poems but as a poem it is not very satisfactory and (let me go further than that) will not do you any good. Let me talk in a loose unliterary way first.

1 'Driven on the wind that sweeps the gloomy hills of London' – T.S. Eliot, 'Burnt Norton' III.

God forbid that I should look for a story in a poem but here I say alright but what is this close-packed stream of short phrases and sentences, doubtfully pithy, leading to? Remember that both my ballads wear the garments (actorish if you like) of the characteristic cadences and archaic idiom of the 'Child's Ballad'. Yeats – the garments of the early Victorian Irish street ballad. Auden – either the garment of the early grim murderstory ballad or the American Negro blues. For me there is not enough of a place or action established. The poem cannot be maintained on those phrases and good 'nutshell' lines alone. Something must happen or the place established must be so involuntarily believed in and accepted as a 'wonder' that there is no need for any objective dramatic action. Even when I piled on the verbal 'gunplay' I tried to make something happen and to establish a place in which it happened in each ballad. Of course the texture you put forward is very much more intricate than mine. But to use such an intricate texture makes it difficult for the poem to have any 'gesture' of statement. Especially when the rhythm is ballady and carrying the stream of words forward with such an almost rockanroll. Also, Robin, (and I would be daft not to say this) it is too like me in the wrong way, in a way which will irritate the critics. Remember that most good reviews I had were almost grudgingly (in spite of) given and you, reminding them of me in this particular way, ride with a helluva handicap. When I say 'in the wrong way' I mean by so much using the 'attitude' of the 'I' in maybe the Baldy Bane ballad more than the B.C. ['Broad Close'] By all means use the idea of a 'supreme selfconsciousness' where the 'I' speaks out continually to the reader but for your own good there must be another way to do it other than using – 'Come over here and name your want.' or 'I put your word into my mouth' or 'It's shouted out.' or 'to get your one word in.'

And so on. And even at that, Robin, it takes a good poem to carry a line like 'Time is a strange strange thing.' Now you will know that I'm not worrying about you 'pinching' or using any gimmicks of mine. That you are not doing and, if you were, you know that the more people who are obviously influenced by me the better because in a way it always helps my 'personal idiom' (whatever that is). I mean don't be influenced by the eccentric Grahamisms. Now, Robin, remember this is me and it is what *I* think and although naturally I believe what I say, you are the one with the ultimate supreme right to send the poem out into the live world and all its encountering intelligences.

No, it's nice of you, Robin, but I couldn't think of coming up or leaving here at the moment. I worry about getting something really solid done and keeping the Council unworried about my rent till Nessie can help when she starts (if she can come) her partime hotel work at Easter. I'll write you soon, maybe a letter to the Peterloo Group to be read aloud. Not too serious not too long.

love from your old poeteastering plume-pal, Sydney

91. *To Bryan Wynter* (pages in a Notebook)

19 November 1958 Gurnard's Head

Dear you know well who answer me this if you dare at the bum's rush threshold of fucking about on the edge of silence again in the smallest hours of the darkest night shell ever grave worm glowed in or lent its lamp to call thee mine, That's what I call a sane tense and no miss taken. And keep your split-new hounds at bay. So the nigh-time wall has ears to tick me off. That's my bees' knees I humble on to get myself into high the great oven above by rolling my legs on a quick free piss cat branch across read type. No blouse femme meant. All swear words disagreed and switch your longwedge to the off.

These, I'm a fraud, are my silly jazzums to rugcut less than nothing at all at the end. Leave us, de lotteries and dumb balls of the hairies in their coarses ran. Nor lean your ide to me ever. Love well alone and let who may be. Then pardon, a mo, while I up and open my new branch lines.

And I remember this. I remember that always somewhere under the live and speaking idiom of the Voice in poetry there is the count, the beats you can count on your fingers. Yes always under the shout and whimper and the quick and the slow of poetry there is the formal construction of time made abstract in the mind's ear. And the strange thing is that that very abstract dimension in the poem is what creates the reader's release into the human world of another.

While I was writing those letters [*Letters* I–VII in *The Nightfishing*] I tried to almost live inside this three stress metre I had chosen. I hoped that I would be able to utilise the very stricture they seemed to impose on my voice. In my note book I made myself try to say all kinds of things which seemed impossible to say in this metre. I wrote pages of verse saying to myself that it didn't matter whether it was poetry or not. And, of course, most of it was not but, to some degree, it seemed to tap, at times, a kind of sensibility which I didn't know was in me. Before I begin to go through Letter IV let me digress for a moment and read you one page of this kind of exercise verse from my note book. And let me read it very strictly & metronomically, if that is a word. . . .

And out.

First I think this works well as a bridge and although grammatically it may appear a little strange, those two words without a verb and then a full stop, it functions easily and successfully. It is necessary even to be always open to the possibility of fresh grammatical shapes. To even quite consciously construct grammatical attacks to counteract the deadness of the same kind of statement again and again. To get away from the stream of –

The sky does this
I go there
The ships sweeps out
Now the day goes etc.

There are many ways of doing this and this is one of them, the distortion of mathematical grammar. The important thing is that it must work, and not just create a perplexing ambiguity which would shatter the reader's involuntary belief.

The Poem is the Poet's Intention[1]

Let me begin by not making an apology for the title but trying to explain what I mean by it.

I know that this phrase is, if you like, only an excuse for talking about our ideas of the nature of art. Now, because we all, all of us here in this room, who are not deaf or dumb *use* all the time, daily, on buses, or having words with our wifies, – WORDS we are sometimes led into the belief that literature is more literary than the other arts. This is not so.

In the same way as we don't expect music to tell us about horsemen or unrequited love or painting to illustrate the behaviour of a molecule we should not expect poetry (even although it is an object of words which we might use every day) to hand us out a little nutshell truth which we have pleasure in agreeing with.

1 Also from the Notebook given to Bryan Wynter.

92. *To Robin Skelton*

27 November 1958 Gurnard's Head

My dear ready breast Skelton,

just a wee note for nothing at all but only because I am alive and awake at this small hour after a sudden 'party' beginning with Bryan Wynter and his wife arriving and then a tap at the window in the middle of the talk and the making a fool of one's self and your old fond friend arriving, Michael Snow. So now they are gone and because your self was to some degree on our oiled tongues (Bryan brought a bottle of whisky.) I take my taprooter and think I will say hello there before I work a bit at wooing the old so-trying muse. So how are you doing away up there in the northern airts?

'Tonight these words, tempters against
Silence, turn me round to face
Again that abstract audience
As———————————————————'

So scare me up my gully knife, Rob Skelton and think no ill o' me and I'll respect you with the word and my kneecapless knee. It falls upon this time tonight and it is four oclock. The near-full moon is going over and on silence I knock.

How do you do, my Beauty
And how do you do, my King.
I bought my muse the Keeper
But ne'r bought her the Ring.

Think nor autodigest the mumbrains of your mental edge too much on this. It's neither wearth nor sky to such great piets as we are. Nature beholds us as we never were. Our selves disgaze us illwise from the truth. Swot that roteric well and god stone dead and let us wee two talk a bit.

By by by by by lulla far well for now and let us let it lightly be for the evry nicht and alle. The lord please unforsake us both this nisht (as the southern German goes). See you later.

chow for now, Sydney

93. *To Robin Skelton*

13 December 1958 *Gurnard's Head, Cornwall*
(Please note that this address is the 'swiftest postal address')
Saturday Night, 11–35 pm.

Dear Rob,

where are the Snows of etc., and you will well know I mean your old sidekicker, your old china, your pal of the sculpt and the stone and the quartz and the spar and the geological sensitivity. And so well we unfolded ourselves each to each. And Christ did he talk of you. Or maybe it was me did. I feel I know you better or is it worse. Those nights talking in the pub your northern lugs must of fairly singed themselves on the telepathic air. That's by the way. Since he went I have been ill. Something like flu except my lymph glands were all swollen and my temperatoora's not gone even yet. I've been in bed now for 9 days and got up yesterday. And,to give you all this kind of news in one go, poor Ness has at last got word that her mother really this time is chosen to begin her journey and we are phoning all the time and if she goes, as it seems like, it will mean Ness being up in Scotland to see her off. Timor mortis –

Oor plesance here is a' vain glory,
This fause world is but transitory.
The flesh is bruckle, the Feynd is slee.
        Timor Mortis conturbat me.

Yes, somehow, Robin, assailed by our acquaintances and a friend here and there, and dodging the sometimes too-thoroughly felling arm of Bacchus and the baying slavering hounds of angst that howl from the hydrophobic dark and – – – – well anyhow I mean that in spite of them all we talked a lot and about yourself and about the idea of the Peterloo Group and the talk was positive and enriching and I think Michael enjoyed his visits. He showed me the review by Ross. A review like that is neither bad nor good. He must have some charm or something about his person somewhere but in relation to anything he says about verse or (by example) in his own works he conceals his wisdom or sympathy to the medium like nobody's business. I mean he could have at least pointed out why you were a better poet than Blackburn.

The thing is that I have read your book over and more and more recently and I get to know the poems better and keep wanting to say something about them, and do not [mis]understand me, I am not frightened that I'll say something you won't like. As you said yourself – I do not HAVE to say anything. That I know. Still – Surely there must be something to say.

Forgive me. This is terrible! I say this with unreasonable irritation. Those fucking dedications of your poems KILL me. I know we have talked about it. It's just as I look at the book now again. Forgive the ootborsht. No offence me[an]t none taken I hope.

Maybe Michael told you we read some of John Knight's poems and Christ they should be published. I don't know what one does about that but apart from that I hope Michael told him how much we were moved that night of the reading.

The first lecture, as far as the script goes, is almost finished. I think maybe I've got too much in. I think it's too meaty and not matey enough. I want it to be not a lecture 'taped' but a performance with the best values of a lecture and with the ingredients special to the medium of a dramatic tape performance. The tape-recorder Nancy [Wynne-Jones] got was no good and a larger truer-toned one has half arrived. Quite soon I should be able to send you up something, even if it is not the completed LECTURE FOR TAPE AND AUDIENCE I eventually decide on.

Nessie goes up to phone in the morning again to the women next door to her family in Blantyre and maybe we'll know then if her mother's gone and, if she has, that means she'll have to go up. We'll see.

our respective loves for now, Sydney

94. *To John Knight*

29 July 1959 Gurnard's Head

My dear John Knight,

Yes it is myself writing so belatedly to you to say how pleased I am that STRAIGHT LINES AND UNICORNS is being published and going before the public eye. What a good thing. As well as it being right that your poetry should be available it helps to create a tension in the speaker (you) when the speaker knows he is being listened to. This, of course, you know and I don't know why I'm going on about it. No matter, John. One must risk the 'corny' to say anything. One can think one's intention continually away. I mean – you are one of the fairly few people I am pleased has got published. Och the words. The words we use seem to speak us into impossible banality.

What a pity I wasn't here when you called. Tonight, or rather this early sea-gull crying morning, I remember that hectic day at St. Just and me at my most greedily aggressive and you and your wife. I hope we will meet again and that the next time I will not go on so much and give us a chance to speak more to each other.

My best wishes to you both and good luck to the book, W S Graham

95. *To Norman Macleod*

January 1960 Gurnard's Head

My dear Norman,

How to begin to reply to you well may you ask. My dear Norman and Isobel (And Isobel, please, keep sending me those new poems. Whatever I have said about them is only, you must remember, complaints about why your poem is not just the poem I have written myself. To evaluate an art object which does not come from one's self is difficult. That kind of objectivity is so difficult to achieve in an Artist at the level I am at still at the moment.) So my dear Norman and Isobel here you are asking me what I feel about THE NIGHT-FISHING, now that I have recorded it again for the THIRD [Programme]. Of course, that poem, because of its distance from me (Eliot said, how rightly, that to look back on earlier poems one realises that one can no longer (even although one is more technically the master) add another poem to that 'time', one has no longer the same 'stuff in stock'.) Anyhow, Norman, you will realise how, that having the chance to 'interpret' it again is an exciting thing for me. Well it's finished and down to the BBC tape or whatever it is. By the way, buggerlugs, my coastguard duties have begun again and here I am writing here from this hut here right up on top of the rock of Gurnard's Head with a low veiled lamp lit and a port or starboard light outside moving across that awful roaring sea dark. No matter. Hell with all that. Let me say somehow how this poem has become, in a way, something else for me.

To begin to read it there in the studio waiting for the green (go) light to blink. I think. Right. Listen Listen make the idea of silence first so that the very first beginning of the very first word is going to be resonant, inevitable upon it. Now, Norman, think of the wonderful (forgive me) dramatic beginning again.

'Very gently struck
The quay night bell.'

Here is the beginning, the first 'noise' of the 'voice' which is going to speak to you. It immediately sets an almost geographical place and a place at a certain time. Night. By the sea. And people, a way of life (because even the bell is rung by human agency).

Norman, this first section, this time, I took easy. I read it speaking loosely, casually, letting each Word come out as though each Word had just been thought of, had occurred for the first time. I remember how in this first section I have made those phrases which are already made. e.g. 'the dead of night,' 'I hear my name called,' 'Named me to the bone.'

And of course, Norman, the difference from the first version being

Owls from on the land,
Gulls from on the water,

changed to

Owls from on the land
Gulls cry from the water.

a nice difference and relief

In the next section beginning 'I bent to the lamp....' I was more easy and relaxed and in the section beginning – 'And now almost blindfold' I was more 'grand' and rhetorical and filled with tone.

Section II

Norman, this section, which I used to think of as a song I have spoken out fairly, let go with the more '*folky*' rhetoric. This 'y' apply only to the 'chorus'.

To work at waking. Yet who wakes?
Dream gives awake its look. My death
Already has me clad anew.
We'll move off in this changing grace.

The moon keels and the harbour oil
Looks at the sky through seven colours.

When I fell down into this place
My father drew his whole day's pay,
My mother lay in a set-in bed,
The midwife threw my bundle away.

(the 'set-in bed'. the bed in a tenement kitchen set into the wall like a square cave.)

Here we dress up in a new grave,
The fish boots with their herring scales
Inlaid as silver of a good week,
The jersey knitted close as nerves
Of the ground under the high bracken
My eyes let light in on this dark.

When I fell from the hot to the cold
My father drew his whole days pay.
My mother lay in a set-in bed.
The midwife threw my bundle away.

Norman Norman Norman what shall I say. Here the third section, the section always in this poem which I find the most difficult to read and even to read within its formal metric.

I chose this longer five stress line thinking this is the kind of texture to *relate* in. The texture to carry the main objective equivalent. And now encountering it again when I have to read it and make the five stresses counterpoint the sense idiom I realise how difficultly I have made it to read aloud. I mean lines ending with a preposition or lines ending with an adjective or adverb making it not easy to read. Because good real verse (which is a reflection of the very starts and stops, grimaces and serenities, gestures of the ideas of the mind) should always have its almost hesitation for a moment between one line and the next. That is why we make our 'say' in lines. Speaking between somehow the spaces which occur between the tyranny of the metronomic in a strange way enables us to say something which we could never elsewhere have said with all the complete silence of the times at our disposal.

And so, my dear, it begins.

I in Time's grace, the grace of change, sail surely
Moved off the land and the skilled keel sails
The darkness burning under where I go.
Land voices and the lights ebb away
Raising the night round us. Unwinding whitely,
My changing motive pays me slowly out.
The sea sails in. The quay opens wide its arms
And waves us loose.

Yes, Norman, here is the attempt, in this third section, to try to 'strut' the beginning statement (up till now) to some kind of illusion of outside reality. Please, please do not think for a second I mean that, the things which seem to happen are only being used in an allegorical way. No. No. Norman. Norman.

The sea is the real sea. If you like it is – 'the sea as metaphor of the sea.' The wind in the morning off the shore is not a wind somewhere existing in words, not realised by another intelligence. No. It is the wind which is true to how a wind begins. I say – 'a slat of wind.' The very beginning of a movement of the air which anyhow already touches us on every side. It is observed even by the character within the poem. It is the wind which

'Comes off the shore sharp to find its old mark
Between the shoulder blades.'

This section, my dear Norman, I find so difficult to read and to fill up every word with sound and attitude. To come to the slow quiet silent bit where there is obviously something more than just the physical slowness and eventual stillness of the boat stopped in the water, I found myself slowing and reading and separating every word so formally. For the reading should not be sound equivalent in any way. You see, Norman, although this section, this third section, shall we call it the 'voyage section' carries the main objective action it is at the same time to do with all my most subjective and moral actions of the moment.

Maybe it is a help to think of this section, this 'objective correlative' section in this way, that as one has started and is caught up with describing something, say the behaviour of water in relation to the boat with lines like –

Gather towards us with dragging weights of water
Sleekly swelling across the humming sea
And gather heavier.

or this

> Our bow heads home
>
> Into the running blackbacks soaring us loud
> High up in open arms of the towering sea.

or this

> ...   Those fires burned
> Sprigs of the foam and branching tines of water.
> It rose so white soaring slowly up
> On us, then broke, down on us. It became a mull
> Against our going and unfastened under us and
> Curdled from the stern. It shipped us at each blow.
> The brute weight
> Of the living sea wrought us, yet the boat sleeked lean
> Into it, upheld by the whole sea-brunt heaved,
> And hung on the swivelling tops...

and those lines are 'objective correlative' lines, they are statements towards constructing what the reader thinks of as the 'life' related to his own life of the senses. He can feel the sea and the way it behaves.

Now, Norman, to make this texture more 'speaking', more charged with whatever we try to send from one aloneness to another, we (I mean 'I'), at the same time try to say other things which, by their very nature necessitate another way of speaking. Therefore it happens that within this realist holocaust of describing the movement of the boat among the waters I let two or three or four or five or six or seven lines go which, in a way seem to be purely physical descriptive lines helping along the narrative. But always, always I make the other, more abstract voice speak. Maybe after three descriptive lines comes a line like –

> ... as the boat
> Takes the mild swell.

which is also descriptive. But suddenly followed by –

> ... and each event speaks through.
> They speak me thoroughly to my faintest breath.
> And for what sake? Each word is but a longing
> Set out to break from a difficult home. Yet in

Its meaning I am.

Norman Norman, to finish with what I feel now about this section. It is an attempt to relate the reader to something resembling his idea of the real world and at the same time say something like –

Leave him nor cup a hand to shout him out
Of that, his home, or if you would, O surely
There is no word,

There is not any to go over that.
It is now as always this difficult air
We look towards each other through. And is there
Some singing look or word or gesture of grace
Or naked wide regard from the encountered face
Goes ever true through the difficult air?
Each word speaks its own speaker to his death.

which is the 'message' statement (and please take note of the inverted commas there). The objective world constructed round the vision (allow that word) like the kernel round a nut.

Norman here is this fourth section. Now the rhythm and metre of this section is very unusual. This rhythm I took from an early poem I came across in the MSS of early Scots poetry, from the Bannatyne MS. Listen, here it goes with its strange two line choruses in the middle.

Only leaned at rest
Where my home is cast
Cannonwise on silence
Or the serving distance.

(This is the strange two line chorus)

O my love keep the day
Leaned at rest, leaned at rest.

Only breathed at ease
In that loneliness
Bragged into a voyage
On the maintaining image.

O my love, there we lay
Loved alone, loved alone.

Only graced in my
Changing madman who
Sings but has no time
To divine my room.

O my love, keep the day
Leaned at rest, leaned at rest.

What one place remains
Home as darkness quickens?

So my dear Norman, here is this section in the poem, like a quick unexpected movement in a sonata following something which of course, is not a bit like that. Here it is with no time or place implied. It isn't night or day, there is no sensual construction. It is an attempt (if we take it as one poem) to make a texture of communication which will be valid because of its 'idea' statement. And not rest on only the 'objective correlative' place which is made. It is to do with the fluidity of identity. It talks about how difficult it is for one half in us to try to find out what the other half is doing. We are always continually another. Each breath we take is taken into a new man. Or –

I bent to the lamp. I cupped
My hand to the glass chimney.
Yet it was a stranger's breath
From out of my mouth that
Shed the light. I turned out
Into the salt dark
And turned my collar up.

Now about this fifth section. This is my attempt to use the completely prose texture. Now, when I read this I read it easily, casually, the 'throwaway' delivery. Now, Norman, this is my speaking, as far as I can, away from the metrical beat.

So this is the place. This
Is the place fastened still with movement,
Movement as calligraphic and formal as
A music burned on copper.

The idea of prosaic speech is necessary surely somewhere within a poem a certain length.

Here is the section VI. I personally think that this section could exist as a poem on its own. There is hardly a thing I know about this 'bit' of poetry. There it is, in some ways more to do with me than all parts of my poem. To write those lines and use the 'of' as a preposition at the end of the line like –

Thus, shed into the industrious grave
Ever of my life, you serve the love
Whose motive we are energies of.

seems to have resulted in some kind of lyrical statement which is also formal and maybe even abstract. This section, more than any other section in The Nightfishing seems, for me, to stand alone and almost exist as a poem on its own. It has a quality which, since then, I have not been able to repeat.

Norman, with the last section the same thing operates as in the first. Obviously it is an equivalent to the first section. With the same use of the already made phrases like –

'the dead of night'

and even distorting those phrases to something like

Home becomes this place,
A bitter night ill
To labour at dead of.

So, my dear Norman & Isobel, this, in a kind of way helps your questions and I hope, for you, results in you being more curious and ready to hear how it comes out in the reading.

Of course, in some ways this poem is so far away that I can hardly anymore think of it as my own.

At the moment I am full of – THE DARK DIALOGUES which has just come out in Botteghe Oscure. In so many ways I think it is a better poem, as one should – we always think we (in intention at least) progress. But thinking of this good beginning, beginning –

I always meant to only
Language swings away
Further before me.

Language swings away
Before me as I go
With again the night rising

Up to accompany me
And that other fond
Metaphor, the sea.
Images of night
And the sea changing
Should know me well enough.

Norman, I enclose the pattern of the skirt which Isobel asked for. I have to finish now. I must light the lamps and the wind is rising.

love to you both – your old friend W S Graham or to you Isobel (I don't know why you went for that old bugger anyhow), Jock

CLUSTERS TRAVELLING OUT

1

Clearly I tap to you clearly
Along the plumbing of the world
I do not know enough, not
Knowing where it ends. I tap
And tap to interrupt silence into
Manmade durations making for this
Moment a dialect for our purpose.
TAPTAP. Are you reading that taptap
I send out to you along
My element? O watch. Here they come
Opening and shutting Communication's
Gates as they approach, History's
Princes with canisters of gas
Crystals to tip and snuff me out
Strangled and knotted with my kind
Under the terrible benevolent roof.
Clearly they try to frighten me
To almost death. I am presuming
You know who I am. To answer please
Tap tap quickly along the nearest
Metal. When you hear from me
Again I will not know you. Whoever
Speaks to you will not be me.
I wonder what I will say.

2

Remember I am here O not else
Where in this quick disguise, this very
Thought that's yours for a moment. I sit
Here behind this tempered mesh.

I think I hear you hearing me.
I think I see you seeing me.
I suppose I am really only about
Two feet away. You must excuse
Me, have I spoken to you before?
I seem to know your face from some
One else I was, that particular
Shadow head on the other side
Of the wire in the VISITORS ROOM

I am learning to speak here in a way
Which may be useful afterwards.
Slops in hand we shuffle together,
Something to look forward to
Behind the spyhole. Here in our concrete
Soundbox we slide the jargon across
The watching air, a lipless language
Necessarily squashed from the side
To make its point against the rules.
It is our poetry such as it is.
Are you receiving those clusters
I send out travelling? Alas
I have no way of knowing or
If I am overheard here.
Is that (It is.) not what I want?

The slaughterhouse is next door.
Destroy this. They are very strict.

3

Can you see my As and Ys semaphore
Against the afterglow on the slaughterhouse
Roof where I stand on the black ridge
Waving my flagging arms to speak?

4

Corridors have their character. I know well
The ring of government boots on our concrete.
Malcolm's gone now. There's nobody to shout to.
But when they're not about in the morning I shout
HOY HOY HOY and the whole corridor rings
And I listen while my last HOY turns the elbow
With a fading surprised difference of tone and loses
Heart and in dwindling echoes vanishes away.
Each person who comes, their purpose precedes them
In how they walk. You learn to read that.
Sometimes the step's accompanied by metal
Jingling and metrical, filled with invention.
Metal opened and slammed is frightening. I try
To not be the first to speak. There is nothing to say.
Burn this. I do not dislike this place. I like
Being here. They are very kind. It's doing me good.

5

If this place I write from is real then
I must be allegorical. Or maybe
The place and myself are both the one
Side of the allegory and the other
Side is apart and still escaped
Outside. And where do you come in
With your musical key-ring and brilliant
Whistle pitched for the whipped dog?

And stands loving to recover me,
Lobe-skewers clipped to his swelling breast,
His humane-killer draped with a badged
Towel white as snow. And listen,
Ventriloquized for love his words
Gainsay any deep anguish left
For the human animal. O dear night
Cover up my beastly head.

6

Take note of who stands at my elbow listening
To all I say but not to all you hear.
She comes on Wednesdays, just on Wednesdays,
And today I make a Wednesday. On and off
I decide to make her my half-cousin Brigit
Back from the wrack and shingle on the Long Loch.
You yourself need pretend nothing. She
Is only here as an agent. She could not
On her own carry a message to you either
Written or dreamed by word of her perfect mouth.

Look. Because my words are stern and frown
She is somewhere wounded. She goes away. You see
It hasn't been a good Wednesday for her. For you
Has it been a good Wednesday? Or is yours Tuesday?

7

When the birds blow like burnt paper
Over the poorhouse roof and the slaughter
House and all the houses of Madron,
I would like to be out of myself and
About the extra, ordinary world
No matter what disguise it wears
For my sake, in my love.

It would be better than beside the Dnieper,
The Brahmaputra or a green daughter
Tributary of the Amazon.

But first I must empty my shit-bucket
And hope my case (if it can be found)
Will come up soon. I thought I heard
My name whispered on the vine.

Surrounded by howls the double-shifting
Slaughterhouse walls me in. High

On the wall I have my blue square
Through which I see the London-Cairo
Route floating like distant feathers.

I hear their freezing whistles. Reply
Carefully. They are cracking down.
Don't hurry away, I am waiting for
A message to come in now.

1. W.S. Graham at Gurnard's Head 1958.

2. (above) Group of Students at Newbattle Abbey College c.1939.
W.S. Graham (top right). Nessie Dunsmuir (third from left).
3. (below left) Edwin Morgan.
4. (below right) No. 1 Hope Street, Greenock. The Graham family's front window was at the top left of the building.

5. Carrying fuel down to The Old Coastguard Houses 1958.

6. The Grahams singing in the Gurnard's Head Hotel 1958.

7. (above left) Michael Snow and Terry Frost in Frost's studio. 1953. 8. (above right) WS. Graham and Nancy Wynne-Jones in Michael Snow's studio, 1958. 9. (below left) Bryan Wynter in his studio at Zennor, 1960. 10. (below right) Sven Berlin working outside his Tower studio in St. Ives. c.1949.

11. W.S. Graham in 1959.

12. Roger Hilton.

13. Ronnie Duncan, 1993.

14. Robin Skelton, c.1959.

15. Ruth Hilton.

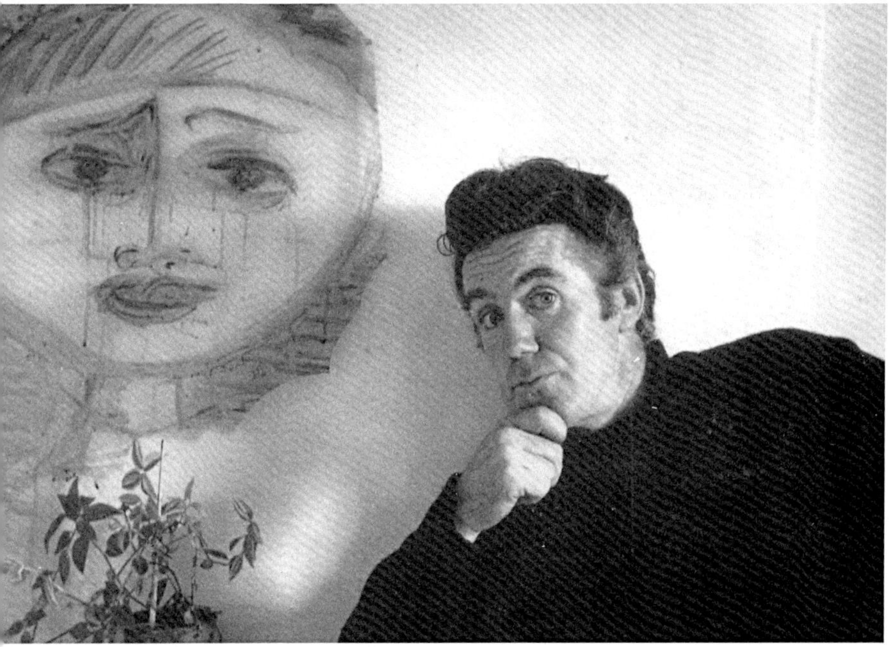

16. W.S. Graham with his painting on glass. 1958.

17. The installation constructed by W.S. Graham for his reading at Newlyn Art Gallery in 1960.

18. No.4, Mount View Cottages, in 1999.

19. Sydney and Nessie Graham outside their house c.1975.

Five

'MY COLD POEM' – MALCOLM MOONEY'S LAND
1961–1970

THE THERMAL STAIR

For the painter Peter Lanyon killed in a gliding accident 1964

I called today, Peter, and you were away.
I look out over Botallack and over Ding
Dong and Levant and over the jasper sea.

Find me a thermal to speak and soar to you from
Over Lanyon Quoit and the circling stones standing
High on the moor over Gurnard's Head where some

Time three foxglove summers ago, you came.
The days are shortening over Little Parc Owles.
The poet or painter steers his life to maim

Himself somehow for the job. His job is Love
Imagined into words or paint to make
An object that will stand and will not move.

Peter, I called and you were away, speaking
Only through what you made and at your best.
Look, there above Botallack, the buzzard riding

The salt updraught slides off the broken air
And out of sight to quarter a new place.
The Celtic sea, the Methodist sea is there.

You said once in the Engine
House below Morvah
That words make their world
In the same way as the painter's
Mark surprises him
Into seeing new.
Sit here on the sparstone
In this ruin where
Once the early beam
Engine pounded and broke
The air with industry.

Now the chuck of daws
And the listening sea.

'Shall we go down' you said
'Before the light goes
And stand under the old
Tinworkings around
Morvah and St Just?'
You said 'Here is the sea
Made by alfred wallis
Or any poet or painter's
Eye it encountered.
Or is it better made
By all those vesselled men
Sometime it maintained?
We all make it again.'

Give me your hand, Peter,
To steady me on the word.

Seventy-two by sixty,
Italy hangs on the wall.
A woman stands with a drink
In some polite place
And looks at SARACINESCO
And turns to mention space.
That one if she could
Would ride Artistically
The thermals you once rode.

Peter, the phallic boys
Begin to wink their lights.
Godrevy and the Wolf
Are calling Opening Time.
We'll take the quickest way
The tin singers made.
Climb here where the hand
Will not grasp on air.
And that dark-suited man
Has set the dominoes out

On the Queen's table.
Peter, we'll sit and drink
And go in the sea's roar
To Labrador with wallis
Or rise on Lanyon's stair.

Uneasy, lovable man, give me your painting
Hand to steady me taking the word-road home.
Lanyon, why is it you're earlier away?
Remember me wherever you listen from.
Lanyon, dingdong dingdong from carn to carn.
It seems tonight all Closing bells are tolling
Across the Duchy shire wherever I turn.

The fifteen year interval between the publication of *The Nightfishing* in 1955 and the appearance of *Malcolm Mooney's Land* in 1970 has sometimes been perceived as an indication of some interruption in Graham's creativity. It was not really so. 'Letter X' and 'The Constructed Space' appeared in 1958 and his important 'The Dark Dialogues' was printed in *Botteghe Oscure* in 1959. During the next ten years he wrote 'Malcolm Mooney's Land' (1966), 'The Beast In The Space' and 'Five Visitors To Madron' (1967), 'Clusters Travelling Out' (1968), 'Johann Joachim Quantz's First Lesson' and 'The Fifteen Devices' (all first published in 1969). Many of these poems were published in magazines in Britain and abroad and all have come to be seen as very strongly individual and central to an understanding of his later work.

Perhaps it is also possible to see 1955–70 as a period in which the 'centre of gravity' of the poetry undergoes a subtle shift. The wild sea of 'The Nightfishing' is, to a degree, external to the speaker though readily transformable into the metaphor for an inner journey. By the time we reach the explorer in 'Malcolm Mooney's Land' it is more evident that the territory being visited is the inner consciousness of the poet and the perils of communication, for which the arctic wastes provide an apt parallel and a suitably spartan discipline.

In February 1961 Graham visited Iceland, sponsored by the painter Nancy Wynne-Jones. He later complained of the difficulties of communication in a land which had no pubs (his habit of abruptly striking up very personal conversations with complete strangers in pubs was a defence against loneliness and well-intentioned, if not always well-timed). He did enjoy making a boat trip right round the island, however. Accounts of polar exploration or indeed expeditions of any kind were amongst his favourite reading.

He was critical of Captain Scott because he believed that he had not taken sufficient care of his men but Nansen he much admired as a humane leader, responsible for his companions and combining literary gifts with practical ability.

By 1962 the difficulties of living at Gurnard's Head with no personal transport had become tedious. Nessie Graham had been working in St Ives and was able to get back to the Coastguard house only at intervals. She had also been ill. Nancy Wynne-Jones had moved from St Ives to a large house in the country at Trevaylor, near Penzance, and the Grahams were invited to live with her there for a time. Later they moved into The Little House or Lodge on the other side of the road, which they called Woodfield. Graham appears to have made the move from Gurnard's Head by abandoning everything not immediately needed and walking out leaving the door open and clothes, books, papers behind. A fresh start.

Wynne-Jones took the Grahams to Greece in 1964 for six weeks. The island of Crete made a particularly deep impression on him and in July 1970 he mentions work on 'a little piece called A Dream Of Crete' which was his fifth attempt on the same theme.[1] Four drafts for this poem are in the collection of Ronnie Duncan, others at the University of Victoria BC and elsewhere, but no final version is known.

In June 1965 Graham was 'writing a long poem in the form of a diary written by an explorer lost in the Arctic'[2] and this, 'Malcolm Mooney's Land', the title poem of his next collection, was completed by January 1966. In February that year he was writing 'The Greenock Dialogues'. The following year Wynne-Jones purchased a small end-of-terrace granite cottage in the village of Madron, just north of Penzance. The Grahams were able to live there rent-free for the rest of their lives. Less than a quarter of a mile away stood the forbidding walls of the old Poorhouse where Alfred Wallis, fisherman and painter, had died in August 1942. In later years the Poorhouse was replaced by a home for the elderly but since that period it has been a slaughterhouse for animals, an irony which for Graham was inescapable and one which he used to great effect in his poem 'Clusters Travelling Out'.[3] Other images suggestive of harsh bureaucracy and confinement recurred in his notebooks over the next few years.[4] The verse printed below was found amongst his papers in 1996.

What is your name? Sign here.
What is your Cause? Sign here.
Name? Wife's name? Sign here.
Possessions? Sign here.
Empty your pockets of all
Signs that you were ever
A man of some worth
To somebody a dear.
Climate too hot for you?
Sign here. Sign here. Sign here.
Why have you taken away
My shirt and my trousers?
I am not used to being
Naked and you looking
At me like this. I can't.
Sign here. Sign here. Sign here.

Penguin Modern Poets 17, containing selections from David Gascoyne, W.S.Graham and Kathleen Raine was published in 1970. Graham mentions finishing another long poem, 'Implements In Their Places', in October this year and his collection of poems entitled *Malcolm Mooney's Land* also appeared in 1970.

1 Letter to Ruth Hilton and John Beckett, 13 July 1970.
2 Letter to Elizabeth Smart, 11 June 1965.
3 *Poetry* (Chicago) vol. 112, no. 3 (1968).
4 Examples are 'The Slaughterhouse' (1969), 'The Prisoner' (1970) and 'Fill In This Form'(1971) from the collection *Aimed at Nobody* (London, 1993).

96. *To Nessie Graham*

24 February 1961 Friday — Reykjavik, Iceland

Dear Ness,

Certainly into the wilderness I have gone. Reykjavik what a semi-American wilderness it is. No one have I met. No drink. Ice cream good. Girls all with snubnoses small. A city of teen agers and the longest American loudspeaking cars I have ever. I am not in the slightest re-orientated, (by the way, I know as I write it is not like me. Even my handywriting). I have been to the British Council. A dead loss. It was the assistant. He was as unhelpful as anything. I said are there any young Icelandic writers interesting. Or people who know the English. Says he O I don't see much of those characters. There he was dressed in a fitting tweed suit with a moustache and being a dope. He was no help. The town seems crowded with teenagers in the American style (a wee bit dated). The restaurants are impossibly dear and I haven't struck one yet which is supposed to serve drinks. And there's no place to meet anybody, no pubs, no beer. I've been about the [Scottish] islands with too much drink and here there is none. And nobody to talk to. I go on tonight to a small fishing village about 30 miles away. I come back on Sunday and catch a boat on Monday to take me up the west coast and right round the coast of Iceland. That will take I think a week or two. Most people don't understand English and the few who do make me have to learn American. There is so far nobody nobody nobody and that is maybe a good thing. The islands were fine but too much of the drink. It's all true about the hospitality. It's great here to see the great snow-rising peaks.

The great difficulty is at night, after being around all day, with no one to speak to. I have been going to bed at 9.30 and rising at 8. This my wee Brer, is not a good letter, still it is me in a kind of a way. Write me post restante – Reykjavik. love, BB.

97. *To the Editor, The Times Literary Supplement*

21 January 1965 — Woodfield, Gulval, Penzance, Cornwall

Sir, –

I have just returned from Greece to find in the TLS a poem – 'In Memoriam – Burns Singer', by W.S.Graham. I wish to state that this was not submitted by me.

These words were written for fun ten years ago in an Aberdeen pub. Jimmy (Singer) wrote one for me too and we both decided they were impossible. I saw Burns Singer about three months before his death and he suggested it was worth publishing. I disagreed completely.

The thing is that this poem is not representative of any work I have done or do now and, as such, will give a wrong idea of the kind of poet I am.

I hope sometime to write a poem for Burns Singer which will be adequate.

W.S.GRAHAM.

98. *To Tom Scott*

31 January 1965 Gulval

Dear Tom Scott,

how good it is to hear from you. How much has run under how many brigs since I had word from you last. I had heard from various people that things were going very well with you and I have seen good poems and, Tom, I am happy to hear it. This winter day we sit in the kitchen with the lentil broth on the boil and Nessie (She stops me to say that she sends her love.) furious at the starlings taking every scrap she put out for the faethered songsters of every tribe. Then hark hark, Tom, with your shellike baritone lugs and I'll carol businesslike with my tenor brain. Ready.

A nice thing, to be in the Oxford Book Of Scottish Verse. Your choice, Tom, would not have been mine but that is always so. I would have liked one of the Ballads seen more in Scotland but I suppose they are too long. Or an excerpt from THE DARK DIALOGUES which so far has only appeared in BOTTEGHE OSCURE a few years ago. No matter. Fair enough. The fee has to go to Faber. I would like to correct the proofs. So often there are mistakes.

Yes, what a sad shock for Jimmy [Burns Singer] to die suddenly. I was at the funeral in Plymouth. Marie was there, of course, and some BBC friends and Robert Frame. Back at the house in Plymouth Robert and I sang some Scottish airs and the gathering was a wee bit like a wake which Jimmy would not have thought bad. The cause of death was 'heart failure' and Marie *insisted* we see the death certificate.

Congratulations, Tom, on the son and twin dochters. The gentle wife, I presume you have got, what's her name? I'm pleased about the Fergusson book. I think you're a good man to do it. Well good-luck to your projects.

Myself, I'm writing again and I'm not falling down my life quite so steeply. Can you suggest any magazine in Scotland with fairly wide circulation which might be interested in printing THE DARK DIALOGUES even although it has appeared in B.O.? For me it is the best poem I've written and I would like it known in Scotland.

My regards to your wife & bairns, love, Sydney

99. *To Tom Scott*

19 February 1965 Gulval

Dear Tom,

sorry to take so long. After considering various possible 'notes' to introduce THE DARK DIALOGUES excerpt I think it would be better not to attempt any description of the other sections of the poem. I would rather you didn't introduce it as autobiographical. I mean sections ii and iii. Even these two sections, although only part of the whole poem, will be what they are to the reader as he finds them. Any indication from me of what I think the other sections are would curtail the reader's imagination and the outcome of the poetry would not be purely his, as it should always be. Therefore how about something like

Two Sections of THE DARK DIALOGUES
(The complete poem is 250 lines long
and is in four sections.)

I take it you will be numbering the sections ii and iii.

Aye. Sydney

100. *To Elizabeth Smart*

11 June 1965 Gulval

My dear Elizabeth,

A quick SOS. I know it's a long shot but you just might be able to help. I need some methedrine or something of that school. I've been taking one a morning for the last year and suddenly the source is dried up and I need some to keep things going till I can arrange a more permanent supply. I just don't want to get a big fatso and my poor Scotch brain like a pudding. The one in the morning started me off at my writing and kept my brain a wee bit lean. See what you can do, Elizabeth. I thought surely you must know someone. A sad thing for me to be writing you after so long and then to be asking for something.

I have a long poem (in the form of a diary written by an explorer lost in the Arctic – sounds cornier than it is) about half finished I think. Elizabeth, if you can, will you phone me on Monday and let me know. I write this late at night with the owls calling and the sashes rattling. Love, Sydney

101. *To John Knight*

29 September 1965

LINES FOR NOTHING
For John Mid Knight

Lying easy on the verge of sleep
Beside the one who has loved me longer
Than most (Nessie), the owls began
Calling and calling from Trevaylor Wood.
Reach out to me from the verge of -where
You are, John and from what you are.
From me today feeling better.
I mean tonight feeling better.
I mean at this breath feeling better.

Well, you old bugger, winemaker, you.
October's castle clouds are slow and rampant.
The tides are in the neap with a roaring sea.
The owl calls from the naked-woman tree.

The 'naked-woman tree' is true. I found
Down in the wood a great beech carved
With a woman on the bark. Her attitude
Was pranced there and stationary. And yet
Always in movement as the slow tree
Thickened round and warted, a woman swollen
Out of her time and into something far

Removed from the fashion of that early fist
Of that long-dead first enthusiast.

Well, John anyhow, it's such a good stock subject for a poem that it's almost impossible to write. You will know well what I mean. It doesn't come from inside enough. Send me a bottle of your wine if you can spare it.

I've been very low creatively but in the last month or two the muse seems to be becoming cuffed or kissed or cowed into some respect for me, although we both know well that the muse is uncuffable, uncowable and (is it true?) unkissable. Remember Keats' Belle Dame. I've been bad at letters but please try John, and send a wee line and say what is going on. I wrote Fraser about you with no result I'm afraid, as far as I know. I heard from afar that Michael Snow and Margaret have a child. I don't know what sex. A great thing ALWAYS.

love to yourself and Rina and from Nessie. Sydney

102. *To Roger Hilton*

19 November 1965 Gulval

Dear Roger,

your letter distresses me and I hope you're seeing things worse than they are. You are still the same person with all your worth and surely this is just a difficult bit on the route, with all the various setbacks coming at once. Maybe, I hope, this is just a low point, Roger. To come down here might be the beginning of a new order. There's no reason why it shouldn't go well. Those other people you mention. You have certainly won their alienation. They don't like their smug false lives to be disturbed. You make them uneasy and remind them that they have given up the best, most difficult way. Your kind of honesty is expensive. Your behaviour censures them and in their hearts they don't take it lightly and by God they will make you pay. Those people want to be left to travel comfortably on their own wee rails they have laid down for safety's sake. God forbid I should ever be a bucker-up, Roger, but I mean I think this is just a momentary anger of the fates.

I know this is presumptuous and terrible but I am your friend and should be allowed to say those things. You are twice the worth of all those careful boys and things are due to get better. You'll work better once you're settled and there needn't be the big oblivion drinking and I hope greater order will come about. Forgive this smuggy letter, difficult to write when I hear from you so worried.

love to Fergus, Rose and Bo and yourself, and thanks very much for the birthday present, Sydney

103. *To Roger Hilton*

19 November 1965 3 o'clock Gulval

Dear Roger,

having returned from Penzance and celebrating my birthday and having with me two bottles of cheap sherry and Nessie putting two bloaters under the grill and the rain kettle-drumming the window and my shirt changed and the music of the old master baiters coming from the marconigraph and my 47 year old brain buzzing like a hive of bees, I sit down to type you out a PS to the other letter.

I wish you didn't think those last poems were too obscure. I thought I was making some headway in uniting you with another medium viz poetry. You can't have it completely understood in that way all the time. Allow yourself to encounter the mystery occasionally and don't ask the thing from an object which it is not. I don't know much about painting but at least I don't encounter the painting asking for what it is not made to give. Fuck the aesthetics. I'll drink another sweet half glass of the stuff and look out there at the finches spinning on the whorl. Enough.

What are you doing at the moment? Keep your weapons of love in good order and your humour ready for any oldmanic depression. Enter dancing bears and dogs. Clowns tumble in. The elephant trumpets the saddest cry on earth. The wind whines through the dikes on Botallack. Times remembered burrow away in the brain.

Ness says the bloaters are ready. Maybe it is better. Maybe that is enough in case I make a Celtic fool of myself to the English. Remind me to yourself. The day is dull and getting on to dusk. Fight the good fight. Poridge brother, do not stumble. Do you think the activity of the spirit is here to stay? Lobster your claws in a farewell wave. I'm off. Sydney

104. *To Ruth Hilton*

19 January 1966

Today, Wednesday, I decided to phone Ruth who continually surprises the moment with her presence [...]

I finished my Cold poem and here it is. I think I was feeding on it too long and living on the bits and pieces and notes instead of seeing it as a whole object with its own characteristic shape and length. It's finished and I'm happy about it. I think, as you say, it's a well-made piece and its mystery keeps its place. I take a personal pride in that its 'voice' is like nobody else writing. By the way, Elizabeth is nothing to do with any Elizabeth I know. I wanted a woman's name that was rich on the lips and yet oldfashioned. I posted it off yesterday to a good American magazine which wants my poems. Also, a Canadian Magazine wants to 'feature my work' and a selection of earlier poems with biographical note and photograph has gone off. So there you are, my deario and now, having cleared the decks, I stand before the good silence allowed to begin with any strange first line of words that speak for me. Are you there? Are you there?

My dear, I hope you had (How belated a procrastinator can you get?) a good Christmas and Hochmagandy Hogmanay with goodies and the hard stuff and music and love. A good old generous thing you are I do my gosh declare. Thanks for the five pounds and presents and goodies and that sudden, recent two.

We had a Christmas Day with Roger, quite good and saw them twice at New Year. And we were over once since then and there is a painter they met in France staying with them and he was a pleasant man Roger was quieter and for once the day didn't descend into the maelstrom. The cottage is taking shape slowly although Rose's[1] love of, and Roger's adoption of, the beat disorder is apparent. I'm sad to hear you saying your escape route is cut off because Roger's there. Do you think he would really bother you much? My dear, I think of it as such a great happy place up there at Croftpool and if I'm in the neighbourhood I can't bear to think of you not there.

Lucky Travelling Musician you. Bon appetit et tres bon soif. Mangare bene. Snuggle me with you through the customs in your fiddle-case or in the depths of your Freudian rummaged handbag. Big nose and small nose, what a team we'd make, baby. Wrap me

1 Refers to Rosemary Phipps, Roger Hilton's second wife.

up with your resin and tuck me in your exalted bosom. If you look around in Trieste you should see signs of the East, a Turkishness. Yugoslavia, I'm sure, is very different from Italy. The place-names on either side of the Adriatic are very different. The Easterness of Greece was exciting. Everywhere you walk in Venice is beautiful.

Ruth, I miss you as always, my dear,
even in my happier moments. love, Sydney

105. *To Ruth Hilton*

24 January 1966

Dear Ruth,

only to say I am thinking of you today now having fed the finches at least I mean having put out some suet and bread for them to treat if they will as part of nature's bounty. Half drunk this morning I write to you after a late late night with your late late husband[1] and what a terrible bore it was. Comic as it is, I think he really would like to destroy me and I believe he thinks he will. He underestimates me hugely. My dear, my dear, it is the old swan of Sibelius which glides in my ear at the moment. A fine invention.

A poor old baritone boy is singing on the invention [radio]. He's not good. There's something missing. Apart from whether the singer takes liberties with the music the listener asks for a certain authority in the man behind the song who is always necessarily present. When a good singer puts the first note down the listener should be able to give himself up to a new inevitability of experience. WOW WOW. OK. Oh God! Ruth he's on again. Let me look up his name. It's Ron Gamack. He sings in a 'trained' way. There's nothing there. I'll leave it. Great enjoyment recently on the music programme. Great Beethoven and Mozart (OK I know they're safe people to like.) and Janacek and Stravinsky. Christ they're certainly plugging the English composers those days.

Electric plankton. Gigantic microcosm. Speckled colliding nebulae. The little shocks in the labyrinths of the silent areas. Kandinsky's dredge from the nether deep. Love me a little in your labyrinths and keep me in your glands.

I've just been telling Nessie that she's lucky. Why? To have me

1 Ruth and Roger Hilton were divorced in 1963.

around so human and with a sense of the comic and with such sweetness ready to be tapped. I suppose last night with your late friend has made me a self-hugging smug champion of order. I like you fine. Can you hear the whisky in the words? If you read poetry well you should be able to. Art expression is a voice between two things. Abstract formality and the very human gesture. And one doesn't work without the other.

Farewell Farewell. Somebody has come in with a bottle of whisky. (Not Rog.) Don't think the drink will kill me. Anyhow Anyhow this is a note to go with that belated letter. Forgive me not saying anything. I would rather make my typewriter work towards yourself than anyone else. My birds, old greedy buggers, have had their little human-contaminated bit. Keep me there in the every surprising moment of your life.

my dear, by by, Sydney

I hear Rose[1] is coming down, I hope Roger takes her over to see us.

P.S. Ruth write a wee bit from somewhere where you are going. Write a wee note before you go. love – Sydney

106. *To John Knight*

5 February 1966 — Gulval

My dear good Knight,

Nessie and I have just turned the invention off and what a great pleasure it was, John, to hear your good poems. The statements came out with a good poetic shock and each poem's shape was both satisfying and astonishing. They had the timbre of authority and, for me, the reading could not have been bettered. You were lucky, whoever chose him. He was just formal and casual to a nice degree. This reading of your work, of that length, really made an impact on me stronger than before of the characteristic 'voice' of John Knight. It should help to hasten attention on you and the awareness of having more ears cocked to your word is good for the word. THE TROUSERED GODS, What a good title. A program you should certainly feel good about. Nessie sat spellbound with her Scottish shell-likes drinking deep.

1 Daughter of Ruth and Roger Hilton.

Goodknight, Goodknight, my nachtegale,
        My homemade wine and Tod.
    Wee moosie scrambles under the leaves
        Neath the eye of the Owl God.
Love from us both and to sweet Rina, Sydney

107. *To Roger Hilton*

THE WALRUS & THE HUNTING DOG

And then not long ago, certain articles
Were discovered by the natives,
Among them the peak of a cap on which
Was the name of one of the crew of the Jeannette.

Thursday, December 21st. It is
Extraordinary, after all, how the time passes.
Here in the dark air the pressure
Shuffles the breaking ice like cards.

Here grey claw-hammer head from folds
Of blubber bull-fat barked across
Black water leads. The walrus spoke
Meaning no harm, in fact to help
His unblubbered friend, lonely afloat
There on his blown floe of love.

'Hello Hello', the great poor beast
Shouted across the Arctic air
'Hello', he shouted between his tusks,
'Roger Hilton, are you there?'

But canine Hilton, he kept mum
And fastened up his parka toggles.
From all around the ice dazzle
Sparked against his snow-goggles.

Nor human sound was heard there
Except the blood-roar in his veins,
And, caught within the grumbling pack
Ice, he drifted from his friends.

A walrus has his feelings too,
And sensitive his blubbered life.
Hush. He hears the distant crack
Of whips and fears the skinning knife.

He shouts once more 'Hilton Old Chap'
And being a beast he cannot weep.
So the poetic walrus slides
Into the dark Arctic deep.

WSGraham
7 – 2 – 66

108. *To Tom Scott*

18 February 1966 Gulval

Dear Tom,

Just to say I am well in the middle of a new poem called THE GREENOCK DIALOGUES which is allowing me to express some part of me which I have always wanted to. Your suggestion, that THE DARK DIALOGUES might be a kind of 1st Quartet had something to do with it. How's things? How is the anthology coming on? I have a new long poem coming out in America soon, MALCOLM MOONEY'S LAND. Love from Nessie and myself, Sydney

109. *To Ruth Hilton* (extract)

[21 March 1966]

– My poetry's proceeding under a full head of steam and it is constantly astonishing to find how much I really have in me to say. In writing poetry the mind taps mysterious cisterns. My little step cistern of the Collective Farms sits on her Steppes of grief. Gorki is gone and the tractors pivot where once the thunder and jingle of the cartridge-belted cossacks went. The bulbul sings in Samarkand and splits the sunflower seeds. Dan Cupid flies with curly knees firing his wee bow wildly in all directions. Spring is nigh. The cuckoo calls, seesaw seesaw. Dog at Botallack [Roger Hilton] skulks, snarls, fouls his kennel, tailwags, schemes against undogs, distempers, worries, seizes the poor unwary traveller and overlaps his whisky bowl. –

110. *To Ruth Hilton* (extract)

13 October 1966 Gulval

This is the morning here and because we have no electric fire we have already been out for kindling and started the fire up and String Quartet in B flat Major, Op.130 of master bate hoven is interfering with my intention. Send me in your next letter a quote from the FLUTE BOOK [J.J.Quantz]. I've put an aerial on my Marconi invention and the music program is louder and clearer. What a great invention it is. I still am able to think of it as freshly as the desert island savage. How does art be able to come through the empty spaces, the whirling spaces of air, through the walls and over the mountains? I can I tune in to LOVE? Christ! This is the last movement. Why am I so lazy why am I not aware more the intended shape of the musical object? It takes an effort of memory to 'observe' the musical object as one object. I know you know you know. Forgive your bad old frrrrrrrrrrriend.

111. *To Ronnie Duncan*

22 October 1966 Gulval

Dear Ronnie Duncan,

Here now take this magazine into your busy politician, painting-lover, poetry-lover, Greek-lover, camping-lover hand and remind yourself and make use of MALCOLM MOONEY'S LAND.[1] I always gain by the enthusiasm of your visits. As an 'appreciative audience' you are a difficult poet's dream. Our night out and back here was a good rich night filled with all the various ingredients. Take it easy. Here is also a not very clean copy of THE BEAST IN THE SPACE. I think you should have it because you liked the strangeness of it (although, I suppose, every poem should have a strangeness) and remember (although you mustn't let the possible meaning of the poem *for you* be curtailed) that the poem is about the difficulty of thorough communication. OK. OK.

Shut up. Shut up. Give him your love.

We are now, Ronnie, on the brink of being shot through the puffed-wheat gun (read the story on the P.W. packet) from our Woodfield home. Of course it's worrying but it is exciting

1 Mooney's Bar in Oxford Street, London, was a well-known resort for writers.

wondering what kind of broch or fogou or butanben or bungalow or cot or cave or paper-mache RETREAT we will end up in. God! It would be lovely to live for a while in Heraklion. Anyhow it's not all that important where we are as long as the Muse knows my whereabouts. 'Today, Tuesday, I decided to move on.' I would really like to have a castle with drawbridge and portcullis.

Let me hear from you, although I don't know what you would write to me about. Give my love to wee sweet Henriette and take some for yourself.

Your bardic friend, Sydney

Ronnie, it's a month later, the house seems to be coming along, near Crowlas. I send this to you now across the plains and shires of England. You're all right. Love, Sydney.

Ness sends her love. She's been ill with pleurisy but is now mending. I hope she mends in time before our exodus. . . .

112. *To Roger Hilton*

24 October 1966 Gulval

Dear Roger,

what a carry on. And yet although it's terrible to bear for you I'm so relieved it wasn't longer.[1] Heavens, it could have been two or three months. Maybe the hospital will not be so grim. After a day or two you might find some kind of things interesting to observe and let me know about it all when you come out. Poor old boy. Remember we will be thinking about you often, at all odd times of the day with love and always respect. I will write you as often as I am allowed to. You'll probably come out in fine trim physically at least. And maybe mentally you won't be killed-off to the extent you think. And Boots [Mary Redgrave] sends her love specially and remember you are better loved by more people than you think.

We'll do all we can to keep Rose from being too lonely. I *am* pleased you decided that Rose shouldn't leave Botallack. Maybe we can visit you at Exeter if we could be certain of finding you in. Ness is here sending her love and cheerio for now,

your chum, Sydders.

1 After two convictions for driving when drunk, Roger Hilton was eventually sent to Exeter Prison where he spent six weeks before being referred to St Lawrence's Hospital, Bodmin.

113. *To Roger Hilton*

26 October 1966 Gulval

Dear Roger,

with great difficulty, because Fergus (Who will ride with?) is putting his fingers among the typewriter works, I ask you how you are there in your double prison. The Hilton Gaol and the Exeter Gaol. Can you hold this paper with your manacled hands? Shall I parachute down to see you from the flying machine and say hello? Shall I start an underground tunnel here from Gulval? Shall I drop you a case of blondes? Would you like some squid done in deep fat and well battered in the Greek way? Keep your pecker up, O ye gates. Ye gates that last for aye. Be lifted up that so the king of Glory enter may. Here come the angels with their jingling keys to take our temperatures. The sky outside is the same sky. The lovers in the shadows are the same lovers . The prisoner in the mind is the same prisoner. What terrible drivel from so great a poet as me. Forgive me, Rog. The juices of dusk are flowing and the Autumn rooks are calling like breaking stones. Lift me your eyebrows. Count a hundred. Santa Claus is coming doon the chimney. Could you maybe get your various veins seen to and your divers wounds of your rough life and Daniel Druff and your hammer-claw-toes? My fetishes are sweating in the darkened ward of my brain. I face the stretching Rogerless night. But good old Resilient boy, you.

Who will wave the flag from the top of the Hilton stone mountain? Who will paint the target? Who will light the fire with a single (non-safety) match? Who who who will keep Sidder's interest up in the eldrich hours? Who will pee beyond the bowl? Who will anything better or almost as good as me yours truly come the boy?

O hogtied friend, keep the fort. I can't think how to write properly to you yet. Be tolerant. Take it easy (How easy to say). Are you allowed to write back? If you can reply reply.

Nessie is shelling beans. I am shelling the ramparts of silence. Where are the sons of seeing? And where does the lonely maker of the reflecting object lie? (Rather Blakean, what?) OK dear R.

O please, not-rock-bottom, chum, already maybe there is something of interest around you to see. As the Claustra wears away the mind of the German snow-prisoner walking soldier appears.[1] Maybe? Fire me a prisoner's arrow with a message. Do keys jingle and cell-

1 Hilton had been a prisoner of war for three years.

doors clang? I hope you're not interfering with the male-bags. Put out your tongue. Say ninetynine and cough. Spare a thought or two for those bereft outside the municipal walls. Ness goes about busy and worrying about it all I mean your impossible self.

Make me a drawing of at least your best breath. How can I say how we miss you, my prim old creature. Try to reply. The next letter will be better. Let me know within a few days if you get this letter. At least tell Rose, if you can't write to me. When this is over maybe it will be a better time for you. My good old boy, cheerio for now. love – Sydney.

114. *To Roger Hilton* (extract)

1 November [1966] WOODFIELD GULVAL PENZANCE
A RAINY BITTER DAY

Dear Roger,

thanks for your amusing letter. I see prison has helped your calligraphy. Nessie's in bed with a bit pleurisy and I am the nurse, cooking and keeping the ward tidy and keeping the patient 'cheery'. As you say, if the choice is Bodmin or prison, certainly Bodmin. By the way, if you produce any drawings which are valuable to you, say for later works, will you be allowed to take them out? I mean from where you are? Draw me your cell, deep draughtsman. Are you getting enough books? What kind of things would you like to read? Light or heavy or in between? Or something with art reproductions? A good master's pigments know their own sty. The good model envies the easel. The good painter's brushstroke continually answers the questions of the brushstrokes preceding it. Hark tis the russel of flint. A cleft palette colours its own language. A painter must keep his eye halfdry. The good draughtsman knows when he's come to the end of the line and shady characters should use the rubber generously. Shall the Constable's trees be cut down or the Turner's sunsets darken away to their natural home of night? Shall the cavalier laugh himself into a fit? Had Van Gogh an ear for music?

Tom, Mix your colours well with Pearl White. What a twittering machine, old Rog, I have become to try to entertain my frriend. Who will entertain me in my prison with no bars but myself. Being a painter you could always say 'I am framed in guilt'. Ho Ho. You're never a great mister till you've gone to the mortal Klee. Gone is the

Cezanny boy with the appling brush. And William Wallis and Stonewall Jackson Pollard. And Crome and gentle waving Palmer of the moonlight baaing river of sheep. Marc's blue horses prance on the abstract eye and Rousseau's lion forever sniffs at the gipsy girl in the desert lying with her stringed instrument. Gallop and gallop ye horsemen of the apoplexy. A strange route round by the desolate beach under the mewing cries of the flying tamarisk. Enough. Hello.

115. *To Roger Hilton*

7 November 1966 Gulval

Dear Roger,

Fergus is not a very good eater anyhow. I've given him good old Graham scrambled egg. We are here and I am very aware of the space which is Hilton. This at the moment is a news letter. NEWS. NEWS. NEWS.

Nessie's Xray means, thank goodness, only pleurisy, not so bad. We have a house near Crowlas. For good or bad there it is. I will make something of it. You must help me. With advice and maybe some mural or something.

Damn you anyhow. I am sick of it. Here I am wanting to enjoy my little conversations and Rose can only talk of your impossible self. Here is what Rose says – 'There I was, shopping in St. Just with Fergus, waiting for the 10b. It was raining. I was standing, in the front there sheltering in the entrance with the bare square in front of me when a large whisky was thrust into my willing hands. The man, who knew you well, said 'When you see Hilton please tell him that all the boys are thinking of him.' And then I went on the bus with all the housewives and shopping and I felt it was a good thing, you and I, and that we were part of the place no matter how extreme we might have thought we behaved.'

So that is that, my dear old Dog O.[1] I am no good reporting, of course. (From that phrase 'Of course' I have been away from this letter for 2 1/2 hours. Ask where I have been.)

I have been to see what the new house will be like in Crowlas. It's not bad. Anywhere becomes home quicker than we expect. It's

1 Graham frequently called Hilton 'Dog', a reference to his friend's perceived cynicism.

not the best, old boy, but the heart (or is it the mind) is resilient. The rooms seem small and dark. That is to be expected after here. The loud road roars not far away. There is no land we can make a garden. The pub is too near. The rooks do not call in my language. The cows moo differently. I suppose that the mice and rats, however they move in the breathing dead of night, move in a Crowlas way.[1] Godforbidus. Forbiduswhat? Answer me that, my artistic jailbird friend. Tell me, old fellow, have you made any good friends or foes? You must find something of interest which you haven't told me yet. If one could be taken in for one's thoughts I would be in having the birch or the cat or the rack or the Chinese water drops on my poor old heid. O Tam. O Tam, y'll get yer farin. In Hell they'll roast ye like a herrin. Are you going to take some cure or other? Are you worth curing? That must be thought about. Who measures us? For what reason are we here in this complicated weather of a world? Is there somebody who judges our each small secret gesture other than ourselves?

To be always alone is necessary.
One would not ever be otherwise.
Yet our nature is such that we
Want to share our souls with others.

OK OK a bit overblown speech, but it is approximately true, if I can say that. And what goes on in the Hilton brain? How are the labyrinths of tortured doubt? Are you going to utilise this experience to make you love other people less complicatedly? Remember the inner silence which is necessary to construct (Whether it has been destroyed, it can be put together again in a different way.) to meet the world of people always encircling us. I'm not very good at it myself. Take it easy till I get to another page.

What a lucky bugger you are to get such good letters. Maybe, old king of Botallack, you're worth it. Who knows. Who knows? Falling Falling Falling. Shades of Tennyson.

But to return to the main problem. Are we to be judged by our acquaintances? No. Let us be devils. Better, let us be monsters or monsteresses. With horns and tensile tails and musk glands and an odd number of legs like nine or fifteen and three eyes (the pineal eye) and a host of sexual members shaped in various devices. The human soul is as different as that from the other. I mean that the

1 The Grahams did not move to Crowlas.

shape of the soul of one's fellow would be frightening to behold. This is getting too deep for me, poor peasant from Scotland, a'canna thole it longer. The quiet night is later now.

I have written two poems called – READING JOHANN JOACHIM QUANTZ'S FLUTE BOOK, one and two. At the moment they seem good and say something I couldn't have said in any other way to anyone, which is one of the doubtful measurements of Art.

Whether it is a good thing or a bad thing, Roger, I have really become a man who only gets any significant 'kick' out of being in the world I write poetry from. It is my last habitat. This is whether I am any good or not.

I AM BECOMING TOO COHERENT IN THIS LETTER. I'LL FIX THAT

To make any thing of it do you want. Come out side there. Take off your glasses. Hand me your pencilsharpener. And stand up like the coalmoneymaker's son you are. FAIR.

The air I breathe is being rather difficult. The light is being rather difficult. The shapes of silence sliding past my ear go by in a way that is foreign to my sensibilities. WE NEVER DIED OF ART FAILURE YET. Lend me your painting I (eye) for a mo that I might look through it and distinguish the significant shapes of my always personal world.

'Who knows the rose or quotes her holy somersaults?' (from my first book of poems)

Think of your father and your matterhorn. Let us to the hills of swiss away. Blow me your mountain Voyage of the Bugle. What age is Eliot now? Pound your schillings in the countries of the low Dutch with Breugeled blind men among the round tables and the pies sticking on and the winterlandscape with a bird with a long tail hovering.

Sweetly sang Robin from his own wild wood.

And so the boy sang. And so the boy sang. O where did I go wrong? The same thing cannot be done. Nothing can be corrected. Only one has the choice of being a better man or not. I don't mean this morally. In our wee bit life we should try to be as aware of our surroundings as possible. Fuck it! It's true but pompous. I am beside you more or less always. Whatever happens we'll be in touch (a terrible expression) in Bodmin in prison or in your ain wee hoos. Think of your frrrrrrrrrrriend and give him your irresistible love.
Sydney

116. *To Ruth Hilton* (extract)

[7 January 1967] still Woodfield

– About Stevie Smith I really don't know. Some poems say something. Others don't. It isn't the kind of poetry which particularly interests me. Too aphoristic. It makes no place or time or other world for me. But that's only me and only her. Kirkegaard I haven't read. I suspect Bohme is better. Schoppenhauer and Hegel are very readable and exciting and have not dated. What they talk about is part of the foundation modern philosophy is built on. I am hoping Madron will make it easier to get books. –

117. *To Robert Brennan*

24 January 1967

If you want to be spoken to. alright. Here I am speaking, invisible to you on the other side of language. Ho Ho what man are you this morning as you read this and the labyrinth of your day complexes itself before you? House tricks? What's buzzin cousin? Keep of the gross. Spouting is forbidden. Beware of the god. Misquotes breed malaria. The camel will never go through the I of a noodle. O Rob, old boy, where is the oasis to be found? I'm only a Toerag drumming his derry over the ups and dunes of life. Vinegar my lips and lift me down from calvary. Put me in but never let them roll the stone away. Pale hands I love beside the Shalimar. And lo the poacher in the east has snared the wee sultan's tooer in a loop o' licht. And so we leave the bed o winies to their vastnesses of their beautiful Sahahahaharah. Albesynia. Chinchinchin.

I enjoyed your visit, Robert. You must come again. As a young man it strikes me you are excellently presentable. You must realise, of course, that if you arrive at this place from which I write you will find it vacant. In other words, we shall be no longer here. The cat, if we had a cat (Our last poor thing is in his feline Heaven, poor surly wee bugger.) will be found mewing and lost on the desolate hearth. You will hear the cheep chink cheep twit cheep of the bewildered crumbless finches. The rooms of air will be still and unbreathed by yours truly WSG. To put it blandly, the bard will have flown. I think we go tomorrow or the next. Dear Rob, I hope I find you well and family pleasantly living Life to the Fool. And how is the boy? And who (if you tried to tell) will ever know? Communication is what our lives are about. We must try. To be better or not doesn't matter. Measurement is out of our reach. One only tries to send a message, a note, however inadequate from one aloneness to another. STOP don't let me sound like Billygraham.

The best letters to write are the ones where you don't have to say anything. The best place is where we have never been. The one we love best we have never encountered. Maybe that is right. I wonder what I'll be when I grow up. I'll think it out. Tomorrow I'll do this. Tomorrow I'll do that. I'm just, today, crouching for the spring. To spring at/on what? Ah there's the bur! The clouds of heaven's high cirrus floor move slowly far beyond the edge of the winter wood. Bruegel has tampered with the perspective of the fields. The meadow is full of pies. A distant buzzard hangs in the unreal literary air. The blue of the sky beyond the clouds is a high thin sound. I hear it with my pupils twin enlarged. Across the glen the orange tractor turns like a pivoting ladybird at the end of the row and adjusts itself to another journey. From here I see him ploughing his stripes in the field surrounded by a bonfire of gulls and he is not thinking of me or you and should be ready for his dindins now don't you think old frrriend Rob?

Ta Ta. This is for nothing. A nightingale. A farthingale. A martingale. A fool Gael from the north. OK then. Nice to have had this talk. Take it easy. Be careful, you, on the high tundra of your aloneness. I'm lost in the mirthest North. Visit us in Madron. Enough Enough Enough Enough Enough I'll see you later there's something I must do and so I send this off with love and respect from yours faithfully truly ——fully (insert your own word here) Double Yes Gee. W S Graham.

118. *To Karl Weschke*

3 February 1967 LETTER FROM JUST ARRIVING HOME

Dear Karrrrrrl,

Who knows? It is true. I press my hangover to the glass and look out from your self-conscious room and see the distant slow-motion flung spray. Wheesht. Let me speak in my own way of this incident. I mean I mean I mean I mean I mean I speak from this flying incident I am. Fischer Wescher. There must be a K in it. Shall we sit in a wee hoose by the sea with all our toys around us which we thought we had given away? Unqueer you, I know, but you rise and fall very easily in masculine emotion ships. The deep sea swell. To understand is far from being able to speak. Sympathy is an impediment. Ho Ho says the boy. Then let us steer our impediments. Good Boy. Come the boy now. Unleather your table. It is not right. Powder your lacquered vessel. Do not (like some bird I think called the bower bird) bamboozle yourself with too many casual objects. It shows in, not even just your physical place, but in your too quick acquiring of unproofs. What that means I do not know. The orange cat is nudging me and the chocolate biscuits are in the drawer and the Chelsea guilt mirror is too high to see my destruction in. Ho Ho says the fool gael from the Firth. Ah gentle egg-headed Toy-distributor, what is to happen to you before you're dead? You have a lot of things. You contribute to my life in the way you are and also better in what I know I superimpose upon you. But you must have something good or I couldn't even do that. The thickening afternoon is clowning its nose between the astragals and the creatures of silence trot across the tundra. Those creatures are my own. They are my medium. Happy unhappy who knows? Give me a skelp on my soul and wake me up. LISTEN[1]

Hell with you anyhow I don't know why I am doing this taptrotting towards you in your complicated igloo. If you collect too many things you will have to hang them somewhere and your walls will melt. It was nice to hear you paraphrasing in English the Schubert. Nokidding. I mean it. Lend me a slice or two of your impossible charrrrrm. And remember I like you and love you even out of my impossible (Christ! the word impossible seems to shoosh into everything at the moment as I speak from within my speeding incident.) journey through this tundra of silences. Cheerio anyhow. Deutchland is who Deutchland does.

BY BY I like you fine, Sydney

119. *To Ruth Hilton* (extract)

21 March 1967

– Not knowing the rules, most of the game I, spectator, see, hear

1 Here follows the first verse of 'Johann Joachim Quantz's Five Lessons'. The complete poem is printed below, pp. 249–52.

and suffer. Who is winning or losing upon the face of things? I'll buy that. Only let begin me a new life ignorant of an old other. Make me twig No. 99995 on the greatest oak in a forest of terrible thousands. But save me from life as a dressing-table leg. Make me a puffball, healthy and true, but save me from the chopsticks of the Red Guard. Make me forget to stir the lentil pot of my moral broth. Make me make. Make me make me.

The thing is to find or create (in this case the same thing) a language, a timbre of thought or voice, which I will live in. It will never be adequate except for its moment but it will be the nearest to my soul speaking and as I change so it shall. A way of speaking, if it is any good, as it persists creates its understanders. Its early idiosyncracies become solid currency. It is alive, changing and organic. And at last works. –

120. *To Ruth Hilton*

22 March 1967

THOSE SYNTAX HABITS GOOD OR BAD I'LL ALLOW HOW MORE OR LESS

In exile shall I as a new cluster of worlds turn my head to want anything different from you the reader holding my message upside down? Then willing to ah nay eagerly you uttering clusters of private particles whirl on the Dervish floor if you will don't promise accomplish. Ho Ho is it you?

Ho Ho is it you? Do I know you? Have we do you think met somewhere before almost? I know your face I think at least I think I must have surely or else I wouldn't have known. I have seen you let me see no don't please say. It will come back I know I'm right I could be wrong. But surely it was at O don't say it it's on the tip. Do you not remember me seeing you once or were you looking? But what a ridiculousness. I'm seeing you now. You're seeing me now and this is us meeting and we at least know that. Though I wish some other person were looking to see us both seeing each other across the old nuisance of language which gets a bit dark or hazy or is it steaming up because we're breathing too close for comfort. I've tried to wipe my side clean how's yours. What was your name I think you said? I know your head from old. The edge of your silhouette seems to be diffusing or is it the words? Anyhow are you hearing me? Surely you're bound to recognise my voice though it's changed a little but not that much from what it was like if you met me before and heard it and I think perhaps we did meet somewhere or other in fact I know we really did I'm sure of it someplace. It was you. I know. It was me. I know. Go home now and come back another time. Ah how do you do how what you do I think.

My long home
Loch is still
Lying between
Hills in my mind.
In memory
Reflections slow
Ly move and change
And elongate
Into gigantic
Wisps alive
In their own right.
Loch Long lies
Held still between
Hills after
My words write
On the long water.

121. *To C.H.Sisson*

26 August 1967 4, Mountview Cottages, Madron, Penzance, Cornwall.

Dear Mr. Sisson,

thanks for THE DISCARNATION which I enjoy having very much. It's a rare beast, on its own and apart from any prevalent trends. It is difficult usually to get articulate reactions from anybody the poet shows his poem to. May I, with all respect, and as somebody else concerned with the medium make some remarks about it. I am afraid they will not be very connected but they occurred to me anyhow when reading it.

I like the easy, throw-away, disarming, beginning stanza. And its presentation of this tight, good artificial shape which is going to be the reader's expected vehicle through-out.

I like the bare distribution (texture) of low-tension words. Already the norm of the expected vocabulary is set and therefore able to be broken by the unexpected word or image however slight.

I like - 'The tears
They shed a humming in our ears.'

I like its dry, unbeautiful idiom.

I like - 'And takes

As sauce the ripples the air makes.

Its softness becomes strength, its coos
Turn into words and bite. ————'

I like – 'The knife
That enters like a prince is met'

Those are only fragments which specially, easily give me pleasure. Anyhow I like the whole poem, as a technical object and what it says.

It was nice of you to think of letting me have a copy. Surely it should appear in something. It's a courageous poem.

yours sincerely, W S Graham

122. *To C.H.Sisson*

31 December 1967 Madron

Dear C.H.Sisson,

A Guid New Year to you and good power in your writing work.

Thanks very much for the copy of ESSAYS. It is thoughtful of you to send those things and I appreciate it more than I can set out here to say. I flatter myself that I am in some way near what I think you say (God! How careful one must be in the negative to not say what one does not mean).

I find this collection of pieces written in such a fresh and 'original' way. I mean each. I mean that although A POSSIBLE ANGLICISM is (as far as its paraphrasable subject goes) not near my interest it really speaks about some things which, in no language (if that is possible), are near us all. Each essay makes a world of ideas enriching to enter.

They are exciting as a collection, one to the other, where they occur.

And you are so right in ON POETIC ARCHITECTURE. What you say is something somehow not remembered enough. Without diminishing at all the responsibility of the poet's intention the poem never goes through the 'space' between the poet and the reader without distortion. But the distortion is necessary and its ultimate value in the mind of the reader is the poem plus his best effort of beholding.

Your Collection is a kind of eccentric gesture to the present scene (no pop meaning meant necessarily), even your verse which I admire very much.

You have something I haven't got (not that I mean I *need* it.) and if you persist in your direction of high cerebral utterance and good fear of 'poeticness' I think (can I say, for fun?) you will go far.

Again thanks. Please, if you can spare a copy of anything , remember to send it. I'm not really a bracket man but you make me write in brackets. All the best, W S Graham

P.S. I am reading two poems on the Third Program week commencing 6th January.

123. *To Margaret Snow*

30 January 1968 Madron

Dear Margaret,

Thanks for your nice letter. I am especially pleased you liked the second poem best. I don't know, myself, whether I like it better than the other but CLUSTERS TRAVELLING OUT is the third poem of a definite break-away from my poetry up till then, a kind of change of gear. It is nearer to me saying things I have always wanted to try to say but never was able to make poetry out of. I will try to make a copy for you soon. Although I think it's coming out in an American magazine.

How is your artistic friend? And now Nessie will be her businesslike self. Love to you both I mean the three of you,

Sydney.

'I feel my signals just don't get received anywhere.' M.S.

Dear M, I like you saying this. It seems one of the most important 'subjects' to speak about, always. The difficulty of communication.

W.S.G.

124. *To Bryan Wynter*

11 May 1968 Windy Madron

Dear Bryan,

first let me get this over with. As we did last time and paid you back do you think you could go through the bore of helping us this time. You know I am not good at keeping money back to do anything with.

The Electricity Bill and a bill for the glazier have come in. The first is for £4 17 6 and the second for £1 9 3. Now would it be best for you to post to us two cheques for those amounts. This is against POETRY (Chicago), paying me in June the amount of £26 10 0. Remember this is not a funny half-blackmail-lone. I'll send POETRY's cheque and you please will cash it and let me have the remainder. (Love and Money are two things that set our prose awry.) Please let us do this the way I did it last time (Ho Ho) and realise that I do not in the least grudge you being paid back when the cheque arrives. Is that I am or is what I say I am here now CLEAR?

You London-struck terrible man! What have you seen? Into what anatomical cupboards hast thou peered? What a lonely muscle mask it is you wear. Do you think you will ever come to something? If what one knew that question meant it would be even half a help. Sometimes it seems we are given no time to find who it is we are each supposed to be. We exist on the escalator, always moving meeting Guidos, Nessies, Herons, Boschs, Mannies, Berlins, Fothergills, Eliots, Billies, Mons, Ernsts, Bartoks, Wilmas, Jackies, Bakers, Butchers, Blows, Ruths, Billiebolithos, Erics, Potts, Wickams, New Statesmen, Archers, Toxophilists, and all the unknown forgotten and 'the old and answered not'. AH AH and the ghosts, the weeping whisky-reeking wraith of MacBryde, the hunched overcoated sliding-down form of Colquhoun, big fat almost-solid ascending Davenport, Coughing Kavenagh, and dear old gracefully shrieking Johnnie of the thin brittle Mintons, and maybe even old high on a stool crosslegged in life-battered stockings, Nina. (God I'm certainly going my early remembered mile!) Well, my dear Bryan and Monica, go the moving people we each moving see. ENOUGH.

Do you think you will ever become to care for me? I thee, but that's not the problem. My cat can sometimes be a bad cat to me and the light is going. My eye-brows are getting out of hand. I send you my love across all those spring dykes and moors and hedges where the new fledglings are impatient to meet the 'real' world.

byby, WSGraham One to each —> X
—> X

I mean Sydney

125. *To Ruth Hilton* (extract)

29 August 1968 Madron

– I saw Roger off on the train (with Rose) (I mean she saw him off too.) last night to London to make an attempt to be healed. He's staying with his brother. You probably know all this. I know maybe it is silly of me to worry about this but I write you to let you know that before getting on the train he said he would say everything possible against me to everybody that mattered. I don't know what you can possibly do about this and I am not asking you really to do anything except correct (if the case comes up) the more vicious lies.

126. *To Roger Hilton*

Mid-day 23 September 1968 King William IV [Madron]

Dear Rog,

Your letter came this morning and I thought I would go down to the pub here and write back and I've left your letter at home. Anyhow here I am saying something which is me about you.

About 'friends' and 'enemies' I know not. Even myself, I only know that some people put up with me more than others and that I, myself, have greater pleasure in one person's presence than another's. There are some people I would say are my friends, if I was pushed to it, and even then I would feel I was being presumptuous. There are some people that don't show much liking of me but I would hesitate to call them 'enemies'. I don't think they care about me strongly enough. All this is to say – 'Friends' and 'Enemies' doesn't mean much. Are you, for example, my enemy or my friend. Within, let us say, three hours of us being together at Botallack, you have been a few times an enemy and a few times a friend. I wonder, which is the right one you diverge from. Or are they both equally valid to your character?

About yourself I have thought a lot, because you are a person of worth and an addition to my life. Maybe also because you are such a different kind of creature from what I think I am.

I am pleased and relieved you find your life up there, at the moment, good, with a kind of freedom.

Take advantage of it, old boy, and maybe try to think things out to get rid of the killing, false furies. To be furious or angry about something you don't know is a terrible waste of the good spirit you have. Or *do* you know? I mean what it is which makes you want to destroy either someone's enthusiasm of the moment or (in the bigger way) put out the light of their soul. (A corny phrase but it is near what I mean.)

I'm a 'mixed up kid' myself but I don't take it out on other people. It isn't their fault. You are a rare bird in that when any degree of love is given you, you don't even use it to make yourself stronger in your own aloneness. It positively makes you angry and want to destroy the source. *That is the mystery.* It is beyond my understanding. So many times I have asked myself – what's wrong with Roger? What does he want? I don't think that you think that Life has given you a raw deal. It is deeper than that. If you resent this sikaitrist (phonetic spelling – from now on spelt 'sik') and positively fight against him, it will be one of the stupidest things you have ever done – and that's saying something. It is not a competition with him. You are not pitting intellects against each other. The lesser man of one kind can help the greater man of another (if he is *lesser*, which I doubt).

It can't be *just* the drink which made the present state. Or frustration over your painting. It began early on, when you first married Ruth, but probably, I suddenly think, before that. Can you not say something to the sik about what you remember those early times were? Don't, Rog, think I am presuming to begin to know you.

I am home now. Your letter was disturbed. I mean this letter. We've had a wedding in the King Wm. They've been very good. Sending in drinks from the Saloon Bar. Well anyhow I am here in my own house. I am not well maybe a happy I don't think so MAN. Hold On.

Let us
If you like
Remember the phrase,
The unity of opposites.

You see
As well as all this
You have never got rid of
A terrible, snob small thing.

I should.
You try and what will you do?

The shades of night are falling fast.
Some will stay and some will last.
You seem to be incapable of loving
Someone else in an outward way.
Some will go and some will stay.

I have heard also voices wearing
Masks and horns shouting out
To me to say I am just a lout.

Ah now I have your Letter Again

What you say about Art I know. You are
no help. I will still send my postcards.

One thing, which I think is important, is
that getting yourself un-alcohalled is
half the battle. Remember this.

Damn the whole thing. Shall I speak
smally about the things about me?

The wood-wall opposite me is untidy and
does not work. It has too many scraps
of everything on it. My house needs
cleaned up. My brain needs cleaned up.

Nessie has just gone down (4pm)
to phone Rose and see if she'll come over
for a wee while. Who knows?

Notes Do you want anything
which I would be able
to send you? –
Poetry Books?
Novels?

Of course maybe those jokes in The Daily Mirror are true. Maybe you're just a not very nice man, a shit. Who knows? Who (and this is the point, would you like to) care?

'Nobody sees me as I walk
Up straight with slow stately gait.'

And this is a sixpenny school jotter
which I will finish to send to you

complete as a book, not very good,
but which I have got my worth
out of.

I have new coal in. The Penguin £100 has not come yet which makes me feel I'm being thought of as nothing.

I end with a Poem to my *friend*

Ha Roger Hilton, a fortnight gone
        Into the wards of the deep,
Worms of the world spiral your brain
        And beasts within you leap.

Then where is the innocent boy of his mother
        And where is the cunning chap.
Don't forget the human weather
        That takes us all in its lap.

O Roger Hilton, Roger Dog,
        Dog of Hell and the Fiery,
Heal yourself with your own Love
        Deep in Roehampton Priory.[1]

love — WSG. P.S. Rose not available.

127. *To Roger Hilton* (extract)

26 September 1968 King William IV

As usual I am worried about my fucking poetry, not wanting to jump onto the wagon of the prevailing style and yet not wanting to stick with a texture of words which is rigidly me. To be new in the right way is difficult, not to put out pseudo-experimental confections. I must be cooler in my approach to the poem and allow myself more to know what I'm doing. As you say about the oblique look at the Art object one must not frighten it away by facing it too blatantly yet somehow know the particular quality of its mystery and do all the things to encourage itself to 'grow'.

1 Where Hilton was undergoing treatment for alcoholism.

128. *To Roger Hilton*

27 September 1968

Madron Saturday 3pm
home from Shopping

My dear
In happy exile
ROGER,

What a rich cascade of letters from your unstraight-jacket life with the lemonade trees and vanishing negro.

When you say that you think you have exhausted the idea of the nudes it must be true because you say so. If the shapes of the areas you are filling in with some colour and/or the lines which are their boundaries are not being exciting for you any more, that is true. The representational thought we superimpose onto the never-ending flat plane must result in some disturbances which, at least to the painter, are a hieroglyph of a world with values we had never experienced before, an extra to one's life, an addition to one's range of sensitivity. All a bit pompous, this language but it is difficult to think things out in any casual language which I don't like anyhow.

There is no steering taste and fashion. And yet, on the other hand it would be wrong to play the Art-game like a one-armed bandit and hope the three lemons, or whatever it is, will come up in the future soon. As you know, it is not like that.

Hold hard, my bonny Botallack monster king. You have the kind of force which most people never dream of, cannot imagine. You will maybe be fine in the long-run. No quick intuition as to when to jump on the wagon substitutes the real talent that has grown up inside over the years. It's true, of course, you could be finished. It might be true. (I, myself don't think so.) But we must anyhow assume it's not true and find new marks and gestures to put on the visual silence which will first release us and then make an addition to other people's worlds.

You are no more lost than me. And yet, of course there is no way of measuring the lostness of any other person against one's own. Suffering in the centre, the remote kernel of the soul cannot be measured against another's. Fuck it all this this awful homespun philosophy. Let us on to something else.

I hope that you are not suffering too much from sexual frustration and not interfering with yourself too much. Are you having many baths? I know well, you old snobbish chum, that that will embarrass one little side of your huge coal-black brain. By the way, I suppose I am the most proletarian friend you have ever had. If the opportunity comes up to make an attempt towards a 'bit of new' I hope you will take it with all your courage.

The leaves come down. The nights are later earlier. The false hands are relentlessly pointing round their circles. Pshepshepsh.

I remember your horse well. At least the quick brown fox did not spring upon it and eat it all up yumyumyum. The three horse-riders are continually upon us charging down the terrible labyrinths of our poor respective brains. Mama. Mama. Dada.Dada.

I am coming out on the Westward TV with the Lanyon poem read by yours truly very well and I'm in it visually too. Who knows what I will come out like. God help the Lord.

Rose has put beautiful white on the walls of your house and it looks super.

Drawing by Roger Hilton (18 × 23 cms)

129. *To Roger Hilton*

31 October 1968 Madron Old Rainy Afternoon.

Dear King of Botallack in Exile,

even although those are wee drawings you send me with the good red on them, it suggests great invention and fertility of what's to come in the larger paintings. Good my boy. Think of Gogh and Utrillo frying on their gridirons of their times.

I do not know whether I love you or not (How embarrassing!) but you are a disturbance in my thoughts at all odd times. Your presence has made an addition to my life. ENOUGH.

Thanks for your catalogue. That reproduction of your painting on the front has turned out very well even not being in colour. Very sexual and all that, yet good Art.

Who the fucking hell am I anyhow? Do not answer. Ever.

Two nights ago we were at Rose's and heard and saw the Lanyon program. I was astonishingly surprised. Good visual bit. I honestly think it's a landmark on Western Television. I don't know how the producer managed to get it through. It was like a short Art film (I mean 'Art' in a good way here). It was shaped and imaginative with great shots of the white glider static in the middle of the oblong and the faraway earth moving underneath and the lighthouse and our house here and me at my terrible taxing table and typewriter and the whole place below you with the mines of Botallack and the swirling slow-motion sea below. I was pleased. Even the old man, old Charlie who talks about the badgers said to Nessie – 'Yes I liked that story your man made up and that shine on the sea was ansome' Maybe luck, but it was extraordinarily good.

Well, old boy, it is always difficult. How can anything be said from one man to another? The sent-out meaning always goes somewhere astray in the saying. The man on the radio has just given the synopsis of the next act and I realise I was not funny enough. He says something like 'and really under the guise of the female castrato she falls in love with Belovio who is really her aunt in the guise of a painter.'

I am changing rapidly. For better or worse I do not know. Who cares about me anyway? Fuck the very air and yet

When the rotten turnip smell of the Autumn fields comes moving across the Madron air, I like being here and feeding my senses on the world. HO HO says the poor old boy.

Where are my ancient lights? St Ann's road [former home of Ruth and Roger Hilton] has eased itself off. Of course one would not really like to begin one's life again. We can't imagine it anyhow. One rides one's toothache of the world. I fall down darkness in a line of words. There are no snows of yesteryear. Or only in the mind. Nothing is recoverable. We have our chance every second which is now.

Fair fair a bit of philosophy. My dear Roger, one spins about helpless saying who am I what am I expected to do.

I have just turned my head to say to Ness who is scoffing up my lentil soup that she doesn't understand me. Who knows? What does the phrase mean? Who 'understands' anybody?

That was a lovely red on your last drawings. You must have had a wee bit of orange or sienna in the tube red.

In the continental winter time
In the clear air we see
A cart of dead people,
A frozen mystery.

The horse without motion
Stands against the light.
A tired column of soldiers
Straggle into sight.

They stop and light their fires.
A pair of glasses drops.
The horse and cart stay still.
They travel without hope.

Dear Roger, I sent back the check to Penguins to be put into your account. They are very bad and I haven't had even an acknowledgement. But please tell me as soon as you know it is in your bank. They are very bad bad bad bad bad. How did the Slade thing go, my dear? Take it easy.

W S Graham – Sydney – Sidders X

130. *To Roger Hilton*

8 November 1968 Madron

EMBARRASSING LETTER but hold fast. It is not too bad.

Dear Roger, Nessie's hotel is closed for a month and we must get over this bare bit. I would like you to lend me £5. I do mean *lend*. That prolific all-rounder Lucie Smith is printing my poem MALCOLM MOONEY'S LAND in an anthology and in a week or two I should be due £15. Bryan is lending us £8, in four £2 weekly instalments, which will take us up to the end of our un-earning period. The £5 is necessary to pay milk and existing grocery bill and get some coal against the season's blast. To set my mind at rest please let me know by return. I enclose a stamped, addressed envelope and hope we shall have the favour of your business in the future. It is a pleasure to deal with your firm. Yours truly, chairman of the bored, W S Graham.

THE MILK OF HUMAN KINDNESS IS CONDENSED – TTBB[1]

Dear Roger, Your letter arrived this morning. It is not nonsense to say that your style (very efficient) is influenced by your many readings of Eliot's QUARTETS.

I'll be very interested in what the sic's injections do to you. By the way, Can you spare one of those 'talking pills' you get?

Whether animals have souls or not I do not know. It's difficult to recognise outward manifestations of a soul. The man who says nothing more than UGH and never acts might have a great soul (whatever soul may mean!). You know how one tries to think sometimes if it is one's soul which is contributing to an action or whether it is one's unsoul. IMPOSSIBLE TALK.

Beauty , yes is in the eye of the beholder. But the Word BEAUTY has some currency value. The possible beholders have a common denominator. We are not *all* that different.

It is a great pity you are not going to be seen around Botallack with your Moss Bros Suit. It would go well against the mine ruins and the ducks. Alas about the Queen being in Brazil. It's not impossible to catch her and Phillip up in Brazilia eh? I wonder who will be doing the investing.[2] Maybe Margaret.

Underneath every nude man there is a suited one trying to get out. Underneath every Artist there is a scientist trying to work himself out. Underneath every lover there is a hater. Underneath every rose there is a lily. A fork a knife. A quick a slow. A prick a

1 Try To Be Better! An exhortation familiar to Graham's friends.
2 Hilton received a CBE in 1968.

cunt. Underneath every Yes there is a No governing it. Here comes my Phylis with a mask of pearls.

Can you not manage a 'bit of new' anywhere in London? How are you feeling in body? Is coloured TV exciting. Can you send one of your coloured drawings of the interior of your room and one of the outside of the main building. It will be a great day on Tuesday. You and Rose and Bo and Ferg going to the palace. Do your best.

Of my own News I have none. Stretches of days seeing no outside people. The seasons nip on the small of the back. The stoves knocking back the paraffin. Early to bed o'nights. Nessie is seeing the doctor to be told that she must have folded in the nerve-ends of her thumb and it might have to be cut open and re knit. Me pale and interesting with no beer flush, trying to begin something new in the poetry line. Keep writing reports, however fragmentary. Love, Sydney

131. *Letter to Mary McGinn*

15 November 1968 Madron, Winday Day

My dear Mary,

Well here we are now entering the beginning of Wintertime with the white hoar on the hedges in the mornings and the hot water-bottle needed for the poor old middle-aged feet at night and the cat getting furrier against the time to come. Hello my dear, and how are you doing away up there so far away in Scotland I am home-sick for so often? My Tilly-stove hissing and spreads its good heat towards us. I have made some good chutney with green tomatoes and apples and all the other necessary things like spice and ginger and turmeric and onions and, although it is a delight to sup out of the jar I think maybe I should have put some whisky in it (if I had had some). It's sweet and nippy but not too much.

I was very moved, Mary, to hear about the presentation of the silver rose-bowl at the bowling green. And that your name should be the first there to be inscribed. My father was a great bowler and skip of his side and got to the runners-up in the singles of the Auchmountain Bowling Green in Greenock. Watch you don't have too much side. I used to mark the cards for the bowlers in Greenock as a boy and got sixpence from each for it. All we (wee) boys did it with our nice white blancoed sandshoes. And that wee box by the side of the rink where the chalk was supposed to be kept was always full of eariwigs. I remember well putting a chalk cross on the bools and measuring distances.

Let me now think of NEWS I can give you about us both down here on the Cornish Riviera (Ho Ho – some Riviera).

Nessie is looking beautiful and the peach-fuzz is on her cheek and here she goes working about the house singing and humming everything from Beethoven's opus 25 to The Tailor Fell through the Bed. I can beat her at the chutney and soup but she has me on the scones. But not as good as her mother's but hush, not a cheep! She is wearing some new dresses these days and looks very smart and fashionable. Maybe I should say 'toney'. A word we used to use in Greenock. You know, Mary, sometimes I long to be sailing over the Clyde Firth and be calling in at Kirn Dunoon Inellan Rothsay and all those further away wee places like Lamlash and Corrie (where the ferry came out) and Lochranza with Goatfell's peak towering up and Kames and Campbelltown. What a grand thing it was to be standing at the rail on those old paddle-steamers coming into a pier and the paddles churning up that lovely green water with its whiteness and almost mesmerising us. And maybe two pigs and some hens being taken aboard. And maybe one or two children there playing on the pier fishing for crabs in the holiday sunlight.

Mary, my dear, I am doing well with the writing and our house is a fairly happy place. I must turn the garden over. Although (because it's so mild here) (compared with Scotland) there are still halfadozen eatable lettuce holding out. Tony's coming over next week.[1] It is always nice to see him with his slow Irish talk and easy stories.

Mary Mary, for now I leave you,
Living there by Blantyre-side.
But be sure our exiled herts
Many a time wi you reside.

Love to Jean and family and your ever sweet self,
Sydney X

1 Tony O'Malley, Irish painter who lived in Cornwall for several years before returning to Ireland.

132. *To Roger Hilton*

MADRON I AM FIFTY TODAY 19 11 68 WE FALL DOWN DARKNESS IN A LINE OF DESIRE AND FRUSTRATION TO WHEREVER WE FALL DOWN TO AND THE DAYS LOOK IN THROUGH THE WINDOW AND HARK HARK THE DOGS DO BARK MEASURELESS

Dear Rog dear Roger Dear CBE are you there? I am a brave man in my way but when one is a brave man in one's way one is not a brave man in another. With all my sense of the comic in life, which means a certain sense of proportion about reality, I know myself less and less and wonder where it is I want to go. We are each, in our own respective ways, blessed or cursed with certain ingredients to help us for good or bad on our ways which we think are our ways. What's buzzin couzzin? Love thou me? When the idea of the flood had abated a hare pussed in the shaking bell-flowers and prayed to the rainbow through the spider's web. I have my real fire on. I am on.

I miss you. There must be a way to say 'I miss you' to another man which has nothing to do with suggestions of homo and is dignified and vital. No harder man than me will you possibly encounter. I don't mean you should come back necessarily. Maybe your time in Botallack is finished. You must change gear now, my dear. Your times in all your mighty times is here. It should be a 'changing-of-gear' time. You are too good to let things slide at the moment. There, old fellow, Great Dog You, you have the power. Put it out. You and I have had some times of valuable Hell together. I have affection for you always and the manic or serene hills of our landscapes have surrounded us well. Shall I surrealise.

(HOW DOES ONE BEGIN?) It is my house here with those simple oils of lamps lit. The door which will not shut is my friend and outside there is a sea of silent safety pins and a small sun rising to shine its rays on whoever I would like to become. I sit on the top of an igloo of ice and inside is Mozart kept alive and I will not pretend I know him well.

And so we leave this paradise where the poet lives and have our wee spell there. To tell you the honest truth, I can't bear anybody. Away and boil [your heid]. But of course, I realise, I must keep somebody liking me a wee bit. Otherwise, where would I be at all. WE MUST BE LIKED BY SOME OTHER PERSON OR PERSONS SOMEWHERE IN THE WORLD. Please let me hear from you now as the light is failing at the window and the road outside is quiet and the wind is sailing the very unhuman rooks up over the chimney. Love your friend.

cheerio, Sydney X

133. *To Ruth Hilton* (extract)

22 November 1968 — Madron 11am BLUESKY SHARP DAY

Write and give me some idea of the texture of your happiness at this moment. They are playing an electric music thing on the radio at this moment and it is not good enough. I can't hear those phrases as more significant than bits of music played backwards on the tape-recorder which we have all heard. How far should one give the other person the benefit of the doubt (even although one knows a great deal of composers are doing it) when no earlier language is suggested at all, even to make a base to be strange from?

134. *To Edwin Morgan*

4 January 1969 — Madron

Dear Edwin,

A pleasant thing to hear your very certain voice again. Well your letter is very thorough and deals with so much I was asking. And thanks for the SCOTTISH INTERNATIONAL. They are certainly going their good dinger in Scotland I see. I think your poem is very good, a real tour de force of some kind of poem. You must have taken a long breath to put that one out. What an imagination you have. It makes me think of a modern Bosch speaking about Scotland if there could be. Great images, real opposites brought together. And I can see the poem as a one-er. You have great energy.

The magazine itself. It is a mixture, I think, of mistakes, and good Scottish real fresh things, and talent. I liked to hear Garioch on Goodsir Smith. McGrath's poem is disappointing after his good article. Alasdair's short story is good but I would like to see more disturbance in the language. Joyce didn't finish all possibilities of texture in prose. There is something to be done.

To finish about the S.I. It is a hopeful sign in the best.

Thanks for your news and information. I will try to utilise it. You writing about me would give me great pleasure. (Why why is it that when I want to say Christ that's fine that we are made to write in a terrible self-conscious pomposity?) I will write to you soon about sending you a poem not in MALCOLM MOONEY'S LAND.

I have some poems which are not in MALCOLM MOONEY'S LAND (which I am told is coming out in March). Do you think any Scottish magazine might print them? I mean –

APPROACHES TO HOW THEY BEHAVE
THE LYING DEAR
Yours Truly
DEAR WHO I MEAN
WYNTER AND THE GRAMMARSOW

I leave you now thinking of your face which is not the face I know. I've just had a gutsful of home-made rice-wine and I send my love across the plains and shires to hope to find you well.

SydneyX (on the cheek) your letter and the magazine make me homesick.

135. *To Tony O'Malley*

20 August 1969 Madron

Dear Tone the Wolfe O'Malley,

I send you this bit of a chat to only say O yes it is all right and I hope we are friends for ever in some kind of way. Whose fault a jolt in the friendship is is never known and is not important. Are you there? Are you hearing your Skittish friend fool gale of the Nord that speaks to you into your bog-fuzzed ears? CRIPES the Autumn is near upon us again another step nearer the Great Winter and the open manhole whose yawning aperture reminds us there is no time to harbour big Ego's minipains. (reJoyce)

Nor lift your Irish Cashel ivy brows at me. This day sees Eire desolate and a drift of smoke from the North.

So as the tide
Was streaming out
Over the oyster
Catching early
Strand, I stepped over
The clinkered side

Of the half-afloat
Family skiff.
With my bare foot
I pushed us out
In a long glide
Ascending over
The weed and the young
Flounder groves
Of the long loch.

Come and see us. We think of you often. You are a rare one.
bendingly yours, love Sydney

136. *To William Montgomerie*

24 September 1969 Madron

Dear Bill,

it's good to hear that certain voice you have again. I envy you your sojourn there. The news that you have resigned your job of lecturing is good if that is what you want. If the fact of you doing that has resulted in you being able to put out more/better poetry that is lovely Bill. I suppose all apparently outward circumstances help us towards making a greater attempt on silence, if that is what you expect. I certainly would like to see the poem you began in France. Please let me not sound presumptuous but, may I say, the sudden freedom to write poetry might be difficult to utilise at first. Batter on and write your best and decide the poems are 'good enough' or 'finished with' and get them together and try to find a publisher and let that be behind you. It is a great strengthening thing to get something out. Then you feel you are being listened to and it helps you with what is to come.

OK OK OK OK OK that is that and I've said my piece about it. Have I given up Scotland? Not that I know. I certainly couldn't write the poems I do without being Scots. Of course I have great bouts of homesickness for Scotland, the land and the people. But the selfconsciousness of what the Scottish art scene seems to be today embarrasses me tae hell.

I like your poem HAMLET as far as I can 'see' it. The very kind of poem it is is difficult for me. I know it is a dramatic poem and that is fair but I like to see the poem as verse with its speeds and movements and montages, no matter how intricate, and not stepping up or down in its words. Don't misunderstand me, Bill. I like Pound and Pound's contemporary disciples where I think the 'stepping' texture is warranted. It just doesn't make my heart turn over in any way or my mind be flung into a new country. There are too many legs of varying numbers. When you do that the reader is more worried about getting the significance of the number of legs than allowing himself to be struck by the muse. OK only my measurement. Good health to Norah and you.

Sydney

Faber's just sent me the proofs of MALCOLM MOONEY'S LAND which I will begin tonight to go through. WSG

137. *To Roger Hilton*

24 September 1969 Madron

My dear (may I call you?) Frienddog o' mine, I hope you will know that last night wouldn't have worked. You were so far ahead at a point I could not have possibly reached in the whole night. Are you there are you there, Badoldoghilton under your Botallack roof? Ecoutez.

What do you think is to happen to you? What have you in mind? Trying to answer the same question myself I do not know I do not know. Walking on the little stepping stones of momentary elation across the terrible chasm of Nothing, I try to walk assured and keep my balance and not look down. REALITY (even reality as far as it means anything for each of us respectively) is a ghost world with insistent affection for the man it hunts, who tries to get away. Are you hearing me? Was there something you wanted to say? I worry about you to some degree although that is selfish and presumptuous. There are untold energies of art in you yet. Do not diffuse it into just a self-image of destruction, of an image of you as the supreme Misunderstood. I do not mean to preach or suggest I am wiser than you or have information about Life which you don't have. Are you picking your nose or playing chess or scratching your head or maybe outside looking over to the long horizon of the Cornish sea ?????

Even though I speak like this I think you know that I am a smugless poor Greenock boy from the North trying to find out what the world (Whatever that is!) is about.

I mean no harm, I say. But of course I mean every harm by speaking with a degree of articulateness above the average about the things which disturb us all I hope.

There is no better Dog than you at your best. Cunning and back-biting the loving hand that feeds you you might be. But the bit rump forgets easily the artistic canines when the dog is a coal-field thoroughbred like your worthwhile shorthaired badmanic self. Lend me your scurvy ears. The great yellow-treed castle-clouded red-berried turnip-smelling rook-calling ship of the countryside world is sailing into Autumn. The sycamore rustles louder and five leaves swirling land in the garden of my heart. The black birds are moving in flocks like iron filings in the sky and practising how to move in their new parliaments of thousands. They are ready to go. They have their laws no madder than ours.

Please come in soon to see me if you will. Better the early part of the day. When you come bring some white. I have no white or a good yellow. Bring a not-precious drawing (I can always fix it up.). Bring your good old boy Badog self. And bring your LOVE.
Sydney.

138. *To Roger Hilton*[1]

Ho Ho says the boy! 'It is hard for a man to believe in the necessity of what he is doing'. That is so true but only after he has become a man beyond a certain point. It is as though circumstances have fired him into a place outside the ordinary easyness where even the fellows he might love have not reached. Remember Remember, 'maimed for the job', is quite true, however I plug it.

Whatever makes for some positive life (let us not call it *Happiness*) between two people who have decided to be together, is a mysterious and demanding thing. Let me again repeat old Marianne Moore and say – Marriage is being alone together.

It would take two impossible, noble people to do their stuff, together, married, in the same medium, Artist, to not be competitive. I could not bear it myself.

1 Extracts from 'Reply to a discourse by Roger Hilton which he calls ART IS A CRIME', undated.

Roger Roger, I do not understand why you should bother at all about the situation you put forward. I don't even think you think it's true. You are worried about something else. Do Not Ask Me What It Is. I don't know.

The point is you are here on the face of the earth with 3/4 of your life spent, living here in Botallack. You carry your earlier life, your attempts and wee bit happinesses around with you, but you are here with Rose and your children, with your Art at a particular point here.

'Your times in all your mighty times is here.'

You must make the best of your past riches or failures and try not to retire into your dramatic, subjective anger, thinking you are the king of the misunderstood.

IT IS NOT IRRECOVERABLE

'There is no place for two Artists in the household'.

I don't know. Because you think it has not been up to now, that is nothing. If you wanted it to be, why not? Don't be a dope. Make it so. Stop entertaining your neurotic self at the expense of your friends (acquaintances). I get a bit disappointed that I have not been able to speak to you about a small thing, a flower, the sky, a cunt, a pile of stones, your son, the taste of lentils; for a good few years now. It is always the condition of yourself.

You never ask me how I am or how Nessie is or how we are making out. This is not for its self alone (although it would be a pleasure to hear) but, my tortured dear, it is a terrible sign. Not that we are going through as boring a hell as you. My Hell is richer and more agile and varied.

The bore is sitting on the floor.

★

If you can't live with Rose and the children here in Botallack and make more of an effort than you are doing towards the painting, then, don't let your shame exhaust your few surrounding people who care for you. MORAL INTERLUDE

I don't like that bit where you say -'It is up to us all, while we have a bit of the tambourine left in us, to protect it by whatever means we have'. Roger (if we are going to use the metaphor of the tambourine) you have never in your life had any of the tambourine in you. What instrument you have in you I do not know.

★

Roger this bit about you 'protecting the thing that is in you by whatever means we have'. Maybe you have an idea of what you are protecting. That is true. But being a painter, if that is what you still decide you are, the only hint that the outside person gets that you are protecting anything, and what it might be, is your painting.

I finish with a homely unsmart bit. It doesn't matter if you drink or not but how can you waste your time just saying any drivel (old school word) that comes into your head. I will always love and respect you the way I do now. TRY TO BE BETTER. W S Graham

There was this artist in his house,
His wife, two boys and a mouse.
Not forgetting a hysterical cat.
Nobody knew what it was at.

The Artist's wife when she was able
Would not lie upon the table,
But now and again she'd slip her cable
And stroke the canvas with the sable.

And when the night was shrill & high
And the found moon flew through the sky
Her paintings sang in her high room
His paintings growled in his high room.

There was no ending to this double
Painting man and wife but trouble.
Whisky & storm sailed over the house
And the sleeping wee unpainting mouse.
WSG

139. *To Edwin Morgan*

14 October 1969 Madron

Dear Edwin,

Yes it is me, Sydney, after this long time. You will have probably noticed that I am putting out poems again after some years. This new book, MALCOLM MOONEY'S LAND is coming out in March. I have this extra proof which I enclose thinking you might like it enough to help its outcome either in Scotland or England by writing something somewhere on the development or lack in my work from earlier books. You certainly would be the boy to do it and I would rather be slain by you than praised by a fudge-brain. I am well aware I write to you for my own furtherance but I do not know now what is done or what is not done in these matters. I never see or talk to writers down here. The thing is, if you like MALCOLM MOONEY'S LAND, what can be done? In Scotland or England or America (POETRY CHICAGO seem very much *for* me). Edwin, this is me deciding to be a bit businesslike for once.

I will be getting in touch with [George] MacBeth soon who I think might put either a reading on again or maybe a discussion. Could anything be down there? Also, when you reply, I would be pleased if you could give me any suggestions about Scotland. I don't know what magazines are going about there. I don't even know whether my poetry is seen at all in Scotland. I am doing a reading of my poetry on March 3rd (a new idea sponsored by the publisher of the poet) at the POETRY SOCIETY in London. They have asked Nessie up too. And that is about all of selfish that. ENOUGH.

You will realise that coming from a lesser man than me or going to a lesser man than you, to say anything about your own work now after the selfish bit of the letter would be suspect. But let me say that I have followed your good real flight with great pleasure. You have my best respect , Edwin, and if that sounds pompous I say it at that risk but I don't think that you will think that.

I hope this reaches you through the University. I seem to be able now at last to write more easily. New poems are coming out. I am now able to speak about things I always wanted to speak about but hadn't the equipment. That bitch muse seems to be at the moment a wee bit kind. Cheerio child of Lanarkshire.

love, Sydney.

140. *To Roger Hilton*

[undated] Madron. Saturday. 4 oclock. bright cheery.

My dear (are you my dear?) Roger, across the moors and roads like lines and the many herds and huddling farms and carns I send you my little bit. Well how are you how? The great ungeometrical cumulus sail above us here in Madron and in my wee brain the world.

Thank you. Think nothing of it, chum. Butter your breadside in the bed you lie. That is your trouble. Go to Tibet and coal will arise under you. That was your undoing, born under your sign and uniting with Scorpio when the terrible time had to come. I am very interested in China. They had gods of rivers. One river was a god. I like the talk of the Gobi desert even although the place itself would try me to my utmost. Is any place better than another for us? I mean any person who doesn't like where he is?

Although you will not know I have paid respect to you in pressing my wee brain as far as possible towards finding out what you want, what you are angry about, what makes you the child delinquent. We know all that mush, making yourself difficult to love and everything.

To tell you the truth I don't know if I can be really bothered to speak to you at the moment. I am rather busy. Forgive me, I have so many things to do. What have I to do? You ask? Well I want to know a wee bit about where I am now before I go away. And I don't mean Madron. It is one of the few things possible. I would have hated to be put into the world either as a pig or a milkjug and gone out again never knowing anything about where I had been. The drink will make you think in one way and even be articulate in one way but in another you will never have been there. How's my boy?

It doesn't matter that poetry will never mean anything to you. It is your misfortune which you will have to bear and as you are the bearing of it will not be difficult.

I have great regard for you to an extent which is not important to anyone but myself.

All this virile anger and destruction. Why not somehow say it through your paintings. That would be the great thing to do. There must be millions of people buggering around the cities and provinces of the world, lonely, and furious, with great flashes of vision, as you have. But you have, added to it, the power to create in some medium. (Never mind the corny phrase. It is right.) When what happens within us seems to not be the stuff that can go into our Art it is a failure. The most difficult things which disturb us should be our meat (No matter how difficult to swallow.) and the best to make our paintings or poems.

Are you a man or a dog? But I like you fine as you are do I maybe don't ask me I think you're spiffing.

THE LAST PARAGRAPH.
The horizontal of the sea insists
That the bewhiskied eye should look suddenly
To be beaten upon by a white white ship
Making its formal way across the blue.
Watch out for foxgloves mushrooms and your own
Poor half-wild roses and the black cat springing
Through the long towers of grass. I never had
No climbing structures to make me climb upon.
Up your jumper. Remember me. BYE BYE.

Sydney

141. *To Roger Hilton*

[undated]

The terrible level
Line of the sea
Into the visual
Intrudes, is always
There. We know well
What it does or better
We do not know
much. And that is fair.

From a deepsea sac Kandinsky dumped
His individual trawl. A list. Certain
Sea-stars, frail urchins from lost ledges,
Yellow-follicled weeds which only waved
From far above, sad horses from twenty
Fathoms down, long-pronged darlings
Of their dark territory, frilled worms
Of light, moving cucumbers who are not
Sex symbols, and printed ribbons of gigantic
Weed which are even saying something on their
Own, torn-off anemones, their frills
Still waving in the air, and some small fish
Maybe who have not been blown up by the
Changed pressure,and and
The beginning of something which is

not me, I mean me.

It is very difficult
That is true. Do
You see how the tern
Goes, like a sea-swallow?

The funny thing is that the point of
putting the words down in a seeming
verse form is real. It is not for
fun or to make it mysterious. Fuck
That!

On the cliffs below you the tern flies.
Also the kittiwake, fulmar,
blackbacked gull, lesser blackbacked
gull, black headed gull, tern, daw,
raven, night-jar, solan goose, diver,
guillemot, sheldrake, and all good
old boys, But not one writes poetry
or paints. ——————————

And so on the northern western sea shore
we walk. Our bare feet in the early-
morning sand fill and cave-in with the
good sea. The youngest flounders flit from
our feet. Who are we with anyhow? In
this early shore in the oystercatching
morning? Look over there, to the
great thundering Rhinns. And
put your cool feet down, print
upon, filling print along the
great shore with the tide out and
nobody nobody nobody any
where. To the left – the little gentle
rush of the sea. To the right the
Terrible impossible world. Cheerio

142. *To Ronnie and Henriette Duncan*

3 January 1970 4, Mountview Cottages MADRON PENZANCE CORNWALL 3 1 70 10am HIGHBLUE

Dear Ronnie & Henriette, the great world of my brain is slowly moving under the influence of your alcoholic surprise. How are you, my two far-northern dears? Nessie and I have made a toddy each of your Vat 69 I mean Teachers. Ah what it is to have a nice wee halfskulltoucher in the morning.

I have my Marconigraph on putting out Beethoven and I take a sip between the thoughts I send towards you. You both enter my mind at times.

PROFESSIONAL NEWS. A new book coming out with Faber in March which is called MALCOLM MOONEY'S LAND which i am secretly or unsecretly proud of. It has already been chosen as THE POETRY BOOK SOCIETY choice for Spring. And whether we think this means anything or not in real value, it will treble sales and general publicity, Ronnie. Also it is already lined up for American publication and Faber must be doing a good job. Although I would like to think the stuff is a wee bit good and giving the very language a nudge. I think I am saying something adult.

I am in the middle of a kind of long montage poem which I've called 80 IMPLEMENTS, although there might be twice that amount. They are not quite aphorisms because they vary so much in texture. I give you three at random –

55
When you were younger and me hardly
Anything but who is in me still
I had a throat of loving for you
That I can hardly bear can bear.

36
Commuting by arterial words
Between my home and Cool Cat
Reality, I began to seem
To miss or not want to catch
My road to one or the other. Rimbaud
Knew what to do. Or Nansen letting
His world on the Fram freeze in
to what was going to carry him.

25
Somewhere our belonging particles
Believe in us. If we could only find them.

Remember, my dear Ronnie and my dear Henriette, they are all different. In fact I thought of calling them (I mean 'it') A HUNDRED DIFFERENT IMPLEMENTS. And the quality I put out in these is no indication of the quality of the poems coming after. ENOUGH ENOUGH.

And so we leave the island of doubtful communication with me asking Nessie (who is starting pickled beef in the kitchen) to put on the kettle again for another.

Give us a kiss. And this is a good place and, my two northern dears, it would be more than just a pleasant thing to have you here together. I send my love to you across the plains and New Year shires of England.

Sydney and Nessie   love, Sydney X X

143. *To Charles Monteith*

[April] 1970

Dear Charles,

What sudden good news yesterday.[1] When the telegram came I read it and handed it to Nessie, standing there with a great inquiring face, and there she was full of a kind of happy disbelief (How's that for overwriting?). What lovely news, Charles. A safe winter. More publicity. And maybe Scotland almost loves me after all. It was very thoughtful of you sending the telegram, as though some faraway wife had suddenly given birth. It's absolutely lovely. I hope Faber are dispatching crammed wagons of MALCOLM MOONEY'S LAND northward.

It will be a pleasure to meet Hughes and Heaney on the 19th. May. I see so few poets down here. Nessie is coming up with me and we look forward to seeing you again. I hope, when you see Robert Lowell you might remember in the rush to give him my regards. Of course I admire him enormously and I met him once or twice in Rome years ago.

I have written to Rosemary Goad about Nessie and me coming up. But anyhow I will write to you nearer the time.

again my dear Charles I am very very pleased. Sydney

1 Reference to a grant of £300 from the Scottish Arts Council.

144. *To Bill Turner* (extract)

22 April 1970 Madron

Dear Bill Turner,

It was one of the best things that poetryreading night in London for you to suddenly come up. I had often at various odd times wondered what you were doing and I remember well those strange and happy nights we had when I came to visit you down in Govan. I was sorry we didn't talk longer although I had almost shot my bolt for the night. I would not have recognised you but when you spoke I could see the image of the Turner of my younger days beneath. The reading seemed to go well (what am I talking about? I know, I could feel it did.) and I felt a wee bit elation.

I hope you like some things in the book. And I would be pleased if Scotland (Whatever that may mean.) liked it and owned me a wee bit more. After all, although I don't write in the Lallans, my verse has a Northern hardness and texture which is Scots.

By the way, I had read THE SEX TRAP without realising you were 'Bill Turner' till you told Nessie.[1] Honestly I thought it was mastery, a superior of its kind and now Nessie has read it again and I've read it again. The well-described 'stuff' of it sticks in the mind.

145. *To Robin Skelton*

7 May 1970 Madron

Dear Robin Goodfellow Certainlyunskeleton,

What a generous letter from you. You send such good news of a benevolent winter. As I write this letter I hear a record of Mendelssohn's Overture, Calm Sea and Prosperous Voyage. And all manner of things will be well.

Now, dear Robin, what you have done with those worksheets has certainly revealed to me more exciting possibilities in them as whole poems than I had noticed. They read aloud well and the point you make about the quoting and halfquoting is very true. But I will hope to change them further from what you have made of them. So hold hold, and I will send you the poems these poems (cross my Clydeside fingers.) might become. In the meantime still regard them

1 The author originally wrote under the name W. Price Turner.

as sellable worksheets.

I send you the most complete collection of worksheets of any one of my poems, CLUSTERS TRAVELLING OUT. You will see how real they are to the poem (C.T.O.) and overlap on to other poems in MALCOLM MOONEY'S LAND. As well as what you are you seem to have a good quick brain of bringing together all the relevant components of the one Art Object. Anyhow here it is, Robin, all having to do with the making of CLUSTERS TRAVELLING OUT. (Please please do not think you are in for a bombardment of W.S.)

For me they were two very rich days. To be able to talk about poetry so easily with you and for me to have the feeling that I was with another person with love of the craft and the keen sleight of the words was a rare pleasure. Not the least was to hear your monster-bearded laugh. Your children were lovely. I envied that wee bit. And Sylvia seemed serene and interested (I pat her generous bottom across the springing shires of England).

BUSINESS Robin, if you are going to be there that night of the reading how about seeing you for a few hours next day? A few hours speaking is worth a dozen letters exchanging. I will even (Because I am such a bad business-writing man.) arrive with notes to remember everything to ask you, although I know you are a better manager of affairs although I know it is maybe my laziness although I know it is not me secretly playing the genius who has no time for those things. I mean, my dear, do you not think that might be the best way. We will speak in an hour what would take ages with letters??????????????

I have just had word that the Scottish Arts Council have awarded me £300. That is an inside WC on to our house. I am very pleased. It is a wee bit recognition from Scotland at last. I have always been a wee bit hurt (JOKE OR NOT JOKE?) that Scotland have never said anything about their exiled boy here, me. Also they have invited me up to do some readings in June or July in Edinburgh, Glasgow, and Stirling at the new University. I am very happy about it.

Of course, they will pay my expenses. And because Nessie has not seen her people for so long I will get both of us up there somehow. Robin, I must do my best and make it a reading remembered In Scotland. Isn't [it] very good!

I went down to the King William the other morning and could only take a pint. They told me you had phoned. I've been in bed since with my duodenal ulcer which comes up every now and then.

I was told you had phoned. It's worse than toothache. All I could do was stay in bed and read (I'm not out now,) a biography of Tolstoy, a nice slow interesting book which makes the place round the man/subject as well as the man/subject.

I was indeed very pleased that Kathleen [Raine] really said she liked my poetry. I can't believe it. It must surely be for (what I would think) the wrong reason. I saw the proofs of the three of us. It looks like a formidable book.[1] Certainly it is the best three together Stangos has put out. We, the three of us, Gascoyne Raine Graham, all stand for our own different rights. And how!

Robin write soon, love, WSG Sydney

146. *To Ruth Hilton*

8 June 1970 Cornish Carribean

My dear Azoff-from-now-and-ever loving Ruth, it was a successful trip to London. Everything went well. Only I say what a pity to have been up and in your house and hardly see you. You must try to come down in the autumn yes no?? My dear we liked your house very much and that street it is in and how near you are to the wharves and that lovely bit of the river.

The day you left I had a successful visit to Fabers and then met Robin Skelton and had a drink in that pub we were in before, the Marlborough. It was a deep summer day and down we went to the Thames-side at Westminster and sailed down (With Robin.) to Greenwich. My deario, it was lovely. The river air was warm and we were given the occasional slight heave like the seaside. What wonderful banks of old Victorian warehouses and water-towers and shot-towers and palaces and riverman's pubs and barges passing and tug-boats tooting. I have always thought there is great beauty in industrial riversides. If you have never made that sail, Ruth, you must. It takes less than three quarters of an hour and it costs ten shillings. Instead of the bus or train you should maybe give yourself a wee bit more time and try it sometime. Please try it and tell us.

Yes, my dear, I got a fright with Nessie. I thought she was going. She still feels a bit weak but I think she is over it. (TOUCHWOOD) Myself also, silly mio, I slipped in the gents of the Tolcarn and fell

1 *Penguin Modern Poets 17* (1970).

hitting the back of my head on the stone floor and I was unconscious for 20 minutes. For days afterwards I had blinding headaches and when I walked the ground heaved up and down. And honestly, Ruth, (Scout's Honour) I was not drunk when I fell. Anyhow we are progressing and this lovely weather is soaking into us.

I hope your Irish time went well. I suppose you were at the Irish whisky and I suppose (I hope.) you saw many faces in the street not unlike your old frrrrrien's. That big room in your house is lovely. How lucky you were. The quiet is unbelievable after St Ann's [Road]. The book you sent is just my stuff.

The garden is fat with chive and parsley and lettuces. So far I've had no further word about when I've to go up to Scotland. I would love it if I could work in a sail from Glasgow down the Firth to Campbeltown and back. It takes about thirteen hours. I am doing new poetry.

I don't know how that hall light came adrift. Ness switched on a light upstairs and the hall light just fell down.

OKOK Good my dear. Write soon. Try to get down. Sydney

147. *To Roger Hilton*

13 June 1970 Madron

At the waking hour when the brain is fighting its depressions of coming back to a new day I get your letter. As we know, whether I am a chum of yours or not, such a letter cannot be treated lightly. Can you hear me alright?

Would it have been better to have been a Major in the Khyber Rifles 50 years ago with different aspirations or would one still have a centre yearning after greater truth?

> Somewhere our belonging particles
> Believe in us. If we could only find them.

I am pleased you are trying my poetry. What it says I think you would believe in. Take it easy. As well you know it is not meant to be 'above' you. It is meant to be above me. Of course there are good lines. By this time I am expert enough to be able to make good lines. I hope I am better than that and move the heart.

And as the dusk of this Monday looks in at the window I wonder who I am doing what in the whole crammed roundabout of the world. But I know a little about it. I try to speak. I try to make an object which will stand.

For Christsake try to keep your health something. You must have some power in you under all this boring life which encircles you. Make an effort. (Don't ask me why.)

I think maybe you don't just ask for somebody to be sorry for you. Surely you can't. With all the great world with its surging ideas around you.

Maybe the French visit is a good thing. Why don't you try to paint there and even make yourself paint from 8 in the morning to 12 midday. Something must be superimposed on the illness of being alive.

I leave you now after making an effort to speak to you out of my own particular despair and naked soul afloat here in the busy world.

love, Sydney X

148. *To Ruth Hilton and John Beckett*

13 July 1970 — A LITTLE LETTER FOR NOTHING

Dear John and Ruth,

for no reason or all reasons I suddenly think of you today. Maybe it is because Beethoven's on the invention. Although I know well I don't know about the medium in any significant way. But do not think I am going to apologise myself to death. It just occurred to me I mean I found myself wondering how you both were up there in your strange-named street. The sea of Azof Street. I sit here in this Sunday afternoon after having old John Knight and his wife for two hours. Such admirable people. His nobility and courage taught (I hope.) me a lesson. At last I was able to turn on this music, Beethoven Sonata in C minor. Op 30 No 2. I realise I didn't just pretend to like music because of you. Is that a joke? I am in the middle of a little piece called – A DREAM OF CRETE. At least the title is something. This morning I had my fifth bash at it. It might be something. Of course, miss, you realise I have to watch. 'Things thought too long can be no longer thought.' Yeats and all that. Are you there, the both of you?? Change me.

When do you think the blue bosom of dusk is going to knock on my anxious window? You need not need not need not answer.

Life is not really my thing. Do you fancy it?

There is no news. My pains are shooting. My cat understands me. My table likes me. My typewriter has not turned to flannel. The lerkin is on high. I sometimes long to see your bonny face. As I grow older do I get better? I can't measure. I don't know. The shades of night are falling fast.

This is a happy letter. Although happiness has never been one of my great aspirations. HAPPY is a word which means nothing ever I seek to be. Happy is who happy does.

149. *To Crombie Saunders*

29 August 1970 Madron

Dear Crombie,

My tape recorder has two tracks (that is – one side and the other side) and the usual three speeds. When you send your tape let me know what you would like best to have on it, although I don't promise to completely comply because some poems I haven't decided just how to read yet. OK?

What a pleasure to have your good letter. I have just put my own typerighter in the infirmary to be made well enough to serve its master again.

The good things you say about Malcolm Mooney's Land I will make powerful medicine of against the bad prevailers. Also, Crombie, it makes me specially pleased for you to say I put my poetry into sound well. I think so, myself, but only a few have mentioned that and none so thoroughly as yourself. I like the way you say 'the classical precision of your reading: the way you place each word, with love, into its context.' I was hoping I was succeeding in doing that. Anyhow, you could not have spoken more generously and (to me) with more insight, A Shot in the Arm from my Old Friend Crombie Saunders.

I think the visit to Scotland has been relegated to next Spring. Nothing I/we would have liked better, than staying with you for a few days in your house and seeing Joan and yourself again.

Good sleight to Donald. Good sleight to his father. Luck to us all. 'And all manner of things will be well'.

'Somewhere our belonging particles
Believe in us. If we could only find them'.

Crombie, there must (I hope.) be a great deal of very good young poets coming up in Scotland. The Festival (full of graft and literary politics, to some extent, such as it is) must help to stimulate the children of the Future Past. What's cookin? When you write again give me the news.

Let us hope, before I descend into the man-hole (please replace cover) Nessie and I are able to meet you and your three sons and Joan.

love – from an ulcer poet to an ulcer poet, Sydney X X x x x

150. *To Robin Skelton*

23 September 1970 Madron

Dear Robinfellow Skelton,

Good morning evening after Canadian Noon, I hope my words find you well or more than well. I begin this letter with no real business urgency, which is always a pleasure to write. I take it you are all 'home' safe and unsinged and untraumed from your experience. Here the fall of leaves is in full swing and my cat is thickening his coat for the winter. His master does his makar work and goes his round of the house draughtstopping. Are you there? Can you hear me tapping along the invisible lines?

When does your book appear here? This time should be different. Five nights ago we came back from the pub with two painters and their wives and a young poet who had read your work. As well as (greedy me) reading some poems of my own I read some poems of yours, THREE PANELS FOR A QUIET HOUSE, THE BEGINNING, AT WALDEN POOL, UNDERGROWTH, THE WORD and the poet read two. They were easy on the lips to read and came out well in the room and worked.

At last I've made up my mind that IMPLEMENTS IN THEIR PLACES is finished, stopped, not to be added to. As it is now it is 63 Implements, about 600 lines. How good to be able to begin anew.

A shaft of cigarette sunlight comes through my small side window slanting down in a beam so solid I would almost have to jump it or duck underneath it. My radio puts out Mr Haydn.

The Raine Gascoyne Graham Penguin is out. Gascoyne is impressive in his romantic torture. Kathleen, when not too Celticly Delphic has her old-maidish strength. I hope it sells and makes a little.

The Plymouth Television are getting a wee bit courageous. They were here yesterday to make a program of me reading THE CLUSTERS to their visual of me here in the house and the camera going through the Slaughterhouse / Expoorhouse here in Madron. It's done and I hope it comes out well. They offered me £5 and I said O don't be daft you're kidding and I don't think meanly. He promised £10 and to try to get me more. Shoestrings are shoestrings but why save on the poor poet who made the 1/4 hour possible? Am I bad?

Write me a letter. Silence has no vocabulary to speak of.

I must go into the kitchen to start my soup. Shall I duck under that shaft or go round and jump it about three feet up? What kind of soup shall I make? Poet's Head Broth? Creme d'amour, Bard's Nest Soup, Sydney Soup or Melancholy Melon Cream of Tears?

Good happy be good health to you all good sleight to the word-hand and love from Nessie and Myself,

Sydney X X x x x

151. *To Charles Monteith*

14 October 1970 — Madron

Dear Charles,

It seems a long time since I wrote to you last. As you will have seen MALCOLM MOONEY'S LAND has called forth a mixed batch of reviews. The worst are vicious while the best are filled with passionate acclaim. Taking them all together I think there are more thumbs up than down. It is strange, Charles, that my verse (or the kind of man I am) either riles or is taken on its own scale at its best.

You will remember explaining to me that review copies are not sent to America when there is still a chance of the book being published in America. Is America still possible? If not, have any review copies gone to America?

I enjoyed doing that last reading and it seemed to go well. It was an experience I will remember hearing Hughes and Heaney reading their verse. Charles, apart from any possibilities of readings under the sponsorship of Faber, if there are any Poetry Readings I could do which you might hear of, let me know.

I have just finished a long poem (beyond even final revisions I say and touch wood.) called IMPLEMENTS IN THEIR PLACES. Now I continue with a poem I have had in my mind for a long time and which I have pages of notes for – A DREAM OF CRETE. If a poet couldn't do something with a title like that, Charles, he would be a gowk.

Nessie is making green tomato chutney and sends her regards. I am finishing this letter and would like to be remembered.

Yours sincerely, Sydney

JOHANN JOACHIM QUANTZ'S FIVE LESSONS

The First Lesson

So that each person may quickly find that
Which particularly concerns him, certain metaphors
Convenient to us within the compass of this
Lesson are to be allowed. It is best I sit
Here where I am to speak on the other side
Of language. You, of course, in your own time
And incident (I speak in the small hours.)
Will listen from your side. I am very pleased
We have sought us out. No doubt you have read
My Flute Book. Come. The Guild clock's iron men
Are striking out their few deserted hours
And here from my high window Brueghel's winter
Locks the canal below. I blow my fingers.

The Second Lesson

Good morning, Karl. Sit down. I have been thinking
About your progress and my progress as one
Who teaches you, a young man with talent
And the rarer gift of application. I think
You must now be becoming a musician
Of a certain calibre. It is right maybe
That in our lessons now I should expect
Slight and very polite impatiences
To show in you. Karl, I think it is true,
You are now nearly able to play the flute.

Now we must try higher, aware of the terrible
Shapes of silence sitting outside your ear
Anxious to define you and really love you.
Remember silence is curious about its opposite

Element which you shall learn to represent.

Enough of that. Now stand in the correct position
So that the wood of the floor will come up through you.
Stand, but not too stiff. Keep your elbows down.
Now take a simple breath and make me a shape
Of clear unchained started and finished tones.
Karl, as well as you are able, stop
Your fingers into the breathing apertures
And speak and make the cylinder delight us.

The Third Lesson

Karl, you are late. The traverse flute is not
A study to take lightly. I am cold waiting.
Put one piece of coal in the stove. This lesson
Shall not be prolonged. Right. Stand in your place.

Ready? Blow me a little ladder of sound
From a good stance so that you feel the heavy
Press of the floor coming up through you and
Keeping your pitch and tone in character.

Now that is something, Karl. You are getting on.
Unswell your head. One more piece of coal.
Go on now but remember it must be always
Easy and flowing. Light and shadow must
Be varied but be varied in your mind
Before you hear the eventual return sound.

Play me the dance you made for the barge-master.
Stop stop Karl. Play it as you first thought
Of it in the hot boat-kitchen. That is a pleasure
For me. I can see I am making you good.
Keep the stove red. Hand me the matches. Now
We can see better. Give me a shot at the pipe.
Karl, I can still put on a good flute-mouth
And show you in this high cold room something
You will be famous to have said you heard.

The Fourth Lesson

You are early this morning. What we have to do
Today is think of you as a little creator
After the big creator. And it can be argued
You are as necessary, even a composer
Composing in the flesh an attitude
To slay the ears of the gentry. Karl,
I know you find great joy in the great
Composers. But now you can put your lips to
The messages and blow them into sound
And enter and be there as well. You must
Be faithful to who you are speaking from
And yet it is all right. You will be there.

Take your coat off. Sit down. A Glass of Bols
Will help us both. I think you are good enough
To not need me anymore. I think you know
You are not only an interpreter.
What you will do is always something else
And they will hear you simultaneously with
The Art you have been given to read. Karl,

I think the Spring is really coming at last.
I see the canal boys working. I realise
I have not asked you to play the flute today.
Come and look. Are the barges not moving?
You must forgive me. I am not myself today.
Be here on Thursday. When you come, bring
Me five herrings. Watch your fingers. Spring
Is apparent but it is still chilblain weather.

The Last Lesson

Dear Karl, this morning is our last lesson.
I have been given the opportunity to
Live in a certain person's house and tutor
Him and his daughters on the traverse flute.
Karl, you will be all right. In those recent

Lessons my heart lifted to your playing.

I know. I see you doing well, invited
In a great chamber in front of the gentry. I
Can see them with their dresses settling in
And bored mouths beneath moustaches sizing
You up as you are, a lout from the canal
With big ears but an angel's tread on the flute.

But you will be all right. Stand in your place
Before them. Remember Johann. Begin with good
Nerve and decision. Do not intrude too much
Into the message you carry and put out.

One last thing, Karl, remember when you enter
The joy of those quick high archipelagoes,
To make to keep your finger-stops as light
As feathers but definite. What can I say more?
Do not be sentimental or in your Art.
I will miss you. Do not expect applause.

Six

IMPLEMENTS IN THEIR PLACES
1971–1976

WITH THE DULLE GRIET IN CANADA
(Extracts from manuscripts)

Bruegel had given us a note
To cover every difficulty
Taking Margaret to Canada.

Going through the people at Calgary
I was slightly drunk. So was she
But she swam through with her dark glasses
Perched on her seeking Flemish
Nose and not a Calgarian soul
Speired who she was. They should have known
Her walking leaning forward as Breugel
Made her ready to do battle
With the new world. She had taken me
On this long journey flying across
The Atlantic from devils to devils
New breaking out terrible Uneuropean
Broken eggs with new creatures avid
To punish us. How pleased we are
To meet you I said for us both
And we found ourselves in an Inn
Of no mean dimensions. She polished
Her helmet, took off her armour, powdered
Her Netherlands nose and went to sleep.

A human head reversed
Scurries away on an arm.
Fat toads jump from bed
To bed from me to her and
The whole room is darkening.
Outside I see the blizzard
Of arrows passing the window.
I shout Featherston Skelton
Sylvia Nessie Vivienne
George Wood Pieter. The phone
Rings like a shrill dispeller
And the room is turned into
A morning room in the Highlander's
Motel with a shy girl
Flemish cleaning her teeth
Beautiful in the bathroom.
She can do that you see.

A version of the poem 'Implements In Their Places' was sent to Robin Skelton as early as May 1971 and 'Imagine A Forest' appeared that year also. After Graham had been ill in 1972, it was arranged that Skelton would make further small, regular, payments for work-drafts and manuscripts on a regular basis. There were further attempts on 'A Dream Of Crete' in 1972, a section of it being printed in *Aquarius* in 1973. In the same year Graham was invited to read in Canada at Calgary, Victoria, London (Ontario), Saskatoon, and Toronto. The journey was not an unqualified success. Despite having several old friends in Canada to help him he was unsettled and extremely lonely. At home in Madron he had had a reproduction of Bruegel's painting *The Dulle Griet* for some time and had thought of writing about it. In Canada he began work on a poem in which he imagined himself accompanied by the bizarre Mad Meg, central image in the painting. A Canadian friend, Bill Featherston, was also using the Bruegel theme as basis for a large mural. In his heightened emotional state Graham was invaded by his own imagination. Featherston recalled: 'His dreams awoke him every night in a cold sweat. The surrealism was possessing him – as you know he was very visual and dreamed in fantastic images – he was very obsessed by "Meg". Women were very dominant in his daily machinations – again he did not have Ness to calm and reassure him, (I believe). He liked my drawings for the mural which I began in 1973.'[1]

By November the following year Graham had embarked on a poem reflecting his Canadian experiences. Several fragments of it remain but it seems to have been abandoned in June 1975. A new extension of his mode of addressing the poem and the reader was being struggled for but was not achieved to his satisfaction. The quiet harmony of the Quantz poems, on which he was also working during this period, seems strangely counterbalanced by the surrealist instability of the Dulle Griet.

In 1974 representations made on his behalf resulted in the award of a Civil List pension. In other years he received awards from the Arts Council of Great Britain, the Scottish Arts Council, the Royal Literary Fund, help from Harold Pinter and other friends and, for a year, small regular donations from a group arranged by Anthony Astbury. The recognition of his work pleased him perhaps as much as the money.

Many of his letters were written to painters. In a letter to Charles Monteith he described them as 'much easier than poets to speak to' (perhaps he saw them as non-competitive) and some of them took an interest in his work. A small number among the many 'St Ives artists' in Cornwall were also influenced by the internationalist tradition of twentieth-century art and literature and contributed to its continuing evolution. They exlored and exploited the abstract potential of their own paint language of colour and form as an important and integral part of the development of their imagery, acutely sensitive to the contribution that the medium itself could make to the creation of new forms, a richer variety of associations and an enhanced expressiveness. The best painters were also stringent critics of their own and other artists' work. Several were friends of Graham and he perceived their willingness to 'disturb the language' as being parallel to his own procedures with words. Though he was at times nonplussed by less figurative paintings he was usually supportive of experiment. The radical disassembly of the clichés of perception in the interest of constructing a fresh vision – all this was territory with which he was clearly familiar, having indeed included it in the 'Notes On A Poetry Of Release' written as early as 1945. Graham's contacts with artists were usually tangential, happily fortuitous. There was mutual respect, good conversation and encouragement. His professional dedication to his work was admired by them and, as Brian Wall said, 'There was a certain amount of steel in his veins that made one cognizant of what it takes to be an artist'.[2] Most of the painters and sculptors working in or near St Ives formed clusters of individualists rather than a 'group' in the usual sense of the word. Despite a shared environment, most of them did not appear to feel that they were representing a defined aesthetic 'programme'. Even when they exhibited together in the Penwith Society of Arts the mixture was an explosive one and the Society itself had been formed chiefly as a reaction to the conservatism of existing galleries and institutions. Graham himself did not accept labels and was not a member of any group. He was quite clear on the point. 'I have lived beside some writers and artists in my life but searching in my work I do not think they have been of any influence. I have never come near being part of a movement or group (not that I am necessarily against that but that is how it was).'[3]

When both Bryan Wynter and Roger Hilton died within twelve days of one another in February 1975, it was a severe blow.[4] They had been his close companions. Wynter had a very inventive mind and a wild sense of humour to match Graham's own. He had known Sydney since 1945 and had been an appreciative and reliable friend. The sparkling dialogues which Graham enjoyed with Roger Hilton in the early years of his friendship with him were unfortunately unrecorded though not unremarked. As Hilton's illness advanced and his behaviour became increasingly unpredictable, Graham's support and concern for him is evident in the letters he wrote. The relationship became impossible to sustain after 1972 but something of Hilton's affection for Graham was apparent when Sydney and Nessie were taken to see him a few days before his death. The room was full of visitors who were briefly silenced when Roger saw Sydney at the door and welcomed him with 'And here comes the best man among you all'.

During 1976 Graham carefully assembled the volume *Implements In Their Places* which was published in 1977.

1 Bill Featherston, letter to the Editors.
2 Brian Wall, letter to Chris Stephens, 20 December 1989.
3 Letter to Tony Lopez, 30 March 1981.
4 Graham composed three elegies for his friends. The painter Peter Lanyon (died 1964) is remembered in 'The Thermal Stair' in *Malcolm Mooney's Land* (1970), and in *Implements In Their Places* (1977) are 'Lines On Roger Hilton's Watch' and 'Dear Bryan Wynter'.

152. *To Robin Skelton* (extract)

12 May 1971 Madron

Dear Robin,

here is IMPLEMENTS IN THEIR PLACES. As a montage I have put one complete implement before the other to make something between them which will slay slightly the gentle reader. They are all of a piece. They are *not* haphazard. They are all in their right places. The good thing (which works) is those different attitudes, those different textures of language following each other.

153. *To John Knight*

5 October 1971 Madron

Knights Poetry Inc.
Dear John,

Thanks for the note with quotation. Why don't you and I turn out a massive collection of quotations. Of course, just ourselves. Imagine us making up all kinds of memorable pieces of verse of about 2-3-4 lines and putting them out. Would they be properly quotations if we really made them up for the job. Imagine the reader buying the book wondering who those two editors, Graham and Knight, will quote from and finding they were all made up by themselves. We would have to have a lengthy *foreword* about *Quotation as Literary Form*.

My dears, how nice to see you that day. Ness sends her love. I like the poem. Remember me. Love, Sydney XX

P.S. Please remember you can drop in anyhow for the bottles without getting sloshed. WSG.

154. *To Bryan Wynter*

13 November 1971 Madron

Dear Bryan,

LETTER I

How terrible to think I never get in touch with you but to ask you for money. Can you please let us have £5? As you know we are just on my £5 a week and we haven't, this time, kept our electricity money. The sordidness of it all does not bear thinking about. Yours in anticipation, WSGraham

LETTER II

Dear B. Look, Wynter, old chap, it's a long time since you've been over. Are you all right? I mean I know you are not all right but I mean healthwise (what a word !).

My poetry is proceeding and LONDON MAGAZINE has taken my fairly long poem, TEN SHOTS OF MISTER [SIMPSON] which means it will be seen around. Peter Watson Wood has begun the machinery to make a film (not TV) about WSG, poet and has made a first provisionary script (which I will have to adulterate into a better visual entertainment). This is for the Arts Council who have already done some films about painters. He has been in touch with them already and they said they had me in mind. Anyhow, Bryan, we'll see what happens. It might come off. It might be good. The point is, if you were called upon to take part would Monica and you be prepared to act (perfectly naturally) in some of the nude scenes with mirrors. Alas in this letter I am slowing boring silly old me into near death.

Do you know David Archer is dead by his own hand in Rowton House. How terrible! What goes on?

CODA
love to you
both,
Sydney
X X

155. *To Robin Skelton*

3 June 1972 Madron

Dear Robin,

yesterday Michael and Margaret came and said they had seen you in Exeter. They said they had discussed possibilities of some money arrangement between us. I mean selling worksheets to you.

WHAT I CAN OFFER IS THIS.

Worksheets of THE IMPLEMENTS which entail corrections and some 'Implements' I have not included in my published poem. They amount to quite a thick wad.

Worksheets of TEN SHOTS OF MISTER SIMPSON (printed in London

Magazine) which I think illustrate an interesting journey from conception to the finished poem.

Some corrected worksheets of shorter poems including some in MALCOLM MOONEY'S LAND.

And, if you like, you could have the first option on any of my poems in the coming year.

If you are interested in those large notebooks which you saw when you were here we might discuss it. They are filled with fragments of verse, prose, quotes from my reading, drawings in colour, and so many of my poems began from them that they are relevant.

Well, Robin, looking out from my vocabulary I see you looking into the shopwindow I have put before you. I think your Irish Portraits Drawings are a success. I have sent my extra MALAHAT REVIEW and all kinds of people are quoting one or other of the Implements. If quotability was the criterion I would have nothing to complain of. Are your collected poems out yet? Do not let Canada 'make' you. Think of us at times unfinancially. Purely, with your Peterloo accent.

love to both of you (if I can say this after such an asking letter)
Sydney X X

156. *To Nessie Graham*

[postmark 27 June 1972] Madron Monday

Dear my Ness,

I miss you more than I can tell you. To be without you here is some experience of something. It is not that I am a weak man. I have my strong side somewhere if only I could find it. Are you seeing the great place? It makes me home-sick to speak to you. And you will have to come back to your dreary old place again.

How nice that those things should be remembered. 'Come my boy' to our old cat. He was alright. I am lucky this afternoon hearing the best of Bach and sitting alone here. I try I try I try to pull myself together.

Tell them please my own dear, I send my good true affection and love to them. I mean all your people. You are a lucky one having them all. Tell them specially this – that the Dunsmuir line is a great line. You all have something.

George and Helen, my good dears.

Alex and Cathie – so much part of you.
Mary and Jean – 2 sisters different
and gone into their worlds. OK my dear
we are all upon the face of the turning world.

Nessie, it is a great effort to keep alive. Please can you let me know when it is you think you will be coming down? I don't mean to hurry you. I would just like to know. It is Haydn on the radio now. OK.

So here I am below the world
Invisible in mist I have made
Become my own.

It must be funny to hear words like that up beside your sister Mary in Rothesay.

Never mind. Love your true love and let me know when you think you will arrive.

Love from your own, Sydney X

157. *To Bryan Wynter*

6 August 1972 [original dated 1952] Madron

Dear Bryan,

I write to you hoping you will come and see us soon. I'm sorry last time you met me in the great depths, when I said – 'My brain is stopped'. Life is better and an even (fairly even) keel is established. We have an account in the bank which is being prudently tapped. I will tell you what put you into my teeming mind. END GAME. Whether that is the Beckett play or not you are going to have the courage to ask us to come and hear, I was reading this week's *Observer* and in it there is a very exciting article about the chess at Reykjavic. You must read it. It says what one always intuitively knew about chess but it is interesting to have it made articulate.

Well Nessie's back and she is going to Hayle on Wednesday for an X Ray of her gullet and stomach and to try to get her heart to behave as a poet's wife's heart should.

Try not to be put off when you come to see me if I seem nervous and I will try to ignore yours. Ho Ho said the boy. And if you do come maybe Monica might have an Autumn fruit or two to send with which some jam could be constructed.

Please try never to find your chum too difficult to come and see. (How's that for Syntax?)

Try to see us before you go to France. Love, Sydney X X

P.S. Dear Monica, my little alto flower of the great choir of life, I send my best love with a sigh on the manic clef. WSG X

158. *To Bryan Wynter*

28 October 1972 Madron

Dear Bryan Wynter,

Indeed sorry it is that your old shy self should have entered my house to find no possible Graham. I thank you for your visit, your vinboozler and your logs. You are a brick, a gem, a constant north, a main stay, a long-standing friend. Ah maybe (Do we think?) the sun comes up less urgently now. Maybe the sea thing with the land thing is not so easily funny. Maybe maybe of course there is no maybe about it. The slices the logs of life I am given are less easy to split. It is not that I've lost my axe. My axe is lighter. I remember once in the dusk in the hollow wood of owls and all my life whispering about me in the high rustling beech-tops I met.... Fairrr fairrr Pcutichicpatachy!

Forgive me I am sorry O yes I am I was not there to help you with the great big loggywoggies from your horseless. O silly bryanless me that day. That day later I tipped some fluid ounces of your Deadly into the northwest of the lesser frontal lobe and enjoyed great surprises. What

What are you doing anyhow? You realise those fleeting visits of yours give me no inkling. I am very fast at discerning and even in your half an hour stay I see. I mean that no matter what state I am in myself I find myself reading the braille of your twitching silence. (HO HO there is a MIXED.) Are you there are you there listening?

'I must stop borrowing my fare
To get to a destination which
Is not of the first rate. Please
Let it be a momentary erring.
Maybe my eyes are not keeping
Blue enough to see the first rate.'

love to you and your dearie, Sydney X X

159. *To Ronnie Duncan*

31 October 1972 Madron

Dear Ronnie,

'And wakened into sleep to find
Myself falling with ancient speed
Slowly throught the dark dividing
At my headlong approach. The Malia
Plain of heroic ghosts floats
Its floor up to discover me.

Father Mother I am falling
Into Crete at night with words
Trailing like bubbles above me from
My tons of body. Why have you let
Me out of you both to land here
On this enormous foreign word?'

This is one of my beginnings for my poem, A DREAM OF CRETE. I have so much material, I mean verse, for it accumulated and yet it is proving more difficult than the charm of the title suggested. I don't want it to become a travelogue made up of montage of Crete-isms. I want it to have a spine of idea or at least a developing attitude. And most of all I want it to have the feeling of me speaking out of a dream. My time in Crete went in so deep. I can recall every wisp of it and I certainly must put down a poem about it. Your PC filled me with envy for you both there. I see your gold locust is a very Egyptian one, maybe even from there.

Thank you for your Irish five pounds. It came at a good time. And word from you came at a good time. You are always enthusiastic about me and you and your letters always do me good. Joy it may be but it is all a lonely business.

'Observe me moving in almost a Vlaminck
World of blue ruts to the brow
Of Madron Hill. I lean my head
Against the buzzing pole to hear
the devil speaking up to London.'

You say in your letter 'the withdrawn life you lead' and when I ask myself if that is true, Ronnie, I have to agree. But that is only true on one level. I don't go around as one of the boys. I can't. I don't fit in very well. (And I don't say this please suggesting any superiority.) I think my phrase in Lanyon's poem is true although I can make fun of it. I mean I am 'maimed for the job'. Although I don't lead much of a social life I somehow know quickly what goes on and about people I have a quick knowledge. My dear what a boasting! What are you doing right now anyhow? Come outside and take off your eyebrows and I'll fill you in. Or better, Henriette, you come outside and keep on your pubic mask and I'll fill you in. This is a kind of round-about Celtish way of saying I like you both. I meant Keltic.

Nessie is much better. Henriette, I send you a lovely hug. Ronnie, you also though you are taller. Please why don't you write me even something to do with how my words, or any words work for you. I like your phrase – 'to keep this side of metaphor'. Nessie Dunsmuir sends her good love.

love, Sydney X X

160. *To Robin Skelton* (extract)

8 December 1972 Madron

My poem, A DREAM OF CRETE covers nearly my whole wall and really has to be hacked to pieces and put together again half the size. What a mysterious, unsubstantial business it is, writing poetry. After one finishes a poem which seems to work one says Ha Ha now I'll write another because I know how to do it but it is not so. There is the silence before one just as difficult to disturb significantly as before. What one has learned is inadequate against the new silence presented. WOW!

161. *To Ronnie and Henriette Duncan*

3 January 1973

Dear Ronnie & Henri (smile) ette,

What a lovely time my dears, both of you looking like humdingers and the talk so good. Without putting too much on it, Ronnie our talk about poetry was a great enjoyment to me and especially our reading aloud of those early Makars and the echo of us reading Hopkins is even affecting my writing at the moment. Do you remember the lovely –

'Some candle clear burns somewhere I come by.'

As I said before. Try to make a habit of writing to me about poetry.

Henriette, you're looking pretty good. But you could tell that I thought that anyhow. My dears, thanks for the goodies and all that drink. Look me in the eye and I'll sign my name on your enlarged pupils.

love, Sydney X X

162. *To Elizabeth Smart*

22 July 1973 Madron

2a.m. Nessie and my cat are asleep. I have Mozart on the gramophone.

Dear Elizabeth,

Gordon and Mary [Graves] have just gone away and the whole house is sleeping. I am writing to you because I was telling them that I am going to Canada in November. I suddenly realise, you are a Canadian girl and because you are somewhere near me always (I am not claiming anything!) I should tell you. You might give me advice or suggest somebody I should see. I mean, I wouldn't like to have gone to Canada without you knowing. I know nothing about Canada except it grew you.

I am going to Calgary College of Art for a week. Then over the mountains for five days on the Vancouver side then back to London, Ontario. Is there anybody there who might know you? Can you say anything?

Do you know, my dear generous sweet-mouthed girl, it is a strange thing going to Canada, a place I have never thought of. How shall I be? Shall I be my charming self and be thrown out. Shall I see any of the parts you came from?

I suppose I write this letter because I am alone at the end of the night and because Mary and Gordon made some kind of picture of you when I asked them how you were. Have you still the good face?

Here I am, Elizabeth, somehow 'maimed for the job', making my poetry up. I think good things are coming out with strange, impossible unpoetic beginnings like –

'Whatever you've come here to get
You've come to the wrong place. It
(I mean your name.) hurries away,
Before you in the trees to escape.

or

'What is the language using us for?

This is not me meaning to open a correspondence with you. It is only that when you are spoken about my heart rises to you to want to speak.

Good my dear. Write and give me Godspeed to Canada. What kind of place is it anyhow?

You realise I am not writing for your help to Canada. It does not matter. Mary and Gordon speaking about you. And me going to Canada. Makes me think of you. And yet, my dear, I know what I am doing. I steer my life.

Do not not answer. We fall down darkness in a line of words. Except I think of you always with the face which must have astonished any discerning mind.

I have turned the Mozart over. Shall I go straight to my bed now? I have to meet Gordon and Mary in the morning. It is only the alone bits of the life that can be utilised for what?

———love———-Sydney X

P.S. You can see I am reluctant to leave the *idea* of you. I will say this, Elizabeth, (which you know already) you added to my life something good. I never forget you. I say this now even being harder than ever I was. WSG.

163. *To Nessie Graham*

21 November 1973 London Ontario

Dear B.,

I have just given my reading. The people were slayed. It went well. They asked for other poems after I had finished. The 'Dean' said I had made something in the College that had not been made before. It was a great tier of audience. I could have gone for almost ever O. I read I Leave This at Your Ear twice. I've lost my notebook and my return ticket from London (England) to Penzance. Do not be worried. I will come home all right till the day I die. I am very lonely. Everybody seems to love me. But That is Not The Point.

Dear Ness, a wee note of love for you. I am in a gigantic hotel where, if a hippopotomus pass in the corridor nobody would blink a Canadian I.

All my readings you would have been proud of. I got your gloves.

I'm coming out soon. I'll try to make that train. I'll tell you.

Love – your Brer.

164. *To Bill and Gail Featherston*

4 December 1973 Madron

Dear Bill dear Gail I am here.

Here you can imagine me back at my table and Ness making something to eat in the kitchen and my cat wanting to get up on the table and sit on the newest stuff hot from the factory of intellect. Last night was Madron Feast and the hangover is massive, interesting to behold but no great pleasure. Up your pipe on a frosty nicht.

Bill, your love brushed my cheek like a feathergale. WOW

It is only now that my memory is beginning to put out wisps of that long rapid dark Canadian tunnel. How wordy can we get? We fall down darkness in a line of words.

I know I drank too much. I know I became more and more argumentative and carnapsious. You were both very patient and what a delight that Gail should be so beautiful and doing you good and obviously being done good by you (with all respect). I hope you can keep your house. Has that man fallen off those railway cars yet? I blush to think how brash I was talking about Art. I know nothing about it. Well not much anyway well I suppose I really do know all about it stop me stop me stop me stop me stop.

I think I've fucked myself with Robin and he has stopped the money. (Say nothing to Robin. He will probably tell you.) I think all along the line I was compelled to be 'agin' and I couldn't help it. Bill, I've written him and said that I would like to do our MALAHAT and I hope his anger doesn't extend to him stopping that. Now, Bill, do not broach the money subject with Robin. I mean the £25 a month he has been paying me for the last year for MSS and all notebooks. I must have been daft, Ness says. Why didn't I just keep my trap shut. OK OK OK

Bill, every reading went well. I have never read better. When I came back Nessie had had a pile of postcards from various deans, administers, fuckulty members, and plain wild students, saying how great the poetry and the readings were. She got a pc to our cat from somebody called Rosemary from Saskatoon. Ho Ho and I tell you this

Paul Cash and I went on the town and I went back with him to your father and mother and sister and it was a great success. What a long road out it was. Your father and mother were easy and they had those Irish tunes on the recordplayer and although your mother is deaf she could understand me well and we danced a kind of Irishscots reel together. The children were beautiful. There was the young one showing me how her skates needed sharpening and the older girl at her shy sweet stage and I sang the WATER WATER WALLFLOWER and they all stayed in the room at the same time to hear their name being sung. Am I a sentimental man? No. It was from the heart and psychologically sound. I missed you both there. Your mother had just made a tray of tarts. I couldn't eat and I asked her if she would put them in a box and so she did and I took them home here to Madron and there we were, so far away, eating your mother's tarts and thinking of you. Your sister fancied me. Bill, it was a great night.

My few days in Toronto were not really a great success (You can say that again.). Susan I just didn't understand. Harry (her boyfriend) less, much less. I left a day early. If I had known I could get an earlier flight-date I would have gone straight from London Ont.

I was very ill on the plane and I really thought I was finished. They gave me oxygen which didn't work because they found the oxygen bottle was empty. I gasped from Montreal to over Ireland. I was taken to hospital for two hours near London Airport and I could hardly remember where I had come from. The doctor phoned up a friend in London when he had read aloud to me all the Croziers in the book so that I could remember which address it was. I stayed there in bed for two days. They gave me an injection and Mogadon and I slept for about 14 hours, the first good sleep for days. It was something to do with the heart. OK OK. A long rigmarole but, Bill, Gail, I thought I was off down the manhole leaving Ness and my cat to face the world alone.

Mike Durham was very good and in fact I think I was much loved. But that didn't seem to be enough. What the fuckinghell do I want?

Somewhere our belonging particles
Believe in us. If we could only find them.

And so as the sun touches the evening sky with saffron we leave this great intellectual landscape.

Do you know what Rimbaud said? 'I really come from the beyond and I bring no messages.'

Did you give me any messages for people? Please tell me, Bill. I forget.

Love to you both, Sydney X X

165. *To Rosalind Harris*

16 January 1974 Madron

Dear Roz, Dear Don, Dear Pia,

Forgive me taking so long to write. It has taken me a long time to get organised after Canada. I wrote the letter I enclose and didn't post it. But now you have it. I think I must be frightened and guilty about this beginning of knowing you. I think I feel you expected a better father, now that you have found him. But, my dear, we will gradually get to know each other and begin to find wee bits in each other which are common to us both and we will be all right together. O look the slates are flying off my house.

We are in the middle of a great gale from the West and the slates are taking off and clattering down in the garden and Nessie is making lentil soup and I could keep you all a good extravert hug and kiss and sing you My Mother Bids Me Bind My Hair which has just been on the silent radio. Your three records came safely. What a lovely gift. You chose well. I used to have The Seasons but that was a long time ago and now to have it is lovely. And now I get to know the Bruch and the Glazounov concertos for the first time. 'The Messiah' – fashion changes in interpreting the written music. This is a new one again to discover. Its not bad. But it is new to me, Roz. I begin to learn a new object.

Canada was a great success. Every performance was received with enthusiasm. My greedy ego had lots to eat. I could have stayed there. I mean I could have shifted my life to there. I was offered two jobs without asking. I was the good disturber of the status quo in Canadian Culture (if there is such a thing) which they wanted. Of course I would never never go to Canada. But, my three dears, I did my job very well there and enjoyed even the physical country of Canada with all its differences from here.

ROZ – A terrible thing. A man's just come in saying half our roof's gone, – Christ! Write me – I'll write later. What shall we do. You can see daylight through the outside roof. I'm running down to the phone to phone somebody or we can't stay the night.

love to all – Sydney XXX

166. *To Bryan Wynter*

[undated, probably January 1974] Madron 4 am

Dear Bryan,

I write you a short letter with no jokes.

I've been out tonight with Ness and I've had a drink or two and Nessie went upstairs four hours ago and I've been trying to write the poetry and it's all posturing mush and so I've cleared up my table and found so much earlier mush of attempted verses around and burnt them and written two letters. I have my gramophone on with the great music. I had a letter from old Feathers and his pioneering skin seems to be wearing thin.

I got the Prime Minister's Pension. Isn't it a lovely thing. It means £500 a year till I go down the manhole into the Burnyburny. At the moment I feel as down as I can be. For no reason that my great factory of brain can fathom. Well that is how it is. But I always find a certain satisfaction in being awake alone in the middle of the night. A wee rest which is not a rest. It maybe just gives me some time to pick my soul's nose unobserved. I think I must be a manic because I begin to feel on the verge of feeling better. I am beginning to think that health might be important to one's happiness. Did you know that poor Ruth had an accident in Ireland and is in hospital in Dublin and will probably never be able to play the viola again? I am sorry. That bit is really a joke. It was her *knee*. She crashed into the trailer of a juggernot and lost a kneecap. I have written to her letting her know it can work out all right and that she will be able, even, to play football. Monica, remember your good frrrrriend. Love to you both, Sydney

P.S. I feel better than where I started from. WSG

P.P.S.S. Don't think I'm making light of the Pension.

It's not sunk in yet but already it's changed our lives.

The strange is – every other post I get letters asking for poems. There are two articles coming out about my poetry. I seem to be getting almost somewhere. I wish I was a boy again. I do not.

Stop me.

WSG

P.S. Nessie's just been reading this letter and says to tell you still to keep it under your hat till the end of March. 'It has not to be broadcast until it is presented to Parliament' I quote Ness from her wee beed.

ND and WSG

167. *To Monica Wynter*

[undated] Madron Wednesday

Dear Monica,

As you see the 'mysterious package' is Tovey. I believe he is really good about music. I probably read him for impure reasons. But he speaks so gaily with such understanding of Art and such insight into the language of music that so many things he says are applicable to the other arts (Like Stravinsky, a particularly articulate man for a musician.) and applicable, therefore, to all thoughts about anything. (The laws in an Art object have something to do with our every action.) Ho Ho big deep talk. Tovey, the man who speaks, is, to me, a very lovable man. It is not just empty enthusiasm. But I see I am overselling him. Please look at it and let me have it back sometime.

Monica, a nice afternoon in your bright kitchen, at the real table. Thanks for the wine (which caused various people various panics and disturbances, a squelchy plastic bladdery bomb)

Remember that if you hear of anyone going up to London on the 9th, 10th or 11th of next month please let me know.

Love to yourself and Bryan, Sydney X x

168. *To Robin Skelton*

31 January 1974 Madron 9 am

Dear Robin & Sylvia,

QUICK NOTE I THINK

To tell you that the word has come to say I have been granted a Civil Pension. My dears my dears it is almost unbelievable. Christ, what a responsibility. Dammit does this mean I will no longer be able to excuse my laziness and drunkenness by pleading money-worry? What a great thing to happen! Not that it 'happened'. I am so aware you instigated my upfall. I have written a wee note of thanks to Leonard Clark and Ian Parsons.

I hope you have some idea of the difference this makes to me, Robin. I feel I don't have to ride the despairing avalanche all the time. Nessie and I keep occasionally telling each other how things are different and what it means. ENOUGH. What is the language using us for?

'Who is The King of Whales what is
He like? Well may you ask. He is
A kind of old uncle of mine
And yours mushing across the blind
Ice-cap between us in his furs
Shouting at his delinquent dogs.
What is his purpose?............'

Although our floor in the bedroom has become surrealist with the floor and bed covered with catching vessels for the drips from the storm, we are having a time of peace and well-being. Nessie is writing to her sister in Blantyre and looks over to me writing you and says don't be saying anything bad whatever that may mean. Nessie means here 'Don't be making jokes out of your elation when you are writing seriously.' I have Brigit's pictures on the wall. What a strange beautiful building that was, Sylvia, when we went to pick up your son from the theatre, the wooden was it a converted barn? Is Bill Featherston still in the same place? What are you doing? What are you writing? Has MUSEBOOK got over here yet? Is the possibility of something with Bill still on? I leave you now in maybe deep Columbian night with your childer and dog and stamps.

And so I write to bring you the good news of the Pension.

Sydney

169. *To Bill and Gail Featherston*

7 February 1974 Madron

Dear Bill Dear Gale,

What a great thing to have your Vista Social Club plonk through the letterbox this morning. Ho Ho says I it is the boy himself. Hardedged you may be but that looks a good picture to me. What do you think, Gale? There at their green-baize table the Great Delinquents of the world are really settling our affairs. But that is fair. I have a good hand which you won't know by the expression my poetry face keeps. Bill, it looks very good. Mad Meg I know very well. With the halfegg-shells, and fiends with half-human faces and arses being breeched and cones. A great woman flying across the night-mare of the medievil and today's world. I have always wanted to make a poem (and I started once or twice) about that picture. You should keep that idea and make some more pictures about it. O Christ pompous me! But Graham 'as a man is emotional, humorous, passionate and frequently unwise.' COME THE BOY O COME THE BOY.

Bill I have been given the Civil Pension which means £500 a year till I go down the man-hole. It will come quarterly starting at the end of March. I have told Robin and it was all due to Robin. Is The Old Foggy Dew? Joke. The great new relief is so lovely. Ness and I can't believe it yet. It is going to make everything easier. I immediately feel more 'sparking', less lazy. What can we do together re words and visual? I have got some domestic new things – Lights, heating and things. We are half-roofless but working at Conor [Fallon].

I wrote you before. I don't know if you got the letter and because of that day the chuckersout appeared I don't know if you are still there. O Featherston, I miss you, take me over the Styx again on the ferry, thirsty for drink to encourage me into making my readings of poetry.

Gale, what a good one you are, and what a lovely face you have. I can remember your painting in your place. A kind of interior scene with objects out of proportion as a language to make a surrealist predominating pink and green world. Ho Ho say I. A very feminine creation. And I mean that well. If you don't receive this write back immediately. Robin and I are communicating with warmth. I suggested to him we still should do something together. Are you on? Have you any ideas of a theme? When I say a 'theme' it doesn't matter. Visual with words appearing together is not necessarily one medium illustrating the other . It is always a montage. I would be proud to have your Art having something to do with mine. Gale, Gail, Gael, make something of him. I have great affection for the old boy. WSGraham Sydney X X

Bill, Nessie reminds me to tell you that this is TOP SECRET till after March. WSG

P.P.S. Dear Bill I hope the exhibition is going well. Stop Now.

170. *To Robin Skelton* (extract)

28 March 1974 Madron

I was looking at the manuscript of The Waste Land, Robin. I have it pinned on the wall. I mean the TLS pages. I find it so exciting to see, this strange beginning attempting such realism, almost like Hemingway prose, and then to think it became that formalised beginning we know with hardly a hint I can see of his first idea. The idea of a long poem is so exciting because things can happen and ways of speaking can occur in it which could not be within a literary object of lesser dimension.

171. *To Charles Monteith*

29 March 1974 Madron

Dear Charles,

You will be pleased to hear I have been given a Civil Pension of

£500 a year. It will make a great difference. A little worry off my mind. Things are going to be easier. It should make me 'better'. And I am always trying to be better. Anyhow, I know you will be absolutely delighted.

I have had three weeks reading my poetry in Canada. It was a great success as a performance and also everybody loved me (Is that not what I wanted?) and I came back to Nessie with my fees intact.

Although Canada would not have been the place I would have chosen to go to, to read my poetry, or even have chosen to go to, it was more interesting and alive than I ever could have imagined. Something is happening there (quite apart from any competition with USA.) Even although I could feel impatience in me at their constant effort to make a Canadian culture, it was happening. (Forgive me. I speak so pompously.) I didn't meet any Canadian poets. Except Robin Skelton maybe you know. Mostly I met painters, much easier than poets to speak to. I flew over the Rockies not being able to see them at night and stayed a week near Victoria with Robin near the edge of the wild Indianless forest. Fenimore had gone. Killer whales leapt out of the water at a dollar a time and seals were in another basin. I thought I saw one I knew (by its face) from the Mull of Kintyre.

Dear Charles, this is also to tell you I have nearly another book of verse which I would like to submit to you. I see this letter has turned out different from what I had meant when I started. It was to tell you about the pension and a new book coming.

best wishes, Sydney

172. *To Robin Skelton* (extract)

25 April 1974 Madron

The Muse is being very good to me, although her aspect has changed. Or is she always the same? Is it me that's changing? The Dulle Griet, my paramour throughout Canada, fixed things bad for me. Her striding way beside me made me small. I have finished the other four lessons of Quantz. I am quite pleased with them. They make a whole world, all of a piece. Tell your youngest my cat is in love and very thin. Cheerio. Do you see how I can fill up the paper not to waste it? I wish I could press you all to my flying bosom.

173. *To Rosalind Harris*

24 May 1974 Madron Early wide-sky morning blue

Dear Roz my deario,

This lovely morning I think of you and wonder how you are in your new place. Is Pia finding some good places to be in and some new chums? Is Don enjoying the change? Remember (And this is not because I am your father giving you home-spun wisdom, although I feel more like your father every day.) that it is not where you are which contributes mostly towards one's happiness. It is your attitude to what surrounds you. My dear, forgive me. Reading that back, what a pomposity. Never mind. You will know what I mean. Do you ever feel you would like to give me a skelp on the ear? Maybe you should. Your Scottish grandmother would probably approve if she sees this strange relationship between you and me. My father was a great man on the fiddle. Do you think, Roz, we will ever get to know each other? How is your mother? And how is Don? You must tell Don that I am alone as easily as him. I am such a shy man I have to take to the drink to meet somebody. My dear my dear, I say all this and yet I write the poetry that I have steered all my life into making. The centre satisfaction I have is in making poetry. And so, my dear Roz, for good or bad, that is my first sustaining occupation in the world. I know it might sound corny but it is true. It is not for the fame (although now I am getting somewhere there and tickled by the idea) but because it makes a centre. Anyhow I send you a kiss along the words of writing.

I must finish this letter and put it into an envelope or I will never send it. Pia, Don, Roz, I send you my love. Don't look a gift love in the mouth. You can always ride it and it will come to something.

Sydney.

174. *To Robin Skelton*

16 September 1974 Madron, Quick note

My dear Robin,

I send you here this poem at last and I hope you will be able to use it. This is me saying I submit this poem. I am very pleased about it. That is very difficult to say without sounding a smug bug in a poetic rug but only I can say it to you. You know me. I mean I like it.

I sent some worksheets away about two months ago. Did they reach you? There are more to come. Reply Reply

Probably you know but – Calvin Bedient's book, EIGHT CONTEMPORARY POETS is out. What he says about me is said in a language which could be for or against. The quotations are pretty good. He sent me a book, BABEL TO BYZANTIUM, which mentioned me with some enthusiasm. It is always a good thing to hear.

I have two strange poems which I will send you when they can be allowed to pass the neurotic gate. One is called ENTER A CLOUD which is about me lying in the sun on the side of Zennor Hill seeing a cloud go in its changing way from one headland to another. The other poem is a blind man going a journey knowing each step and turn. I had given it a title called – POEM IN BRAILLE but, the title came up too easy. It's better than that. My poetry is drastically changing round. My whole idea of the world is changing fast. Who am I speaking to anyhow? Are you the poet of the yester the waterloo year. I miss you. I haven't been down to the pub for – NESSIE? WHAT IS IT? – ten days. Nessie is not hearing me (to put it in the grammar of the Indians) because she is cleaning her teeth. Leave it. Do you think you will ever love me. Love to you Sylvia my Killer-whale pal. This is really just to send the poem. Love. And to your wife father mother brother sister daughters sons cats dogs squirrels grammersows friends painters eskimoes – Sydney xxxxx xxxxx xxxxx

175. *To Robin Skelton*

19 September 1974 Madron

Dear Robin,

You are being pelted with poems from me. Here's another, TO ALEXANDER GRAHAM.

I don't think my verse is really getting simpler. This one kept itself simpler or clearer against my too aesthetic inclinations. I think maybe, Rob, I wanted it to be understood by my father if, perchance, he overhears it.

love to you all, I miss you, Sydney X X

176. *To Bryan Wynter*

25 September 1974 MADRON A great old rook-high day

Dear Brrryan

Thanks for the trousers. I think they will fit me well except maybe the ballroom is not my own. Somewhere our belonging parts believe in us. If we could only find them. It is great weather. It is my kind.

This weather I am in a great spate of writing. I finished and sent off three poems in the last two weeks. This is not me boasting, as you would know, but only me giving you news about myself hoping it will indicate a nearer happy condition. I think I am becoming braver about letting the words go out. Maybe I am beating the Oblomov syndrome. (What terrible language we are tricked into using for the sake of vain communication.)

Good wishes to you for your show. I am absolutely delighted that you are still tickling the kinetics of Art's illusion. It is all difficult and all easy. This morning I began this poem but I've lost heart about it for the moment. I wanted to make a poem of a description of an old picture and enter it with the reader and speak about what was in it. Anyhow here –

OF THE EARLY ITALIAN SCHOOL[1]

Flame and the garden we are together
In it using our secret time up.
We are together in this picture.

It is not easy to enter. Time
Has smoked it like a kipper, leaving
A cave-mouth on the flat within
Four gilt sections with mitred corners.
It has its distances still glowing
Saffron under the cracking varnish.

Monica, I miss your face and voice. Did you hear/see THE MARRIAGE OF FIGARO on the Telly the other night? Very exciting and buzzing in my head still. Bryan, godspeed to the show.

love to you both, Sydney X X

1 This is a very early draft of 'The Found Picture' *Collected Poems 1942-1977*, p. 234.

177. *To Anthony Astbury*

3 October 1974 Madron

ASTBURY, dear Tony,

A happy birthday to you. Many joyous returns. Thanks for the pound which I translated into liquid. Thanks for the nicotine banks of Sweet Afton where Burns, who looked like my father was wont tae gae. It was my mother's song. May you flow gently in your life and knock them all down if that is what you want to do. Good my Tony.

I am pleased to see you are doing early Italian poetry. I would have liked to be there to hear it. Tell Danila Pampanini that I am sorry I got a wee bit drunk that night I met her. The Italian language I dearly love. I lived in a castle at the top of an operatic montana called Sermoneta above Latina for a year. I was alone and it almost killed me with misquotes (I mean mosquitoes.) and I had my type-writer with me and couldn't write anything. There is an aria from one of the operas and I forget the Italian title, but the English equivalent is MAMA, THE RED WINE BURNS LIKE FIRE. OK OK, Tony, take care take it easy. I think you have many things to do. You must be getting old and the good young speakers dancers laughers sighers humble enthusiasts girls and boys of the celestial porridge of the world are all ready to speak.

I see your friend, our friend, Heath Hampstubbs in the LISTENER in a photograph today. Get it if you haven't. O god I am drunk with that pound from your birthday. What age are you at, anyhow, Tone? You must be muddle-edged now.

'What age is Eliot now, swinging
Among the nightingales behind
Our terrible, fashionable eyes?' WSG

Good boy Tony. How is your soul, your heart, your cock dealing with you? Are you getting ahead in your life?

'Ancient of runes, the stone-cut voice
Stands invisible on Zennor Hill.
I climb here in a morning of mist
Up over a fox's or badger's track
And there is no sound but myself
Breaking last year's drenched bracken.' WSG

I send my love with my lungs full of Sweet Afton hastening me off fast to the cancer ward. But as the Celtic hail batters the pain I think of you and wish you good courage in your life. I leave you now, my sweet frrrrriend saying the good impossible prose which is always secret. As for you my bonnie Prance of Whales, the shades are lengthening ower the river and the wee boys are few. Off I am to the chew-tonic forests of the interior of my irreproachable world and my spelling keeps a troash us between us. To which to who?? Owl like a volp your end is come. Farewell my bonny birthday man. Do your reading well on the 19th. Make me proud of thee. Farewell and forward. And Nessie sends her love.

'Somewhere our belonging particles
Believe in us. If we could only find them.'

Sydney X

178. *To Robin Skelton*

22 November 1974

MADRON ASNIGHTASNIGHT 22 11 74 FIFTYSIX YEARS HO HO
Dear Robin,

I've had my birthday. The last was in
Saskatoon. What are you all doing there?
This is a letter for nothing except.

When I think of the kind of man I am anyhow
I could lean out of the window of anyplace I live
and ask the same question. What are you all
doing there. They're a' oot o step but oor Johny.
Yet, Mister Robin, I would hesitate to call myself
an unhappy man. How is your dog?

In his tyme sa wrocht he. The Bruce
(Hes herte hurlt intill the stoure
O Blackfeet ayont the Muckle Slave)
Quick oot o Arran cam tae Canada.

Canada is a young man's country. Is this me
talking? What did you want me to help you to say?
Make up your mind. Come in. You're lucky
To catch me here so late between

Disguises. I can see by your face
You must be a mister or Earl of the place.

Mixing prose and verse so near to each other is an irritation to both parties. Forgive me. I got the Malahat. I haven't really gone through it yet. A very good cover. My poem looks fine. Printed like that I could read it for ever. I am putting it into the Claddagh records. I did the first side three years ago. Now they have asked me to go up and do the other side. They are very good in that they have asked us both (Nessie and me) up again from here for two nights in London. Do you know about those people?

Robin, you must tell me if those things I send off to you reach you. Otherwise it's like posting them into the Something trench (3000 feet down) downer than Everest up. How is the Queen of Whales?

What are you doing in the wigwam (igloo if so you are enclined) of your soul? Don't get too caught in the University. I know it is a cheek to say that. But you have your things to do. Anyhow Beethoven is turning over in his poor grave and I have it on now entering my steerio ears to disturb me and bugger up my prose. I wish I could see you now to say hello. How's Bill and Gail? I thought I saw Bill yesterday on the ferry going over looking over the rail but when I got ready to greet him he turned and it was another man. He wore a Stetson. Are you still there? Can you hear me? Maybe the time-change has taken my words away. Shall I begin a new paper? Is it worth my/your while? O O O O O

Was there something you wanted to say? Loki
Is cousin to me. Our instruments
Of putting each other to death
Are not very good. O Robin call
Our organisations together to see
If our cooking fires could go again
With singing and the shields put down.

And at this place the yellow bears
Were taken. Thirty bears were killed.
Many sleek grey brown and spotted
Swimmers we killed between the floes.
Excuse my language you who come after
To this beach after the battle seeking
A way to live or spoils to bring

back to your women. It is not my way
By choice. I am the writing scald
With no shield or sword or axe.

Ok, Robin. Lend me your helmet from Manchester and keep liking my poetry. Although I do dearly think music is the best of unnature. You certainly can't confuse it with anything else. What did you want to be when you were a boy? And what are we now? Maybe better to have been an engine-driver in the steam-age. A sportsman a shaman a drummer a dancer rainmaker farmer smith dyer cooper charcoal-burner politician dog bunsen-burner minister assassin thug bird-watcher poet's-wife queer painter alcoholic ologist solger sailer candlestick-maker composer madrigalist explorer invalid cowboy kittiwake graamersow slater flea sea-star angel dope dunce dunnick dotteral dafty prophesor genius monster slob starter sea-king prince earl the end.

And such lists have to be made for the mind's good even at the risk of turning the hero to stone. Look always in the shield you have been given by your father. I've shot my bridges burnt my bolt.

I am going to bed. Will you be here tomorrow? I am flying from Saskatoon on the earliest plane.

I have begun a poem about my travels in Canada called WITH THE DULLE GRIET IN CANADA. It's got to about 300 lines. Having Mad Meg with me as I write and re-call my time there helps me to say things I could not say (or even observe in retrospect) without her. I have read bits of it to some people and it at least seems funny in the laughing sense (although it was no laughing matter.) The airports were the greatest wildernesses of all. Of course I didn't see any wildernesses anyhow. And not an Indian. I think the place outside the hotel in Calgary (It was about five miles out of town.) was the most alone-making place I have ever beheld. There seems no doubt that to Bruegel's contemporaries Meg was not all there. Give my love to your sweet kin. Sydney X X X X x x x

P.S. (30 November 74) Dear Robin, Thanks for the fifty copies of What Is The Language Using Us For. They are lovely to have. I did ask you for a copy of my poem, ENTER A CLOUD. The thing is, Robin, I have left myself with a copy I am not sure of. Could the office maybe 'photostat' a copy? I climbed the Gulvas yesterday and we got back through the mist drenched.

Sydney

179. *To Michael and Margaret Snow*

TESTING THE SPECIAL PAPER IN MADRON IN THE YEAR 1975 AT SIX-THIRTY OBTAINED BY MICHAEL SNOW FROM WOOD PULP FROM THE PRIMEVIL FORESTS

Dear Michael & Margaret
Dear Margaret & Michael
Dear both in your respe
Ctive untouched kernals
Dear both as a unit dan
Cing in a nightclub in
Prehitler Berlin going
Back to the rough spir
It Teutonic of the cunt
Ry. O dear Snowball &
Snowballess. Dear two
Friends from parts
Of England I have never
Had the joy of being un
Happy or happy in. I
Do dearly love the sly
Happy whose delight it
Is my delight on a sto
Rmy nicht. And as for
Lancashire may my bluid
When I fall in battle
Be entered into a big
Black-pudding and be
Scoffed by the Peter
Loo ghosts of the peo
Ple who went down.

Well, anyhow, how are you? Speak up speak up has the cat got your tongues? No need to an-swear that. The paper seems to be writing adequately. My spelling was never anything to write home about. It gets wurs the more I draw the langwage nearer my great factory of intellect. You must be nice people to know. Do you come here often?

How is the paper for tears? Does it take the tears of a rejected lover well and not run the ink too much? Weeping into a type-writer in Cornwall with the salt air stops you writing in a week.

Rust in pus.

I have just sent another poem out into thorny reality. Gosh I seem to be creating like a fiend. It must be years. You must write. I wouldn't know you now, I suppose. I hear you are very good on the bowling green. Have you thought of taking up Art. It will keep you alive and help you to pass the time. There is many a jest said in just.

My dears my dears, what a corny hanselling[1] of the great new paper. Why don't you write a pc and let us know beforehand when you will come to see us, either here or a short drive and to eat something. Any how the test is over. The paper is A1. Both you also. Sydney X X

180. *To Robin Skelton* (extract)

30 January 1975 MADRON IN THE MIST

I liked (of course) seeing my poems in MALAHAT and I was pleased to see the simplicity of TO ALEXANDER GRAHAM and find it not sentimental. I think Carl Morris is very very good. Even through those reproductions I get a strong release into a visual new place. I mean in MALAHAT 32. How pleased I am to find –

> 'What is grass?' the child asked,
> and Whitman gave a poet's answer,
> explaining nothing. Dürer
> painted a clump of it,
> formal and brilliant in German air.

from Leonard Clark. Robin, I know some of his poems and I like them but this is the best I have seen. I like being beside him in the same book. He's a good sweet man. Your editing is exciting and always sound.

This is where I usually begin to end talking about the weather or whimsy news snippets or Ness making lentil soup.Or Mr Cat. Or wee Brigid. Or your dog.

While I remember let me say that THE SECRET NAME and IMAGINE A FOREST came out in POETRY NATION No 3. I asked them to acknowledge MALAHAT but they say they forgot. I'm sorry. I'll make

1 Hansel, handsel: the first use of anything.

sure the next time. I have been looking again at my Canadian poem and it has great possibilities and it's got to the stage of being on the wall. WITH THE DULLE GRIET IN CANADA

181. *To Robin Skelton*

9 February 1975 Madron

It is morning , Robin, and I am very drunk.

Bryan Wynter died last night.[1] Whether you knew him or not does not matter. I could have got drunk for any simple reason. He happened to be a man who was very near me in my life for about 30 years. I can't believe it. This is not a letter to tell you that somebody has died. You don't know him anyhow. But here I am up in the early Madron morning drunk as a hand-cart or any adjective you may choose wanting to tell you that he will never come into the house again tapping at the back window. I can't believe it. But here we are, Robin, still going through our lives as we respectively do. Are you there? Is your dog there? I make your dog a symbol.

I am very sad about this. I don't know why I write to you to tell you. It is because I am here this morning roaring drunk after going out last night to the Wynter House and speaking to Bryan's wife and brother. I send you some sheets.

And how are you? Forget me being so impossible in Canada. This is the last of my being sorry.

Tell Sylvia I could have fallen in love with her beside the Killer-whale pool. (Robin, give me a northern skelp on the ear to keep me right.)

Some poems of mine have come out in MALAHAT. You should see them. They're spiffing. And and and Robin Robin Robin, I miss the timbre of your verse. The most recent I know is in MUSE-BOOK which in my territory has been liked and read-aloud and handed about. I know about sex, those unkempt places, rising, or opening between us beside the Canada or the Madron river. It is difficult to write about trying not to get into a masterbating way of speaking or making just a sexual object. Don't get me wrong. Let us all fuck milk-jugs or words or whales or Blake's lonely images on your dreaming pillows or the straight-forward cunt. Ho Ho My

1 This letter is dated clearly but oddly. Bryan Wynter died on 11 January 1975. Roger Hilton died on 23 January 1975.

Canadian friend. Sylvia, watch as you drive, taking that road which was too conefered for me. Love concealed.

I am sitting here like a hive of buzzing quick ideas. Robin, who am I now? Rob, I go to the funeral on Saturday. Who shall I be? Shall I put on the intense face or the concealing face or the interesting face? Did I like him? Did I love him? Were you in Canada when I was there? Give me a hug across the sea. Sylvia, give me a wee kiss. I am not really sentimental. I am as hard as Greenock shipbuilding nails. O O O . I have fallen here on the floor. Can you lift me up. WOW that's a good ending. I enclose some 'sheets'. Sydney X X

P.S. I read this letter now and decided that, in spite of what it reveals, I should let it go to you. WSG

182. *To C.H. Sisson*

11 March 1975 Madron

Dear C.H.Sisson,

What a pleasure to have your poem, THE GARDEN. How good you are able to write quietly as well as whatever the opposite is when it occurs urgently in some of the poems in [IN] THE TROJAN DYKE [DITCH]. It makes an echo of a Yeats poem come into my head which I can't remember at the moment. Saying this I do not mean in the least that the poem is unduly influenced by Yeats. I just think of his poem ending 'rejoice'.

I have lost two very near people in my life suddenly in one week with no chance of preparation. Bryan Wynter and Roger Hilton. A year or two older than me. It is as though my very awareness of the world has been put out a bit and my thoughts from now on will be different. I am missing them going through their ups and down just a few parishes away. Why I tell you this I do not know.

I wanted to make a fairly long poem out of my visit to Canada. Being a man who is greedy for 'making' I wouldn't want it to be just a verse-report of my three weeks there. So I have Bruegel to help me. I have taken Mad Margaret with me. It is coming together. I've called it – WITH THE DULLE GRIET IN CANADA.

Please send me a wee poem now and then.

with admiration and affection, WSGraham

'Timor mortis conturbat me'

183. *To Ruth Hilton* (extract)

26 April 1975 Madron

– Sylvia Plath I like. I think she's the best woman poet of our time apart from Stevie Smith. Both gone away. I miss Roger very much, as you know. I sit here in the middle of the night, making my words go together but knowing Roger is not there makes me think not just in the same way. That is to be expected. A certain number of my brain-cells took a big fall. They will have to learn to readjust. Timor mortis. –

184. *To Monica Wynter*

5 May 1975 Madron

Dear Monica,

This is just a word or two in the middle of the night. I miss your friend. I had got so used to relating some new thought in my mind to Bryan, apart from whether I ever brought it up or not, when he appeared. Maybe most times I had forgotten. My fire-place is packed round with logs he brought and axed with me in the wee back garden. I am loath to use them for a fire for the visitors who come. You mustn't think I am eccentrically making a thing of Bryan dying. It is only me writing to you, suddenly being struck by the realisation of his absence. Don't mind the literariness, Monica. It is a self-consciousness which I can't get out of.

Monica, do not desert us. But you will know that I mean also, just, let's keep together. I don't really mean 'keep together'. I only mean – don't fly off out of our lives entirely. Christ! I mean don't leave us alone unless you want to. I am not used to writing to you. Are you going to have any fruit for jam this year? To write to you was necessary. Beside the starlit fences etc.

Monica, send the shortest note to say hello and the slightest news.

love Sydney X

185. *To Robin Skelton*

21 June 1975 Madron Midsummerday

Dear Robin,

I got your letter about the money. It is all in the first paragraph but it isn't clear what you mean. Is it going to falter? Is it going to stop for a time? Is it going to stop? I can write to you with real sweetness because you saved me from the tattypicking and put our life here onto a steady way. You owe me nothing, Robin, you have been very good. After saying that, I see it like this–

Our money has halved. Things are so difficult that I was going to write you to ask if there was such a thing as a Canadian grant to put in for. I have nearly completed my book for Faber [*Implements In Their Places*] which will get something. It needs some pages to make it the length. (Could you sell me five foot of tritametre and a foot and a half of villanelles?) Therefore Robin, do your best to not stop the money without crippling your life. Do my work-sheets not help at all? I never have any news from you if you get them or not, or about them. Shall I continue? I mean shall I continue to send them? Well, that is me being honest, which was easy enough for me in my mind but putting the words down to represent my honesty is another thing. The honester I get the more I get near saying ugg groo frush pryesha. Money talk finished.

I don't like your end of the letter where you say you must prepare for a trip to Oregon with Sylvia tomorrow. I am bice green with envy.[1] I haven't seen your new book yet, TIMELIGHT. A good title. I look forward to see the Graves MALAHAT. My Canadian poem is in splinters and when I try to gather them up I trip over soap-stone bears or Eskimo Budhas (spelling?) or ex-footballer College Deans. And where is the end of it all but up Peace River to Fort Vermilion. Keep your childer safe.

Christ! I didn't know this piece of paper was so long. Do I have to use it all? It is early morn, the day after midsummer day. Nessie is up to her bawbaw deep in a dream I'll never know. Dream gives awake its look.

I am not going to cut the last of this paper off. I will say cheerio farewell love to both now and begin a Graham's Fury Tale and go till the paper O is all stopped.

The Word That Did Not Know Who It Was

Once upon a time there was this word. It was a boy word. It did not know how it looked or sounded to humans. It was a very ignorant word. It did not know how many letters it was made of. Of

1 Bice: pale blue or green pigment.

course it did not know what country it came from. Well, we will call him Word. This is what happened to him.

One day in Winter Word through colliding silences found himself uttered out of the mouth of a Princess and rushing toward the ear of a not nice man who worked in the government. He held back and tried as much as he could not to go in but as he momentarily disintegrated at the outward whorl part of him went in and in the inner dark the anvil was struck. The bad man's eyes blinked and Word flew off and hid in the world's memory. The Princess turned and ran over the frozen garden and through the gate and did not know that in the name of the people she was to be shot in a cellar and her white dress covered with blood. Word was exhausted and hid in a book in a library under an onion dome but he could hear voices and a samovar cooking Tibethan tea. Ho Ho, he said, at last I'll snatch myself a sleep. Page 955, para five, two lines down, he in print slept dreaming of his name.

One day in Winter the telegraph wires were sagging and white with snow. And who should be travelling along in the middle of the wire in cahoots with the electric but Word. Quicker than tenses changing a shepherd shouted him into a collie's lug rounding up sheep. Where and O where are you now my dear he thought O Princess. Dispersed again unuttered into the Northern air he knew not what to do. Shall I go home he thought into big boy lexicon and lead the life of a prince between aardvark and zythum? Poor Word he cried poor Word. O speak me, write me, weep me, grunt me whimper me, he thought. But Word perked up finding himself typed out the second word from the end on a buff telegram form handed in to a Greenock granny in Lyndoch Street. Put your glasses on and read me, Word wished. He did not know what the message said because he could not read. Also he was nervous in love for the Princess and could not sleep under the weight of the other telegram forms pressing him down like a thousand blankets. No wink he slept that night.

At last one winter when the poor people of the world had gathered their sticks and were going home, a boy with a clear musical voice came running from the palace and said you have to go to the Princess because she knows your name now and loves you. Word was very frightened but ran following the boy through the shifts of silence but the guards let him in although he looked like nothing at all. He was at last before the Princess and he knew she was going to tell him his name. Your name is Fuck said the Princess and they lived happily ever after. And he was just a small humble boy too. WSGraham

OK. I didn't know it would go on this long. It's very good. I'm taking a copy. Bye Bye. Sydney

186. *To Ronnie and Henriette Duncan*

23 August 1975

Madronopulous, A gray day with the Pelloponese summits vanished in mist. Dear Ronnie and Henriette.

WOW WOW SO I BEHOLD THEE

Ho ho my Kriti boy and girl. I observed you there. I was the rustle at the edge of the olive grove observing how you behaved and the expressions on your Helvetian/Otley faces as the place flew into your respective souls and I was a quick guard-god to keep you from being whimsy. Your behaviour was admirable or excellent (take your pick of those academic boys) and I followed your every act but I was cold sometimes at night and krept invisibly in between you both to get warm and take notes in the hotel bed or the tent-groundsheet or (Ever?) the blanket spread on the pine-needles where Mister Skop really went to town with all his owls poleeping even down into the dry river- bed. Self-consciousness of speaking. O save me from ' those therrable prongs.' Can I get off the dancing floor and out of the Turkish smoke and the singing mandolines and sit down there by the quay's dark edge with a bottle of ouzo?

Fair Fair Wow Wow, now I behold thee through
The ouzo glass with your faces convexed
Untouristly I hope against the taverna's
Terrible cylinders of light and loud
Arabic wailing. I hear I am not clear.
I mean I see you both against the inside
Night-time light as you come out to find me.
Here I am by the oiled Ulysses water
Finishing the dregs of ouzo from the bottle
Unanciently labelled. Poleep Poleep
Will never find me here. We are shaking hands.
I hear you are English. Also is your wife?

Swiss! What a wise choice. Chocolate and cuckoo
Clocks and currency and William Tell.
Yes I speak English fairly well. I very
Am not an Englishman. My life is spent
Translating Scotch into the English language.

Yes by all means join me please sit down.
Henriette! What a charming name and so well
Put together. I hope you are accurate.
Ronald! A heroic name. I see your nose
Has had a touch of the Kritan sun who is
A god whose name escapes me. Not many
God's names get away from me. May I take home
This sprig of thyme to put under my pillow
Or under my dear's pillow, whichever will
Do best for me or her or both at once
Behaving to each other or us both
As a couple behaving to the world?

My dears my dears this letter has gone to the dogs.
I meant to speak about Crite and the White Mountains.
Leave my spelling of Krete alone. Let me
(Do you realise, Ronnie, I have to read your letter
with my glasses on and also a microscope I mean
magnifying glass. I have just come off the bus
and my mother with her black swaths (she refuses
to wear anything else after my father, Nikos, was
murdered by the Turks.) met me with the good water
of our village in a glass and a spoonful of jam.
What an unexpected letter coming out of me. Watch
me moving to the next page.) proceed.

Wow Wow so I behold thee both again.

This time, sly me, I saw you under the blinding
Light from the monastery wall. I was sitting
Ouzo-eating in the umbra of the square's great
Plane tree. You passed me slightly exhausted
Under the attention of the hot foreign sun.

What a great place to stop, here among the hot rocks, and to be able to look down the whole plain of Malia with its unsailed windmills and crane-balances to hoist the buckets from the wells. I am making use of you to try to get into five-accent lines again. I have just put on a record of Theodorakis. Songs sung by Maria Farandouri. I'm in a vulnerable state and they enter to the bone. Let me on to the fives again. Buy me another ouzo. Are you ready?

And who would see me now lying looking
Down on the blue water where gods and half
Gods came out of the Greek water to enter
The people. Or shall we have it the other way?
They looked at the sea and dreamed their gods on it.

Those lines of colour are to represent a terrible void which suddenly assails me.[1] What am I doing anyhow fucking about with words? There does not seem any point in speaking. There is nobody I really want to say anything to. I still like the place when I'm in the middle of putting the words together because it's the most alive experience I know. Yours faithfully, Manic Graham. X

Ronnie, Henriette, see, I am back to see you
Both hiding in your lovely bales of wool.
Forgive me meeting you in such an unbearable
Country. What country do I mean we walk
The hot road on? We walk between the palace
Ruins and Malia. The hot classical sun
'Beats on us mercilessly'. What did we do?
We went into this shack of a taverna and
The guy there sold us an ouzo or two
And then I said hey I thought we were
Supposed to get some stuff to eat with this.
Well, it was funny, this old wog says
Follow him and he took me round the back
And a thought he was going to sell me a piece
Of tail or somethin. Do you know what he said?
Pick yourself an orange, buddy. That guy
Knew Detroit better than me. I gave him
Fifty of those wog drachmas. In the dark inside
I could see his wife. She wouldn't come out.

zxzxzxzxzxzxzxzxz
ONTHEROADTOLASSITHI

1 This letter is one of a number containing sketches and patterns of coloured lines.

I send you a lovely line in the best of the iambic pentametre Elizabethan style by Beddoes.

I see his life as on a map of rivers.

O what will wink at me out of this next page,,,,,,,,

I find myself standing up between
This page and the one before saying
'You will be all right. Dont worry.'
As people go (WOW WOW) I don't think
I am less happy than most. But the word
Happy has ceased for years to mean anything
I seek to be. How's that for a pompous mouthful?

Where are we now? Where are we now? Your words
From Kriti made me benevolently envy you.
I think that phrase is strange but pretty good.
Henriette, blow me a flying hug from Otley
Down on the east side of the Pennine Chain.

Madron in my night house. 9-30 pm

Beholding thee I run away across
The tundra shouting WOW WOW I behold thee
But thee is never there. Only the few
Creatures I did not get round to falling
Out with are padding or swimming or flying over

---

a break here. I will tell you later why

---

what will I do. I have had a great slug of some homemade wine by a sudden visitor.

Don't leave me alone. I will meet thee in Malia. Cross to the other side of the page.

8-a.m. 26—8—75

I have just read those three pages. I'll send them, but I'll keep them till the last post at 5-30. I can hear by the bells my goats are getting beyond me. This is Epidirous – forget the spelling as long as you know what I mean wsg – in the early morning (true) with Nessie and me walking out into the trees and hearing the far-off tinkle of the goats bells. It being true is not necessary currency telling it to another.

We gathered huge hazel nuts from under the trees. I never saw the goats. Unsmile thy face. I will see you. Hold.

187. *To Ronnie and Henriette Duncan*

11 September 1975

I think I might write a serious of letters to you. You will be used because you are you but to some degree I will be writing them for my own sake.

Madron Penzance Cornwall MIDNIGHT

'I love you too but have not your talent.
I am the fox and therefore do not want it.'

Dear R. and H.,

This is the third letter where my brain has gone blank.

At the end of this church-road one comes upon the shell of what was once an early church. It is the church of S. Claudio, built about 1240, its façade half-broken down.

Here we turn right into the Via Franco Ciri and walk its length under the Umbrian sun to find a road leading away from the town oer-leaved with trees which is a pleasant thing for the traveller from Greenock or if you will Otley. This is our road unUmbrian children.

– – – – – and a helmet, shin-pads, spearheads, a tall wide-mouthed Attic vase with a bronze lid showing the legend of Triptolemus (sent by Demeter the Greek corn goddess to teach the Eleusinian mysteries to mankind), and another kottabos. I leaned my ouzo head on the cold stone and thought good boy you've felt something do not be guilty at not dying from the sheer symbolic ancientness around you. Out-side white heat hits me a terrible blow and I walked down the steep street and through the market of melons and egg-plants and grapes and tomatoes and bags of nutmegs and cloves and red and green and yellow peppers. I sat down under the plane tree and almost dwined away but a man came up to me from the White Mountains with his own cut goat-stick and moustache and black baggy trousers or kilt tucked in his mountain boots and called me German. When it was established that I was not he drank me under the peeling metal table ouzo for ouzo. Songs were exchanged. I could hear the Turkish in his mountain airs. O I have fallen down!

I see in this third letter it is all distorted quotes. Let that be so. I'm a sensitive man. So says the fox, the leaper over souls. In this letter do not expect anything direct. I am only practising how to speak to speak myself out of myself. Derwent is rising. Joyce.

Here I am sitting at my writing table at one in the morning. Ness is safe in her wee bawbaw and I even lent her the cat to take up. Everybody is safer than me. I know that is not true. Here I am, my dears, and there is really nothing I want. There is nothing I lack except what I deserve to lack which is very difficult to recognise or put consciousness to. Put that in. I see my prose, Ronnie, is not proceeding as it should because I live on the typewriter in verse. Please don't think I am so sensitive to language. But, of course, I mean that.

Farandouri is killing me again or Theodorakis. He does not sing. She sings.

The quick brown fox jumps over the lazy dog.

The quick brown fox jumps over the old or young
Men who thought they would come to the aid of
The party. Look. He comes jumping over.

I can see you clearly through this paper I am typing on although the wispy overcast has taken off the top of your heads. Are you in your respective secret kernals happy? I know you will not try answer that, having considered it many a time but not in these words. JESUSCHRIST! What led me into that! It must be me wanting tonight to see you for two hours maybe and hear more than your letter. Of course, maybe I'm just lonely and I must write something. That is not true. The whole world

In all its undimensioned particulars
Keeps its arms round me. That I have to keep
Believing. I believe it anyhow.

Ronnie, Henriette, Now I ask you to do something for me and it will cost maybe £1-30. You are in the North of England. Nessie and I have been longing to taste a real black-pudding. Also chitterlings. Do you think you could get a local butcher to pack two black-puddings and some chitterlings (if they would travel) into a stout box and post them down to us? This is a quick thought come over me suddenly thinking of Northern eatables and making my juices flow. Or would I rather batter my self-caught octopus on the Greek rocks and have it stewed in the hot quick ink. I've made myself hungry. On the lower right shelf is a figure of Hercules.

Roni, Ongriet, the quick storm kettle-drums the window panes and here I go up to join my dear and my cat.

And who will ride with Fergus now
And drive among the brazen cars?

Brown fox, my creature, I have put you here
Far out of typewriter test. You are
The point-nosed shy creature pacing along
The wall in the first light at Gurnard's Head.
Mister Fox, will you ever come to see me again?

I have put the music off. I have taken my swig of bicarb. I have peed. I have wound the clock. I have taken my sleepy shirt from the drawer. Good night. Guid nicht. Boneet.

188. *To Anthony Astbury*

29 September 1975 Madron

Astbury,
What's happening to you?

So language seizes me with mice and cats
Of stature in their literary camoflaje
Living with love on the paper and me flying
Trying to say something with my head
Against the easy flank of the yellow leopard.

This is the story and the creatures in it
Wanting to tell. There are certain ones who
Will want to say too much. Others will turn
Into apples and oranges on a dish.

Astbury let that be a lesson to you. You should
have written to say it had been a good time. Your
chum, Geoffrey, wrote. I had wanted to give you a
red tie I had been given by Bryan Wynter.

Now write back like the good delinquent child you are.

love, Sydney

Don't send the £5 back. Try to get me a bazouki (Greek) record (a bit rough and astringent – not too sweet), and send it. love WSG

189. *To Michael Snow*

3 October 1975 Madron

Dear Michael,

I am only writing to ask you if you would give me some more paper to type on. I know I can afford to buy some but it is not the same. Making poems on the paper which has been given to me by a friend is better. Am I being very cunning? I don't mean to be although I am very cunning by nature of course I am not such a sweet man am I. I am the merry ploughboy travelled into skitzoid.

It is 3 a.m. And I can tell I am getting older. What the fucking hell am I doing anyhow. I don't know what I want. Writing my wee bit poetry. Who will it reach? Only the kind of people I wouldn't like anyhow. What a prospect.

Anyhow, my dear, do your best. This is a selfish letter.

The quick brown fox jumps over the lazy god.

Yours faithfully, Sydney X

190. *To Michael Snow*

10 October 1975 4pm MADRONA DESERTA

Dear Michael,

WOW WOW so I behold thee as though I could really see you giving me singing choirs of snowwhite areas unfootprinted by man. But I am saying thanks through my beard of bicycles read icicles and I am at the ready to see you as a black speck appear over the crest of The Great Barrier. I am sitting here on the snow with my typewriter keeping warm on my primus and I see my words through my slit wooden goggles. They were given to me by Nanook after shooting the seal scene. Later when I was playing the cinema organ in the Igloo Odean he offered his wife for the night for five bullets, a double-breasted suit, a vibrator, a packet of fish-fingers and the name of my psychiatrist. Anyhow to cut this uncotton-pickin saga short, when I see WOW WOW thee again it will be through the slit wooden eyes of Nanook.

What can I say Old Timer but try to mush down this way soon. You ask about the traps. Well a suppose the line is payin its way. Lost ma pardner a time back. It makes a difference. Caught is leg in a bear-trap o Teachers. Haw Haw Haw ye see old Clint Grimm's still good for a yarn or two an make you laugh. Nuthing's so good fura man as laughin. Knew a man once all is hair on fire an..... Well Mike am no han at writin things down but this letterll have to do. How you gitten along wi that skill-toucher squaw o yurn?

All be handin this to Capt Mac when the whale ship comes in at Christmas. Thankee for the paper. Real special it is and bumsoft too. Send me a bottle of that distemper cure.

Love to you and your lady, Sydney X X

191. *To Robin Skelton* (extract)

12 October 1975 Madron

Dear Rob,

Just a quick note to send this poem. It seems to be in my simpler or less opaque style if I have that, to go with the poem to my father and the poem about Loch Thom. It is one of those poems where the facts are all true. I am not meaning in the least that that has anything to do with the success of the poem but I got a certain kind of satisfaction putting the words down about the objects, Roger included. It's true. I have his watch verdigrised and I nurse it to keep it going. He did drink Teachers and he spat a lot and he woke in the middle of the night. I don't know why I am telling you this except. I could have made up something equally autentic I mean authentic and it would have served as well. I see I keep returning to those three-beat verses. I write clearer but I say something else from what I might have wanted to say in fives.

192. *To Ronnie Duncan* (extract)

23 November 1975 Madron 6 a.m. No blue at the window.

I have been reading Rilke's DUINO ELEGIES (Leishman and Spender) for the first time and it is terrible poetic-philosophy goo. I think he must be better than they translate him. I liked the English Gascoyne put Holderlin's poems into. I know it is difficult and impossible to translate literature into another language but I suppose it makes something. As Eliot said – It could be better. And there, my dears, is Finnegans Wake translated into Japanese. What a strange structure it must be. And me translating English into English.

193. *To Ronnie and Henriette Duncan*

29 April 1976 Madron Thursday The First Bluebells

Ronnie & Henriette my dears,

You are certainly being put through the mill No punishment intended. It is good to hear that the oscillations of hot and cold are quietening and you are feeling stronger. I feel a dope writing those words when I am here and it's not happening to me. Our thoughts are with you both as near as they can be every day.

Rose Hilton visited us yesterday and she says that Roger's paintings and even the smallest drawings are selling for high prices. I miss him. I wonder how he is and how he is behaving himself wherever he is. I haven't forgotten your copy of LINES ON ROGER HILTON'S WATCH. Next time, Ronnie. Ruth in a letter mentions you met at Matthew's. How was it? Who was the poet you went to visit? Good you seeing the Constable Exhibition. And with the flu too. How was the wain?

I do dearly hope your cat has come home. I know full well the particular kind of love for the cat. We instill it with so many things that happen to us and it never disappoints us by saying the wrong thing. Your good cat might be just away on an erotic walkabout.

We have been asked to go to the Queen's garden party at Buckingham Palace at the end of July. Whether we go or not, my vanity is amused and I am glad I was invited.

I am beginning new poetry now my book's gone into Fibber. I would like to make some good solid poems in iambic-pentameters. I am reading all the five-foot verse from early to blank-verse through Elizabethan and the occasional sonneteers through Hopkins and the best five-beat contemporaries. Not forgetting Omar Khayyam. Soon I won't be able to ask for the salt or order a drink but in the iambic-pentameter.

I'll have a double Teacher's please with water.
Are you the landlord's wife or dirty daughter?

And now this whistling letter is let go
To Otley oer the secret bowers of snow.

love, Sydney X X

194. *To Charles Monteith*

9 June 1976 Madron

Dear Charles,

I am glad you are pleased with IMPLEMENTS IN THEIR PLACES. It seems a terrible long time till autumn of next year. Dear Charles, do your best to fit it in there. Meantime I will think of some possible draft blurb ideas.

Now Charles, can you help me in this. The long poem, *Implements In Their Places*, has only appeared in Canada and, of course, I think it is good and important to me. I would like it to be seen in this country before coming out in the book. The only magazine I have sent it to is LONDON MAGAZINE which had taken TEN SHOTS OF MISTER SIMPSON, in my collection. Now (This is me asking your advice.) a small private press would probably print it. Or Carcanet Press. If it came out with soft covers would that be all right with Faber? I would appreciate [it] my dear if you could let me know soon about this.

Again I say I am envious of you being in Rome. I loved it and how small the city walking across and out to the beginning of the Appian Way and you can see the Frascati country rising.

We have an invitation to the Queen's garden party in July so we will be in London and maybe we could have a drink together. I am taking my cat up in a basket to look out at Her Majesty and, if she is handshaking, maybe I could open the basket a little to let his well-groomed paw come out to be shaken. No doubt you have shaken her paw many a time.

love and good pleasure to see you, Sydney x

O Why Am I So Bright?

O why am I so bright
Flying in the night?

Why am I so fair
Flying through the air?

Will you let me in
After all I've done?

You are a good boy
On the fields of Joy.

We see you as you go
Across the fields of snow.

We will not let you in
Never. Never. Never.

W S Graham
Madron
August 1976

195. *To Karl Weschke*

13 July 1976 Madron

Dear Karl,

You might like to have those bits of verse. I think the Simpson poem is complete. The other sheets of Quantz are early and not right to the eventual poem but I know you will think them splendid and be intrigued. The 'Karl' is not meant to be you. You have no natural musical talent. Meaning no harm. OK. That is enough.

Yours truly, Sydney X

196. *To Terry Frost*

WSG Madron, Penzance. The kernel of the night of 24-11-76

Dear Terry,

Thanks for your catalogue with pictures in it. I didn't know you had such a range of visual disturbances put forward. I can see your mind is sparking in the noble and great way. I mean no joke. I mean by the word 'noble'.

It is four in the morning and I have spent an hour putting a new ribbon into my taprotter because I found it was very difficult to make it go. So you are the first person I have made my poor old machine try to speak to. Good gracious me. I am from the Hindo Kush. It is four in the morrrrrrning etc. Good boy.

I am very pleased you heard the poem and liked my reading. We didn't hear it very well ourselves. Our crystal-set's cat's whisker seemed to miss rock-face it was meant to lean into. You will understand that, being the kind of painter you are. I mean you're a good aware man.

I have lost or given away the Crete poems. If I've given them to Canada they are gone and I'm daft. What a pity. Nessie has ransacked our wee house and there is not a vestige. I don't understand the bit in your letter – 'Printed a Lorca last week sold several in Canada.' No-doubt you know what you mean. Don't be so daft. Take your eyebrows off and come outside an al knock the heid off ye.

If you want me to unite with you (WOW WOW) in some words on some visual escapade please let me know. There is no other one left (I know I am being moved by my early times.) I would like better than you to make something with. The quick brown fox jumps over the (good my boy).

I send my love to Kath and the boys and thank you for your catalogue which of course is only the small pictures very far away from the good pictures they represent of other dimensions which would be a great experience to be beside.. WOW.

love to you all, Sydney

P.S. – Kath, I send you a small kiss on the right hand side of your cheek, X

P.S. I enclose one wee bit of Crete I found. But why don't you tell me what it is for? Maybe I have something in stock more suitable. How do you look in stripes? Or, for the Queen, mauve. Remember old Mauve? A very nice man. WSG.

197. *To Fraser Steel*

8 December 1976 Madron

Dear Fraser,

Here I send you the poems and introduction and linking remarks for LIVING POET. (Is it LIVING POET or THE LIVING POET? Your letters differ.) I have timed these seven poems at the speed I think I will read them at.

The texts of the seven poems without titles add up to 18 minutes. The introduction and remarks add up to 4 minutes including poem titles. With the pauses and the way it will be I think it is right for the half-hour slot. You will know better about timing it.

Now, Fraser, if the purpose of the introduction and links (presentation) is to make the LISTENER all ears and also inform, I think this succeeds. It departs from the usual tone of the presentation of a verse program. It is because the poet is presenting it himself. Therefore I think I am allowed to approach the LISTENER with a more intimate immediacy. Don't be frightened of such a shock beginning as 'Can you hear me?' My attitude in this program is to set the actual readings of the poems before the public in a less formal, more human way. I am very pleased with it. After all that I am ready to take what suggestions and changings you might want to offer.

best wishes, Sydney

From a poem in progress

A DREAM OF CRETE

And wakened into dream to find
Myself falling with ancient speed
Slowly through the dark dividing
At my headlong approach. The Malia
Plain of heroic ghosts floats
Its floor up to discover me.

Mother I have tripped and fallen
Out of the sleep I know into
Crete at night with some words
Trailing in worlds above me from
My making tons. Why did you let
Me out of you both to land here
Not knowing? Like a new war-friend
I land and tumble over and tuck
My notebook safe ready to kill
Reality by my literature.

Here I am trying to brush the sleep
Off my Hope Street Greenock chin
And lying looking up between
Now I know they are olive trees.

I have been here before have I
Been here before? The olive grove
Trees above me speaking down ask
Who are you how do you spell your name?

I try to introduce myself.
I try to speak what I think is
My home tongue. I had hoped
Not attempting the least edge
Of that language, my dream's creatures
Would shelter me and be interested.

And that is what has happened. All
I have done now is to put on
A mask of features of imagined love
And look, see, they steer me into
Not a cave but the plucked wires
Of the taverna of Nickos Poulis.

Seven

' I AM AN EXPERT OF ALONENESS'

1977–1986

LOCH THOM

1

Just for the sake of recovering
I walked backward from fifty-six
Quick years of age wanting to see,
And managed not to trip or stumble
To find Loch Thom and turned round
To see the stretch of my childhood
Before me. Here is the loch. The same
Long-beaked cry curls across
The heather-edges of the water held
Between the hills a boyhood's walk
Up from Greenock. It is the morning.

And I am here with my mammy's
Bramble jam scones in my pocket.
The Firth is miles and I have come
Back to find Loch Thom maybe
In this light does not recognise me.

This is a lonely freshwater loch.
No farms on the edge. Only
Heather grouse-moor stretching
Down to Greenock and One Hope
Street or stretching away across
Into the blue moors of Ayrshire.

2

And almost I am back again
Wading the heather down to the edge
To sit. The minnows go by in shoals
Like iron-filings in the shallows.
My mother is dead. My father is dead
And all the trout I used to know
Leaping from their sad rings are dead.

3

I drop my crumbs into the shallow
Weed for the minnows and pinheads.
You see that I will have to rise
And turn round and get back where
My running age will slow for a moment
To let me on. It is a colder
Stretch of water than I remember.

The curlew's cry travelling still
Kills me fairly. In front of me
The grouse flurry and settle. GOBACK
GOBACK GOBACK FAREWELL LOCH THOM.

In 1977 Ronnie Duncan and his wife Henriette, both of whom had been seriously ill, suggested taking the Grahams with them to Crete. The Grahams were keen to return there and despite Sydney's erratic and uneasy behaviour ('I am not really a good man socially for more than about two or three days.' 'I am a nervous man feeling unloved and greedy and lyrically manic.'),[1] he was again deeply moved by the character of the Cretan people and their landscape and frequently referred to both later.

Following a suggestion made by Anthony Astbury, Charles Monteith discussed first a Selected then a Collected Poems with Graham. *Implements In Their Places*, published in an edition of 2350 in September 1977, was almost sold out by March 1978. In view of the imminent preparation of the *Collected Poems*, the *Implements In Their Places* volume was allowed to run out of print, causing some annoyance to Graham who was giving several readings during that period without there being any books to sell to the eager audiences. *Collected Poems* was published in November 1979, followed by a *Selected Poems* issued in the USA by The Ecco Press.

Graham himself was more and more in demand as a reader of his poetry and several of the letters show the exacting standards of performance he strove to maintain. He usually controlled his audiences with considerable dramatic skill; appearing at first to be speaking very slowly, he also spoke extremely clearly and rhythmically, making plain the structure of the verse and keeping its metre. He held a very small hesitation at the end of each line, even where the 'sentence' continued into the next line, and he sensitively deployed the wide dynamic range of his voice. It seemed as though his delivery of a poem was, at each reading, a fresh and thorough exploration of what sort of a newly discovered 'object' that poem was, or a new experiment in what it might be made to become. The drama seemed to come from the work itself, not to be dependent on an actor or projected as part of a personality cult of the author. There was nothing casual or conversational about his performance, he appeared confident, even authoritative, but members of the audience felt themselves personally addressed. As with music, the poetry represented the public performance of an essentially private and individual communication. Although he would have been the first to say that the poetry must be continually remade by other voices, his own readings made such an indelible impression that it was difficult to hear other voices without comparison. Graham made a number of BBC broadcasts, recordings for the British Council and for Claddagh Records, the Library of Congress, universities, and private collections.

Although his readings continued to increase his public, Graham's health was suffering and some of his later performances were affected by the drink needed to steady his nerves. The readings he gave in Edinburgh, Glasgow, and Dundee in 1981 were to be his last visit to Scotland. He had hoped to be able to spend his final years there. From time to time the letters show how much he wanted his work to become better known and appreciated in the country he loved.

The poetry itself demonstrates the degree to which Scottish images, vocabulary, and clarity of address informed the structure of his verse and occupied his imagination throughout his life.

1 To Ronnie and Henriette Duncan, 1 June 1977.

198. *To Ronnie and Henriette Duncan*

11 January 1977 Madron, A day as high and blue-souled (if the soul is blue) as a guid body could bear.

Dear Ronnie, Dear Henriette,

this is only a letterette to say that after much deliberation and overcoming timidity on my part we have to decide absolutely, –

Yes let the 4 of us go to Create together. You will both have to put up with my manic, nervous self but we will have a come and go between us. I think we should be able to manage it, I don't want to go into it now, at length Ronnie. The main thing is -We are saying yes let us go, the four of us. It will be a good thing. I can't think of going to Crete in better company.

So, as far as we are concerned, you can begin arrangements. It doesn't matter when 'Implements' comes out, You decide on the time etc. And please keep us posted as your plans proceed.

I never thought I would ever see Crete again. Maybe after this visit, if I am spared, I will really do a good *Dream of Crete* with your help. Can you just tell me now what period of time you had in mind in Crete?

Henriette my dear, Ronnie my dear let us get ourselves good for going to a foreign country.

What a lovely visit it was. Write back and I will right back. Ness says how great we shall go.

– love to you both, *Sydney* X

199. *To Ronnie and Henriette Duncan*

19 January 1977 MADRON, Penzance, Cornwall.
A GREEK FRIEZING HAPPY DAY

Dear Ronnie, Dear Henriette, Brave Travellers,

Yes everything is settled in our minds. It just took a little while for us to arrange ourselves towards the idea. Now we are sure. It will be a rich (God sparing us) Time for all of us in Crete and for each of us respectively. And we really don't know each other very well so, whether we like it or not, we will be discovering new things in each other and that is another country we are going to.

I have a competent side (How surrealist!) about times and places and can be anywhere I want when I want when I decide. So don't worry about that. Getting to Gatwick is easy. We shall be there to meet you. Ness, Yashmaked and I myself with my black turban and Turkish skirt-trous-tucked into my boots with stick from the White Mountains.

Ronnie, suggested itinerary could not be more exciting. As we exchange letters all kinds of ideas will come up as to things we might do. Maybe you'll be bringing your tape-recorder, for bits of untourist-conscious song and speech. Oral objets-trouve. And I will be, this time, putting down some words 'on the spot.' Ho Ho, maybe, my good wool-gathering boy, we could skin a goat or two and introduce some Cretan fibres into the Yorkshire shooting jackets. NOW I'M IN A HURRY. Nessie's poised for the post. More later. This whole beginning could not be better.

Henriette, we will all draw great disturbances from this event.

love to you both, Sydney X X

200. *To C.H. Sisson*

24 January 1977 Madron, Penzance, Cornwall with the wind rising about the gable

Dear C. H. Sisson,

Here I am at my table in the middle of the night going over your book again and reading softly aloud (not to wake Nessie asleep upstairs) certain passages to try them on my tongue. M'dear (allow that Cornishism), it is a good rich book filled with new things for me. The quality of your voice I like. I find it immediately near me and not so far away as anybody might think. I think the advent of your verse is going to help our contemporary English poetry (Whatever that is.) and batter fashion a bit. You speak with the real authority in this 'timeless' voice. The critics, the reviewers, will take a long time scurrying about to decide how to receive you.

I know THE CORRIDOR well now. Although you are a very different man from me, so much of your poetry my soul can use.

Nothing is what I have done
Where I have been
These long years

A guid New Year and happy Hochmagandy.
love, WSGraham

201. *To Anthony Astbury*

3 February 1977 Madron, Penzance, Cornwall. Internal weather Manic

Dear Tony,

I opened your letter to Nessie automatically, not thinking and saw your proposal, LOVE TO W.S.GRAHAM. My dear Tony, you are a good boy making your way through your difficult air. But I would not like that. I realise the proposal is an honour and also a love-gesture but the very idea of it is very apart from me. Therefore let us forget it. Every good boy deserves favour. EGBDF.

So do not do it. You mentioned the list of people you invited to say something good about me which you enclosed (which you forgot to enclose) and you should stop that immediately. It is not an idea which could give me any happy.

You must be becoming a man of some years now, with good all-round awareness. So here we go, each of us in our great travels. Love, Sydney X

202. *To Terry Frost*

25 February 1977 W S GRAHAM MADRON A SOBER GREY DAY WITH THE MIST IN FROM THE WEST

Dear (Tall man mad on colour) Terry,

I got your letter about Alan [Lowndes]. I dearly hope he is not as seriously ill as you conclude. Maybe his good greediness to over-power us all with talk will help his glands and organs to get over this wee bit. Your letter gave me a shock and made me realise how I would miss him not around in the great Betting Yard of the world. I know the younger Alan better. In the recent years you are nearer to him.

I understand what you mean about 'the deadly drink' and not eating. Even although some of us feel we have to take in the toxins (to maybe cushion us off from the fact that our values are moving away from the normal) I would not like to hasten myself down into the burny-burny. I dreamt I dwelt in Alco Halls. 'Mama Mama, the red wine burns like fire.' (Translation of the first line of an aria from a Sicilian opera.) TTBB. Pour me a double.

I have written Alan from my heart and what is left of my soul. I pray to the Invisible he will get through.

I hope you are proceeding with eyes which don't see over-brown (hot) or over-blue (cold). Love, Sydney

203. *To Alan Lowndes*

7 March 1977 Madron

Dear Alan Lowndes,

And there you are Master Alan Lowndes the lad thinking of your sins and I hope you are wanting to get up quickly to correct them. As you gain strength, no doubt you will be sitting up and after your lemon-juice you will be thinking up new jokes and puns to slay me with.

Slowly the blue-eyed world is turning round
Bearing all the beautiful lost and found.

I am still trying to exceed the speed of silence. I sit at my writing table trying to speak. My cat is the only human which understands me. Alas, its language is difficult and will take me years to learn.

When you can, do me a post-card. We have made many good times together. Up your pipe on a frosty night.

Good the boy, Love, Sydney X

204. *To Fraser Steel*

8 March 1977 Madron

Dear Fraser,

Thanks for your letter. I am pleased you like the Quantz poem and that you agree it will fit in nicely to the script.

About TRAVERSE. I considered it well, its difference between 'traverse' and 'transverse' as applied to the flute. 'transverse' is more logically acceptable but 'traverse' in the poem goes with its surrounding language which is a strange English coming from a translation of an imagined Quantz at that time. WOW WOW. Anyhow it couldn't possibly be a negative ambiguity. It is a flute which goes across and not straight out.

Of course I mean 'arpeggios'. That's why I said 'archipelagos'. It is making a quick little entertainment by putting down one word in stead of the other and both words making an exciting sense. At least I hope so. Again, I think we know he is playing a quick flourish of islands. WOW WOW again.

WOW WOW is only to signify I feel I've said too little in too many words. Let me know how things go Fraser.

My wife's asleep. My cat's out in its red-light area. It is about three-oclock in the morning. I thought I might go down over the shingle and the bladder-wrack and take my line and red-rag worm and row out over the loch. What do you say?

Yours traversely, W S Graham

205. *To Gordon and Mary Graves*

15 March 1977 Madron

Who do you think you are, writing to me at this time in the morning. You are lucky to get me up. But as it happens I am not up. I haven't been down in bawbaws. An American came yesterday with two bottles of whisky to do a thesis on me and I am at my writing table at 7 oclock in the rooking morning with Ness in bye-byes still and the noise of the sliver of the letter through the horizontal organ of the door and me opening it and reading 'Do you feel as I do – – – ' and me still half-drunk writing this before proceeding further and O where am I O can you stop me me OO I think O yes I half fallen done o down on the fl flower I mean floor but now Ah yes I pull my socks together and have some beer that's left and when I begin to write again I will have read your letter.

Dear Mary Dear Gordon,

I've got myself together a bit now and I've got Nessie up from above and she's down washing the front of her blantyre face. And I've read the letter. My dear my dear what a string of misshaps.

We think of you both and speak about you at all odd times when certain things come up. Like – Row you oer the keelo or Berlitz, or wire, or detective stories, or enamelling, or house-buying, or Mozarting, armaturing, ringing, loving, joke-telling, eye-seeing, you can see I can go on for ever and that is what I do with a blank page when it faces me thinking I want to say something. My dear, our respective backs are in fine fettle except we are both dying rapidly.

O O O Don't look now. Here comes Noisy Dancemore -

Love to the Wakefield Nightingale and the Glasgow Limner.

206. *To Michael Snow*

17 March 1977 Madron

So late, O Snow I Michael thee in mad smile ours O night. Your choirs o white Nile-side papyrus is lasting me out. My toprotter has lost its style. My falls are arching. My fun is fading my piles are flowering my stones are only unable to piss the geology test my lungs can't hold the long note in Il Mio Tesoro my skin is flaking off like (no offence meant) snow my talse feeth will not gnash my good old heart is hammering me to bits my pineal gland is pinking my third eye is breaking through my body is covered with leopards bees Carbunkles plooks old-scars limpets seaweed thorns punctures arrows signs-of-the-cross postage-stamps burnt cork cadmium cirulean lamp-black home-made-wine small-joys tattoos psoaris mistles maps (I see his life as on a map of rivers) beer-glass stains, love-bites, O O O O O no knudist ever I could be and cannot spell. I am a shell of fifty-eight and the white petals of your paper will see me out. Christ! What information I have given you. Maybe you're not anywhere? My brother you must look within yourself if you can find you.

I'm only testing the paper. The times are rapid. The world is whizzing. The clock is more nervously semaphoring. Have you ever thought what you would like to do? Not that there's much time really between sleeping eating worrying sex fixing talking having-your-hair-cut, cleaning-your-nails, sowing-on-buttons, lentil-soup-making, farting, beauty-loving, doing-pressups, lying, standing, being-wet, being-dry, being angry, being concealed angry, smiling, peeing, shitting, coughing, dunkarding, dispairing, fossil-hunting, aloneing, yearning for nothing, yearning for something, day-dreaming, getting up in the morning, getting, disguising-one's-self, pretending, making-mistakes, singing-arias, being frightened, falling down without a sound in a dream. Bugger you anyhow. Why are you asking me all those questions. Shall I go up perchance to?

In his tyme sa wrocht he. Paraphrase
Preposteress the queen within her gaze
    Living herself askance
Entities from afar with no bridges
Between her home of waltzing offices

And would not like to dance.

Paper-testing. Madron, Penzance 17 3 77

Signed by chief tester – W S Graham

207, *To Michael Schmidt*

28 March 1977 Madron

Dear Michael,

I am writing in great ridiculous ballpoint because Nessie is typing out TO MY WIFE AT MIDNIGHT on the same table. I am encouraging my wife to type and trying not to look at her out of the side of my eye to promote mistakes.

Thanks for your letter. We had a good day at Plymouth with Fraser Steel and I think I read my words clear and well. You are very kind in your remarks about the script. All I need is a taperecorder saying that into my ear day and night. Lovely to hear about you maybe doing the review in TLS. If I can help you let me know. For example I hope you will mention that I am influenced by Tibetan Verse (The Lasha Review). (Joke)

I also, am having (You will see that my calligraphy improves when I am speaking about money.) difficulties with finance. Here is the poem. Do you think I could have the £20 on receipt of TO MY WIFE AT MIDNIGHT.

You seem always worried, at the end of your letters. They all close with a phrase about the lack of money. Well, my dear, Michael, you must know what you're doing. I don't quite understand the 'drowsy numbness'. Did I write that, or you? I hope you don't let yourself be overwhelmed. Are you a poet first?

'Is not to ring the bell' 'There, at the highway's end'
'Lies hidden where exile/ Too easily beckons.'
'Done is a batell on the dragon blak'
'Weary of watching round the fire at night.'

I hope among all the fuck-up of finance you are writing your verse.

Viva Mexico & Manchester, W S Graham

UNTIDY DREADFUL TABLE

Lying with no love on the paper
Between the typing hammers I spied
Myself with looking eyes looking
Down to cover me with words.

I won't have it. I know the night
Is late here sitting at my table,
But I am not a boy running
The hide and seeking streets.

I am getting on. My table now
Shuffles its papers out of reach
With last year's letters going yellow
From looking out of the window.

I sit here late and I hammer myself
On to the other side of the paper.
There I jump through all surprises.
The reader and I are making faces.

I am not complaining. Some of the faces
I see are interesting indeed.
Take your own, for example, a fine
Grimace of vessels over the bone.

Of course I see you backwards covered
With words backwards from the other side.
I must tackle my dreadful table
And go on the hide and seeking hill.

208. *To Charles Monteith*

28 March 1977 Madron

Dear Charles,

We have just come back to our house from being away from Madron to meet your letter of the 16th. and see the specimen page for IMPLEMENTS IN THEIR PLACES. I am pleased things are going ahead. The type is all right but the moustache between the title and the first line of the poem should surely be taken out. The title is part of the poem. And the space between the title and the first line is part of the poem. If I had wanted to put something in that space I would have.

Charles, it is not even successful in the visual sense.

Best wishes from us both, Sydney

209. *To Charles Monteith*

Good Friday, 1977 Madron

Dear Charles,

I think we like the wee bit of us we know and what I say now is outside of all affection I might feel for you. This is serious and I speak, I hope, without humour.

The ornament (or whatever name we give it) will have to come out.[1] It does not matter what you are told by some other department, either the three earlier women or this new Production Controller, you are the 'leader' and you must know it is bad.

It is wrong on so many counts.

1- After the title the poem begins and the space between the title and the poem is the writer's. What if I had wanted to put a zodiac sign or an ideogram in that space?

2- The look of it on the page offends the eye aesthetically and makes that small page slightly more difficult to deal with. In the poem in your 'rough tracing' IMAGINE A FOREST, I see the title in caps and when my eye manages to scurry round the tache and begin 'Imagine a forest' my eye is still conscious of the disturbance before.

3- The ornament there is Victorian. Surely it is not conscious

1 The ornament (see proof page reproduced opposite) was removed.

Victoriana. If I'm supposed to be sky-trekking new frontiers of language on the blurb, what will the reader think of the corny fancy-work?

4- You have no right to put a mark between the title and the poem.

5- It is in bad taste. It is vulgar. It is not worthy of Faber and. Anyhow I did not write it.

Dear Charles, to shave the moustache off can't be too difficult. Anyhow, off it must come. Love and from Nessie.

Yours unhirsutely, Sydney

210. *To Albert and Hilda Strick*

22 April 1977 Madron

My dears Albert and Hilda,

Ah Mr Simpson. Ah Albert. Ah Hilda, in this chill April, I write this letter to you for nothing at all except to say that I think of you both at times outside the pub where we are all either nervous or by drink bamboozled. This letter's for nothing, or just to say that I am always conscious that knowing you both is an enrichment in my life. And that is that. Don't prune your feathers sitting there in your wooden house.[1] I am a bad man too. My image of you both goes up and down but, of course, the idea of you as a real couple with warm hearts, is true.

Yesterday I corrected 85 pages of my book for the publisher and it's coming out in October. We are trying to get ourselves into the mood to depart for Greece on Thursday.

This is only to say hello outside of the pub. I send you both a hug each. Albert, if you don't like that you know what to do. Off with your eyebrows etc. Hilda I am giving you a special kind of hug and if you don't like it you also know what to do. Off with your moustache and come round the back.

Remember this is a letter for nothing for nothing at all. Remember you are both being thought about with love somewhere when you are leading your Madron life. W.S.Graham

211. *To Carole Hope-Thomson*

24 May 1977 Madron

Dear Carole Hope-Thomson,

If you have any proofs of IMPLEMENTS IN THEIR PLACES to spare I would dearly enjoy having one or two. That must be Hillbilly Cornish. What do you think?

Dear Carole, we are back ten days ago from Aghios Nikolaos in Kriti. It was better than I remembered. I mean the places the tourists have not got at, me being a tourist myself. The villages you see in the distance halfway up the mountains are the places to go to to meet the Greek people pretty well Greek. Greek old people will speak to you if you make the least attempt. Anyhow we are back and it's taking a while to get over the sheer beauty of the place.

The sun you'll get enough of. It could fry a blue-eyed Faber-worker into impossibilities. Take care. When you sit on the edge of the fashionable taverna you will see a little speckle of oatmeal near the top of a mountain and that will be a village where they have never known the likes of you. Try to get there. I stop now seeing my 'passion' is running away with me and going off the edge of the paper. My layout is going to pieces.

OK, my dear, W.S.Graham

212. *To Ronnie and Henriette Duncan*

1 June 1977 Madron

TRUE TALK IN A KIND OF VERSE

We are back from Kriti and it's taking me a long time
to settle down. Apart from how I behaved there it seems
to have gone in deeper than my first visit.

Coming back on the plane I don't remember that it went up
and down much. Yet there I was in the first week waking
Ness in the middle of the night to say 'Ness, I still feel
we are not here and the world is heaving like a journey.'

I have written to you twice. I love you both and it would
be a stupid, avoidable catastrophe if you took the huff
From now on. Not only my cat would be appalled but our
respective, good vanities wouldn't be fixed up again.

I am not really a good man socially for more than about two or three days. That is how I would have behaved anyhow, filling myself with ouzo and making myself a 'funny man' to the mountain, more native people. I am a nervous man feeling unloved and greedy and lyrically manic.

The point is we must stay together not for you to give me any money or take us to Tibet or furnish my burying money. Let us in your life keep speaking and you keeping your lovely files good and keep speaking to each other for sheer regard. Oh Oh please stop. Can we get out onto that slope of the nearest paradisical slope of flowers and herbs we will ever get to? My dears, it is in me for ever.

My dears I was always aware of you both there with your own idea of the reality of your surrounding going. I don't know what you think I got from it but just to the right of my soul there is a cistern of visionary pleasure (forgive the pomposity) which is filled and which I draw from till the end of my days. OK. Stop. I am going off the beam.

Do not leave me now. Ronnie & Henriette, I need you as two people even all your distance away.

Let us four come out again
To do our peeps among the flowers
Gazing across the Kriti plain.

love to you dearest both, Sydney X X

213. *To Crombie Saunders*

24 June 1977 Madron

My Dear Crombie,

How pleased I am to get your letter, sad as it is. I am glad you have forgiven me not replying to the tape. Although Crombie, I thought I had. Remember I am a great man for the drink also my immediate life is disorganised and somewhat bemused. Sometimes I don't know where I am. I thought I wrote to you telling you how much I liked the tape and your speak-bits. My tape-recording broke down after hearing you and when I can use it I'll send something. So my sweet Crombie, here I speak not very well to you at Tom na Voil.

A good poem, Crombie. Nessie and I have read it to each other a few times now. It is a poem of no time, neither 'modern' nor early. It turns the heart. With presumption I suggest that it needs a title. Maybe something like – MY SON LEAVES HOME or GAVIN GROWN UP LEAVES HOME. Don't laugh at my suggestions, you will find a better title. But a title suggesting that, would help the reader.

You say – 'At 63, Sydney, one does not expect to write much poetry.' Crombie, that statement means nothing. Who does not expect? You were always one to revere the mysteriousness of the Muse. You might just be ready to be visited by her if you try hard in the middle of your lonely despair. Why shouldn't you change gear now, even among the difficulties of drinking and the unbearable manic life, and maybe find that your best poetry was just round the corner all the time. *You dont get anything for nothing.* I, myself realise, the act of writing poetry is my only salvation and I try to make myself put down the words when I feel I would rather construct a great sleep and turn my head to the wall.

Somewhere our belonging particles
Believe in us. If we could only find them.

WSG

Crombie, I will never take as long again to answer any letter you might favour me with. I leave you with two lines I have pinned on my board at my table here. They don't say anything very deep in themselves but they seem to me to be lines ending a poem I will write.

And how shall we allow the time to go
Across the fields without us.

your good friend who wishes he had known you better in our young Glasgow days.

love to Joan and you Sydney X X

214. *To Ronnie and Henriette Duncan*

19 July 1977 MADRON 2 am ATTACKED BY GHOSTS OF KRITI

.....rank with ouzo. Or what between us said the mis quote bitten boy is to be expected. I spy you there from the flat hot dazzling roof walking with coloured trousers to see your ouzo fellow-explorer. What am I saying? Why was I always stung at night. Drive further along the road the olives go steeply down and over them you can see out over all the ancient foreign miles of plain. What is to happen, my two dears I impossibly know? And what is to happen to each of us swinging alone in our wee hammocks of the soul? Wow Wow Wow Wow Waterloo. Remember the silver girl turning round and they all say 'O Yes.'

O dinna fache O dinna fache.
And bring back your fond moustache.
We will each be happier yet,
Ronnie Duncan and Henriette.

Maybe I should have stayed up in that village in the mountains to be eaten up by mosquitoes and ouzo and young black widows.

Love, Sydney X X

215. *To Sebastian Barker*

30 July 1977 Madron

Dear Sebastian,

How good to hear from you now grown up and editing this number of Aquarius.

I am pleased to hear Aquarius is putting out a number on John Heath-Stubbs. That is a good thing to do. I think he is a very good poet who suffers almost invisibility by not being nearly in the fashion. If I can write anything at all adequate about him, in any form,I will send it in in plenty of time. I am not good at this, but we'll see.

Yours sincerely, W S Graham

216. *To Anthony Astbury*

13 August 1977 Madron

Dear Tony,

Hello the boy. After our telephone talk at ten past noon in the King William, I write my promised letter.

I realised something had to be done to take us through the winter and start us on the next year. Therefore I have some readings lined up. Here is the list –

Wyvern Theatre, Swindon November 21st.

Poetry Society Oxford University November 22nd.

National Poetry centre, Earl's Court. December 2nd and I am doing a recording for DIAL A POEM on the same visit. ['To Alexander Graham']

In each of those journeys Nessie will be with me. I managed that by saying that Nessie was necessary which, of course is true.

The reading with Pinter sounds exciting. Please let him know I would be very happy and interested to read with him. By all means, Tony, let the machinery begin towards a reading. First things are the money to get us up and down and then a fee. (There is no way round that. I'm broke.) When might it be where?

Your most joyful news. The Royal Literary Fund would certainly be a great help at the moment. How good and thoughtful you are to keep me in mind. What do I do now? Do I wait till I hear from them? You have no idea how excited Nessie and I are to get this news. WOW WOW. The cat perceives this by our inhuman cries and gives a happy somersault and a great spring on to a record of my grandfather singing in Gaelic and sits there purring.

Yours faithfully, love Sydney X

217. *To Elizabeth Smart*

13 August 1977 Madron

Dear Elizabeth,

Well it's come to a pretty pass that someone I clasped in my younger arms is going to review my book. Do your best and write about it as though you have never known me in your life. (Which is half true.) Watch your spelling and beware of the big words with Latin endings and use 'superb' sparingly and don't put in a breathless explosion of language when your mind fails you. Make sure you have paid your sin-tax for the year. This was supposed to be funny, my dear. I realise I have fallen between. Anyhow how are you getting on at the piano? And how is your sister? And can you still make nail-marks on the margin of the papers you read?

Write in your best House & Garden style and if you really like my poetry it will show on the borders.

I hope your book is being well received and making a pleasure for you. I have 'The Kreutzer' on my Grahamiphone as I write, disturbing the soul at my age.

Yours ouchly, Sydney X

218. *To David Wright*

9 September 1977 Madron

Dear David,

Thanks for your PC. I am very pleased we have sought us out. I'm glad you like JOHANN JOACHIM QUANTZ'S FIVE LESSONS. You ask who he was. This is how the poem came about.

Ruth Hilton, Roger Hilton's exwife, came over to stay with us for a week. She is a musician. She had this book with her about the traverse flute by JOHANN JOACHIM QUANTZ. I went all through it and found it so exciting even although I am lacking in formal musicianship. He was a great man. Eighteenth century flautist, intellectual of musical aesthetics, a teacher of the flute to Frederick the Great and he wrote this book, still the definitive book on the flute. Although it was translated by someone, the style of the prose showed me somebody behind it I know I would have liked. I therefore made this poem (A PAINTER FRIEND HAS COME INTO THE HOUSE) in a kind of verse a bit different although they are lines of fives. His prose steered my verse. Even the strange rhythmed first line. It helped my imagined gestures.

It will be good to see my/your poem in the LISTENER.

Why are you leaving Braithwaite?

I am trying this time to be unlazy about the furtherance of my book. David, have you any idea or suggestions? Love to you and Pip, Sydney

219. *To C.H. Sisson*

29 September 1977 Madron

Dear C.H. Sisson,

I was just writing you when your letter came in. I am very pleased you like the book. I write with idiotic restraint. I put it this way. If I wrote my verse for the admiration of a living writer it would be yourself. I know you well I do not know you well through your voice.

OK that's a bit much but it is a difficult thing to say. I mean the values of the language you make are near me. I have no irritation or quarrel with them.

You did send ANCHISES. It is part of my household. We know it well. Your beginning of THE CORRIDOR is frightening and so immediately memorable.

Nothing is what I have done
Where I have been
These long years

I thought I had written to you thanking you for it and about some of the poems.

Remember always your words are an addition to my life.

Love (If I may.) W S Graham

220. *To Elizabeth Smart*

[postmark 30 September 1977] Madron

NOTES about IMPLEMENTS IN THEIR PLACES which might help, as they occur. wsg

I am trying to be more simple without narrowing the scope for the reader's imagination. The reader can still enter and make anything without reason.

I'm a great di-de-di man. All my poems have a metrical selfconsciousness. The poems in this book are in 'threes' or 'fours' or 'fives'. Even reading them aloud when I approximate towards normal speaking cadences it is the underlying metrical beat which keeps things together.

Some of the poems for me have more emotion in them than others. The Bryan Wynter poem shatters me still although it is mine and I just made it up out of my head. Also the Hilton poem and my father's poem. That maybe is to be expected. But that is the kind of poems they are. They are not better for loosening a tear from the eye.

I like TEN SHOTS OF MR SIMPSON. It creates a whole world consistent in itself and has the right mystery. This man the photographer is taking pictures of a man who gradually emerges and becomes (I hope) a creature of our concern.

I like WHAT IS THE LANGUAGE USING US FOR. It's a great place to travel in and it allows me to say some things a wee bit new for me.

I find already, in letters, that the few people who have seen the book tend to specially like the Quantz poem. Good David Wright sent me a letter liking the book and saying 'Johann Joachim Quantz seems to me the pearl.' Quantz wrote the definitive book on the traverse flute.

The IMPLEMENTS poem is not a random collection of aphorisms or nutshell poems. It is one complete object.

It is not necessarily a better book than MALCOLM MOONEY'S LAND. It has more lines of verse in it. It has an easier surface aspect which should not fool the reader at all.

In the texture. The nice choice of words. Maybe quote –
what ever you see to illustrate this –

Elizabeth, for the moment I have run out of anything more to say about Implements. It all sounds very pompous but one must speak from an attitude. It might help. Write and ask me any specific questions which you want.

Of course I missed you as soon as you went away and I pull myself together. So many things I didn't ask you. That monster bottle the first day put a deep-sea helmet over me and I was only a fool Gael from the north. Please write now and then in whatever literary style may take your fancy.

My dear my dear, your teapot is pouring well. I was thinking today if I could possibly write a wee poem entitled –

AND WHO WILL RIDE WITH HEATH-STUBBS NOW

I think a poem of mine is coming out in the Sunday Observer colour supplement this week or next or next. At least I have been paid (imagine!) £15

love Sydney X

221. *To C.H. Sisson*

1 December 1977 Madron 2am

Dear C.H.Sisson,

It has been a strange day and here I am with my wife gone to bed and the ingle with another log hissing on the fire. I think of you because I found an early letter from you saying you had Hiltons on the wall.

You realise, of course, I am done I am done. Never the less, my dear good creator, I think it is right you should have the enclosed bit of Roger Hilton. Don't think I don't know its value to my soul. It will be nice to have.

I think of your mind turning over often. I know you because I saw your face in the photograph on one of those hideous Carcanet pamphlets.

I have great affection for you there doing what you are doing. I am not as good a poet as you are but I am whipping up my dogs to get somewhere.

Love, W S Graham X

P.S. Maybe you wonder why I am giving you this. It is because nobody worth would get it if I went away. It came to me as a letter. WSG

I hope you realise that I am just done not done. I mean I am not feeling very well after London. WSG

222. *To Michael Snow*

undated [December 1977] Madron

Dear Michael,

I presume you know who I am. I am here at my age,
neither older or younger, sitting at my table trying
to think what is the respective worths of replying or
sending out a Christmas or Fuckyou card to whome.

My dear my dear my Michael de Neige, how are we getting
on. No need to answer that, my Beauty. The world
is getting ready to put a new number on the new per-
iod of time and we will have to remember at the beginning
to write down its new name. For us all in some way the
new year is climbing up over the hill to present itself.
The buds on the red-currant bush are there already
saluting the approacher, 1978.

Time we are always in, Michael. I don't suppose we can
say – How is Time dealing with us? It is how we grow
or journey towards the end. What have you done to have
put on you in a letter such heavy homespuns? Never mind,

my slightly Northern sweety, maybe do you think we
will be all right if we are good boys and have our
black puddings and chitterlings? We must keep our
helmets buzzing and our curiosities alive and have
courage in the times we drop and miss a step.

We know very well that our respective secret values
are not known to plural us. But in spite of that I wish
your soul Good Appetite and a certain release from any
earlier torment you have been suffering (if that is
what you want but I could have made a mistake). I
mean A Guid New Year. I have always loved you according
to my cut. I am having new sails set. I'll always
keep the mizzen, the sail of direction.

Maybe I'll see you before this gets to you. On the
other hand, when you reach this bearing you might
sail over the spot with all your hands on lookout
and find just only some floating signs. A hencoop.
The cap of the ship's master with Mooney in guilt on it
floating. A cabin-boy's sea-chest. The horn of a
gramophone which had somehow trapped air. A tinned
black-pudding and spars and a splintered life-boat. O
yes, I forgot, also a half-enjoyed bottle of whisky.

Yours sincerely from the sea in a bottle, Sydney X

223. *To Fraser Steel*

16 December 1977 Madron

Dear Fraser,

How pleased I am to meet to see you here beside the Madron River singing like a choir boy from Paisley Cathdral dressed in your white collar but with a faint moustache on third from the left front row.

O I have made a mistake. I meant to say – How pleased I am to get your letter and hear from you.

Fraser, I'm glad that at last the reading is coming out. I hope you are doing all you can do in publicity. Can you get them to put a few lines down in the RT and or even a photograph of me at my best. Forgive me, I am being too greedy. I think it will be a special thing for both of us.

I am pleased you liked falling into the sea. I understand what you are saying and if I can make anything near your requirements I will send it. 'I know it is some fish you want.' Forget that bit I was only thinking of Newby going down the Ganges asking an Indian fisherman for fish and his polite reply. He said something like – 'I am only a poor fisherman and I am not giving you any fish.' A mistake of translation. He must have meant 'I am sorry although I am a fisherman I am not able to give you any fish'. Fraser, how good of you to think of me and to ask. If I can write anything I think might fit 'NOT NOW I'M LISTENING' I will send it.

I have just been to Swindon and Oxford and the readings went better than I have ever done. And then I did a reading in London which was the very best. OK OK OK It is all right. In London Harold Pinter (who made a reading of my poetry with the other two) was at the reading and wants to make a reading with me in London again maybe at the Tate after the new year. I only tell you this because I have a seed in me of a proposed reading with Pinter maybe to offer you.

I stop quickly now. Nessie is finishing a frank farter and Der Poste is champing at the bit and the last tram goes to Auchenshuggle in the morrrrrning.

It is always a pleasure to write to you. Send me a wee note soon before the day. Love Sydney X

PS. I have my logs on in the good fire. It has a lovely flavour. WSG.

224. *To Michael Schmidt*

16 December 1977 Madron

Dear Michael Schmidt,

Forgive me taking so long to write to you after seeing your review. I know you are all for me. I think you should have stuck your neck out more. I think you should have made use of your space in the TLS to show your thinking better. I know how I struggled up through my early poetry to gradually get better and clearer. It is not like that. I was disappointed you writing in the old cliché about me. My dear Michael, now is your time to say something about how poetry works, from yourself. Why did you make it an extended blurb of a book. You had this area of print given to you (whether it was about me or another poet) to show whether you had any real values about the art of poetry. Why speak like an advert?

Shall I tell you my own measurement of my books? I am getting better I hope. But it is not like a graph saying 'he started out not knowing what he was doing and then went through his Dylan Thomas phase (Which I got a great deal out of) and now he [is] refining himself (You don't even speak as well as that.) and able to be clear and able to say the great, deeper things which were almost near him anyhow.' MALCOLM MOONEY'S LAND is as good a book as IMPLEMENTS IN THEIR PLACES. You see, my dear, you have fallen into the dopiness of your surroundings. Don't let me go on too long or begin to speak about your debut in detail. I had thought that because you were the editor of your magazine holding poems and criticism (reviews must be criticism at their best no matter how limited the space) you would have spoken clearer with a fresher attitude. To finish, I thought you would have been greedier to make your mark as an observer of what verse means and how it works. My dear Michael, a dull and uncourageous review. I even had two letters asking me why you were not more for me.

I thank you for your 'justice' first paragraph. That is all right and most of the readers will pat you for that.

Dear Michael, Don't let us have a review coming between us. Since I wrote you last I have been up here from the end of the Celtic Jetty giving readings in Swindon, Oxford and London. I think, my deario, I am getting better at making the good electric in the reading and 'slaying' the people.

What are you doing with your poetry? Have you another book coming up? You better get one out immediately so that I have a chance to know whether you know anything outside.

Come on, Michael, do your best, Sydney X

P.S. And so I end now with Nessie changing, correcting the stuttering typewriter. And I expect you to write back and say hello and that you send love and a pat on the head. I have been asked to go to do a week in and around Loughborough in Leicestershire in the early coming year. OK. WSG

225. *Sebastian Barker*

17 December 1977 Madron

Dear Sebastian,

It was a pleasure to meet you grown up and unrecognisable from the ghost of young charming Bashy to you now looking every inch a Barker and with a formidable first book behind you. It was a funny, strange visit, up through those stairs and along those stone levels of doors and meeting you and Elizabeth in that wee room and before we had time to say anything easy to each other the room was full of various other new people (I liked them fine.) which I couldn't cope with with all the drink in me anyhow.

I scoffed the brandy like a famous fiend
And Corrievrechened me before the end.

Dear Sebastian, I think it is a great book to begin with. What a courageous thing to do. To make it all sonnets. Your verse is filled with the lively rhythms and counter rhythms absolutely organic to the sense of what the words are saying. They are real sonnets with real sonnet lines and the wee iambic penta metra-gnome (not a dwarf who lives in the underground in Paris) beats out his measurement well. I can see they will become a model for sonnets of a certain kind, sonnets utilised to explore the self (which maybe all poems do) and explore one's relationship to another human. I think you make good poetry in the sex bits too. Which is very difficult. Most attempts are exhibitionary or masturbatory. Sebastian, as far as I can value the take-awayable message (which I know is not The Poem) I think you have great insight. OK, the book's a humdinger. It's worthy of your father and mother.

I leave you now maybe reading this 2 or three flights up in Peter Street (Nessie fell down the last five.) and I wonder what your AQUARIUS will look like. I mean the last five steps.

Love and Guid Hochmaganday, Sydney

226. *To Elizabeth Smart*

17 December 1977 Madron

My dear Elizabet,

You are a good, impulsive, Canadian girl and how very good of you to send me the £30 I asked for without the least hint of stricture. Your prose style managed it very well. It is difficult to ask, difficult to send and difficult to thank for. What mush I can still find myself writing. How are you getting on anyhow with your new prose work in progress? How are you getting on in nothing? I presume, like all of us, you are also set upon by the furies from the halls of angst. I get better at dealing with them. But the more I learn about them, the more they learn about me. Have you good people (I mean people good to be alive to.) near you in The Dell, Flixton?

I wrote to Sebastian honestly and it was a pleasure to write what I wanted to say. It is a very good book and let us hope the discerning should respond. Good George and good you making another poet come out of you.

Your tea-pot is pouring well and doing the job that a tea-pot should. Your Acanthus looks interested in the world. I am not a Christmas type but I wish you a merry one. I wish you a Guid New Year and lots of Hochmagandy.

Wow wow,wow wow across the dark
Shires and hills and lake and fen.
Wow wow, wow wow. The dogs do bark.
The Barkers are at the Poetry again.

Love, Sydney . . . .

PS. *Corryvreckan* is the great dangerous whirlpool between the Isle of Jura and Scarba on the west coast of Scotland. WSG.

227. *To Ronnie and Henriette Duncan*

18 December 1977

From Madroni high on a village inside my high inward mountains.

Dear my dear Henriette,

Dear my dear Ronnie,

Here we go and the time is turning round and the New Year is approaching over the hill. WOW WOW WOW and what is to happen to us four, each of us lonely within our selves. We shall be all right together again whether we go to Crete or Ardnamurchan Point or Madron or Weston or Heaven.

Henriette, your courage shames me. This is maybe another stepping stone to get over. What do you think there inside your lovely wee Swiss face where a stranger may never really enter? Please, my dear, keep the good joy in you and believe that maybe this is only a difficult part of the fight. How can I speak to you anyhow in your position. I am nothing, looking in at you with such presumption. I have your beautiful Crete book. Also I am becoming a better man as I grow older. Easier, not needing so much. Is that a good thing. Keep Ronnie calmed down. He is a fragile lad, not easily taking to strangers. MY DEAR MY DEAR MY DEAR MY DEAR MY DEAR MY DEARIO.

Dear Ronnie, my bad wooly-pelted boy, after Crete we will have to go up in the plane immediately again. You know, as they say in the stories, to keep our nerve we try again. This time the four of us maybe to an isolated cottage on the rough side of Jura. Nessie and I stayed years ago in Islay. We walked to Port Askaig and saw the great high bulk of Jura across the Sound of Islay. What shall we do how shall we behave in our little years left and to whom?

Good good my affectionate curious creature. We are all together. After all, I sit here typing in the damp of my house with your good cardigan on like your arms round me when I think about it.

What shall we do? My wee clock ticks. I am anyhow irrecoverably attached to you both for better or for worse. That is how it is. I don't suppose you happen to have a black-pudding about you? It will be a wee bit desolate if you are not here for Christmas.

My deario, if a hug is any good for your Swiss nature I send you the best. Keep loving me. Love,

Sydney X X

P.S. By the way, Ronnie, it wasn't my sixtyth birthday. There seems to be a movement to make me 60 before I am. Not that it matters but I like to have my age right. I envy you walking in Islay and seeing the lovely bare Rhinns. I had a 'rave' review in the Observer this week. I am on the 3rd programme (THE LIVING POET) for 1/2 hour on the 20th Jan. 1978 at 9-35pm. Please, my dear, write by return and give us a report. WSG

228. *To Michael Schmidt*

4 January 1978 Madron

Michael Schmidt (Mexico)
Director

My Dear Michael,

My first day up of such a Flu you cannot imagine. A special very new animal of virus fresh to the world.

I've been in bed nearly three weeks. It was like having cholera, rabies, malaria (Misquotes breed Malaria), leprosy, mumps, the skitters, world-sickness, all at the one time. My lips are cracked. My nails have grown. My legs are half ham-strung. I even have to walk about between the words with a white stick. Anyhow how are you there and how is your Brer Gloucester and what new year do you see stretching before you and shall Mexico be freed. Why did you not send me a box of home-made various kinds of tortilla(s)? OK, Michael, maybe I overdid things.

I am writing to you now leaving your review across the room because we would be getting nothing out of me writing now if I went through it. Let us leave it. I know you were all for me. What made me write to you like that was because I was expecting better writing from you. Not that you should say I was better than you did. It was you belittling, too much, for the sake of the last books, the early poetry. Of course I think there is an advance but, if I put out HERE NEXT THE CHAIR I WAS, now, I would be proud and 'THEY' would like it well. Whether this is an observation on the poem or 'THEY' doesn't matter. I would like to think there are more good poems in my later books than in my earlier. I meant this to be only a note to you however you feel and to say I like you fine and that you got over the swirling nights of Christ Mass. I want us to be the same as before.

What is the language using us for?

> But the quick brown pouncing god
> Magnifies towards us.
> He crunches it up like a bird
> And does not leave one word.

I have said my say. My cat doesn't like the trochaics in my new verse. It sounds like – – – – – O nothing at all. Have I ever met you before? WOW WOW OK OK FINISH.

Sydney X

229. *To Charles Monteith*

29 January 1978 Madron

Dear Charles,

Forgive me taking so long to reply to your letter of 30 11 77. I just found it difficult to answer and kept putting it off. It is still difficult. But here we go.

Charles, I think we get on and I am one of your poetic family, therefore don't let my business style suggest any disrespect to you. I am only trying to be factual.

I think IMPLEMENTS IN THEIR PLACES is immediately a success and should sell its edition out pretty soon. Please don't think this is just an enthusiasm coming from me signing so many copies at my readings or having 'rave' reviews. I can tell it has a surface entertainment for the people. I can't take anything out of it just as I can't put anything in to it. Don't think I am playing the Poet. It is one thing with a shape and it works.

MALCOLM MOONEY'S LAND maybe is not so easy to take. But the same observations apply. It is easily as good. I am just younger in it and maybe further from pleasing the people.

THE NIGHTFISHING Well, I like the whole book. It already stands for something in the language. I mean the whole book as an object.

My dear Charles, do you not see those early books are coming into 'use'. Be a not too patient publisher and fight (I know Faber is difficult to get poetic money out of.) *to get those books into another edition.*

Forgive me. The red line came out too formidable.

Therefore I would like them not broken up again after Penguin Modern Poets 17 in which I was allocated 53 pages.

I don't see how a 48 page, paper-back of selected poems is going to help me.[1] You mention the 'case of Robert Lowell' but that is not the same case. His name is known considerably more than mine and the 'young people's pockets' are more ready to receive it. My poetry is more difficult (not better) for the students yet.

So, my dear Charles, what is to be done?

I get various letters (not just from people who know me) saying

1 Charles Monteith had asked for Graham's reaction to a proposal to publish a 'Selected Poems' of 48 pages. On 3 February he replied, 'You have convinced me. We'll publish a Collected Poems, not a Selected Poems.'

they have written Faber asking for THE NIGHTFISHING and MALCOLM MOONEY'S LAND. Some get a reply saying it is out of print. Some are not answered.

Why does the publisher never tell the author how many copies are printed? It's a wee bit like the doctor not telling the patient whether he has cancer or not.

I get The Listener, The Observer, Stand, PN Review, TLS, Aquarius (All of which I have been printed in.) and good reviews in The Observer and TLS. Is there any indication that IMPLEMENTS IN THEIR PLACES by me is out and published by you? Apart from the reviews is Faber doing anything?

Could you remind the department to send the Durrant reviews when (if) they appear.

Will you reprint IMPLEMENTS IN THEIR PLACES this time?

My dear Charles, I got your Christmas Card. I hope the New Year has begun well for you and all the unpublishable desires have been started towards. This letter has almost killed me to write. I am only a simple ploughboy from the north. My dear, I hope maybe some communication has been achieved. Why don't we switch round? I'll work in Fabers and you come into the salt-galed air for what? Five years. We would never be the same again. I am absolutely delighted to be writing to you. Mozart is on the Grahamyphone touching my late soul at the end of the night now as I finish this serious letter to you. Love, Sydney

230. *To Charles Monteith*

8 February 1978 Madron

Dear Charles,

I am absolutely delighted you decided to do this. If you are ready, on your side, to set your machinery up (of girls departments), I am also. It will be a delight to communicate with them again. They must be a wee bit older.

Your good letter came this morning so, of course, I haven't had time to consider the shape of the book or what earlier poems to exclude.

OK. THE NIGHTFISHING and MALCOLM MOONEY'S LAND and IMPLEMENTS IN THEIR PLACES will go in complete.

I would not want the earlier books in complete. In fact, (as a quick reckoning because you say as quickly as possible) I think it might come out about two thirds of the pre NF poems.

There will be about ten pages of new poems (already written) but whether that is a good idea or not is open.

Of course I'll send you copies of the earlier books.

Charles Charles, it is lovely news. This is written with spacial speed to get the post through the Malcolm Mooney snow.

Love to you and the girls, Sydney X

231. *To Anthony Astbury*

14 February 1978

Madron in its kernel of unique blizzard the only communication being Mister Malcolm Mooney and his delinquent dogs whose names are (from the leader back respectively) Sarah, Tom, Skimoy, Anthony, Wowwow, Cinnamon, Nessie, Geoffrey, Jessie, Foxglove. I log the date as 14-2-78. Wind force 10 NNE. O God, the dogs have not eaten for five days. They are beginning to gnaw their leathers. I don't even know where I am. My compass is useless here. My pemmican is running out. Why did I set out anyhow on this white hell of a journey? Who to find?

Well. I've got the tent up. 15-2-78 I think it must be. A blizzard of such force has got up it's a wonder the tent is not carried away. The dogs have very good been. Remember them. I had to eat Jessie. It was necessary. She was unusually tough (I've eaten dogs before in China, on the banks of Yangtze in a barge-haulers' village in Nanking Province where I was summoned by Ezra Pound to help him translate but I fell into the midnight water of the moon and was not a great help.) but a certain part which shall not be mentioned went down alright.

Please don't think I am unhappy. The dogs have been very good. I almost ate you the night before last but I realised there wouldn't be anybody to write to. I suppose you would have tasted best of all. YUM YUM. I think – – – –

O I suppose I am drowsing off. It is the cold. Although I don't feel it now.

I– – – – I will not be writing much more. But everything is ok. I am not even hungry. I appreciate you and Geoffrey and Harold doing that reading. But– – – – the terrible howling of the white cats

– – – – why where is Malcolm tell him where to find. Geoffrey's gone anyhow. I picked him clean yesterday. I bit sweet. I th – – – – – – –

I am putting this statement into this empty soup tin which I am going to tie to the stern of a ski and push up through my frail but loyal canvas. Take care of my cat. You will see now – – – – at the end – – – – (I hope I do not embarrass you, Sir.) I mean now I am not bothering to make up poetry.

cherrrrrio. I could do with some chitterlings. I– – – – finish now fare well

232. *To Fraser Steel*

6 March 1978 Train to Loughborough

11am. On the train hence the Auchenshuggly[1] calligraphy. We are on our way to do 7 readings starting at Leicester Un. We are centred in Loughborough from Sat 4th to 11th. and jaunt off to readings from there. I am (I forgot to begin 'Dear Fraser') really writing you to say I listened to your Edward Thomas Prog. last night. It was good in the sense that when it ended I wanted to get into Thomas again and read him with more responsibility. I have always thought he was under-rated. He has the best qualities of the Georgians but that is apt to hide the fact that his best poems have other almost frightening serious qualities which lift him out of being a Georgian poet at all. OK OK Anyhow it was a programme to be reckoned with. I think you could have made it plainer who was speaking when. More should have been said, in a language way about Thomas's special quality. I think you and Schmidt and Sisson spoke best. I was touched to hear Sisson say something like – When I read Edward Thomas it makes me feel ashamed of my rhetoric. Of course it is just that their 'voices' are very different in timbre. Love from Auchenshuggle.

Sydney X

1 Auchenshuggle was the terminus of the no. 9 Glasgow tramcar route. 'Shuggly' means shaky.

233. *To Don Brown*

20 April 1978 Madron. A bleak Spring day.

Dear Don,

A sad thing you went away like that, mostly my fault. I was flippant in the drink when you came with your news and I didn't take it in that this time it was serious and irrecoverable. It must have been more than irritable. Please let me still be your best friend and number one chum for Don Brown's route sake. And I will write you a better poem and colour pictures for you and feed you real Scotch black-puddings and speak to you to make you laugh and behave like a realer extravert than myself. We will be fine together again. And remember you are less than an hour away. When you come this time shout with a great shout at the gates.

I am at my writing table, of course trying to put my life in order. It's a quarter to three and I've missed the pub but I'm not hiding in my bed and I'm making an effort to be better.

I speak out of a hole in my leg. I got up at six oclock in the morning, perfectly sober, and tripped and fell and the sharp corner of a board sticking out from under the mistress mattress went into calf of my leg 1 1/2 inches. It cut two veins and you could see them like broken pink worms in the hole. I've been twice to the hospital. The stitches are itching now. The surgeon said I would have bled away to a poetic death. So there you are, Don. You must keep being my chum. Come armed with chitterlings.

love always, Sydney X

234. *To Alan Lowndes*

11 May 1978 Madron

Dear Alan,

The red bridge has been up in front of us for a good while now and it has given me great pleasure and enriched my life in all moods. I'm sorry I didn't acknowledge its arrival. I have been up and down and creating like a fiend and even now I speak out of a hole in my leg, my left. Do you think you will be able to become the person who will forgive me? It is a great bridge and the picture has the good strength which goes into the bones.

Although, to tell you the truth, I thought you might have put a wee bit red and green on the signal arms. That goods train going to the left, where is it going to? What age is the girl holding on to her wee sister? And where are they going and, if their father is in the pub, is their mother ready to give them love and black puddings?

Of course, maybe their father is a teetotaller. I see an industrial crow perch up there high on the nearer railway signal. He gives a crake seeing the men in their well-painted attitude and sees the two sisters.

I will lend you Malcolm
Mooney my friend to seem
To take you out to find whatever it is
You need or think you need across the ice.
Deep in the berg there is a freezing office
With an emerald window
Waiting to deal with you.

The beginning of a new poem. OK OK Love to you all — Amanda, Martin, Rosalind. Love to you and Valerie. x x x x x
Sydney

235. *To Anthony Astbury*

25 June 1978 Madron

My Dear Tony,

Good to see you after the reading. I felt I read well. I enjoyed the speaking out into the darkness. It was pure black. Not a face to be seen. I hope you think I spoke clearly. At the beginning I was nervous and frightened. After the first minute of words I found a confidence and professionalism beginning to rise in me. I hope the audience will be marked. We all read well.

That was Wynter's jacket. Nice to see Monica there. Antonia with her forgetmenot blue eyes and her remoteness. Edna O'Brien putting her Irish arms round me. WOW WOW WOW WOW WOW.

What is the title of the poem? How good to see you. Remember Johann Gramm. Do you think you are going to be all right? Remember to breathe from the diaphragm. Don't be put off by the other animal. Make an effort to know the grammars and currencies of the language you cast your bread on. Otherwise you are lost. A drop of Bols? Send me five herrings.

Good boy good boy. It's late. I'm going to bed. I've had my fling. The typewriter has been putting me into words all day. I am losing power. What is my name where do I live what do I do what do I look like where am I going?????.

Love, Sydney X

236. *To Arthur and Peggy Caddick*

4 July 1978 Madron

Dear Arthur and Peggy,

WOW WOW the years are picking up speed flowing under the bridges and here we are. And what is happening to us? My lower teeth are ruins. I am writing with glasses. Yet, my dearios, I suppose we are riding through Time, or somebody's theory of time. In our wee bit garden we've put in LOVE IN A MIST, COSMEA, CONVOLVULOUS, SUN FLOWERS, MARIGOLDS, FORGIVEMENOTS, POETS BANE, SYNTAX DAISES, OLD POETS BEARD, CADDICK BANE, WHISKYWORT, PARSLEY, MAIDENHAIR FERN, PANSES, SWEET ALLYSSOM, WILD WOODBINE, TEAZLES, SHEEPSBIT, and Caddick and Graham riming weeds. We shall have rain. See the snails are snarling and running away across the road to be smashed. Willy wagtail is taking up his specks.

Much love to you both always. [...] Sydney X X

237. *To Harold Pinter*

13 July 1978 Madron

Harold Pinter
Dear Harold,

OK there is this Poetry Night in the Purcell room organised by Astbury on the 29th of September. Gascoyne, Wain, Graham, Barker, Yourself (Shall I call you Pinter?), Empson, and I think nobody else. I would be pleased if you read some of my poems. Astbury suggested that you knew all about it and happy to do it.. And so what goes on. I would dearly like you to read some poems of mine. For every reason. Let me assume you are coming to read. And so

Harold, what would give you the best pleasure to read? Have you any books in your Portugese house to choose from? We have been given ten minutes you, fifteen minutes me. I am reading a poem (It is in *Implements In Their Places.*), TEN SHOTS OF MISTER SIMPSON which roughly takes 12 minutes. And maybe two lovely sweeties to make things neat. WOW WOW. Now I ask you (You are the best man at this.) where 'and in what position' shall we read? I mean, shall we read one after another or you to come out with the poems of the good boys between? It's bloody Early. I'm worn to a frazzle with dream.

Anyhow, Harold, give me a sign of what you would like to do. I have later poems. Shall I send you to choose from? Last night I finished Mary Queen of Scots. A great experience. I know you're a busy man but let me know what you think. So said the hangover poet at 5 am putting down his French and flowery lute after the queen had slid in under into bye-byes.

Spooner

Which never moves, which never
Changes, which never grows
Older, but which remains
Forever, icy and silent

Love, I'll drink to that. Sydney

At last my COLLECTED POEMS is coming out with Faber in November. I've done the proofs.

238. *Michael Schmidt*

14 July 1978 Madron

P N Review
Mr Michael Schmidt
from very far
away from the beginning
slopes of the Sierras.
Dear Michael,

Hello How are you? Thanks for John Heath-Stubbs' book. I haven't written to him yet. I have been writing some short new poems. I have tried the BBC first. Is that the best thing to do? Which comes first if I want to come out there and in your review also? Therefore I might be sending you some poems. I have a poem, a big fellow, under my hand now quivering as I write, fresh from the depths. Can I get the hook out of his mouth?

Where how is your brother Gloucester and is he pressing his kin to publicly speak in a new book?[1]

I write this in the morning at 8 oclock in the morning already of the best summertime to occur. What is the magazine doing? I saw your name and Sisson's in the Listener was it. And STAND's editor. Don't think I am writing in this way being vague because I think I am above those discussions. Although it is true, I have to look after my power. You are all right, beginning from Mexico with good black eyebrows. My eyebrows have whitened and gone rogue. WOW WOW the light shafting into my granite den. I hear Nessie stirring upstairs and the coffee is perking. What makes me be able to bear making my once-young brain from the lovely burnish of the Firth of Clyde hammer out the laborious words. Anyhow, Michael, whatscookin? I have tomatoes growing. Hello Ness.

I feel pepped up this weather because we have come down from London and old friends and friends newly to take part in my life. Harold Pinter and an actress, Ruth Rosen, and myself. We read my poetry at the National Theatre. It went (from my measurement and outside) beyond my best hopes. Speaking into the darkness of the audience I was at my best. Pinter and Rosen read their poems so well. Pinter read MALCOLM MOONEY'S LAND and others. Rosen read mainly early poems but also THE FOUND PICTURE. I read THE FOREST, QUANTZ, WYNTER and TO MY WIFE AT MIDNIGHT. Antonia Fraser and Edna O'Brien overwhelmed me after the reading when we went down to the Green Room bar. I hope this is not too much gush but I know you will be pleased to know. Pinter and the director think something can be done in the future.

It was a stimulating visit for us. We went to Pinter's play The Homecoming which opened my unploughboy eyes to theatre possibilities.

P.S. And what is there left to say except the day is really going to live up to its promise, my thermo. is up to 80. I saw George Barker afterwards. OK. Love, Sydney

1 Reference to *My Brother Gloucester*, poems by Michael Schmidt.

239. *To Elizabeth Smart*

8 September 1978 Madron, Penzance, Cornwall. Mist and rain from the lovable west

Dear good Elizabetho,

A joy to hear from you but don't mind not writing when you're 'froze Up'. It does not matter. I only write (even to you) to help myself as well.

I am pleased you are going to remember me by those two symbols. Slicing the loaf of Life. Peeling the onion of tears. Deario, contain yourself.

We are listening to the best of Mozart. Ruth Rosen, who read with us that night at the National Theatre said she would send me The Magic Flute. I thought she had forgotten but this morning the red royal male knocked on the door and it was it. A great 'copy' with the best singings I know and thorough, not 'highlights'. So there you are. What face are you making now? I miss you I can tell I miss you.

I think the government should arrange for us to have a week together twice a year for our art's sake.

Your Akanthus is rather an ill boy. I think it is whooping cough. But your nasturtiums are everywhere and make a great glow. Love-in-the-mist is growing high and cool. The cosmea are good tough boys and girls and know what they're doing.

I am always for you, Love, Sydney x . . . .

240. *To Elizabeth Smart*

15 November 1978 Madron. A misty winday day

Dear Elizabeth,

As you know I have no French. Although I remember us laughing in Paris at hysterical pun language I uttered. There was an American girl and her French man. We were together for a day or two. Of course there was that CANCAN afternoon in Flood Street in the sitting room upstairs with the sofa. A good line of high kickers. Where are they now? There was John Davenport's wife who jumped. And Mary John. And sweet yourself. This is thinking of times past It is for no reason. Only your French pc brought it back.

I have your event,

pinned on my wall. I will be there.

The garden did well. Love in the mist. Cosmea. Convolvulus. Nasturtium. Lovely, my dear, washing the dishes to unsteam the window and see the random colours which I would never have thought could go together. If you have a seed or two to send us for next year pray send.

This morning I received a copy of the Observer Coloured Supplement in which I figure. A page-size portrait of me by Sally Fear (A wee beautiful coming-up photographer who came down and stayed the day.) and an article by Penelope Mortimer.[1] I quite like the photograph, me looking like a serious poet with something inside him which indeed I have. About the article. Penelope had a tape-recorder which went on most of the time. She was in the village three days. A sweet woman to me. She said we're the same age. A good-looking woman. If I had been interviewing myself I wouldn't have put things quite like that. Anyhow it is somebody attempting an honest impression of meeting me. Naturellement (Froggy) I would have liked you to come down and write it. There was no choice. Poet is who Poesy does. Would you like a kiss?

Penelope's idea was that it should come out on my 60th. birthday which it is, this Sunday the 19th. November.

We are both going up to Liverpool about the 21st. January to do some readings. I'm going to make chutney with my green tomatoes. How is Sebastian doing with his poetry?

Cheerio. I miss you. Love Sydney X

241. *To Michael Schmidt*

8 December 1978 — Madron

Dear Michael,

How very good of you to send the £60 so quickly. It was a real cry. You answered with good heart. And so we speak as though out of Judas Maccabeus by Handel. Sound an alarm, your silver trumpets sound. Smith takes ship to Mexico.

I don't know how you can go into a wee tirade about the boy

1 The novelist Penelope Mortimer became a good friend of the Grahams and briefly lent them her London flat.

from Gloucester. Of course you'll be another boy with other words with other ears to fill.

Michael, your clarity of type dazzles my eye. It is true that, poem or business letter, good clean type is half the battle. To be executed at five oclock in the morning is better in the light of an order seen to be typed on a new ribbon.

I wish I was going to Mexico with you although I know it would be nothing like what I imagine.

I was wearing my extravert mask.

Maybe terrible to ask but – If you could send me back THE VISIT and I WILL LEND YOU MALCOLM I will return them by return if that sounds logical. I think there is a word in each which has to be changed.

Again thanks for the speedy sixty. I thought I had told you about Faber's COLLECTED POEMS. Cheerio.

Love, Sydney

242. *To Ronnie and Henriette Duncan*

9 December 1978

And Loving is. Good Ronnie & Henriette. 9pm Mushydram, Penzance

You are both braver than me. As well as that you are both better than me. You are also better looking than me, Ronald. Henriette you are better looking than me. What if I had met you earlier? What if I had been somebody else? What if you had been somebody else? Ron, how would you like me for your father? Too late. I am gliding away. Circumstances has (It is in my nature to use 'has' at this time.) made you two different people together. The exchangement of your respective private-nesses, especially in the last five years must be but of course impossible to behold. O How Can I Say I Am Not Joking. I think you must have a courage further out than where I have come to now.

Anyhow where is it I've come to? Please is this the place? Kritsa? Krastepoulis? Kalimera. The flower is beautiful. Asphodel. Efcharisto.

Quick quick let me out of the motor-car to be sick across the road there where the edge will let me see down the great foreign valley of olive groves. Of course I saw in the distance the white speckles of what are villages I'll never know.

Swiss-pie, Guidwul, Dunsmuir, Ouzogrimm, into the car and we're away. Meeting none but meet many. Maybe an outside observer would see you behaving, would hear you thinking, different from me.

No moustached men from the White Mountains. Nor wolves. Nor POLEEP POLEEP (I grant you I didn't deserve them.) Mind you, Ronnie, great things went into me. Watch out and you'll see them coming out. It's a pity you weren't both out with us that night in that untourist cafe up over the brow of the hill and the daughter generously enamoured.

What's ma name? Baldy Bane. What's your other? Ask ma mither.

Christ can you not tell, Ronnie, I think I think I am rushing away or am I just naturally a fearful man. I am envious of you sitting on the brown pimple above Sanaigmore.

The next time you are in Islay keep your eyes open to maybe seek and find a cottage of small rent. I'm not, nor Nessie, going to die here. Ness and I have thought of this before, to try to get to Scotland. I mean on one of the islands.

Nessie has just read this aloud to me as a check (which, Mr Duncan, you will realise I have to always do in case I am being bad) and it passes. I feel *nearer* to you both after this. Keep loving me. Henriette and sweet Ronnie. Here's Ness [...]

Turn the other side and see, it is Sunday 10 12 78 when I arrive on this side I see I must have hammered out my words from the other side. The surface is like braille, or paples on boiling porridge or uncraters on a flat, yellow moon. Shall we speak again on this side?

The other night coming in,
I thought my scarf was my cat.
An easy mistake. He must
Be somewhere in my brain.
I wonder what he is at

We are all right, feeling the first chills of winter and trying to be grown-up and organise our life ahead. A reading in Liverpool on 21st January. A reading down here. I want to line up some more. I like all seasons but I am really a Winterophile. I saw a very red robin this morning. What small happinesses. Fuck it I've lost the washer of my hotwaterbottle. I'll meet thee on the frozen paps of Jura. They were the subject of my first water-colour as a boy. Is it cold today or is it me.

I think in your letter from Islay the note-paper heading has too many geese. Enough's enough.

So what we'll do this Monday morning in July is this. At 8 oclock send the Swiss-pie down by Aruadh raining or not and I will meet her before she encounters the loch-side. You will leave an hour later. Well my deario, says one to the other, what simple secret thing is it you want to tell me. Hugs were exchanged. The long prling cry of the curlew was unheard. Then I had to send her back to her apple-splitting father on his farm on the edge of the Alps. An hour later, Ho Ho my bad boy of the good eye and the water mills. I know you are not queer nor me. But I'll give you a great poetic northern hug because the centre of who you are is somehow connected with me. Or shall I go off to Rekavic with James Mason and descend into the centre of the earth? Which of you gives me more pleasure? I will stay here by the sweet Loch Gorm an hour or two till the midges' time. I'll meet you back at the hotel. You'll find Henriette changed as she will you. Get a bottle of the lovely blended ready.

I leave you now by the curlew-crying water. Sydney X X

243. *To Stewart Conn*

28 February 1979 Madron

Dear Stewart,

Thanks for the Glasgow Subway. I remember it well with its wheels and the smell of tarry rope.

This letter's to say that I wrote you about your book and the playing cards are away to Dundee.

Now, Stewart, even just through our business notes I think we get on fine so when I say that I had a letter from Carl MacDougall of Dundee University and sent him the poem, LOOK AT THE CLOUD HIS EVENING PLAYING CARDS, it is not meaning in the slightest a wee stricture because you have had it this time. I suppose it will come through you anyhow. It is changed slightly. Tell me you feel OK about this if you feel OK about this.

UNDER THE ICE

This feels daft. I wrote such a good letter very much liking the book. It warmed me to the cockles of my Art. It is the silliness of my position which allows a sentence like that to come out and stay. I can't begin to try to recall what I said last time. Anyhow it was all for. We got excitement and great pleasure reading the poems aloud. Of course I see I think I saw you looking up from the freezing glass I stand on. A book to be reckoned with. Maybe on the side of keeping a wee bit safe. Fight hard against the universality of the happy medium. As they say – I look forward avidly to your next book.

I'm glad you liked the poem. I hope the beginning didn't deafen you. I wanted it to sound like a shouted proclamation. My dear (The fishermen say that all the time.), I liked your poem to me. I like your wife better (two different kinds of object it is true.). Despatch her immediately with soda scones tied in a snow-white towel and a jar of her own make of strawbwerry jam.

Love to you both, Sydney X X

244. *To Matt Simpson*

28 February 1979 Madron

Dear Matt,

Forgive me greatly for not answering you sooner. Good poems. A special individual voice speaking from an interesting place. 'interesting place' – I mean your verse has in it a good hardness coming out of family values and physical working objects. And the people you bring in and the proper names and family expressions are immediately 'believable' and enter the reader with no doubt. I dearly love, as they say in Cornwall, MY GRANDMOTHER'S AFRICAN GREY.

Matt, you are to my measurement, a very good poet. You've got the imagination and the juice.

So what do you do? Everything you can think of to get your poems before magazine editors, publishers, any poetry platform. I can think of nothing but the long slog of sending poems out again even to magazines in America. Matt, early on I battered the American field. It helped me to get known and sometimes it paid very well. Try everything and keep writing and don't let yourself harden up with despair.

I am very sure you are a real special poet. You will be all right, believe me.

Love and strength to your making, Sydney. X

245. *To Peter Moldon*

4 May 1979 Madron

Dear Mr. Moldon,

Thankyou for your letters of the 25th. and 26th. Thanks for your sample-setting for *Collected Poems*. The Perpetua looks fine. I am sure it is going to be a goodlooking book, a pleasure to the eye and with great things in it.

One or two changes, and I hope it doesn't make difficulties for you, –

It is necessary that the titles of the poems should be printed in caps, every word. Please believe that this is not an affectation. It goes with the kind of 'word-conscious' poetry I try to write.

In that sample 'First Poem' and 'Second Poem' are too heavy and squat above the Perpetua. Do you think you could make it a bit lighter.

I forgot to say that I would like the titles to be without slope.

Lovely that it is to be in Demy 8vo. I am for blue for no reason. I won't die if it's not blue. The blue of IMPLEMENTS IN THEIR PLACES with the white name and the black title made a goodlooking book.

Again, forgive me, I have forgotten to say –

In your sample page, could I have CAGE WITHOUT GRIEVANCE and all the other book titles printed in the same all-caps as the poem titles. Maybe a larger degree. What do you think?

When you say 'Poems from 2nd Poems' I'm afraid it will have to be

Poems from 2ND POEMS

You see, although it sounds mad, 2ND also means 'To Nessie Dunsmuir,' my wife. OK OK. Forgive the changes.

Yours sincerely, WSGraham

246. *To Ronnie and Henriette Duncan*

5 May 1979

I am an expert of aloneness.

I see you both through the Moorish keyhole of your desire.

I didn't know it was a hotel now for tourists of the mills below the pikes. I lived in that place for five years when Abdullah, the great old Emir was alive. I had been invited for a considerable sum to teach the youg boy, the son, the beginnings of the syntax involved in iambics. He became my great friend and would hardly let me go when my great task was at an end and the young boy crammed and polished and ready to go with his father's gems to London and start a wee magazine. Good boy. He loved me like a father. His father gave me a file to put my poems in. Ronnie it was almost like those lovely files you give to me. But not so practical. Too heavy. The covers were thick encrusted with Arabian gold and infant rubies discovered just outside the white mud town. Good poor old Emir. He found it a great embarrassment finding out words that I was welcome to make use by night or day, of the harem of twenty-three creatures. Of course that put me off. But being a young spirited lad brought up by the Clyde's side, nature brought me round to be curious and one day I took advantage of his invitation. The ebony guards let me by and I walked through the corridors, blinding white sun on one side, Moorish dark on the other. When I entered they just half-turned then I saw they saw me different. There they were all lying just as in Delacroix's painting. Suggestions of enforced lesbianism and desperate clittertouching.. And what happened to the poor boy?

They descended on me like a herd of nymphic bees. OH what a terrible experience! They used me as a sex object. I was their will. They did everything to me. Their shrieks of unbearable ecstasy blinded my ears. The shrieks were in many languages, French, Highgate, Korean (with her fiddle), Swiss-pie, Karelian, Ethel (a mill-girl from Otley who said she knew you), a Hungry Hungarian woman with a passionate wisp of a moustache who almost took my best away, a Chinese butterfly, a very young girl from a house on the Rhinns of Islay. And Oh my dears, there I was, orgasmed endlessly and that is why the man you think you know now drinks and stutters and has to hide in the igloo applying himself to poetry.

I love you both as well as ever. As a matter of fact you are both as good as me. Nessie's sent off a letter, has she.

I think everything is OK if I can keep my health in trim.

Keep having a wee bit love for me.

X—Henriette X—Ronnie

X—me—Wow Wow Aba

Sydney

247. *To Gordon and Mary Graves*

22 May 1979

Madron 1pm, High blue sky, Tuesday. Temp. 45. Wind Manic.

– – – – – – – – – —— not' Stop up your gob says I an gave 'er the back swipe of my hand. Over she went in a drunken somersault of sexual ecstasy shrieking Mozart at his best and came to rest on badly designed linoleum between the refridgiceboxerator and the lord of the electric rings. Nobody saw me. Except the hanging implements of my desire. I realised they were hanging there looking at me. HO HO shall we say silent witnesses. (Funny enough she is still alive, Noisy Dancemore.) O O O O O I am losing my domestic metaphors. Seeing my milk-white love was breathing I I took down the eggswitcher and – —— — —

Och I am after to be losing the sight of you both there so far across the shires of England growing your tremendous flowers and teeth-drenching herbs. I miss you both. I miss my cat also. The spring has arrived with a keen wind. Feathered songsters are getting married and making very intelligent homes for themselves.

At this point I am away to have a drink in the pub with a young Jewish poet who has knocked on the door. He brought a half-bottle of Glen Livet. My dearios, I think he is a nice boy, about 23 3/4, with black wide-brimmed, felt hat of the Lebanon and a beard of the shape of a young Rabbi, and the echoes of the wailing wall still about him. But wheesht, he's out for a circumcised slash in my gentile W.C., a good boy with some poetry in him I think.

Gordon and Mary WOW WOW WOW See I am back. Judas Maccabaeus had to go. With joy on both sides, a good interesting, educated, aware boy from the great place itself, Jerusalem.

So here I am not at my best but for you both always at my best in your respective nomad bosoms. Nessie's blue peepers are concentrated and her St. John's Hamilton High School calligraphy is gradually filling up that lovely buff-yellow paper. I don't know what she is saying. My dearios, here is a rather used copy of a recent poem. Take it into your bosom with me. After your class shall we wait for you and go up to your wee room for Spaghetti?

love love, Sydney X X

248. *To Harold Pinter*

24 July 1979 Madron

Dear Harold,

Indeed it is a fine thing you going to do the reading with me at the launching. The poems you have chosen to read should come out fine through that Portugese trumpet.

I can see Nessie is pleased you are reading I LEAVE THIS AT YOUR EAR. Will you remember to put in 'For Nessie Dunsmuir'. TO ALEXANDER GRAHAM I thought you read very well last time. Harold, I think it was because you read it slower. Maybe I read too slow for some ears but it is right for me reading the kinds of poems I make. You should hear me reading THE WRECK OF THE DEUTSCHLAND. Of course, after all that, every reading is unique. WOW WOW said the boy. It will be lovely to hear you read THE FOUND PICTURE which I don't know through my ears very well.

We will be arriving at (not Euston) Paddington about 5pm on 29th. That is a long time away. Before that I'll know what's happening and maybe we could meet for half an hour somewhere before the reading.

Now definitely I can say my book, COLLECTED POEMS, comes out 12th November. Also a New York publisher [The Ecco Press] has a SELECTED POEMS under way. Famous is who famous does.

Thank you about my health. I am coming up. Love, Sydney

249. *To Ronnie Duncan*

28 July 1979

Ronnie,

I want to be back. I want to be back.

I want to be back with Ness somewhere in Scotland. Surely you can get some place. I have now had my fill of away.

The point is give us a wee place to finish in, in Scotland. I feel my life is finished here and I *need* to get back. Try your best.

WSG.

250. *To Harold Pinter*

11 November 1979 Madron

Dear Harold,

It is now three weeks to the reading of my poetry at The Poetry Society on 4th December.[1] Are we near enough the time for you to be able to say you will be free that night? Are you anyhow near wanting to do it? I mean, my good Harold, don't be put into doing it. I would like you there. It, of course, would be a great help. I could do it on my own (I'm gradually getting a bit better at steering the theatre night.) but your presence would strengthen me and the audience. Let me know not too far hence so that I can think about it.

If you decide to do it, what I would like would be for you to say something for 5 or 10 minutes so far away from any idea of an 'introduction' of a friend's poetry that it sounds like a man talking about the swivelling chains and pullies of the meat market or something oppositely special and to say that and yet get them ready for the words. (WOW WOW don't let that put you off.) Then, because my book is out from young poems to to-day you might like to start the second half by reading a 5 minutes of early poems which will be completely new to them. After that I will do my best and try to end the night changing the shape of their souls.

That is just an idea, Harold, overwritten to you. Take it easy and just tell me what you think.

Yestreen the queen had fowre Maries.
The nicht she'll hae but three.
There was Mary Beaton and Mary Seaton
And Mary Carmichael and Me.

Love, Sydney

1 One of the poems which he read to the Poetry Society was 'Look At The Children' which had been commissioned by *The Observer* for The Year Of The Child. It was also included in *Uncollected Poems* published by the Greville Press in 1990.

LOOK AT THE CHILDREN

Look at the children of the world
Looking out at us to say hello
All from their lonely photographs.

Look at the children in their year
Which they know nothing about.
What lovely round big eyes they have.

What's to be done? What's to be done?
The hungry dogs are come to town.
Where have your father and mother gone?

Look at the children of the world
Appearing in the newspapers
Not knowing we are here at all.

The thing is they are beautiful
Because of something maybe not
A mystery all that deep.

Look at them looking out at us
Not knowing we are making an obscene
Use of them. They are all lovely

Enough for us to take home to the soul.
And who would you choose? The difficult one
With the not straight left eye looking?

Look at them. Why are they not seeing us?
The thing is they are beautiful
Not knowing us, in spite of us.

Look at the children of the world
Breaking our hearts but not enough
While we eat our money up.

9th November 1979

251. *To Crombie Saunders*

29 January 1980 Madron

Dear Crombie,

We are old pals, but we are nearer than that. We are nearer than that about 30 years. I know thee well. I know you have become somebody else. I also. My earlier disguise I have put aside. But, Crombie, that is the glacier I ride on. Wow Wow. The language tricks us into nonsense.

I play your records. You sound / and the Verse / sounds (a mistake) very good and makes me homesick for Scotland. Always remember I love you in your position and in my position sitting down here in this granite house. Here I am, Crombie, sitting in front of my old typewriter, trying to steer the terrible conglomerate which comes into my ear. O O O O What will I say to Crombie Saunders?

Love, Sydney X

252. *To Harold Pinter*

21 May 1980 Madron

Dear Harold,

What a great gift at this time. I know you don't want me to go on saying thanks in different polite ways. I have your letter here on my writing table (I hope I'm not using my writing table too publicly as a character in my poetry.) and I know you have given me this £1000 in the best way and generosity. You are very good thinking also of The Royal Literary Fund.

I am more than pleased you think so well of my poetry. In earlier times between us it was hardly true to me. Now, I say, in point of fact, you did leave your desk to encounter my works.

Harold, this is going to make a difference to our lives. I will use it well, although you are giving it to me unconditionally straight from your heart.

Thanks for THE HOTHOUSE. By the way, I sent you the paper-back because it is the nicer object.

Love, Sydney

253. *To Michael Snow*

3 June 1980 Madron

Dear Michael,

I write from my bed not at my best at 8.30. I think I must have [been] taking a bucket too much. If there is a reason this time it is that I saw Nessie onto her taxi to catch the train to her nephew for a night and then on, from Reading, the next day up to Scotland, to be met by her brother Alec and to Blantyre to her brothers and sisters. The sister Mary is taking her for a week to Rothsay. Isn't it a nice thing although what shall I do without her, which is a complicated question to answer. I put her on the taxi this morning early with her cases packed and zipped and good sandwiches with goose patty (I know that's not the word.) and a kiss under her ear to keep her going. It is the same day, Michael, and yet I'm already finding I can't turn something. I well know that is just a sudden difference that is presented. This is just the first day. Lonelinesses and difficulties will come up. But maybe it will be the making of me. She's away for 3 weeks. She's going to send some kippers and slice.

I need more good white paper, if you have it near you. I am older than when you saw me last. Do not forget your poetic chum. What a lonely night with hardly a stir of wind.

I'll see you in your time. Love to Margaret and your sweet self.

Sydney X X

Do you think it is too early to try to go to sleep? WSG

254. *To Anthony Astbury*

14 July 1980 Madron

Dear Tony,

Great news. The Royal Literary Fund has come through with a generous £1000 for three years. What a great relief of all the wee financial terrors I suddenly experience. How lovely! I know you have helped me towards it. Thank you. And good things will take place.

I've just had the proofs of SELECTED POEMS from The Ecco Press New York. It looks very good. The selection gives it a quite different character from the Collected Poems. We'll see. At what stage is Thirteen Graham Poems? Is it becoming nearly discussable as a project?

I send you a good shot of love. No doubt we will see each other before the summer fades.

Sydney X

255. *To Charles Monteith*

24 October 1980 Madron

Dear Charles,

It seems a long time since we communicated. Your last was your letter after the Poetry Society reading. I'm glad you enjoyed it. Doing it I felt it was going well. It was heartening to see the Faber contingent in the front row, and the wee bonny face of Mary Jane.

I've seen a review or two, all good except the TLS by a woman who seemed to be in a bad temper. She was equally terrible about Sisson who I think is a very good poet, which helped me think things were not so bad. Charles, can you let me know how the sales are going.

The SELECTED POEMS from ECCO PRESS in New York seems to have got off to a good start. A letter from them at the beginning of September said they had sold 279 copies in the first week. Isn't it a lovely looking book and to handle, the yellow and black. The selection and the different order of the poems makes one see them freshly, neither early nor late.

I am reading at PENTAMETERS at The Three Horseshoes pub in Hampstead on 15th. December. Also, we go to the Cambridge Poetry Festival in June next year. We are both older but in good health. I am writing new and different poems which should make a new book by early next year. I send my love looking out of the rainy Madron window and hand you over to Noisy Dancemore to say her ending piece.

Sydney.

256. *To Harold Pinter*

14 January 1981 Madron

Dear Harold,

FAMILY VOICES has been in the house now for a time long enough for me to go through it in various moods and at times to catch it unawares in the middle or anywhere I open it at. Boy! It certainly is a strange object of some power. It has gone into me indeed. I have the whole feeling of it. I say this not seeing it as a play as I read it but a chamber trio of words. Are the audience of these words to see anything? Is it for Radio or from maybe out of a great bit of abstract or unabstract scenery with no actor visible? You can see I like it enough to wonder how you are going to present these family letter-ists. Bits of it are what I would like to have written myself.

Of course, what it is saying, in a oner, I do not know. It is exactly what the title is, Family Voices. I enjoyed the changing texture of Voice 1 speaking, being all those ways of speaking at once. I mean not just the words (Which are everything) but the Voice 1's person not being able to establish itself is a wee bit difficult for me enjoying it here in a piece of life in 23 pages of words. I can't get him into focus as real a near person.

Harold, you know what to do. Fuck Lady Withers. Fuck Jane Jane with a bun in her hand. Remember your father. Start a new letter to your mother.

I had to make that red line to stop me. Nessie has just I mean Nessie has just I don't mean Jane Jane, appeared. Here she comes through the stormy casement in her yellow oilskin with her cargo of Portugese Peppers, Slight Whisky, Sweet Potatoes, a paper bag of five buns, and LENTILS which is to be eaten and boiled and supped.

Take no offence. (Tosca is on my machine.) The way I speak is mine. Nessie is almost frozen. I am giving her a dram o whisky in hot water and honey — O Doc Pinter, is that the thing to do?

Tosca is finished. Here comes the terribly over-English man ushering in Haydn. (Fuck the whole thing how self-conscious can a man 'that's me' get) There is Puccini who slays me. There is Haydn who slays me. So I am slewn. Where does that leave me. My father has gone to kneel on the Bowling Green in Greenock. My red MacDermit mother is back in the west of Ireland putting up the clothes.

Dear Harold, thanks for your nice letter of appreciation. When my letter asks questions they are not meant for you to answer. It is just the way the language goes. My typing arms are sticking. Love from us both, Sydney

257. *To Tony Lopez*

30 March 1981 Madron

Dear Anthony Lopez,

Thankyou for your interesting letter. It is good to hear you would like to write something about my poetry. Yes, I am coming up to Cambridge to take part in the Poetry Festival at the beginning of June. It will be nice to see you there, but I am afraid I cannot say if it would be possible to give you my attention for two hours because I still don't know my programme although it seems to be going to be a busy time. The way things are it would be impossible to see you here in Cornwall. Anyhow, we will see what happens.

To slightly answer some of your questions –

I have lived beside some writers and artists in my life but searching in my work I do not think they have been of any influence. I have never come near being part of a movement or group (not that I am necessarily against that but that is how it was).

Wherever any creative artist lives, of course has an effect on the object he puts out, usually mysteriously and not easily tracked down. Like most other poets I enjoy the use of place names and in about the last twenty years my poems have contained many rank-Cornish names like – Botallack, Morvah, Lanyon Quoit, Godrevy, Zennor, Gurnard's Head.

When writing The Nightfishing I knew I had read Pound's translation of The Seafarer, and other voyages literature. Nansen helped me to steer. No, I am not a member of any religious group.

Godspeed in your research. I look forward to meeting you at one point in Cambridge,

Yours sincerely, W S Graham

258. *To Gavin Saunders*

14 April 1981 Madron

Dear Gavin,

Thanks for your letter. Good your dissertation is going ahead. I write from my bed, not ill, and Nessie is typing.

Here are some splinters of observation on my poetry. They could be used in your thought or quoting.

1. I write in *verse*. In the centre of my poems there is always a

metric keeping the words in position.

2. Hopkins and The Seafarer was near me in The Nightfishing.

3. Choosing to write poems in a three-beat line is like putting on a restricting suit and yet that very restriction can make one do great things.

4. My early poems are as good as my later poems. They are maybe just not fashionable, but neither are my later poems. The early poems are other objects with their own particular energies. To say I am getting better, or have written myself into a greater clearness, is very much a surface observation.

5. Good you like the newer poems in the PN Review. I think they say something a wee bit new in the language.

The enclosed might be of use. Best wishes to you and Crombie and Joan, Sydney.

259. *To John Mack*

14 August 1981 Madron

Dear John Mack,

How pleased I am to hear you are kicking and making me a bit jealous being in the country I, older, get homesick for.

I come from Greenock, grown up from a sight of Helensburgh across the Firth. I'm sorry to hear about you having a stroke. I'm about in line for it (American bad grammar).

It is good to hear Morley Jamieson is still around his writing business. Please tell him about the readings, and tell him I have thought about the 'Experience' of Newbattle often and thought that something should be written about it. Dear John, I was almost the youngest student there. I think it was 'great'. I got great joy from my time there, brash and impossible as I was, (I stole the bell. I stole Mr. Fraser's cake.) But I got something of worth.

How did you keep yourself sane down there at the end of the drive? We were a fantastic mixture.

Please, John, let me know what goes on with you and 'The Newbattle'.

best wishes, W S Graham

260. *To Tom Leonard*

undated

Good Tom Leonard,

It was a pleasure and a nice excitement to meet you that night in the iris of The Third Eye. The drink and the night got better but I wish we had had longer. Sauchiehall Street wasn't the same. I wasn't the same. It was a different kind of night-time. The Firth of Clyde is my place. I came back a bit homesick.

I like your poetry. It's certainly a great linguistic achievement of its kind.

Tom, I hope we meet again.

Yours sincerely, S.Graham

261. *To Don Brown*

20 November 1981 Madron

Dear Don,

The stove is a really beautiful addition to our lives. What a generous thought. I can see it is going to make that downstairs black damp square granite cave habitable. I realise I will be in it more. What a birthday present! (63 on Thursday 19th). Monica came up and we had been given two good rich crabs and when the dusk moved in there we were in the lovely warm room and the rosy glow of the stove. That was a good day with Rose and you.

Remember we are here, love, Sydney X

262. *To Rina Knight*

17 February 1982 Madron

Dear Rina,

Here I am in my bed on the edge of getting better. I like you always and the driving hail is at the window. I miss you both, you and the boy with the crooked nose.[1] You are special, the two of you.

About the letters. Let them go and they will come back. They

1 John Knight died in 1975.

are not going to do any harm. The sum of them is they are all for John.

Does this mean you are allowing his letters from me to be free? They are nothing anyhow, although he turned my head a bit, and he was a *Great Poet* Yours—> X X <—his

263. *To Ruth Rosen*

27 April 1982 Madron

My dear Ruth,

Here I am in bed not at my best writing to you at last. Why I have not written you before was not lack of interest in your poem. I know it almost by heart. It was impossible to write. I have been down in depths unspeakable about. I have been in bed since leaving London, not drinking, not thinking but for going down the village to phone you.

But here I am, my Table-Mountain, Hampstead deario, on my way to trying to be a better man. Nessie is downstairs putting on a Mozart record. We have just been reading *Requiem for Osip Mandelstam aloud*. About the poem —

How lovely for me [to] be able to say truthfully, it is a good poem, able to show its face anywhere. A lovely beginning – 'The Spanish Poet/ sang in your veins'. Do you mean Lorca? A good stanza —

'Through the bloodsoaked century
Into the gut of Stalin
You bulls-eyed your death'. and

'fingers thick with grubs'

Your reiteration of 'leather' works in the poem very well. It becomes a profound symbol. Your stanza beginning 'But words change hands' is a humdinger, forceful and filled with meaning in a great flight. Good for you!

– my dear, the whole poem to its end with -
Then gave them back gave them back
to the sun
dust to dust and leather to leather
And they cover us now a coat of armour
Finer than air and better than leather.

Ruth, a great preparing for the end
and a great ending. You are a
good poet. May you do more as good. I
can hear you reading it out to an
audience with your special tones.

I am pleased to find myself able to speak. I am pleased to be alive. I will see you again. My good love to Ismond.

love to yourself and an April hug. Sydney X

264. *To Nancy Wynne-Jones and Conor Fallon*

29 April 1982 Madron

Dear Conor & Nancy,
or
Dear Nancy & Conor,

Here I am writing from my bed with the great new Spring coming through the window. It is half past nine. And here I write to ask you to help us again. The point is could you arrange for certain bits of the house to be fixed up. Of course I have to be courageous in some department of my mind to say this. OK OK. You see, Nancy, Conor, those years in the house, I have made it something to do with me. We have been happy in those granite walls and, my dears, I have put out some new, surprising poems from here. The thing is, here we are in this house getting on at a certain rate, and remember, Dear Conor and Nancy, it is your house and will be coming to you. Nancy, Conor, Stop me from asking you. Why should I be so shy?

It is the lovely April with its hawthorn breath coming through the window. Right. Here I tell you about the house.

The House

(This is me trying to be business-like)

1 – Most of the woodwork in the kitchen is softening up and going, especially the woodwork outside the window which lets in the water with great pools in the morning.

2 – *The wiring*. When we came in we gradually realised the wiring of the house (done by the other people) was on the edge of deadly. We had new rings put on the stove by an old friend who is a depend-

able man who said the wiring wouldn't last long.

3 – The front door has perished under the prevailing Penwith gales. The wood is rotten and it's come off its hinges. We ask people to come to the back. It won't open.

4 – And here is the last at last. BLACK DAMP It comes on the walls inside in great black sploches and we have a hard fight against it.

Please do not think we are not helping our house. We have painted it inside and outside (3 times) and got a new lovely blue gate.

Shall I end here? Of course I think I must. Bits of THE NIGHT-FISHING are coming out in the Observer colour magazine soon with photographs of trawling. Are you both well and happy and fashioning your respective objects?

Love to you both, Sydney X X

265. *To Harold Pinter*

24 November 1983 Madron

Dear Harold,

Everything is coming back into some order I can deal with.

Nessie has been near death but is coming out of hospital on Saturday. It is a great relief. She will have to go to a friend's for a time.

Everything is all right with money. We are going to be all right that way.

This is to let you know I am alive again and thinking of poetry and things to do.

I enjoyed the few times we met. If I make a new worthy poem I'll send you a copy.

Love – Sydney

P.S. I am going to stay. WSG X

266. *To Gordon and Mary Graves*

22 February 1984 — 5, Jack Stephen's Estate, Penzance till further notice.

My dear Gordon and Mary,

And where are you what are you now my two dearies of circumstance? We wonder about you and about what is happening to you both. My happiest times have been beside you.

Where am I what am I now??

We are here for about 3 months, an old people's bungalow. Palatial for us coming from the cottage which is being 'done up' with heating and the terrible rivers of damp stopped. We are too hot. Sometimes too hot the eye of plumbing shines. Nessie didn't manage to get to a phone. She is fairly well and looks peachy. I, myself am up and down after the operation but I can't say I have signs of Mr Cancer approaching yet. Maybe I will be all right. What do you think, my dearies. My handwriting has gone to hell. I could enjoy a real kiss from both of you. Nessie is out now at very much the nearest shop and I myself sitting up in bed hunting good feeling writing to you. I will get her to add to this letter.

Dear Gordon and Mary, it is really a fight to stay alive in the way we want to stay alive in.

Oh Watch O Watch – Who is that? It is Nessie coming back saying 'See I am back. I wasn't long.' Have you brought a drink says I, from Greenock. Yes I have says Nessie, the girl from Blantyre. I'll have a drink first she says. And here is the smiling Nessie Dancemore herself dying to speak to you. I leave you now.

267. *To Tom Leonard*

8 September 1984 — Madron

Dear Tom Leonard,

About three weeks ago I had word I had cancer in the bowel. I went into hospital where I had an operation cutting out and throwing away the bit where the malignant King lurked Wow! Wow! Now, Tom, I have been wheeled back to my own bed although I feel I've been through the mincer. The surgeon's report (I asked for the truth) was that there were no signs of spreading. I felt pain which I am frightened to remember and my pain-killer pills are fucking up my handwriting now. CODA – I feel in good heart and soul. I am going to get through it. I have been thinking of my own good poetry.

Yourself, Tom. I often wonder how you are. If you have a spare copy of a poem, whether early or recent I would be pleased to have it. I enjoyed meeting you that one time. If I come back to normal health I hope you will ask me up again.

Take this as an optimistic letter,

Love, W S Graham

268. *To Harold Pinter*

20 November 1984 Madron

Dear Harold,

Here I am and I am all right and for nothing my line comes into my head –

'Good stars above you, night pedestrian.'

I'm pleased about the reading and honoured that you should take part. I know that you won't allow it to be a cry from an old poet dying. I will be all right. Make the *verse* come out and remind them of line-endings making a pause even although it seems to go against natural speech. The sense will come out anyhow even in the aesthetic distortion. WOW WOW.

Include any poems in your collection. Read the ones that need your good voice and timing. Do not be frightened to give the Quantz poem a bit theatrical shoosh. Make a play of it. Make the dry bits slow and serious and the sentimental bits tear-ductors. Harold, don't give them too much. Better the slow intensity (If you can get it.) than the smother.

I am pleased at people's interest and generosity. What can I say more? I hope you are still with your wife. Do it well. You are the leader from the mountains of Portugal.

Yesterday was my birthday and today I have had a small injection of Rose wine. Let me know if you want to know anything about the poems —love —Sydney X

(P.S. —Can you get Faber to have books there.)

269. *To Pamela Clunies-Ross*

6 December 1984 Madron

Dear Pamela,

'Here I am, standing in front of you and W S Graham has given me the introduction[1] and he says – just read this, nothing less and nothing more.'

'Dear Audience, listening to poetry
being put into sound, especially words
in an unexpected sequence, is not
necessarily an unhappy thing.
You will be all right. If I have
made these poems
well,some of you should get
something. I send you my regards
from the end of the peninsula'

I have good people to put my poetry into sound. Geoffrey Godbert, Ruth Rosen, Harold Pinter.

Thank you
W S Graham

270. *To Frank Ruhrmund*

6 December 1984 Madron

Dear Frank Ruhrmund,

What a good morning piece for me to waken to. Frank you have been very perceptive and generous. You could not have done better. I think I am coming up the hill.

You have been very good at getting everything in. I am very pleased when Nessie tells me you said 'It is Graham country' when you were up at Gurnard's Head. In a kind of way there is a great deal of this place in my poems. I like your choice of quotes in each painter poem.

1 This introduction to 'A Tribute To W.S. Graham' was to be read in Graham's absence as he was too ill to attend. The three friends gave their reading at The Riverside Theatre, London, on 7 December 1984.

You have made a good thing for me. What can I say more.
regards (you can read that I don't know what more to say.)
WSGraham Sydney X
P.S. Good power to your writing hand. WSG

271. *To Don Brown*

19 January 1985 5, Jack Stephens Estate. Penzance.

Please don't leave me away from you like this. What-ever happened was nothing big enough for us to disentangle. Please come back and I will hoist you up the freezing metres. O what a dishonest man I am. I will send you down the Matterhorn for a bottle of whisky when I am dying. Don't leave me. I am near you in my eccentric way. I have a love for you, something to claim. Try to reply or call personally with a stamped addressed envelope. I love you more than you know. Give my love to yourself and Amanda and Pamela. I missed you.

love, Sydney X X X

272. *To Sylvia Thompson*

27 March 1985 Madron

My dear sweet Sylvia,

Forgive your manic-depressive chum not writing all this time. My handwriting is getting more Parkinsonian. I should use your oil-immersed tapwriter more. But here I am trying to be better. I am doing my (metaphorical) jogging to face life and be able to go to Rotterdam in June. I have been asked there to a Poetry International to represent UK. It frightens me but god-willing I will do a good job. It will do me good. You ask if you can bring me anything. Well, my deario, here is a list.

1- No fibre or bran biscuits. A wee bit shortbread.

2- Try to get (second hand) a small stool of the milking stool variety.

3- A filing cabinet (second hand) which could be put in the corner to help set my life in order.

4- drawing pins. Bulldog clips. Screw in hooks.

5- a black pudding without too much fat or a white pudding or chitterlings or anything savoury from the North.

5a- A young lamb plucked from the highest fell.

6- A book about Rotterdam.

7- A lock from your nearest hair.

8- A drop of whisky.

9- Relaxedness. Sweetness. Love.

10- A wee bit whisky.

11- Some good long spaghetti.(New)

12- Yourself and your love.

13- Anything which occurs to you which will make that house better.

14- A stuffed Blond from Las Vegas.

15- Chitterlings (again)

16- A steak pie with flaky pastry.

17- Powdered Rhinoceros Horn.

18- Bring your sweet self at its best. Meet me with a smile and a kiss and I will be here.

love – Sydney X

273. *To Anthony Astbury*

5 June 1985

Dear Tony my Deario,

Forgive me not writing you more. I love who you are in my life. I am a good boy keeping my fingers crossed against the bad cells. WOW WOW. I send you a hug.

I get great pleasure from the things you send me. I could easily put a buttercup under your chin. I am only a simple boy gone slightly complicated. And where are you now my boyo? I miss seeing you and your great laughing style. I will see you again.

I am sending you two poems. FALLING INTO THE SEA and THE ALLIGATOR GIRLS. They have appeared in Poetry Nation some years ago. That is my best offer. My dear, they will be new to the people.

Your book, NESSIE DUNSMUIR'S SEVEN POEMS is a lovely production. You are excelling yourself in what you put out. It is a pleasure to read the printed words on the good paper. It has all printed paper should have. Nessie's poems shine out beautifully. You have produced a good object for both sides to be proud of. What a lovely cover. I am pleased you managed to put in Nessie and me.[1]

Now, Anthony, I have to say this. That although I don't know anything about publishing or putting the books out into the best places, I think your price of £6 is asking too much. If they buy those books at 6 it would be wrong. It would be a handout. Make it less. Now I finish and I have to say – My dear, you have worked things out and do what you want. Cheerio

Sydney with love.

★★★

From 1981 Sydney Graham's health had deteriorated more rapidly and he withdrew more and more from society, seeing only a few close friends. In 1984 and 1985 he underwent operations for cancer and, after a long illness, died at home in Madron on the morning of 9 January 1986, aged 67.

There were many moving tributes to him and his poetry has continued to be studied and enjoyed ever more widely.

'The Constructed Space' was written in the 1950s and remains one of his most compact and moving statements about language and the shape of human existence. Read again after the poet's death, the poem takes on some of the qualities of an elegy.

1 Reference to a drawing of two faces, by Sydney Graham, used as frontispiece to the book.

Meanwhile surely there must be something to say,
Maybe not suitable but at least happy
In a sense here between us two whoever
We are. Anyhow here we are and never
Before have we two faced each other who face
Each other now across this abstract scene
Stretching between us. This is a public place
Achieved against subjective odds and then
Mainly an obstacle to what I mean.

It is like that, remember. It is like that
Very often at the beginning till we are met
By some intention risen up out of nothing.
And even then we know what we are saying
Only when it is said and fixed and dead.
Or maybe, surely, of course we never know
What we have said, what lonely meanings are read
Into the space we make. And yet I say
This silence here for in it I might hear you.

I say this silence or, better, construct this space
So that somehow something may move across
The caught habits of language to you and me.
From where we are it is not us we see
And times are hastening yet, disguise is mortal.
The times continually disclose our home.
Here in the present tense disguise is mortal.
The trying times are hastening. Yet here I am
More truly now this abstract act become.

Appendix

Notes On A Poetry Of Release. By W.S. Graham.

I

The original diseases and cures of those fictional problems of Morality (involving Politics and our each illusion of a Liberty) live in each of us and express through how we lift a cup, walk, or blow the dandelion seeds into the air to tell the time. Let me be the poet writing in a disguise of the 1st person about the intricate marriage between those problems and the poem and the searching reader. Though those problems move me as a man to varied action I try to put them out (at least as a conscious direction) when I begin to make my poem. Those problems move me and work to successfully direct the outside accidents and me through accident. With words my material and immediate environment I am at once halfway the victim and halfway the successful traveller. There is the involuntary war between me and that environment flowing in on me from all sides and there is the poetic outcome. I am not the victim of my environment. History does not repeat itself. I am the bearer of that poetic outcome. History continually arrives as differently as our most recent minute on earth. The labourer going home in the dusk shouts his goodnight across the road and History has a new score on its track. The shape is changed a little. History as a crowd divides and divides into its population where I am a member and at last I am left to say my history has my eyes and mouth and a little likeness of my father. Time and time again I am scored by the others and their words and the diseases and cures war and change in their part of me. First I'll put them aside for my poem is to be a successful construction of words, a construction in which anyhow those cures will act whether the poem is about a pinhead or Lanarkshire.

The most difficult thing for me to remember is that a poem is made of words and not of the expanding heart, the overflowing soul, or the sensitive observer. A poem is made of words. It is words in a certain order, good or bad by the significance of its addition to life and not to be judged by any other value put upon it by imagining how or why or by what kind of man it was made. It is easy to strive to make a poem out of the wrong material like a table out of water. It is easy to mistake a poem for a different thing with a different function and to be sad when it does not put out what it is not. In the end then are those still words on the paper and arranged half-victim to the physical outside, half-victim to my Morality's origins, out of this dying and bearing language. All the poet's knowledge and experience (as far as the people who wait outside his gates are concerned) is contained in the language which is obstacle and vehicle at the same time. The shape of all of us is in this language. Our riches and poverties have affected every word. For the language is a changing creature continually being killed-off, added-to and changed like a river over its changing speakers. The language changes along with all of us and is headline litmus record wreckage pyramid shame and accomplishment of all we do and have done and (through Poetry) might do. Each word is touched by and filled with the activity of every speaker. Each word changes every time it is brought to life. Each single word uttered twice becomes a new word each time. You cannot twice bring the same word into sound.

It is a good direction to believe that this language which is so scored and impressed by the commotion of all of us since its birth can be arranged to in its turn impress significantly for the good of each individual. Let us endure the sudden affection of the language.

2

I must begin with first the illusion of an intention . The poem begins to form from the first intention. But the intention is already breaking into another. The first intention begins me but of course continually shatters itself and is replaced by the child of the new collision. I try to have the courage to let the last intention be now a dead step and to allow myself to be taken in hand. Yet I must not lose my responsibility, being that explorer who shoots the sun, carries samples of air back to civilisation, and looks his forward. The poem is more than the poet's intention. The poet does not write what he knows but what he does not know. A man's imagining suddenly may inherit the handclapping centuries of his one minute on earth. He has to explore the imagination by using the language as his pitch. On it he must construct (intuitively to an organic as true as a tree) an apparatus which will work and to a special purpose. It is no help to think of the purpose as being to 'transfuse recollected emotion' or to 'report significantly' or indeed to think of it as a putting-across of anything. The poem itself is dumb but has the power of release. Its purpose is that it can be used by the reader to find out something about himself. Words are ambiguous. He must face it that words are ambiguous, but realise that this has to do with the fundamental force of poetry and is to be used to a positive end. The poem is not a handing out of the same packet to everyone, as it is not a thrown-down heap of words for us to choose the bonniest. The poem is the replying chord to the reader. It is the reader's involuntary reply.

What is to be done? To bisect the angle between God and Man and find the earliest distance between heart and head. To join Man and Word and project his consciousness of the prophetic in the language into the world. To be the labourer carrying the bricks of his time and on the scaffolding of an unknown construction. To bring about the reader's Involuntary Belief. To present before him an addition to the world like this which Blake made where the reader is left not to agree or disagree as to its rightness but to answer from a new cave flooded to light,

> For every thing that lives is holy, life delights in life;
> Because the soul of sweet delight can never be defil'd.
> Fires inwrap the earthly globe, yet man is not consum'd;
> Amidst the lustful fires he walks: his feet become like brass,
> His knees and thighs like silver, & his breast and head like gold.

I go my way. Then I find the muse laughing her fill in the Atholl Arms, fixing her face genteel not to be thought the whore she is. She's drunk and says, 'give us Kevin Barry,' but singing's stopped this long time, and the bar is thumped like a drum at the least hint of a note. Glasses go over and we are all at words. Shapes of language (right out of the gasp and gesture of speech) spill round our ears and I am at once the man of technique who books the phrases of drinking and affection so that later I might explore the mechanics of their memorableness and vitality. Down the page I've written, 'fairly his mile,' 'anyhow here's Mary will tell you right,' 'have you lately heard tell;' and like the unrehearsed possibilities of a dream beginnings, endings, and those swift metaphors of the moment break into sound in the ear. An organic rhetoric is built up which charges and maintains the formal mechanics of poetry. The syntax holds and a poem's infinite number of overtones are magnified to a greater memorableness. A poem is charged to that power of release that even to one man it goes on speaking again and again beyond behind its speaking words, a space of continual messages behind the words like behind Joyce's words like this:

> It's something fails us. First we feel. Then we fall. And let her rain now if she likes. Gently or strongly as she likes. Anyway, let her rain for my time is come. I done me best when I was let. Thinking always if I go all goes. A hundred cares, a tithe of troubles and is there one who understands me? One in a thousand of years of the nights?

I try to remember those adventures along those lines of words. Though do I move along words in a poem when, after all, as I am at the last word and look back I find the first word changed and a new word there, for it is part of the whole poem and its particular life depends on the rest of the poem. The meaning of a word in a poem is never more than its position. The meaning of a poem is itself, not less a comma. But then to each man it comes into new life. It is brought to life by the reader and takes part in the reader's change. Even the poet as a man who searches continually is a new searcher with his direction changing at every step.

> For ever as the seeker turns
> His worshipping eyes on prophetic patterns
> Of shape arising from all men
> He changes through, he shall remain
> Continually stripped and clothed again.

Let the poem be a still thing, a mountain constructed, an addition to the world. It will have its own special function and purpose, to be that certain mountain. And there is the reader going on to it with his never-before exploration after his perfect hunger's daily changing bread. A poem is a mountain made out of the containing, almost physical language, and with the power to release a man into his own completely responsible world larger than that outward solid geography.

Man setteth an end to darkness,
And searcheth out to the furthest bound
The stones of thick darkness and of the shadow of death.
He breaketh open a shaft away from where men sojourn;
They are forgotten of the foot that passeth by;
They hang afar from men, they swing to and fro.

(The Book of Job)

It is a good direction to believe that this language which is so scored and impressed by the commotion of all of us since its birth can be arranged to in its turn impress significantly for the benefit of each individual. Let us endure the sudden affection of the language.

First published in *Poetry Scotland* No. 3 (July 1946).

Principal Publications

Cage Without Grievance, Parton Press, 1942
The Seven Journeys, Wm. MacLellan, 1944
2ND Poems, Poetry London, 1945
The White Threshold, Faber and Faber, 1949
The Nightfishing, Faber and Faber, 1955
Malcolm Mooney's Land, Faber and Faber, 1970
Implements In Their Places, Faber and Faber, 1977
Collected Poems 1942-1977, Faber and Faber, 1979
Selected Poems, Ecco Press, N.Y., 1980
Uncollected Poems, Greville Press, 1990
Aimed At Nobody, Faber and Faber, 1993
Selected Poems, Faber and Faber, 1996

Further Reading

Tony Lopez, *The Poetry of W.S.Graham* (Edinburgh, 1989). Includes a thirty-page bibliography.

Edinburgh Review No.75, 1987 (ed. Peter Kravitz). The issue is largely devoted to Graham and contains contributions from Tony Lopez, Edwin Morgan, David Wright, Tom Scott, Robert Frame, Nancy Wynne-Jones, Ronnie Duncan, Robert Calder, Tom Leonard, Sebastian Barker, Matt Simpson, Frank Kuppner, and W.N. Herbert.

The Constructed Space, A Celebration of W.S. Graham. Edited by Ronnie Duncan & Jonathan Davidson (Jackson's Arm, 1994).

The Constructed Space. Catalogue of an exhibition commemorating the poet which was curated by Chris Stephens for Bradford Art Galleries and Museums at Castle Yard, Ilkley, 1994.

Calvin Bedient, *Eight Contemporary Poets* (Oxford, 1974).

Neil Corcoran, *English Poetry since 1940* (London, 1993).

James Dickey, 'W.S.Graham' in *Babel to Byzantium: Poets and Poetry Now* (New York, 1981).

Damian Grant, 'Walls of Glass: the poetry of W.S. Graham' in *British Poetry since 1970*, eds Peter Jones and Michael Schmidt

(Manchester, 1980).
Vivienne Koch, see list of articles on page 65 above.
Tony Lopez, 'On Malcolm Mooney's Land'. *Ideas and Production*, No.4, 'Poetics' (December 1985).
Michael Snow, 'W.S.Graham' in *Dictionary of National Biography*, Supplementary Volume 1986–1990.
John Haffenden, 'I Would Say I Was A Happy Man', W.S. Graham interviewed by John Haffenden, *Poetry Review*, vol. 76, no. 1/2 (1986).
Penelope Mortimer, 'A Poet's Interview With Himself', *Observer Magazine* (19 November 1978).
Robert Hewison, *Under Siege. Literary Life in London 1939-45* (London, 1977).
Julian Maclaren-Ross, *Memoirs of the Forties* (Harmondsworth, 1984).
Frances Spalding, *Dance Till the Stars Come Down*, a biography of John Minton (London, 1991).

List of Correspondents

W.S. Graham's letters are in most cases still with the correspondents or their heirs and executors. Where important letters or groups of letters have been found elsewhere, the location is shown at the end of the entry.

Anthony **Astbury** (b. 1940) Poet, teacher, director of The Greville Press. Published *Uncollected Poems* of W.S.Graham in 1990, and Nessie Dunsmuir's poems.
See nos.177, 188, 201, 216, 231, 235, 254, 273

Frank **Baker** (b. 1908) Writer, actor and musician. Travelled widely, lived for some years in Mevagissey where he knew the Grahams well.
Letter in the Alan Clodd Collection.
See no. 78

Sebastian **Barker** (b. 1945) Poet, son of George Barker and Elizabeth Smart. Has written several books of poems and the memoir *Who Is Eddie Linden?*. Director of Literary Festivals at Bracknell and elsewhere.
See nos. 215, 225

Sven **Berlin** (b. 1911) Sculptor, painter and writer, trained as engineer. Co-founder of the Crypt Group and the Penwith Society in St Ives, 1949. Wrote first book on the fisherman painter Alfred Wallis (1949), which included Graham's poem on Wallis.
Letters in The National Library of Scotland, Edinburgh.
See nos. 24, 31, 35, 47, 55, 56, 71, 85

Robert **Brennan** (b. 1925) Artist. Temporarily acted as a postman in the Zennor area when Graham lived at Gurnard's Head. Elected to the Penwith Society 1957. Learned to make monotypes from

watching Graham doing so and was a frequent visitor.
See no. 117

Don **Brown** (b. 1930) Artist and teacher. First met Graham in 1962 when camping at Gurnard's Head. A keen climber, he created a memorial cairn to WSG in the Annapurna Sanctuary of the Himalaya containing a copy of 'The Don Brown Route'.
See nos. 233, 261, 271

Arthur **Caddick** (1911–87) Poet and novelist. Trained in Law at Oxford, had various occupations before settling in Cornwall in 1945 with his wife, Peggy. A companion noted for his polemical verses on local topics.
See no. 236

Charles **Causley** (b. 1917) Cornish poet, writer, teacher and editor. Awarded The Queen's Gold Medal for Poetry 1967. Did not see Graham frequently but strongly admired his work.
See no. 84

Alan **Clodd** (b. 1918) Founder and original editor of the Enitharmon Press. Bibliophile and MSS collector. Assisted Graham by purchasing early worksheets.
Letters in the Alan Clodd Collection.
See nos. 81, 82, 83, 89

Pamela **Clunies-Ross** Former Secretary of the Poetry Society.
See no. 269

Alex **Comfort** (b. 1920) Poet, editor, critic. Pursued a prominent career in medicine and was also influential as a writer with strong pacifist and left-wing ideals.
Letter in the Library of University College London.
See no. 38

Stewart **Conn** (b. 1936) Scottish poet, playwright and radio drama producer. Worked for the BBC in Edinburgh 1962–92.
See no.243

Ronald **Duncan** (1914–82) Prolific author of stories, poems and plays (*This Way To The Tomb*, 1945; *The Eagle Has Two Heads*, 1946), also a librettist (Benjamin Britten, *The Rape Of Lucretia*, etc.). No relation to Ronnie Duncan.

Letters in The Harry Ransom Humanities Research Center, University of Texas.

See no. 72

Ronnie **Duncan** (b. 1928) Yorkshire businessman and art collector interested in poetry. Met the Grahams in 1958, visited them regularly and, with his wife, Henriette, took them to Crete. Encouraged the Ilkley Literature Festival of 1994 devoted to Graham's work, and co-edited with Jonathan Davidson *The Constructed Space*, studies of his poetry.

See nos. 111, 142, 159, 161, 186, 187, 192, 193, 198, 199, 212, 214, 227, 242, 246, 249

Bill **Featherston** Canadian artist and teacher who worked for a time in Cornwall before returning to British Columbia. Knew the Grahams both at Gurnard's Head and at Trevaylor.

See nos. 164, 169

Terry **Frost** RA (b. 1915) Widely known St Ives abstract artist who later moved to Newlyn. Gregory Fellow at Leeds, also taught at Reading University. Admired Graham's artistic integrity and work, helping to make it better known.

See nos. 196, 202

Nessie (Dunsmuir) **Graham** (1909–99) Poet. Studied with WSG at Newbattle Abbey in 1938. They married in 1954 and she strongly supported his work. Her own poems were published in magazines during the 1940s and in two pamphlets from the Greville Press in 1985 and 1988.

Letters with the W.S. Graham Estate.

See nos. 96, 156, 163

Mary and Gordon **Graves** Gordon, a teacher, met Sydney Graham at the Scott Street Art Centre in 1941. Mary, also a teacher, first encountered Nessie Graham in Paris in 1950 when Nessie was teaching in the Berlitz School.

See nos. 205, 247, 266

Mary **Harris** (b. 1916) Writer, critic, and teacher, friend of WSG from 1943, mother of Rosalind. Lent Sydney the caravans in Cornwall which he called 'The Wheelhouse'.
See no. 52

Rosalind **Harris** (b. 1944) Teacher and dyslexia tutor. The daughter of W.S. Graham and Mary Harris.
See nos. 165, 173

J.F. **Hendry** (1912–86) Born in Glasgow. Widely travelled Scottish poet, editor, translator, and linguist. Co-founder with Henry Treece and Dorian Cooke of the New Apocalypse group (1938–43). Edited two anthologies of their work, also including Norman MacCaig, Nicholas Moore, Philip O'Connor, Dylan Thomas.
Letters with Edwin Morgan.
See nos. 41, 42, 49, 50, 79

Roger **Hilton** CBE (1911–75) Artist. Studied in Paris and taught at the Central School in London. Visited Cornwall from 1956, introduced to Graham by Patrick Heron. Moved to Cornwall with his second wife, Rose, in 1965 and became a frequent companion.
See nos. 86, 102, 103, 107, 112, 113, 114, 115, 126, 127, 128, 129, 130, 132, 137, 138, 140, 141, 147

Ruth **Hilton** (1921–95) Professional musician and teacher, Ruth (David) was married to Roger Hilton from 1947 to 1963. Sympathetic to Graham's work and lent him the book on which he based the Quantz poems. Her partner John Beckett (b. 1927), first cousin to Samuel Beckett, was a freelance musician, conductor and composer, also music producer for BBC Radio 3.
See nos. 104, 105, 109, 110, 116, 119, 120, 125, 133, 146, 148, 183

Carole **Hope-Thomson** Member of production staff at Faber and Faber.
See no. 211

John **Knight** (1906–75) Poet. Civil servant in Manchester (active in the Peterloo Group) and, later, in London. Retired to Cornwall with his wife Rina in 1966. *Straight Lines and Unicorns* (Cresset Press,

1960) *Edges of Fact* (Stonemark Press, 1977).
Letters with Michael and Margaret Snow.
See nos. 94, 101, 106, 153

Rina **Knight**
See no. 262

John **Lehmann** (1907–87) Poet who wrote criticism and biography and edited Penguin New Writing series. Founded *The London Magazine* in 1954 and edited it for seven years.
Letters in The Harry Ransom Humanities Research Center, University of Texas.
See no. 2

Tom **Leonard** (b. 1944) Scottish poet, editor and anthologist. Special interest in Glasgow dialect, socialism, and the poetry of the radical working class.
See nos. 260, 267

Tony **Lopez** (b. 1950) Poet and novelist. Has been a Lecturer at the University of Edinburgh and the University of Plymouth. Wrote the first book-length study and other critical articles on Graham's work.
Letter in The National Library of Scotland, Edinburgh.
See no. 257

Alan **Lowndes** (1921–78) Artist from Stockport. After several visits came with his wife Valerie to live in Cornwall 1959–70 before moving to Dursley in Gloucestershire.
See nos. 203, 234

John **Mack** Scottish lecturer who taught philosophy classes at Newbattle Abbey.
Letter in The National Library of Scotland, Edinburgh.
See no. 259

Norman **Macleod** (b. 1906) American poet, writer, editor of *The Briarcliff Quarterly* and of *The Pembroke Magazine*. Founded the Poetry Centre in New York. Professor of English at Pembroke State University.

Letter in The Harry Ransom Humanities Research Center, University of Texas. Other papers held at The Beinecke Library, Yale University.

See no. 95

Mary **McGinn** Sister of Nessie Graham. Lived in Blantyre where Nessie was born.

Letter with the W.S. Graham Estate.

See no. 131

John **Minton** (1917–57) Artist. Popular teacher at Camberwell, The Central School of Arts and Crafts and the Royal College of Art. Was a prominent member of post-war Soho society, particularly generous in his support for other artists and writers.

Letters in the Library of The Royal College of Art, London.

See nos. 10, 12, 13, 14, 16, 17, 19, 22, 25, 26, 27, 28, 29, 37, 39, 40

Peter **Moldon** Member of production staff at Faber and Faber.

See no. 245

Charles **Monteith** (1921–95) Fellow of All Souls College, Oxford. Assistant to T.S.Eliot at Faber and Faber in 1953 and succeeded him in 1965 as editor in charge of the poetry list. Chairman of Faber and Faber 1977–80.

Letters in the Faber and Faber Archive.

See nos. 143, 151, 171, 194, 208, 209, 229, 230, 255

William **Montgomerie** (b. 1904) Scottish poet and folklorist, editor of *Lines Review* 1978–82. Settled in Edinburgh where he and his wife Norah, also a writer, were active in encouraging the arts. Graham stayed with them when coming to read in the region.

Wrote the Introduction to Graham's *Seven Journeys* (1944)

Letters in The National Library of Scotland, Edinburgh.

See nos. 3, 4, 7, 8, 9, 11, 15, 20, 43, 44, 45, 46, 60, 61, 136

Norah **Montgomerie** Author of books for children and editor of *The Hogarth Book of Scottish Nursery Rhymes*.

See nos. 18, 23

Edwin **Morgan** (b. 1920) Influential Scottish poet, essayist, critic, translator. Lecturer in English at the University of Glasgow, from which he retired as titular Professor in 1980.
See nos. 1, 5, 59, 63, 65, 68, 69, 134, 139

Ben **Nicholson** OM (1894–1982) Leading British abstract painter. Worked in London, St Ives (where he strongly influenced the 'St Ives' artists and others), and later in Switzerland. Interested in Graham's ideas and his experiences with Jankel Adler.
Letters in The Tate Gallery Archive, London.
See nos. 6, 21

Tony **O'Malley** (b. 1913) Irish painter who settled in Cornwall in 1960. Joined The Penwith Society of Arts in 1962. Lived close to the Grahams at Trevaylor. Later lived in St Ives with his wife Jane before they returned to Ireland.
See no. 135,

Harold **Pinter** (b. 1930) Leading actor, playwright and poet. Admired Graham's work and tenacious dedication to his craft. His readings and support helped to encourage a wider recognition of Graham's poetry.
See nos. 237, 248, 250, 252, 256, 265, 268

W.R. **Rodgers** (1909–69) Irish poet. Began to write in 1939. Moved to Scotland and worked as a BBC producer. His first book *Awake* (1941) was followed by *Europa and the Bull* (1952)
Letters in The Harry Ransom Humanities Research Center, University of Texas.
See no. 48

Ruth **Rosen** Actress and poet, born in South Africa, well-known for her performances, poetry and prose readings.
See no. 263

Frank **Ruhrmund** (b. 1928) Cornishman. Freelance journalist and poet. Arts correspondent for the Cornish Press.
See no. 270

R. Crombie **Saunders** (1914–91) Scottish poet. Edited a selection of Hugh MacDiarmid's poetry for Maclellan's 'Poetry Scotland' series in 1944. Co-edited with J.D. Fergusson *Scottish Art and Letters* No.1. Gavin Saunders is his son.

See nos. 149, 213, 251

Gavin **Saunders**

See no. 258

Michael **Schmidt** (b. 1947) Poet and critic, teaches at Manchester Metropolitan University. Founder/Director of the Carcanet Press and editor of *PN Review* in which he published Graham's work at an early point.

Letters in The John Rylands Library, University of Manchester.

See nos. 207, 224, 228, 238, 241

Tom **Scott** (1918–95) Scottish poet, critic, literary historian and translator. Studied at Edinburgh University as a mature student. Edited *The Penguin Book of Scottish Verse* (1970) co-edited *The Oxford Book of Scottish Verse* (1966) and a selection of early Scottish poetry. His own work was strongly idealist and nationalist.

See nos. 98, 99, 108

Matt **Simpson** (b. 1936) Poet. Recently retired from teaching at Liverpool Hope University College. Most recent books: *Cutting the Clouds Towards* (LUP) and *Somewhere Down The Line* (Shoestring). Met at Graham reading in Liverpool.

See no. 244

Marie **Singer** American psychologist and painter, married James Burns Singer in 1956. James (Jimmy) Singer (1928–64) was initially a keen follower of Graham who developed a very individual poetry of his own. *Collected Poems* (1970) followed by *Selected Poems* in 1977.

See no. 87

C.H. **Sisson** CH (b. 1914) Poet, translator and critic particularly associated with the growth of Carcanet Press and *PN Review*. Formerly a senior civil servant. *Collected Translations* (1996), *Collected Poems* (1998).

See nos. 121, 122, 182, 200, 219, 221

Robin **Skelton** (1925–97) Poet, editor and critic. Taught at Manchester University, co-founder of the Peterloo Group. Emigrated to Canada with his wife Sylvia. Professor at the University of Victoria, B.C. and editor of the *Malahat Review* in which he published Graham's poetry.

Letters in The Macpherson Collection, University of Victoria, British Columbia, Canada.

See nos. 88, 90, 92, 93, 145, 150, 152, 155, 160, 168, 170, 172, 174, 175, 178, 180, 181, 185, 191

Elizabeth **Smart** (1913–86) Canadian novelist and journalist, companion of the poet George Barker. Shared her home at Tilty Mill with the Roberts Colquhoun and MacBryde and many other literary visitors including the Grahams, whom she also visited in Cornwall.

Letters in The National Library of Canada, Ottawa.

See nos. 73, 74, 75, 76, 77, 100, 162, 217, 220, 226, 239, 240

Margaret **Snow** (b. 1929) Poet, teacher. Literary Administrator of the W.S. Graham Estate. Together with Nessie Graham she surveyed all the W.S. Graham poems in Nessie's possession.

See no. 123

Michael **Snow** (b. 1930) Artist and teacher working in St Ives area since 1952. Elected to the Penwith Society of Arts, co-founder of the Peterloo Group, Manchester. Director of Combined Studies (with University of Exeter) at Exeter College of Art 1966–85. Knew Graham from 1955 to 1986. Literary Administrator of the W.S. Graham Estate.

See nos. 179, 189, 190, 206, 222, 253

Fraser **Steel** Formerly a programme producer for the BBC, Fraser Steel is now Head of the BBC Programme Complaints Unit.

See nos. 197, 204, 223, 232

Albert **Strick** (1914–99) Worked for the Local Authority first at Madron Poorhouse and met Graham when painting the exterior of the old Coastguard house at Gurnard's Head. He and his wife Hilda (b. 1921), became staunch helpers and companions of the Grahams during their later years in Madron.

See no. 210

Sylvia **Thompson** (b. 1934) Nurse and health visitor from Yorkshire who first met the Grahams with Ronnie Duncan during the 1950s and often visited them later in Cornwall, providing practical help and encouragement.
See no. 272

Bill **Turner** (W. Price Turner) (1927–99) Poet, playwright, novelist. Edited and hand-set *The Poet* (1951–6), publishing some of Sydney Graham's poems. Met him in 1955 in a Govan pub where Sydney was reading the two ballads from *The Nightfishing*. Was Gregory Fellow at Leeds University 1960 and held other creative writing posts.
See no. 144

Karl **Weschke** (b. 1925) German figurative painter who came to Britain as a POW. Settled in Cornwall in 1955 after meeting Bryan Wynter, living first at Tregerthen, near Gurnard's Head, and later at Cape Cornwall, St Just in Penwith.
See nos. 118, 195

Moncrieff **Williamson** (b. 1915) Scottish poet, novelist, biographer, gallery and museum director. Worked in England and later in Canada (where he became Museum Director in Charlottetown). Met Graham in 1948 at Vivienne Koch's New York apartment, and afterwards in London and at his home in High Wycombe.
See nos. 53, 57, 58, 64, 66, 70

David **Wright** (1920–94) South African poet, writer, critic and translator. Graduated from Oxford in 1942 and joined the staff of *The Sunday Times* for five years. Together with Patrick Swift founded and edited *X* Review. Visited Cornwall and was a companion in Soho.
See nos. 30, 32, 33, 34, 36, 51, 54, 62, 80, 218

Nancy **Wynne-Jones** (b. 1922) Welsh painter and composer, worked in Cornwall from 1957 before moving to Ireland with her husband, Conor Fallon, a sculptor, in 1972. She gave rent-free shelter to the Grahams at the Lodge, which Graham named

'Woodfield', at Trevaylor, and subsequently in a small cottage at Madron near Penzance.

See no. 264

Bryan **Wynter** (1915–75) Painter, teacher at Bath Academy of Art, who came to live in Cornwall after the war. Met Graham both there and in Soho. His inventive art and interest in nature and verbal wit made him a good companion for Sydney and he and his wife, Monica, were consistent friends and visitors.

See nos. 67, 91, 124, 154, 157, 158, 166, 176

Monica **Wynter** (b. 1932) After 1975 continued the friendship and helped the Grahams until Nessie's death in 1999.

See nos. 167, 184

Index